Performing Mixed Reality

Performing Mixed Reality

Steve Benford and Gabriella Giannachi

The MIT Press
Cambridge, Massachusetts
London, England

Performing Mixed Reality is supported by

RESEARCH COUNCILS UK

horizon
DIGITAL ECONOMY RESEARCH

For information about special quantity discounts, please email special_sales@mitpress.mit.edu.

This book was set in Stone Sans and Stone Serif by Toppan Best-set Premedia Limited. Printed and bound in the United States of America.

Library of Congress Cataloging-in-Publication Data

Benford, Steve.
Performing mixed reality / Steve Benford and Gabriella Giannachi.
p. cm.
Includes bibliographical references and index.
ISBN 978-0-262-01576-9 (hardcover : alk. paper)
1. New media art. 2. Mixed reality. I. Giannachi, Gabriella. II. Title.
NX456.5.N49B46 2011
709.05′1—dc22
2010045904

10 9 8 7 6 5 4 3 2 1

Steve dedicates this book with love to Penny.
The continual interweaving of our trajectories has enriched my life in so many ways.

Gabriella dedicates this book to Nick.
Thinking of Sinzias

Contents

Illustrations

Acknowledgments

We would like to thank first of all of those who directly collaborated to this book by offering generous feedback and providing us with original interview materials: Brendan Walker from Aerial and Holger Schnädelbach, Andy Crabtree, Boriana Koleva and Marthin Flintham from the Mixed Reality Laboratory at the University of Nottingham. We are profoundly indebted to Blast Theory and, in particular, to Matt Adams and Nick Tandavanitj, who offered original interviews for all our chapters and provided us with unfailing support and essential feedback throughout the writing of this book, and also to Ju Row Farr for her many valuable inputs to our collaborative projects and discussions over the years. We would like to thank Chris Greenhalgh, the creator of the MASSIVE and EQUIP software platforms that have underpinned so much of this work, and also Martin Flintham, who has developed the application software and supporting tools for many of the projects discussed here. We would also like to thank Tom Rodden from the Mixed Reality Laboratory, Nick Kaye from the Centre for Intermedia at the University of Exeter, and Doug Sery from the MIT Press, who offered crucial support and feedback that informed the shaping, writing, and editing of this book. Special thanks go also to Katie Helke from the MIT Press for answering all our editorial questions with great precision and speed. We gratefully acknowledge Hazel Glover and Sheila Popple for their support.

Throughout the years, the work presented in this book has received significant institutional support. In particular, we are indebted to the RCUK, as it is through the RCUK-funded Horizon project (2009–2014) that we were able to conduct the research on trajectories that underpins this volume. We would also like to acknowledge the EPSRC-funded Equator project (2000–2007), the EU-funded iPerG project (2004–2008), and the AHRC-funded Presence project (2004–2009).

The interviews and correspondences extracted and published in this book were recorded and edited by the authors and corrected and approved by interviewees for publication. We are happy to acknowledge that parts of chapter 2 were previously published in Giannachi and Benford 2008 and Benford and Giannachi 2008.

With regard to the figures reproduced in this book, we are pleased to acknowledge the following credits: figures I.1, I.2, 1.10, 1.11, 1.12, 1.13, 1.14, 2.3, 2.5, 2.6, 2.7, 2.8, 2.9, 2.10, 2.11, 2.12, 2.13, 2.14, 2.15, 3.2, 3.3, 3.10, 3.12, 3.13, 3.14, 3.17, 3.18, 3.19, 3.20, 3.21, 3.22, 4.3, 4.4, 4.5, 4.7, 4.8, 4.10, 4.11, 4.13, 4.14, 4.20, 4.25, 5.1, 5.2, 5.3, 5.4, 5.5, 5.6, 5.7, 5.8, 5.9, 5.10, 5.11, 5.12, 5.13, 5.14, 5.15, 5.16, 5.17, and 5.18 courtesy the Mixed Reality Laboratory; figures 1.1, 1.2, 1.3, 1.4, 1.5, 1.6, 1.7, 1.8, 1.9, 2.2, 3.1, 3.4, 3.5, 3.6, 3.7, 3.8, 3.9, 3.15, 3.16, 4.12, 4.19, 4.21, and 4.24 courtesy Blast Theory; figure 2.3 courtesy Mauricio Capra; figure 3.11 courtesy Anthony Steed; figures 4.1 and 4.2 courtesy Brendan Walker; figure 4.6 courtesy Newsteam and the Alton Towers Resort; figure 4.9 courtesy the BBC.

Introduction: Designing Mixed Reality

An emerging generation of artists is turning to digital technologies to fundamentally transform theater. At the same time, by collaborating with technologists, they are also reshaping the nature of human interaction with computers. Working at the cutting edge of live performance, these artists are increasingly employing digital technologies to create distinctive forms of interactive, distributed, and often deeply subjective theatrical performance. Although early examples are diverse in their detail, they share important underlying characteristics, in that they establish complex relationships between multiple physical and virtual spaces; employ networking to create distributed structures that flexibly interconnect many local settings to create a global "stage"; integrate live performance by actors and audiences with digital media and the kinds of rule-based structures that are found in computer games; and establish rich temporal structures in which the artistic experience is interwoven with ongoing everyday activities. We refer to these experiences as *mixed reality performances*, a term that is intended to expresses both their mixing of the real and virtual as well as their combination of live performance and interactivity.

This book charts this new field of practice by documenting landmark examples of mixed reality performance while recording interviews with key practitioners, both artists and technologists. It then draws on this material to develop an overarching theory to guide the future study and design of mixed reality performance. The foundation of this theory is that we can express how artists design, and participants experience, mixed reality performance in terms of multiple interleaved trajectories through complex hybrid structures of space, time, interfaces, and roles that establish new configurations of real and virtual, local and global, fact and fiction, personal and collective.

We follow an interdisciplinary approach that draws generally on the humanities, computer science and social science, and specifically on the fields of human-computer interaction (HCI) and performance studies which are the backgrounds of the two authors. In its detail, the book draws on a series of works that have been codeveloped by the Mixed Reality Laboratory (MRL) at Nottingham in collaboration with a series of artists, most notably Blast Theory. Indeed, a further outcome of the book is to document the series of collaborations between the Mixed Reality Laboratory and Blast Theory that for more than a decade have gradually evolved a distinctive interdisciplinary approach to combining practice with research. Studies of individual works and elements of our theory of trajectories have previously appeared in various papers in sources such as the Association for Computing Machinery's (ACM's) annual conference on Human Factors in Computing Systems (CHI) conference and more recently in humanities journals such as *Contemporary Theater Review*, *Leonardo*, and *PAJ*. Our book draws this material together for the first time to present a comprehensive and extended account of the works, studies, and theories from multiple perspectives. This introductory chapter provides the general background to our study of mixed reality performance, covering

- the definition of mixed reality performance in relation to the wider fields of mixed reality and performance;
- an overview of our methodology, both in terms of wider contributing disciplines but also a brief history of how the Mixed Reality Laboratory has evolved its particular approach;
- an introduction to the foundational concept of trajectories that underpins our theory as seen from different disciplinary perspectives;
- a guide to the structure of our argument and of subsequent chapters.

Mixed Reality Performance

Mixed reality performance might simply be defined as the staging of theatrical performances in mixed reality environments. A more sophisticated and useful definition than this requires us to explore in some depth what we mean by both mixed reality and performance.

On the Nature of Mixed Reality

Beginning with mixed reality and turning first to computer science, an ideal starting point is Paul Milgram and Furnio Kishino's taxonomy of mixed reality displays, which includes the "virtuality continuum" as covering a spectrum of different forms of mixed reality from purely physical, real environments at one extreme to purely virtual environments at the other (see figure 0.1). In between these two extremes lie augmented reality, which signifies physical environments that are overlaid with digital information, and on the other side, augmented virtuality, in which virtual environments are overlaid with physical information (Milgram and Kishino 1994). A good example of the former is Wikitude, which allows via geotagging the augmentation of physical spaces through digital information, and a characteristic example of the latter is

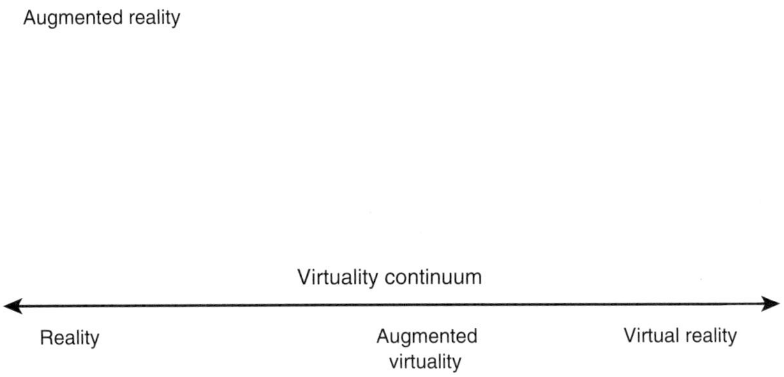

Figure 0.1
Milgram and Kishino's Mixed Reality Continuum.
Drawn by Steve Benford.

enhancing virtual environments such as Second Life with video views and other live information from the real world.

What is interesting about this framework is that it encompasses both "real" and "virtual" elements and so allows for the possibility of generating and analyzing environments in which physical and digital objects cohabit and interact in real time. We shall see many times in this book how mixed reality performances may simultaneously occupy multiple points along this continuum by combining many real, virtual, augmented reality, and augmented virtuality environments into complex hybrid and distributed performance stages. This combination may certainly involve overlaying real and virtual environments, but may also involve other spatial relationships, such as making them adjacent so that participants can look or even pass from one to the other. The idea of adjacent rather than overlaid real and virtual spaces is explored in Boriana Koleva's study of traversable interfaces, which shows how such environments may spill onto one another but remain seemingly separate from one another even when forming part of the same mixed reality environment (Koleva et al. 2000). So whereas the virtuality continuum remains a useful means to understand the broad relationship between reality and virtuality, a more rhizomatic model would allow for the real and virtual to be overlaid or juxtaposed rather than opposed to one another. Indeed, Milgram and Kishino's original taxonomy itself argues for a more sophisticated classification of mixed reality environments based upon multiple dimensions of "extent of world knowledge," "reproduction fidelity," and "extent of presence metaphor" (1994).

Many of the performances that we consider in this book involve using mobile technologies to enable spatially extended performances, or embedding computer interfaces into everyday artifacts and structures, which naturally leads us to the idea of ubiquitous computing (ubicomp), one of the most significant ideas to emerge from computer science in the last twenty years. In his seminal essay "The Computer for the Twenty-First Century," Mark Weiser talked about "embodied virtuality," as "the phenomenon by which the 'virtuality' of computer-readable data—all the different ways in which it can be altered, processed and analyzed—is brought into the physical world" (1991, 20). Computers, he stated, will become "invisible" and will be "interconnected in a ubiquitous network" (20). In this context, he predicts, people will use computers "unconsciously to accomplish everyday tasks" (21). This vision of ubiquitous computing is seen as a direct contrast to, and even rejection of, the earlier vision of virtual reality. Ubiquity and immersion could thus be seen as two opposing forces that point to opposing ends of the virtuality continuum. However, the mixed reality performances that we consider in this book appear to comfortably combine the two, with participants sharing or contrasting perspectives between them or moving from one to the other during a temporally extended performance. In short, mixed reality performances deliberately adopt hybrid forms that combine the real and virtual in multiple ways and through this, encourage multiple and shifting viewpoints. Ten years after Weiser's essay, Jay David Bolter and Richard Grusin discuss how ubiquitous computing is turning "our whole world into a computer interface" (2000, 213). Whereas virtual reality immerses the user into a simulation, ubiquitous computing, they note, offers a world in which "everything is a medium because everything is or contains a computing device" (217). Here, they claim, "the question of the subject does not need to arise, because with ubiquitous computing, we do not have to occupy different points of view" (219). In this book, we show the opposite, which is that the question of the subject must arise in ubiquitous computing precisely because different points of view can be occupied, so the subject's way of experiencing this new mixed reality is always already based on the convergence, divergence, and reconvergence of multiple embedded and emergent trajectories. It is by adopting different positions on these trajectories that the subject can remain empowered in this new world, so aptly described by Weiser, in which real and virtual are continuously intersecting one another.

In whichever case, the essentially hybrid nature of the environment generated by the coexistence or superimposition of real and virtual merits further analysis. Here, studies of installations, performances, and games from the humanities shed further light. So, for instance, in his study of "virtual art" Oliver Grau dedicates a section to mixed reality in which he identifies the fact that users do not need to wear "oppressively heavy HMD" and are "not forced into the computer-generated body of an avatar" (2003, 245) and identifies hybridity as a distinctive characteristic of this type of space. In writing about Monika Fleischmann and Wolfgang Strauss's *Murmuring Fields* (1998), developed as part of eRENA, an EU-funded project that also involved the Mixed Reality Laboratory, Grau then notes how the work attempted to construct a "hybrid" space, a "combination of projection screen and viewing room, which does not alienate the observers from their own physical perception" (245). Distinctively, he also cites Strauss noting its aim was to emphasize "the body and its materiality and integrate its dynamics into virtual action spaces" (Strauss in Grau 2003). Unlike virtual reality, mixed reality in fact offers the possibility of creating such hybrid performative and participatory environments in which real and physical data appear, but not so much as integrated into one another but rather juxtaposed on top of or next to each other. Here, we aim to analyze how to design and manage these particular types of hybrid environments.

A number of other works developed over the last ten years distinctively blurred the boundaries between virtual and real. A popular example is *Majestic* (2001), a commercial alternate reality game reminiscent of the serial *The X Files* (1993–2002) that was played through a chat client integrating chat rooms, email, a buddy list, and a web browser in which players could also receive calls, text messages, and faxes providing clues that helped them to resolve the mystery of the game. In this case, the fiction of the game was seemly interwoven with players' ongoing daily lives. Other games that used similar strategies are *I Love Bees* (2004) and *Perplex City* (2005). Geocaching pervasive games such as *Big Urban Game* (2005) and *PacManhattan* (2004), aiming to disrupt social conventions in public spaces, also belong to this group. A number of early site-specific and interactive works developed by artists such as Myron Krueger, Lynn Hershman, Peter Weibel, Jeffrey Shaw, Monika Fleischman, and Wolfgang Strauss, among others cited in this book, also used varied mechanisms employed in mixed reality performance, as did, in more recent years, Rimini Protokoll's powerful piece *Call Cutta* (2005), a forty-five-minute experience in which participants were guided through an urban environment by call center employees based in India. Far from constituting a contained field, these kinds of works are increasingly affecting other forms of entertainment, such as film and television, social networking, heritage and museums, and even theme parks.

On the Nature of Performance

The second key aspect of mixed reality performance that we need to discuss is performance itself. In its most conventional form, this can mean scripted and staged performances given by actors within the mixed reality environment, and we shall see examples of these later on (although even these often involve actors performing everyday roles such as a receptionist or technician in contrast to more conventional fictional characters). However, there is also a second sense of performance in mixed reality performances in the way in which the traditional audience members of conventional theater are first transformed into being interacting participants or players, and subsequently into being performers in their own right. In large part, this is because the spread of technologies into everyday settings such as the city streets renders interactions publicly visible and so naturally turns them into accountable acts of public performance—for example, in the way that using a mobile phone on a train or in a café becomes an act of locally staged performance as well as of communication with a remote other. This directly reflects arguments from sociologists such as Erwing Goffman, who accounts for social actions in terms of the "performance" of everyday life (Goffman 1959). Furthermore, some mixed reality performers deliberately implicate passers-by in the experience and thereby potentially transform them into performers, albeit unwitting ones. In short, mixed reality performances establish multiple and coexisting modes of performance often spanning real and virtual environments.

Jane McGonigal, who has written extensively about various aspects of (what we term) mixed reality performance in performance and game studies, has tended to distinguish between ubiquitous computing games "which are deployed to colonise new objects, environments and users in the name of ubiquitous computing," pervasive games, which "aim to critique and disrupt the social conventions of public spaces," and ubiquitous games, which "work to materially replicate the interactive affordances of traditional digital games" (McGonigal 2007b, 233). Crucially, she notes that they have distinctive "reproductive practices" including "the proliferation of gameplay *citations*, the situated proliferation of gameplay *spectacles* and the proliferation of gameplay *affordances*" (233; emphasis in original). She also discusses how ubiquitous computing adopts Donald Norman's user-oriented concept of affordances and cites how Rich Gold, in discussing ubicomp proliferation, foresees that computers will be "embedded and hiding as it were, within the objects of our everyday life." In addition, she points out that "the everyday objects themselves become a kind of ruse" so that, as Gold predicts, "a baby doll (or toy block) might look like a familiar remnant of childhood, but it is really only one of a thousand distributed nodes which control the functioning of the whole house" (1993, 72). These kinds of object-machines then become, for McGonigal, "prompts" (2007b, 235) affording action between digital and physical worlds. McGonigal, who notes that Gold's closing remarks of his essay is "a vision of distributed networks of play and performance" (235), finally suggests that "ubiquitous gaming asks players to take up two core mechanics: first, searching for and experimenting with the hidden affordances of everyday objects and places; and second, exhaustively seeking to activate everything in their immediate environment" (236). These findings are also crucial in our analysis as we show how affordances can be used in design to transform the role of the spectator into a participant and even a performer by a series of trajectories that position the participant on different points of the mixed reality continuum.

McGonigal raises a number of other important points in her research that merit attention at this stage. In discussing her own alternate reality game *I Love Bees* (2004), she introduces the term "power plays," which she describes a being a "cross between a digital dare and street theater." In defining their characteristics, she depicts them as "live gaming events, conducted in public places and organized via digital network technologies, in which players are directed via clues to show up at a real-world location" (2007a, 252). She then identifies flash mobs as a "quintessential example of a power play" (252). Among its distinctive features, she mentions the fact that participants play in environments in which they usually would not be and interact with others, often strangers, in ways in which they normally wouldn't, but also by making "spontaneous spectacles of themselves" and rewriting the social rules of a given space "in highly visible ways" (252). These games are often guided by what she calls "puppet masters," which she describes as a group of "shadowy, often anonymous figures working behind the scenes as the writers, programmers, directors, and stage managers of the live gameplay" (252). McGonigal reads the relationship between these puppet masters and the power game participants as one of power, though she notes that as the term "puppet master" originated from participants, it denotes their desire to establish this particular type of transaction in this type of artwork. In this book, we shall discuss at length the nature of the "orchestration work" that is undertaken by artists and performers to shape the experiences of participants and players from "behind the scenes" and its impact on traditional performance roles. McGonigal then goes on to discuss how Blast Theory's *Uncle Roy All Around You*'s command-and-control structure raised criticism by Marc Tuters, who in his essay "The Locative Utopia" states that the design of the work has concerned those who feel that it represents "an unwelcome substitution of military logic over the 'real' world" (in McGonigal 2007a, 257). We will show here that although mixed reality performances and other similar experiences are designed in such a way that they do involve a certain degree of steering, they also facilitate emergent creativity and play and stimulate thought about the consequences of performing with "command-and-control" technologies. This is often achieved by means of ambiguity, which we and others (Gaver et al. 2003; Björk 2007, 277–278) identify as distinctive feature of pervasive games. Additionally, we show that here, as in much twentieth-century art, the very role of the spectator is problematic. We know from Söke Dinkla that historically in Futurism, but also in Brecht, and subsequently in American experimental performance and art from the late 1950s and 1960s, the passive role of spectatorship is challenged and audiences are turned into participants, thinkers, and even interactors (2001, 128). But in mixed reality performances, audiences are often encouraged to move from one role to another within the same work, thus gaining multiple perspectives over a given experience.

In summary, though mixed reality performances do indeed involve staging performances in mixed reality environments, the nature of mixed reality and of performance is complex and hybrid, involving multiple spaces, shifting roles, and extended time scales, all of which are connected in multiple ways through diverse forms of interface. Although existing theory from computer science and the humanities contributes to our understanding of the subtleties of mixed reality performance, they are not in our view sufficient to provide a fully comprehensive account.

Research in the Wild

Our approach in this book is to draw on a series of projects spanning more than a decade, during which the Mixed Reality Laboratory has collaborated with artists to create, tour, and study a series of mixed reality performances. Key to this body of work has been the gradual evolution of a distinctive interdisciplinary approach that tries to combine the goals of artists to create compelling and tourable new experiences with those of researchers who wish to develop new technologies (interfaces or software tools), conduct ethnographic studies of these technologies in use, or ultimately, develop new frameworks to explain them. Our book takes many of these projects as case studies, weaving them throughout its chapters. This involves documenting the experiences, revisiting and extending earlier studies and theories, and also interviewing key figures who were involved at the time. Given its steadily evolving nature and central importance to this book, we now offer a brief historical account of how our underlying research methodology has evolved over the years. Our aim here is to provide some general historical perspective on the case studies that follow and to thereby help place them into an appropriate context. We would say from the outset that our approach has emerged and evolved in quite an organic way and that it still continues to do so.

Although the Mixed Reality Laboratory was formally established in 2000, it grew out of a series of earlier projects and collaborations that had spanned the decade before that, many of them involving what was known as the Communications Research Group or CRG. The focus of the CRG during much of the 1990s was on the technologies and applications of collaborative virtual environments and shared online virtual worlds, but mainly focused support for business productivity in the form of online meeting and visualization tools. During this time, and reflecting a far wider trend in the field of human-computer interaction to incorporate ethnography—specifically, ethnomethodologically informed ethnography—into interactive systems design that had emerged from Xerox PARC in the United States and the Universities of Lancaster and Manchester in the United Kingdom (Hughes et al. 1994; Crabtree 2003), the team began working with ethnographers to conduct naturalistic studies of interaction in and around collaborative virtual environments. Much of this took place within the European COMIC project, a formative Basic Research Action that drew together multiple teams from across Europe who were driving forward the then–rapidly growing field of computer-supported cooperative work. These studies often involved relatively small-scale deployments of prototype technologies among the research teams, taking on the form of iterative quasi experiments in which the results of ethnographic studies were rapidly fed back into technology design. Early ethnographic studies provided rich descriptions, often through illustrative fragments of interaction transcribed from video recordings, of the nature of embodiment and talk in collaborative virtual environments (Bowers, Pycock, and O'Brien 1996); later ones addressed topics such as jointly manipulating virtual objects, pointing, and the challenge of establishing mutual reference in virtual worlds (Hindmarsh et al. 2000). These studies also informed a series of more theoretical papers that proposed theoretical abstractions for the field such as the "spatial model of interaction" (Benford and Fahlén 1993) that provided a framework of concepts to underpin the negotiation of awareness and communication among the participants of shared virtual worlds.

With the end of the COMIC project came two important reflections that led to a significant change of direction. The first was the recognition that the main applications of collaborative virtual environments would lie in the domain of cultural rather than business applications. Though there would no doubt be applications in engineering, medicine, and other areas, virtual reality is essentially about immersion in a fictional or fantasy world, and the most compelling applications (and surely the largest markets) for this would most likely lie in games, theater, and other forms of social and performative storytelling. The second was the realization that our studies needed to look beyond how the researchers themselves experienced the technologies to instead address the experience of real audiences. In other words, we had to move emerging technologies out of the lab and into public settings as rapidly as possible. Together, these reflections led the team to the realization that it needed to stage and study public events—performances and installations—that built on these technologies, an understanding that was carried forward into two further sibling European projects funded under the European Intelligent Information Interfaces (I-cubed) program, eRENA (more performance-oriented) and eSCAPE (more installation-oriented). Early performances such as the 1996 MASSIVE poetry slam (Benford, Reynard, et al. 2000) and the 1998 Out of this World "inhabited television" show (Greenhalgh et al. 1999) were tremendously exciting technological experiments that certainly produced some strong research papers, but were less compelling as artistic experiences. A response to the challenge of producing work that was both artistically strong yet could sustain innovative research emerged in 1996 through a chance encounter with the artists Blast Theory, who were experimenting with the potential of video projection into water spray as part of a residency at Nottingham Trent University. The synergy between this and the idea of traversable interfaces that was being discussed by the research team was immediately apparent and catalyzed the creation of *Desert Rain* (1998) under the umbrella of the eRENA project, the first project in a longstanding and highly productive collaboration between the Mixed Reality Laboratory and Blast Theory, and one that brings us to the beginning of the timeline for this book.

The approach of collaborating with artists to create and tour new theatrical works which are then subject to ethnographic study was picked up and further developed by the EPSRC-funded Equator project, a major UK research collaboration between eight UK universities into the "interweaving of physical and digital interaction for everyday life" that ran between 2000 and 2007. Coinciding with the official formation of the Mixed Reality Laboratory at Nottingham, Equator was instrumental (along with other funding from the UK's Arts and Humanities Research Council) in delivering *Can You See Me Now?* (2001–), *Uncle Roy All Around You* (2003), *Fairground: Thrill Laboratory* (2006), *Savannah* (2003), and a host of other experiences. Its approach was directly carried on into a further European project, the Integrated Project on Pervasive Games (IPerG) that delivered *Day of the Figurines* (2006) and *Rider Spoke* (2007). IPerG also saw an increasing turn to the humanities to enhance and broaden the basis of the theoretical work from which concepts, frameworks, taxonomies, and other theoretical abstractions would emerge. In particular, the involvement of the Centre of Intermedia at the University of Exeter introduced a new set of perspectives from the performance studies, drama, and new media fields, and brought to bear an extended focus on the documentation of mixed reality performance that has been directly carried forward into this book.

What emerged during this period was a methodology that came to be known as "research in the wild," a term that has since been picked up by the UK's science and technology research council (EPSRC) in its Digital Economy program. This has a few key defining characteristics:

- *Led by artistic practice* Projects would be proposed and developed by professional artists who would have a high degree of artistic control over their content and direction and who would also bring opportunities to stage them in public. Although the broad goals of funded projects and the results of previous projects would clearly provide a framework that would shape or constrain ideas to some extent, the aim was still to facilitate an artist-led exploration of novel applications of technology (when seen from a technologist point of view). This was because artists bring a very great degree of creativity and adventure to research projects alongside opportunities for public deployment and, through this, public communication of research ideas too. The overriding aim was to be adventurous, to take risks, to go public, and to encourage maximum exploration. This was no doubt facilitated by having large-scale, long-term funding, which enabled a degree of self-managed risk taking that is not always possible with shorter, more highly specified grant proposals.
- *Ethnographic studies* Ethnographers would conduct naturalistic studies of public performances, increasingly capturing and analyzing a wider range of documentary material including video, interviews, and system logs. The challenges of working on relatively short timescales and tight turnarounds increasingly involved carrying out

"quick-and-dirty" ethnographies, although it was often then possible to follow these up with multiple studies as a project begun its touring life. The need to handle diverse forms of data also led to the development of new tools such as the Digital Replay System. Key here is that these studies are not hypothesis-led; that is, they are not conventional scientific experiments. They are however informed by sensitizing concepts, which provide lenses through which to attack the challenge of analyzing a novel application. Ethnographic studies are a powerful way of studying practice-led projects, but this approach is not without its tensions—most notably, the need for ethnographers to be able to closely follow, record, and interview participants, which artists may feel will compromise the actual experience itself.

• *Abstracting theory* The final activity involves abstraction of theory such as the trajectories conceptual framework developed in this book. Frameworks, models, taxonomies, and so forth are an essential part of HCI and indeed of computer science in general (the skill of abstraction is perhaps the most important one for computer scientists to develop). Theory is, of course, also an important aspect of scholarly research in the humanities, which also aim to conceptualize broader findings from across a range of specific practice-led examples. Theories typically emerge from long-term reflection across a range of studies. Another important form of abstraction, and one not so directly covered in this book, is that of creating technical platforms and tools. Many of the projects described in this book have been supported by and also contributed to a series of general-purpose software environments, including three generations of the MASSIVE collaborative virtual environment platform and two generations of Equator's Equip platform created by Professor Chris Greenhalgh at the Mixed Reality Laboratory. In several cases, these platforms have been released as open source to the wider community and therefore represent a valuable form of abstraction and generalization of results beyond specific projects.

In general, our research methodology, at least when applied to a specific project, tends to proceed from artist-led creative practice, through naturalistic studies in the wild, to abstractions of theory and platforms. However, there is a danger of oversimplification here, as in the longer term, theories and technologies do feed back into additional projects and/or studies. Thus, although this general trajectory from practice to theory may often hold, there is in the detail a more complex set of relationships at play, as summarized (in a highly simplified way) by figure 0.2. Here we see that practice provides data for studies, but also that these can feed back directly into practice through iterative design. We see that multiple studies ground emerging theory, but also that theory provides sensitizing concepts for studies. Finally, we see that theory can lead to concrete design guidelines and design patterns that inform future practice, while it is also possible to derive some theoretical insights directly from documentation and critical analyses of practice.

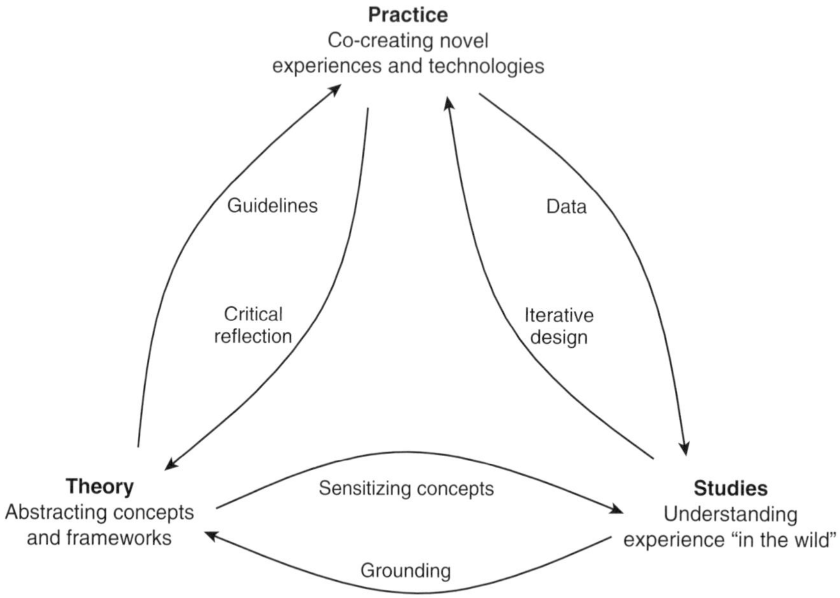

Figure 0.2
Relating practice, studies, and theory.
Copyright MRL.

Of course, our approach continues to evolve from project to project, so this diagram is not only a simplification of what actually takes place, but also merely gives a snapshot of where we are at the time of writing this book. How might we expect the approach to further evolve over the coming years? One of the most exciting recent developments has been the launch of the RCUK-funded Horizon Centre for Digital Economy Research at Nottingham. This provides a further long-term opportunity to support new projects over the coming years, with a particular focus on how ubiquitous computing can enhance the creative industries. Moreover, this new project actively seeks to widen the net and draw from the disciplines of business and management studies, film and television studies, sociology and psychology, performance studies, and new media to further broaden our perspective on how we understand emerging forms of interactive experience such as mixed reality performance.

A Theory Based on Trajectories

This book documents landmark examples of mixed reality performance and develops a new theory illustrating how they work. By "theory," in this context, we mean a framework of concepts that can serve to explain how existing mixed reality performances are designed, account for how they are experienced, articulate design strategies for creating future experiences, and relate developments in this new field to other fields and existing bodies of knowledge. To do this, we recur to an interdisciplinary body of work. Within the humanities we draw principally on new media theory, performance studies, and game studies, although we also use anthropology, design, and geography. Within social science we draw on ethnographic studies, and within computer science we draw on HCI, CSCW, ubiquitous computing, and virtual and mixed reality. Interestingly, two of our principal disciplinary perspectives in this book, human-computer interaction and performance studies, both came to prominence in the late 1960s/early 1970s. HCI emerged from human factors engineering and, since the 1990s, has also encompassed design, leading to the practice-based approach of interaction design. Performance studies, on the other hand, originated from theater studies in the late 1960s. For Richard Schechner, who initiated the discipline at that time, it includes the studies of "gatherings of every kind," but also "the structure of sports, ritual, play, and public political behaviors" (1973a, 3). Thus both HCI and performance studies are inherently interdisciplinary, and both are concerned with processes and practices that are experienced and performed in everyday life. Between them, they provide ideal and complementary departure points for the challenge of developing a theory of mixed reality performance.

We have already seen earlier when defining the term "mixed reality performance" that existing disciplines already have a great deal to say about the subject from their various perspectives. Indeed, there is a wealth of existing theory that might underpin any new theoretical approach. Computer science provides a number of theories and paradigms that are relevant here. Though the desktop PC remains the dominant form of computer interface today, this is rapidly changing, and the discipline has already yielded several competing visions of how to move "beyond the desktop." The paradigm of virtual reality and associated theories of presence concentrate on stepping "through the screen" to become immersed in a computer-generated virtual world, best seen in the spread of interactive computer games. Ubiquitous computing, which was originally framed as the antithesis of virtual reality, considers the explosion of computing from out of the desktop into the everyday world around us, broadly encompassing a variety of other ideas such as mobile, wearable, tangible, pervasive, embedded, and ambient computing. Mixed reality performances tend to combine both of these approaches. They are more akin to Milgram and Kishino's definition of mixed reality, which, as we have discussed earlier, considers a continuum as a way of capturing this relationship between immersion and ubiquity.

At the same time, mixed reality performance also exhibits distinctive temporal, spatial, and perfomative structures that are not addressed by the previously mentioned theories of mixed reality, but can be addressed through perspectives offered by performance studies, theater studies, and drama. Previous studies have discussed the theatricality of computer interfaces and stressed that because of it interface design has become "an *interdisciplinary* concern" (e.g., Laurel 1993, 5; emphasis in original). Other studies used theater and performance studies to describe pervasive gaming experiences (e.g., McGonigal 2006) and addressed the implicit theatricality and performativity of interactive experiences (Dinkla 1997, 2001; Giannachi 2004). Likewise, well-known game studies have utilized conventional dramaturgical concepts like space, time, characterization, and role-play (Wardrip-Fruin and Harrigan 2004; Salen and Zimmerman 2004) to explain how games operate. Most crucially, relevant studies in new media—such as Martin Rieser and Andrea Zapp's *New Screen Media/Cinema/Art/Narrative* (2002), Steve Dixon's *Digital Performance* (2007), Matthew Fuller's *Media Ecologies* (2005), or Susan Kozel's *Closer* (2008)—have investigated aspects of the field theoretically, often drawing from a number of disciplines. Although mixed reality is specifically mentioned in a number of these studies, only a few refer to it more extensively, such as Mark Hansen's influential *Bodies in Code* (2006), arguing that embodiment is now indissociable from technology, or, less explicitly, Lev Manovich's *The Language of New Media* (2001), which however formulates the necessity for the "emergence of a new cultural metalanguage" (93) able to define a culture that is increasingly "encoded in digital form" (70).

In other words, there is no shortage of existing theory that might help explain the nature of mixed reality performance. Yet we do not find existing paradigms sufficient to capture what, from our experience, is the essence of this new theatrical form. We shall argue throughout this book that mixed reality performances are neither virtual reality not ubiquitous, tangible, ambient, or embedded computing, or any single point on the virtuality continuum, but rather involve combinations and juxtapositions of all of these to create complex hybrid structures. In turn, they are also not simply traditional performances, conventional computer games, or even new forms of pervasive or alternate reality games, but rather mix all of these performance aspects into yet more hybrid structures that span diverse performance roles, time, and technologies. Our core argument is therefore that a new theoretical approach is required to capture both the essence and detail of mixed reality performance, and for this we turn to the idea of *trajectories*.

Why Trajectories?

Our analysis of mixed reality performance is based on the underlying idea that these forms of events are constituted by a number of embedded and emergent trajectories through an experience. We consider an experience to be a complex mixture of space, time, interfaces, and performance roles that are connected into a sophisticated structure using computing technologies. A participant's experience is constituted by a journey through this structure. Each participant may follow his or her own routes or trajectories, which intertwine and interweave in different ways to create social structures. Trajectories emphasize aspects of journey, continuity (with key transitions), future and past, perspectival points of view, and weaving and crossing, and thereby offer a distinctive starting point for considering mixed reality experiences. Moreover, trajectories can embody future planned action as well as past action, and thereby express not only a spatial and social, but also a temporal continuity of experience spanning past, present, and possible futures. Unlike routes or journeys, trajectories embrace both embedded and emergent narratives, thus representing not only a direction or path, but also a way of experiencing and performing mixed reality environments.

Etymologically speaking, a trajectory differs from a line, journey, thread, or trace in that it implicates the act of throwing across (*trans jacere*) and therefore indicates the movement of a body or object through space and in time. *Trans*, of course, alludes to the act of going beyond or across, of traversing and therefore also encompassing different worlds. But trajectories do not merely indicate a mode of transport. Whereas transport, as anthropologist Tim Ingold suggests, is "destination oriented" (2007, 77), trajectories express the progressive itinerary of a body or object as originated by an agent. This implies that both the agent, whether human or other, and the body or object itself can determine the precise direction and duration of a trajectory. In other words, a trajectory is influenced by an agent and by context. One can predict a trajectory, even mathematically, but never be in absolute control of it, as it is impossible to fully manage the context that determines how it is practiced and experienced at every given point in time. It is also impossible to define in absolute terms how a trajectory is likely to evolve over time. The object of a trajectory is therefore in a persistent state of unrest.

In this book, we use the term "trajectories" to indicate predicted and actual itineraries through mixed reality experiences. These emerge as the result of diverse types of navigation, journeying, and mapping. To describe the differences between these types of movement and understand what they might mean within the context of mixed reality performance, we recur to Ingold and start by saying that as knowledge about an environment is determined while we are "on the move" within it (2000, 230), and the environment is "perceived not from multiple points of view but along a path of observation" (238), the primary means by which to experience a mixed reality performance environment consists of the trajectories or paths of observation and experience that facilitate one's route through it. It is important to remember that these are both embedded and emergent and in some way represent the development of perspective within an art form, mixed reality performance, that is formed by the juxtaposition of digital and physical environments.

Trajectories throughout the History of Art

Most art forms have engaged with concepts that are related to our definition of trajectories. We now briefly introduce some examples to explore the similarities and differences between our definition of trajectories and uses of similar concepts in other disciplines and across different historical moments.

Trajectories in Theater Theater, performance, and new media all involve the creation of paths of observation. These are frequently related to paths of actions carried out by the actors or performers, with respect to the context dictated by the plot, its setting, and interactions with other performers both on and off stage. In the theater, the audience tend to experience paths of observation and of action collectively from the auditorium, whereas in experimental performance, where the audience is often dispersed and sometimes even on the move, possibly for prolonged periods of time, they are usually experienced subjectively. An example from theater is offered by Constantin Stanislavski's use of lines in *An Actor Prepares*, in which the naturalist director distinguishes between short, long, and broken lines, all to remain, however, "on our side of the footlights, and not to stray once into the auditorium" (1980, 258). Another example, this time from an experimental theater director, is constituted by Richard Foreman's use of strings on stage, which, in Foreman's words, intended to signal "that amorphous aspect of true-to-life perception, interfering with objects and actors, but also superimposing what I imagined to be 'lines of force' echoing the many trails of energy that do shoot through our lived visual field" (1992, 61). Interestingly, in both cases lines were used to indicate paths of observation that directly positioned the audience outside of the environment represented on stage, whereas in mixed reality performance the audience is usually located within both the physical and digital environment.

Trajectories in Performance Art In performance art, lines have been used to indicate the audience's route through a site, as is the case of Lynn Hershman's early site-specific work *Re:Forming Familiar Environments* (1975). In this work, Hershman hired members of the group COYOTE to perform tableaux in various rooms in Eleanor Coppola's house "doing simple everyday tasks such a taking a bath, sleeping, or peeling potatoes" (Tromble 2005, 44). Hershman in fact claims to have used trajectories to convert "ordinary and often overlooked spaces into extraordinary sites for expanded awareness." Thus, she says, "floor plans of the house were designed into game boards" and because the game's objective was "to (as minimally a possible) transform an inhabited dwelling; to alter perceptions about the potential uses of familiar environments" (Hershman 1975), trajectories were adopted to map the locations in which this contamination between the everyday familiar environment and its uncanny transformation into art occurred. Subsequently, Hershman used this term to define the relationship between networked identities, in an article about her synthetic female agents, *The Dollie Clones* (1995–1998), *Synthia* (2000–2004), *Agent Ruby* (1991–2004), and *DiNA* (2004). So, she notes, these "expand the possibility of singular identities into a networked trajectory composed of flowing data that eats itself, cannibalizing in the process information that mutates and is re-expressed in unpredictable ways" (2005, 209). Finally, Hershman used this term again in an interview (Giannachi 2010) in which she was discussing her interactive work *Lorna* (1982). Here she described them as a way of "trying to understand a direction that something's going, imagining how it's going to go, the staging of a process in the future." Though from an authorial point of view trajectories marked an imagined future path, from a given participant's point of view they constituted both the audience's path of observation and their path of experience. Crucially, as in the case of Foreman's work, they were used here to play with, but also to alter perception with respect to the relationship between the artwork and everyday life. In this sense, trajectories are not just scenarios, but rather hypotheses of movement and behavior that create a rhizomatic three-dimensional structure within which participants journey for prolonged periods of time.

Trajectories in Architectural Works Although trajectories are useful in determining an audience's path through an experience, they also constitute an important means to enmesh a work within a broader matrix of intertextual references. Architectural works often use lines in this way, such as—perhaps most famously in recent times—Daniel Libeskind's Jewish Museum in Berlin, the design of which was based, in the architect's own words, "on the invisible figures whose traces constitute the geometry of the building" (1999, 17). Thus the Jewish Museum follows the contours of an invisible broken Star of David, designing intertextual trajectories that intend to connect individual addresses in the city. The building itself is located at the intersection of Markgrafenstrasse and Lindenstrasse at the edge of Friedrichstadt, the district named after the first King of Prussia, Friedrich I. During the war, the entire area (part of which belonged to former Eastern Germany) was raided and almost completely destroyed except for two major buildings: the baroque Collegienhouse built by Philipp Gerlach in 1735, in which the writer E.T.A. Hoffmann served as a judge, and the German Metalworkers' Union Building, a major piece of European Modernism built by Erich Mendelsohn (1930). Markgrafenstrasse connects the museum with the square Gendarmenmarkt hosting the Karl Friedrich Schinkel Schauspielhaus (1821), as well as the German and French cathedrals built by Karl Gontard in the eighteenth century. The other street, Lindenstrasse, connects the site with the Berlin City Hall and what is left of the Old Town. The intertextual tension created by this matrix of addresses produces lines through which the building may be navigated and which embrace structural voids left by the building's architecture that symbolize the void left by the Holocaust. Creating connections between the warm curved lines of the baroque and the colder straight lines of modernist architecture, the museum spreads its wings across hundreds of years of history, stretching itself, like Benjamin's famous Angelus Novus (Benjamin [1955] 1992, 249), toward the future, while staring into the pile of debris left by Germany's past. Libeskind's work is an important example of how trajectories can span physical and cultural environments, a distinctive feature of a number of the mixed reality performances analyzed in this book.

Trajectories in Painting and Film In painting and subsequently in film, writings on the importance of lines—particularly in relation to Renaissance perspective but also at the time of the avant garde—abound, with the painter Wassily Kandinsky, for instance, drawing attention to the fact that lines are the "anti-thesis" to points because they entail an application of one or more forces, hence implying movement, but also tension and direction ([1947] 1979, 57–112). Similarly to Foreman's "lines of force," Kandinsky's use of the term thus reminds us that trajectories imply forms of "gravitational pull," or steering, and that they are useful not only to structure and analyze experiences, but also to study how these evolve over time. Another art form that influenced our definition of trajectories in mixed reality performance is film. Among a number of directors who wrote about lines in film is Sergei Eisenstein. Influenced by the use of lines in Renaissance painting, Eisenstein describes how lines can be utilized as a way to visualize "the character of a movement." So he notes that the construction of "concrete picturizations of roads along which were distributed the events that the artist wished to portray in particular sequence," typical of early graphic art ([1943] 1968, 148–150), was used to define complex spatiotemporal coordinates. As an example, he cites Domenico Ghirlandaio's *The Adoration of the Shepherds* (1485), showing that "the infant surrounded by the shepherds occupied the foreground, and on that twists forward from the background appear the Magi; so that the road ties together events which are, in subject, thirteen days apart" (150), indicating the development of a timeline or narrative trajectory within the painting's spatial setting. In a subsequent period, Eisenstein points out, the road is replaced by a "path of the eye," marking the change from a sphere of "representation to one of composition" that, once perspective started to be used, often included the viewer into the journey. So, he notes, "there is usually something in a painting which attracts attention before all other elements. From this point the attention moves along that path desired by the artist" (150). In mixed reality performance, the hybrid environment is designed or, to utilize Eisenstein's terminology, composed, in the sense that physical and digital aspects are considered as if in dialog with one another. Just as in film, dolly zooms are able to traverse environments and create trajectories across space, in mixed reality environments paths are designed along which real and virtual environments may be viewed and/or experienced in their relationship to each other and details from one made to have an impact on the other. In film, as Eisenstein notes, frames are able to "gauge the movement of the eye over a determined path" (151), which can then be matched to paths created by other forms like music or narrative (139); in mixed reality performance, cultural, physical, and digital data can be juxtaposed or intertwined to generate a complex hybrid compositions of fictional, physical, and virtual worlds.

Trajectories, Mapping, and Wayfaring

Although spatial navigation and the consequent design of routes, journeys, and even trajectories straddling across sites is not a novel practice in art, the span of these in mixed reality performance across real and virtual environments constitutes a crucial difference in the way trajectories are designed and practiced. The mixed reality performances we discuss in this book are locative, with some, as in the cases of Hershman and Libeskind, being also site-specific or site-sympathetic. Participants to these experiences tend to behave like Ingold's traveler who, in mapping, "knows as he goes" (2000, 231). This idea that to perform the mixed reality space the participant must map it is crucial in our analysis. To explain the implications of this assumption, we shall refer to Ingold, who describes how through cognitive maps the traveler does not plot their routes mechanically from A to B, as if executing a prescribed course, but rather "'feels his way' toward his goal, continuously adjusting his movements in response to an ongoing perceptual monitoring of his surroundings" (230). Proceeding by feeling their way is the principal means by which participants in a mixed reality performance perceive the hybrid environment in which they are located, and because this strands between real and virtual, this operation has to occur in both the physical and the digital worlds. This means that though participants to mixed reality performances may use maps, or even make maps as part of their experience, they are also mapping, in the sense that they are feeling their way through an unknown environment precisely in order to know it, constantly renegotiating the real and virtual elements that form it, learning to move *between* them, affording one *through* the other.

In this book, we show that artists design mixed reality performances through a variety of mapping strategies and that subsequently participants to a mixed reality work tend adopt a number of mapping and navigational practices to explore the environment, including wayfaring, trail-finding, and preplanned navigation. To explain the absolute difference between the forms of movement that mark the use of these trajectories, we shall refer again to Ingold. For him, though the navigator plots a journey through a cartographic map and then explicates the plot, in wayfaring "one follows a path that one has previously traveled in the company of others or in their footsteps, reconstructing the itinerary as one goes along" (2007, 15–16). Whereas all wayfaring is mapping, navigation, Ingold notes, is map-using (2000, 231). So travelers in antiquity and the Middle Ages were wayfarers rather than navigators, in that "they did not interpret the writing on the page as the specification of a plot, already composed and complete in itself, but rather saw it as comprising a set of signposts, direction makers or stepping stones that enabled them to find their way about within the landscape of memory" (2007, 235). Participants in mixed reality performance works are required to use both wayfaring and navigational skills. They map in that they reconstruct, often collaboratively, predesigned journeys by using physical and digital signposts not only to orient themselves in a given mixed reality environment, but also to design it at the same time. Moreover, they navigate by plotting their own journey in space via predesigned maps and occasionally design their own maps to further aid the navigational process or create mementos of their experience.

Trajectories in Past and Future

In order to conclude this initial discussion of trajectories, we need to dedicate some attention to the role played by traces, or practiced, historical trajectories. The trajectories that artists inscribe into mixed reality performances as well as those that participants actually follow also leave behind traces that affect future experiences. Of course, the processes and interactions engaged with in the making of and encounter with most art forms generate traces. These often act as documentation, and occasionally also operate as canonical examples of spectatorship, engagement, or participation. In much conceptual art, these traces become the work itself, whether in their own right, as in Giuseppe Penone's *Alpi Marittime* (*Maritime Alps*, 1968), in which the artwork consisted of the documentation of Penone's aesthetic interventions in a forest, or in their relationship with the "original," as in Robert Smithson's *Mono Lake Nonsite* (1968), which was composed of both the site representing the location from which materials had been taken and the nonsite located in the gallery. But in practicing mixed reality performance spaces, participants not only produce traces in physical locations, but also generate what we call "contextual footprints," digital records of their passage through both virtual and physical worlds, the latter increasingly captured through a variety of sensing systems such as the Global Positioning System (GPS), wearable biosensors and others. Some of these footprints are accidental, in that they were generated through technologies belonging to third parties that unintentionally captured the event (such as CCTV); some are external, in that they are generated via interactions occurring through social networking that do not in themselves form part of the artwork but that could be used to understand the broader context in which a work is generated, advertised, and received (such as artist- or user-generated images, sound files, and videos placed on Flickr, Facebook, MySpace, YouTube, or Twitter updates); others are intrinsic to the technologies used to produce the experience itself (such as GPS). Within the latter category, some footprints may form part of the work itself and become visible by participants; others may remain invisible to participants but could be used at a later point in time for evaluation and analysis. For instance, environmental footprints are likely to become increasingly important, and artists are already working with emotion footprints indicating how people respond to stimuli in a given cartographical and social context (e.g., Christian Nold's emotion mapping) and thrill footprints generated by utilizing adaptive rides aimed at the generation of thrill in entertainment parks (e.g., Brendan Walker's work presented in chapter 4). Within the context of mixed reality performance discussed in this book, some of the contextual footprints operate primarily as a documentation of the work, as in the case of the positional readings in *Can You See Me Now?* or *Uncle Roy All Around You*. Others, however, become part of the work itself, like the recordings left by riders in *Rider Spoke*, generating traces and trails leading participants onto particular journeys through the work. The concept of trajectories then becomes a useful tool to explore the value of these contextual footprints, which encompass data produced by artists, technologists, participants, and even bystanders, as well as users engaging with the work at a much later point in time, thus constituting the basis of a "*live* archive" that is able to evolve and reflect about itself over time.

However, contextual footprints have value not only because they tell us about past and emergent behavior, but because, like traces or trajectories, they may inform future behavior. Anthropologists tell us that traces play a fundamental role in the way that memories are transmitted from one generation to another. The wayfarer, Ingold notes, "lays down a trail in the ground in the form of footprints, paths and tracks" (2007, 79). Thus, he argues, "one learns by discovery while following in the *path* of an ancestor" (2000, 146; emphasis in original). Trails, therefore, are not just routes to remembrance, but are "routes to knowledge" (Lye in Ingold 2000, 148). In this sense, the past becomes the key that unlocks our future. This suggests not only that we learn through mapping but also that we learn future directions by mapping existing trails. Trajectories mapping traces of digital footprints can therefore play a crucial role not only in the way we study and learn from mixed reality performance, but also in the way in which we are likely to develop future knowledge and behaviors. Just as paths "impose a habitual pattern on the movement of people" (Jackson 1989, 146), such trajectories, and the contextual footprints that form them, may influence the "habitual pattern on the movement" of others.

For Ingold, "mastery consists in knowing what the environment looks like from all practically available *paths* of view, that what the traveler remembers are vistas and transitions" (2000, 239; emphasis in original), or a "passage from one vista to another" (238) rather than location-specific images, and that keeping track is a matter of regenerating the flow of perspective structure over time" (239). Within the context of a mixed reality experience, "mastery" then becomes practiced knowledge of canonical and participant, but also, crucially, historic trajectories that allow for the possibility of replaying and thus regenerating the perspectival view of the intersection between trajectories over time. Roy Wagner, writing about the aboriginal people of the Australian Central Desert, takes the impact of routes further, saying that for some cultures "the life of a person is the sum of his tasks, the total inscription of his movements, something that can be traced out along the ground" (1986, 210). Much locative work discussed in this book adopts hunter-gatherer habits, such as direct procurement, through missions, of means of survival from the "wild," so participants are required to remain "at one" with their environment—a distinctive feature of hunter-gatherer societies being that they do not approach their environment as "as an external world of nature" (Ingold 2000, 42), except that here the environment is both digital and physical, so the expression "at one" has to be adjusted to encompass both and to take into account the contamination of one through the other. Trajectories thus become the lines necessary for participants to orient themselves in this hybrid mixed reality environment generated by the juxtaposition between digital and physical worlds. The contextual footprints generated by such experiences then become the inscriptions through which our movements in space and time are marked. Through them, we can look at ourselves from another perspectival viewpoint, and analyze the very fragments and traces of our presence that may one day be adopted by an other to see what we saw and be who we were from within the world we temporarily inhabited.

To conclude, we are increasingly affected by the way that ubiquitous computing experiences, including mixed reality performances and other forms of elite and popular entertainment, are integrated in our daily lives. Trajectories, as we have seen, are useful not only for the design of these kinds of environment, but also for the design, management, and understanding of other aspects of past, present, and future living that are becoming increasingly part of a mixed reality. As Dourish noted (2001), trajectories could be used as a means to understand how social worlds may develop as a way to reflect about how to use trajectories to design a better future. For this, we recur to Gilles Deleuze and Felix Guattari's writings on lines in *A Thousand Plateaus* (1988). Here, the philosophers note that we do not just journey on lines but are rather traversed by them (meridians, geodesics, tropics, and so on) and are composed of bundles of multiple lines that are in part imposed on us from the outside and in part the result of our own making. To support their argument, they cite Fernand Deligny's study of autistic children in which "he transcribes the lines and paths of autistic children by means of *maps*: he carefully distinguishes 'lines of drift' and 'customary lines'" and, as well as walking, generates maps of perception and gestures and even language (in Deleuze and Guattari 1988, 202, and Deligny 1975). They write, "The lines are constantly crossing, intersecting for a moment, following one another. A line of drift intersects a customary line, and at that point the child does something not quite belonging to either one" (203). In this rhizomatic economy of lines, they note, "we must invent our lines of flight" (202). It is crucial that trajectories that are about designing but also about understanding the relationship between systems and individuals should allow for lines of flight, marking the possibility for evasion, difference, and change. Here, far from proposing merely a model of control, we explore how—through trajectories—paths can be designed that, by subverting the way we look and experience things, and by repositioning us within the *polis* of everyday life, have a powerful aesthetic, social, and even political impact.

The Structure of the Argument

Performing Mixed Reality has begun with an introduction to the definition of mixed reality, undertaking an initial investigation of what the term, and the practice it defines, have come to mean within HCI, new media, and performance studies, and especially to the work of the Mixed Reality Laboratory over the last decade. Following an analysis of why this field is best presented through an interdisciplinary approach, encompassing HCI, performance studies, new media, and game studies, as well as aspects of anthropology, geography, and ethnomethodology, the introduction has moved on to motivate and present the core concept of trajectories as a theoretical foundation for studying and realizing mixed reality performances. The following chapters now investigate in more detail the role played by trajectories in four key aspects of mixed reality performances—space, time, interaction, and performance—with each presenting key artistic events, educational games, or forms of popular entertainment that variously utilized mixed reality. At a theoretical level, the chapters draw principally from HCI, performance studies, and new media theory, though most analyses are also indebted to a number of ethnographic investigations conducted by Mixed Reality Laboratory staff over a period of eleven years as part of a series of EPSRC- and EU-funded projects. All chapters present original interviews with key figures in the field, including artists Matt Adams and Nick Tandavanitj from Blast Theory; United Kingdom–based thrill engineer and artist Brendan Walker, who has been collaborating with the Mixed Reality Laboratory since 2006; and staff from the Mixed Reality Laboratory itself, including architect Holger Schnädelbach, ethnomethodologist Andy Crabtree, and HCI researchers Boriana Koleva and Martin Flintham, who variously contributed, alongside the artists, and other staff from the lab who are cited throughout this book, to the development of the technologies, theories, and practices described in this monograph.

Chapter 1—on space—shows how mixed reality performances generate hybrid realities that span physical environments and virtual worlds. These hybrid spaces tend to encompass events that occur on different points of the mixed reality continuum, and are often juxtaposed or adjacent rather than superimposed upon one another. The seeming dichotomy between the physical and the virtual turns these hybrid environments into spaces of disjuncture, in which participants are made to feel "off balance." The chapter shows how hybrid spaces can be designed but also navigated through a combination of embedded or emergent trajectories. Focusing on Blast Theory's locative works *Can You See Me Now?* (2001–) and *Uncle Roy All Around You* (2003), as well as introducing the educational game *Savannah* (2003), this chapter analyses the salient features of these kinds of spaces, shows how they are designed through a number of interweaving canonical and participant trajectories, and notes that they are often constructed communally, as the result of a network of collaborations spanning between physical and digital worlds, and intertextually, linking the performance environment to matrixes of cultural, geographical, and historical addresses. Finally, the chapter explores how the nature of the ubiquitous computing infrastructure of wireless positioning and communication technologies that underpins hybrid spaces shapes the mixed reality performances that occur within them so that the site of performance may constantly shift during a given event due to changing coverage or accuracy of the technology used. We show how the "seams" in this infrastructure—that is, gaps in coverage and limited accuracy—have an impact on different participants' experiences, and discuss how trajectories are designed to cross such seams.

Chapter 2—on time—turns its attention to the idea of a hybrid, layered time within mixed reality performance, exploring various mappings between story time and clock time. The chapter, which adopts Blast Theory's pervasive game *Day of the Figurines* (2006) as a case study, also reflects on findings in sociology and philosophy of media claiming that we are witnessing the introduction of new forms of temporal organization that allow for fluidity between previously separate fields of social existence, such as work and entertainment. The chapter then introduces a general framework for describing the hybrid temporal structure of mixed reality performance in terms of five distinct layers of time—story time, plot time, schedule time, interaction time, and perceived time—and proposes the concept of temporal trajectories to express different mappings between them. Finally, the chapter presents an analysis of the value and nature of recording and replaying mixed reality performances.

Chapter 3—on interaction—focuses on the design of computer interfaces supporting mixed reality environments that are spatially and temporally hybrid. These interfaces are often tangible, embedding digital information and computation into physical artifacts, and sometimes traversable, establishing the illusion that virtual and physical worlds were adjacent, or joined together in such a way that one could move from one to the other. Focusing on Blast Theory's *Day of the Figurines* (2006), their early performance work *Desert Rain* (1998) and the museum installation *Flypad* (2008), as well as the site-specific *Shape Living Exhibition* (2001) designed by Mixed Reality Laboratory staff, the chapter explores the "transformative" role played by interactional trajectories in connecting these hybrid ecologies of interfaces. The word "transformative" is used to indicate how they facilitate the transitions that turn passive spectators into active participants or even performers, and herewith prompt or afford the action that is at the heart of the interactive process. Finally, the chapter discusses a taxonomy of spectator interfaces based on four strategies of designing secretive, expressive, magical, and suspenseful interfaces.

Chapter 4—on performance—considers the nature of participation in mixed reality performance by exploring trajectories through different performance roles. The chapter starts by analyzing the construction of theatrical, performative, and participatory roles in mixed reality performance, focusing on a triangle of core roles: performers, spectators, and orchestrators. It then discusses how participants move between these roles in a number of case studies, such as Brendan Walker's *Fairground: Thrill Laboratory* (2006) and Blast Theory's locative works *Rider Spoke* (2007) and *Ulrike and Eamon Compliant* (2009). Focusing on the function of framing, ritualization, and transactions, the chapter discusses how participants are given license to perform, thus constantly readjusting their position between everyday life performance in the physical world and performance in the digital world, resulting in the two contaminating one another. The chapter also analyses the changing nature of participation, and suggests that mixed reality performances involve a complex ecology of hybrid roles. Following a detailed analysis of the increasingly important role of orchestration, the chapter concludes with a discussion of how transitions, transactions, and journeys through these roles can be explained in terms of trajectories.

Finally, chapter 5—on trajectories—brings these discussions together by drawing out the general properties of trajectories, defining a framework of concepts that can guide researchers and artists who work in this field. The framework introduces three fundamental forms of trajectory: canonical, participant, and historic; identifies key transitional moments that may occur along these trajectories; and discusses how the interweaving of trajectories can express the social and collaborative aspects of an experience. These concepts are then put to work to analyze and explore alternative designs for two of the works introduced in previous chapters: *Uncle Roy All Around You* and *Day of the Figurines*. The framework aims to provide sensitizing concepts to guide future empirical studies; compile artistic craft knowledge into a form that is useful to a wider range of designers; identify requirements for new technologies; and ultimately establish the foundations for a dramaturgy of interactive user experiences. To conclude, the chapter draws attention to the actual and possible uses of trajectories in other subject areas.

1 Hybrid Space: Between Real and Virtual, Local and Global

This chapter investigates the construction of space in mixed reality performances. We show that mixed reality performances generate hybrid spaces that span, often intertextually, physical environments and virtual worlds. Our observations, which are grounded in two case studies, *Can You See Me Now?* and *Uncle Roy All Around You*, that combine these seemingly dichotomous worlds in a performative context, lead us to argue that such hybrid spaces are navigable through trajectories. Following a contextualization of hybrid space, we discuss how each participant pursues their own spatial trajectory, but also how these cross one another and are shaped by each other, for example as participants chase or guide one another. We then consider how trajectories embody future planned action as well as past action and therefore reveal one of their core properties—that they express a temporal continuity of experience spanning, past, present, and future, and so provide a powerful resource for planning and reflecting on mixed reality performances. We also explore how the nature of the ubiquitous computing infrastructure of wireless positioning and communication technologies that underpins hybrid spaces shapes the performances that occur within them. Drawing upon ethnographic studies of *Can You See Me Now?* and *Uncle Roy All Around You*, we show how the "seams" in this infrastructure—that is, gaps in coverage and limited accuracy—have an impact on different participants' experiences. Finally, we discuss how trajectories need to be carefully designed to cross such seams and introduce five strategies for achieving this: removing, hiding, managing, revealing, and exploiting seams.

Can You See Me Now?

Winner of the Golden Nica Ars Electronica 2003, *Can You See Me Now?* (2001–) was developed by Blast Theory in collaboration with the Mixed Reality Laboratory. In this location-based game, online players were chased through an online virtual model of a city by four street performers or runners who negotiated the streets of the city equipped with handheld computers that had wireless network connections and GPS receivers in order to capture them (Benford, Crabtree, Flintham, et al. 2006). Up to fifteen online players could take part in the game at any one time. These online players could move only at a fixed speed and had access to various views of the city. They could see the positions of other players as well as those of the runners and could exchange text messages with one another. Meanwhile, runners, who were Blast Theory performers, could move through the city and see the positions of the online players and those of other runners on a handheld map (see figures 1.1, 1.4, and 1.5). They could also see the online players' text messages and communicate with one another through walkie-talkies. The descriptions of what happened to the runners on the streets reached the online players in real time so that the latter would hear reports of traffic conditions and be aware of the physical effort undergone during the search. A player from Seattle commented, "I had a definite heart stopping moment when my concerns suddenly switched from desperately trying to escape, to desperately hoping that the runner chasing me had not been run over by a reversing truck (that's what it sounded like had happened)" (Blast Theory 2003).

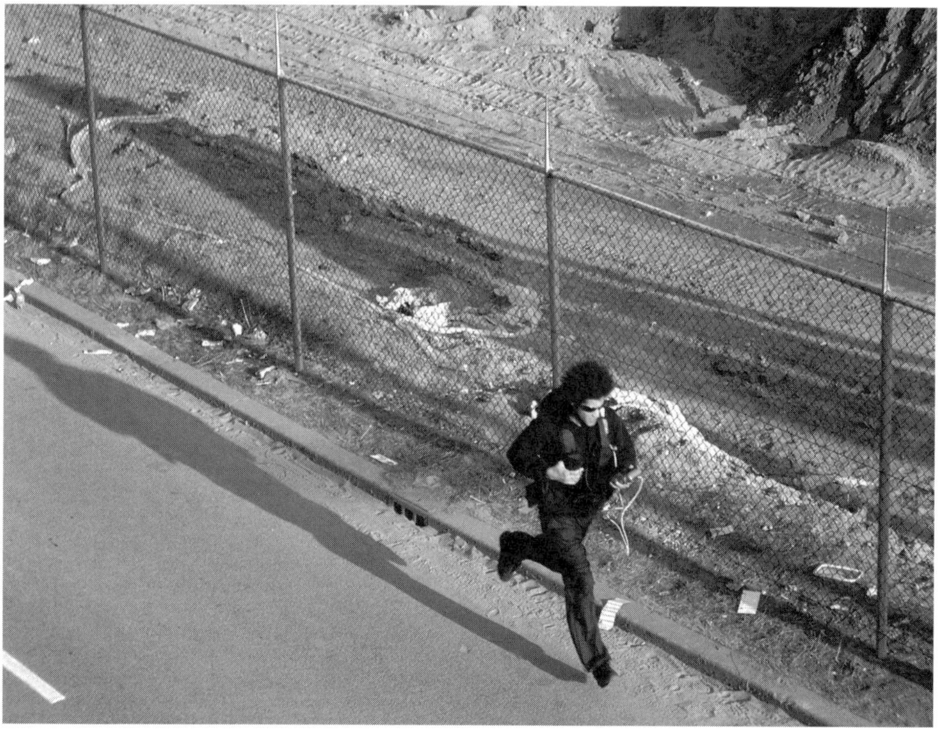

Figure 1.1
Can You See Me Now?, Rotterdam (2003). Runner.
Copyright Blast Theory.

The online players' experience started when they were asked to enter a name for themselves in response to the question "Who are you looking for?" After waiting in a queue for some time, they could join the game and were dropped into a city map at one of several predetermined positions. The game zone was approximately 500 meters by 1000 meters. Online players could use their arrow keys to move around the map, but would not be able to move off the map or enter solid buildings and other restricted areas. In the Sheffield game (2001), players were represented by a white icon showing their current position according to their local client, providing immediate feedback about their movement, and a blue icon showed their position according to the game server. The blue icon would lag behind the white one by a few seconds. Other players were also represented by blue icons, and the anonymous runners were shown as orange-red icons (Benford, Anastasi, et al. 2004). In subsequent games, online players were represented by running avatars (see figure 1.2). Online players could exchange text messages, and audio from the runners' walkie-talkies was streamed over the Internet so that online players could listen to their conversations, which were partly prescripted. If players were seen—that is, if they moved within 5 square meters from the runners—they were removed from the game and offered another opportunity to join the queue. The players' score was represented by the time elapsed since they joined the game.

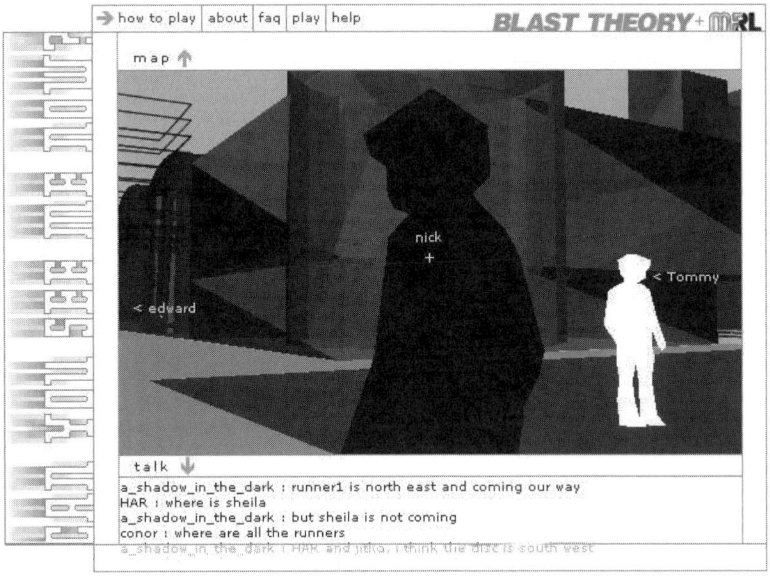

Figure 1.2
Can You See Me Now?, Rotterdam (2003). Avatars.
Copyright Blast Theory.

The runners saw a map of the city showing their own position as well as the online players' positions and text messages (see figure 1.2). They could talk to each other on walkie-talkies and communicate with the control room on a dedicated technical channel so that the online players would not hear them. They could zoom between a global view and a close-up local view centered on their current position. The relationship between the virtual and real city was fluid. At some levels the two seemed identical, so, for instance, the virtual pavement and the real pavement matched exactly and behaved in similar fashion. In other ways, the two cities diverged and appeared distinct from each other. For example, traffic was always absent from the virtual city (Blast Theory 2003). As well as their walkie-talkies, the runners carried digital cameras to photograph the physical locations where online players had been caught. Pictures of these sites of capture then appeared on an archive website after the event. Each player was therefore finally linked to this anonymous square of the cityscape indicating where their game had ended (Anastasi et al. 2002).

Can You See Me Now? encouraged "online players to experience the city through another person." Although they were dispersed, possibly playing from different continents, the runners were all located in the same section of the city. Online players were able to identify as a community of players because they had all been virtually "relocated" to this remote urban destination in which the runners were actively chasing them. The game logs showed that through texting, players collaborated in orienting one another with the runners, helping each other to avoid the runners, taking evasive action, organizing collaborative gameplay, and finding and meeting one another, as is the case in the following example (see figure 1.3):

#13. *VESPER*: Let's all gather—makes things more exciting.
ANNICK: Where?
VESPER: And when the runners come we scatter.
PHIL: This could be interesting when they come running for us.
VESPER: Between Las Palmas and Sumatra. (Benford, Crabtree, Flintham, et al. 2006, 109–110)

Online players had a "prosthetic" relationship to the physical site. They would be hearing how the runners were moving, become aware of obstacles that they encountered such as traffic, hear when they were tired and out of breath *through* what the runners themselves said via the walkie-talkies (Benford, Crabtree, et al. 2004). This of course also indicated that the runners could prescript and generally simulate certain conditions. Typically for Blast Theory, these game dynamics entailed a level of trust, but also of control and manipulation. On the one hand, the runners could stage what was happening to them. On the other, online players could manipulate them into certain experiences. So they frequently came to realize "that their online actions [were] having a remote physical effect (e.g., that the simple act of crossing a line on a map

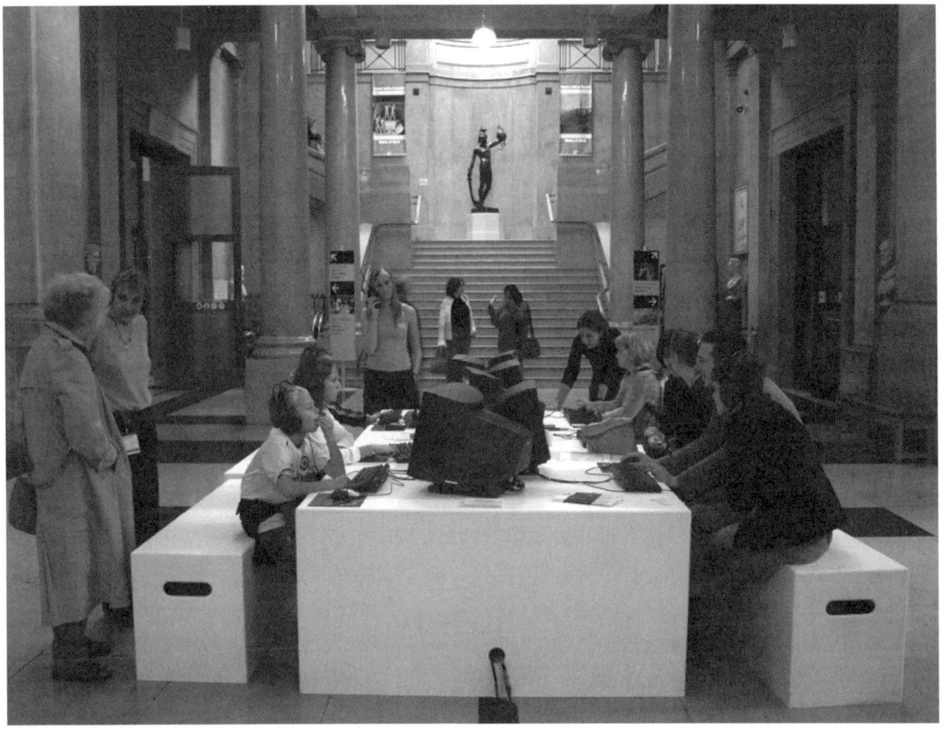

Figure 1.3
Can You See Me Now?, Cardiff (2005). Online players.
Copyright Blast Theory.

may cause another person to negotiate the traffic to cross a busy street)" (Benford, Crabtree, et al. 2004, 2).

Although the piece primarily operated spatially, in that it brought geographically remote players in contact with one another, it also entailed a form of temporal expansion. Although the game appeared to be purely result-based, in the sense that when online players were caught the game ended for them, it also attempted to break the game's temporal frame by rendering concrete the memory of someone from the players' past, who did not belong to the game world, at a crucial moment marking the end of their experience in the game. At the point of registration, players had been asked the question: "Is there someone you haven't seen for a long time that you still think of?" This person, who seemed irrelevant for most of the game, was then brought back when players were caught or seen by runners. At this point, the name was mentioned again in the live audio feed from the streets. A player from Dublin described this uncanny moment as follows: "The absence of this person from my life was suddenly converted into a palpable presence through the dynamic physical and mental responses of my body to the emotions, which came from hearing her name" (Russell 2007).

Spatially, the game played with telepresence or presence at a distance. Just as online players could render the runners breathless and even put them in some danger by forcing them to cross busy roads or visit isolated spots, the runners could terminate the online players' game, but also mislead them by giving them inaccurate information that would then lead to their capture (see figure 1.4). Temporally, just as the figure from one's past was seemingly absent from the game, it was the shouting out of their name that marked the one moment in which the online players' presence was documented in the game, a moment that was captured through a photograph marking the player's absence from the site that would then represent that player's "presence" over time in the game archive (see also Russell 2007).

An early study of *Can You See Me Now?* indicated that one of the most interesting design features of the game was that both the online players and the runners inhabited separate "worlds" or environments that were connected together virtually to create

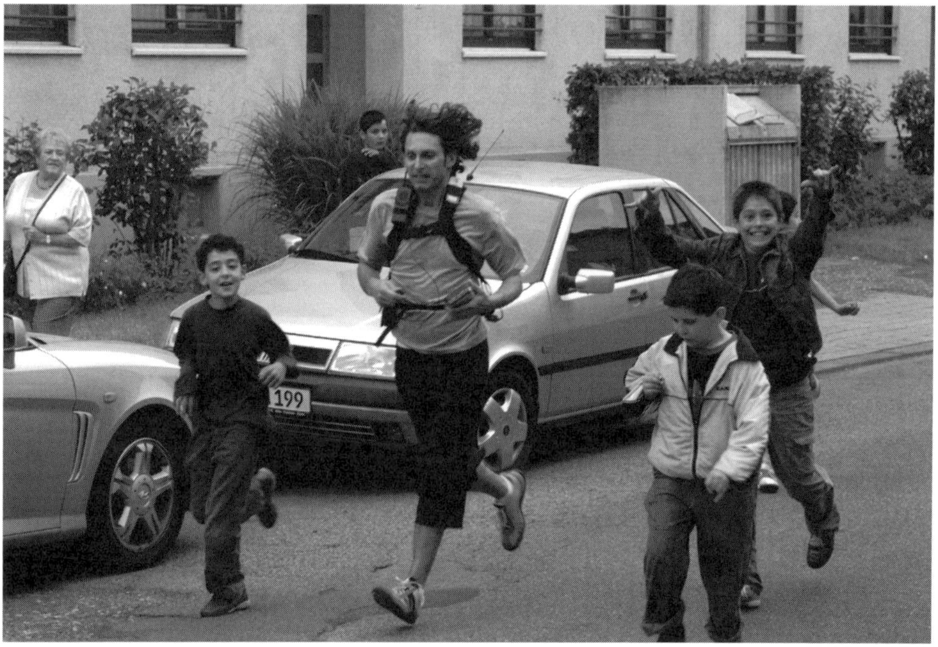

Figure 1.4
Can You See Me Now?, Cologne (2004). Runner with kids.
Copyright Blast Theory.

"an *adjacent reality* rather than an augmented reality, which in its ideal tries to seamlessly connect one world to another." The study noted how this structure, combined with the audio system, encouraged "online players to imagine the runners' experience through their verbal description of the physical world in relation to the virtual model" (Benford, Crabtree, Flintham, et al. 2006, 108; emphasis in original). In the Rotterdam game (2003), this disjunction between the real and the virtual city was emphasized by the fact that buildings that had not yet been built were shown in the virtual city as wire-frame representations, thus aiming for a potential rather than a current representation of the city (see figure 1.2). This had the effect of stretching the temporal frame of the game to include future design of the site. But much more endemic to the piece was a form of uncertainty that emerged from the fact that both online players and runners had to deal with the ambiguities created by the intermittent functioning of their GPS and Wi-Fi. Although online players were mostly unaware of these uncertainties, there were some occurrences in which their effects became apparent to them. Runners, on the other hand, were very aware of the uncertainties inherent in the game, so much so that the management of interruptions became "an essential feature of gameplay" for them (Benford, Crabtree, Flintham, et al. 2006, 114; see also Crabtree et al. 2004). The study concluded that uncertainties are "a fundamental characteristic of location-based experiences" (Benford, Crabtree, Flintham, et al. 2006, 121) and that five different strategies could be identified for coping with it, namely: remove, hide, manage, reveal, and exploit uncertainty (Benford, Crabtree, Flintham, et al. 2006, 130–131). Following is an example of a runner dealing with uncertainty and cooperating with others:

#19. *MARCEL*: Attention. Runner 1 is cheating by using his invisible coat.
HBAB: What's an invisible coat?
MARCEL: Never mind what the coat is—he can pop out of nowhere. (Benford, Crabtree, Flintham, et al. 2006, 113–114)

These forms of uncertainty were correlated by a complex series of disjunctions and discrepancies. We have already seen how the online players had an almost intimate knowledge of the runners' experience but were physically removed from them. Moreover, the virtual and the real cities did not entirely coincide with one another, but they were the only means by which online players and runners could find and control each other. Online players who had lost contact with someone were brought back in "touch" with them once they were captured by a runner. This capture would allow players to be "placed" in the game in the sense that their location was immortalized through a photo even though they were not physically present in this location. These disjunctions were exploited by a player in Dublin who, utilizing Wi-Fi, located himself in the game space, alerted the runners that they could find him at the Harbour Master Pub, and finally suggested that they should call in for coffee. He commented on this experience as follows: "I watched as runners moved about my physical space, aloof, disengaged, unaware of my presence. . . . My participation as player had switched to controller or at least instigator or voyeur or surveillance operative" (Russell 2007). The same dynamics emerged from a conversation with Matt Adams, founding member of Blast Theory, who felt the entire experience of *Can You See Me Now?* explored "the limits of our commitments and obligations to one another" and showed that "electronic places are fraught places of trust" (2005). Focusing our attention on the game's dynamics of control, he explained:

> I am sat online, playing in my bedroom, 2,500 miles away from where someone is on the streets of a city in the rain in an anorak and trainers, running as it gets dark through rush-hour traffic. And as I exert pressure with my index finger on the left arrow key and turn into the virtual park, this human being is required by the rules of the game to leap the hedge into the muddy grass and run up the steep slope through the park to maintain this game space. (Adams 2005)

As is evident from Adams's description, *Can You See Me Now?* did not just frame its players, whether online performers or runners, into a playful and seemingly unproblematic game of chase that required some level of trust and cooperation. Rather, the game dynamics made it possible for the online players to quite literally direct the runners' journeys (see figure 1.5) and thereby affect their physical and psychological experience of the game. By steering the runners' experience, the online players created the soundscape to their own experience that constituted the means by which they perceived the city in which they had been relocated as *live.*

Uncle Roy All Around You

The location-based game *Uncle Roy All Around You* (2003–), developed by Blast Theory and the Mixed Reality Laboratory, was a hybrid experience merging aspects of computer games with live performance. Following a brief induction, participants were required to venture into a city in search of an elusive figure called Uncle Roy. Online participants were able to track their progress in a parallel online virtual model of the same city. As in other Blast Theory works, the induction constituted an important gateway into the piece. After handing over their possessions, and having a photo taken, participants received a handheld computer or PDA, and were told to locate the mysterious figure of Uncle Roy in approximately sixty minutes. The PDA showed a map, which corresponded to the game area. Meanwhile, remote players could monitor their progress through the online virtual model, and offer advice via text messages that could reach participants in real time. The map could be dragged around to show other areas and there was a zoom facility and an "I am lost" button. There was also a built-in microphone, allowing participants to communicate verbally with the online players. Once participants left the venue, and became street players, they received a

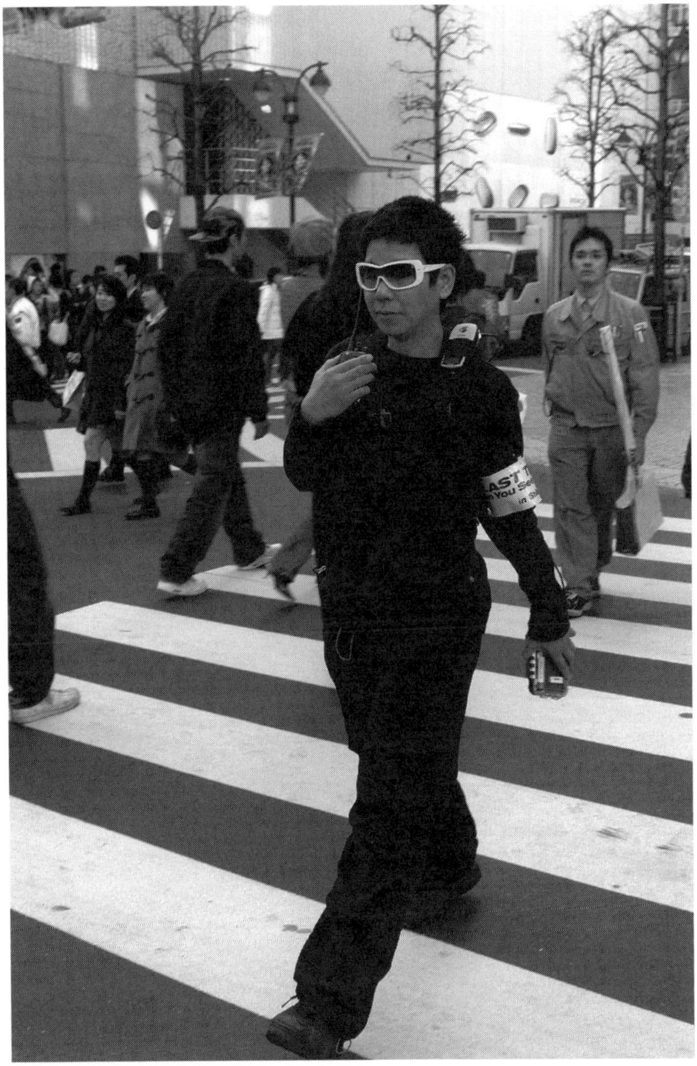

Figure 1.5
Can You See Me Now?, Tokyo (2005). Runner.
Copyright Blast Theory.

message from Uncle Roy saying, "Meet me in the park by the lake. I've marked your map with the location. Click on the 'I'm here' button to confirm you've arrived and I'll come to meet you." On the map, a red button indicated the location of the meeting. Street players could declare their position by using a "drag me" icon on their PDA map to their current location and then pressing the "I'm here" button. Meanwhile, online players could monitor their movements and even collaborate with them. Each time street players declared their location, Uncle Roy would send them a message, offering further clues about his position.

Street players searched for Uncle Roy following a series of clues (see figure 1.6). These were predominantly prescripted and developed site-specifically. Their main function was to direct participants across the city, engage them into live interactions in unfamiliar settings, and turn their attention to specific sightings. For instance, in the Manchester version of the game, street players were asked to find a postcard that had been placed among a stack of papers in a gay bar. Subsequently, they were led toward Chinatown and asked to adventure into a "dark, rubbish-strewn street, filled with fetid smell of decomposing peppers" (Dodson 2004). Clues had the function of reminding players that they were running out of time to find Uncle Roy. If participants

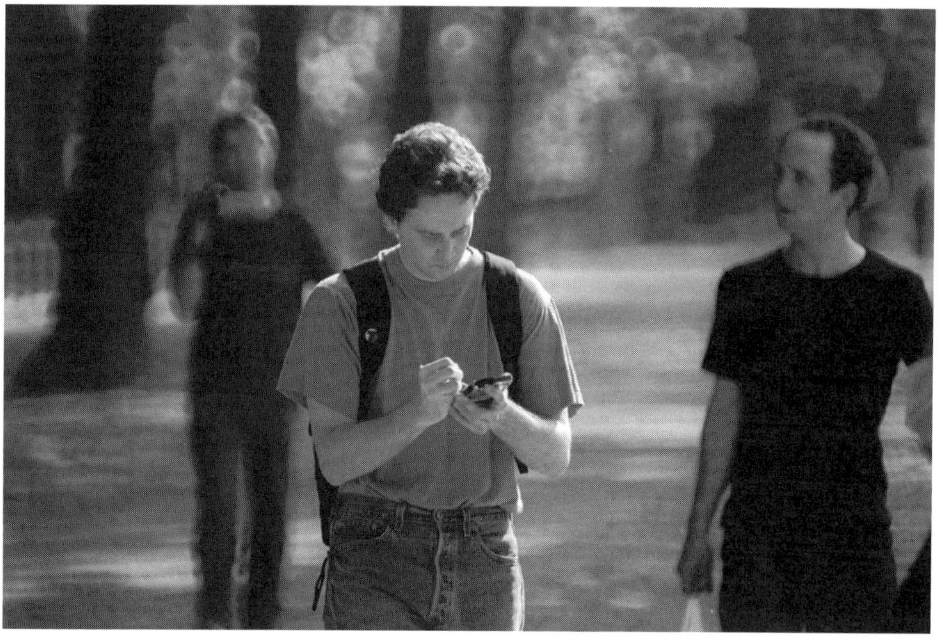

Figure 1.6
Uncle Roy All Around You, London (2003). Street player.
Copyright Blast Theory.

journeyed too far away from their prescripted routes, clues would also be used to indicate to them how to return within the game's mapped area. Clues were often deliberately ambiguous, "misleading to the point of being mischievous." Street players were directed to follow diversions, which increasingly implicated them in the materiality of their locality. They were also directed to notice passers-by. This had the effect of "heightening the sense of being watched" while at the same time "casting doubt on the intent and personality of Uncle Roy" (Benford, Flintham, et al. 2004). For example, clues might say: "You are doing well. Drift towards Buckingham Palace. After a couple of minutes click I am here. You have NN minutes remaining" (Benford, Flintham, et al. 2004).

Players were monitored by Blast Theory members, or street performers, who could intervene in their game to help them to find their way, remedy a technical fault, or address crucial contraventions to the rules of the game. Even at this level, actions were always carried out from within the frame of the game so that players reported experiencing a feeling of "uncertainty and mistrust" when facing the street performers (Benford, Crabtree, Reeves, et al. 2006, 433), who might, for instance, interrupt them with sentences like "Uncle Roy informs me you have a problem" (Dixon 2007, 666). While searching the city for Uncle Roy, street players also received messages from online players. These were taking part in a slightly different mission, namely to enlist street players in order to retrieve a postcard from a given location in the city which should then be posted back to them. Postcards were placed in bars, telephone booths, and even inside bicycle bags to encourage street players to "cross the boundaries of normal behavior in the city" (Benford, Crabtree, Reeves, et al. 2006). Online players were connected to the game through the Internet and navigated a parallel 3D model of the city by moving their avatar through this model, thus encountering and exchanging text messages with other online players (see figure 1.7). They could also access details of current street players, including their name, gender, description, and a photograph taken when they registered for the game. Finally, they could zoom out to a bird's-eye view showing them the positions of all street players and landmarks labeled on the map. Online players and street players were required to collaborate to find Uncle Roy. To maintain orientation and be able to progress in the game, street players had to trust and often act on instructions received by the online players, which were frequently ambiguous, such as, "Follow the man in the T-shirt at the traffic lights" (Adams 2006).

When street players in London reached the zone with Uncle Roy's office, they'd receive a message stating, "Go to number 12 Waterloo Place and ring the buzzer marked Roy." As the door slid open, they were asked to enter a deserted office. Inside, the room was furnished in 1970s style with an architect desk, a red vinyl chair, a small table, a brown carpet, and a Roberts radio broadcasting Radio 4. The walls were dark green and there were some empty shelves. On the ceiling, there was a webcam

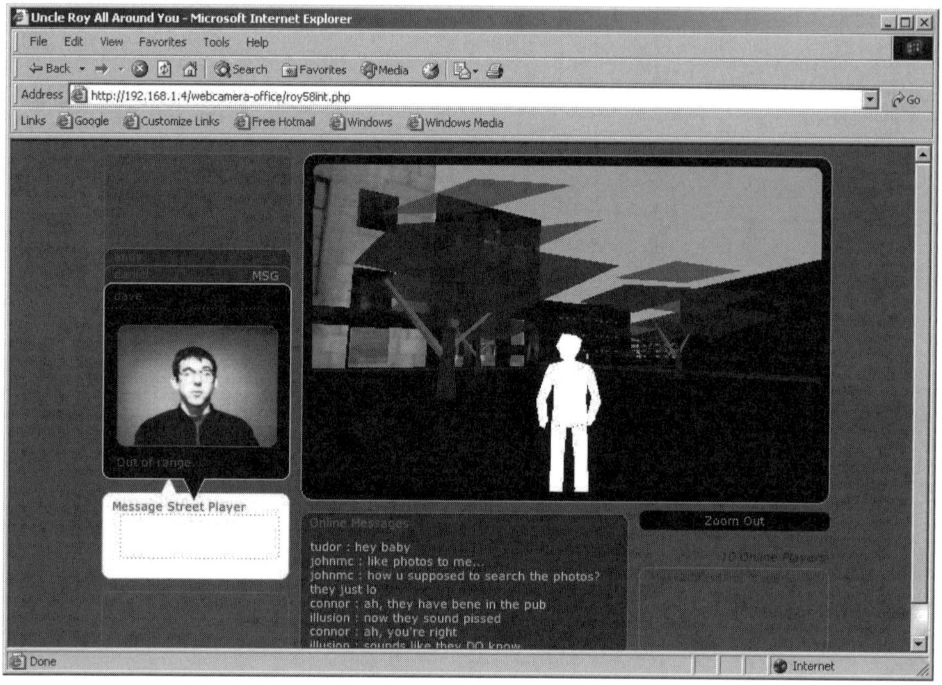

Figure 1.7
Uncle Roy All Around You, London (2003). Player interface.
Copyright Blast Theory.

monitoring everything they were doing. A model of the surrounding city made of Post-it notes was displayed on the desk. On a nearby monitor, there was an augmented display showing the Post-it note city populated by current street and online players of *Uncle Roy All Around You*. Online players could see the street player through a live webcam link. At this point, online players were asked: "Somewhere in the game there is a stranger who is also answering these questions. Are you willing to make a commitment to that person that you will be available for them if they have a crisis? The commitment will last for 12 months and, in return, they will commit to you for the same period." If players agreed to make this commitment, they were invited to enter their postal address. Meanwhile, in the office the street player could see a postcard that read, "When can you begin to trust a stranger?" printed on it. Via the handheld device, Uncle Roy then asked the street player to answer the question and go to a phone booth outside the office with their card (see figure 1.8). Here, they received a call instructing them to get into the back of a white limousine parked across the street (see figure 1.9). Once they were in the limousine, a man sat next to them in the back

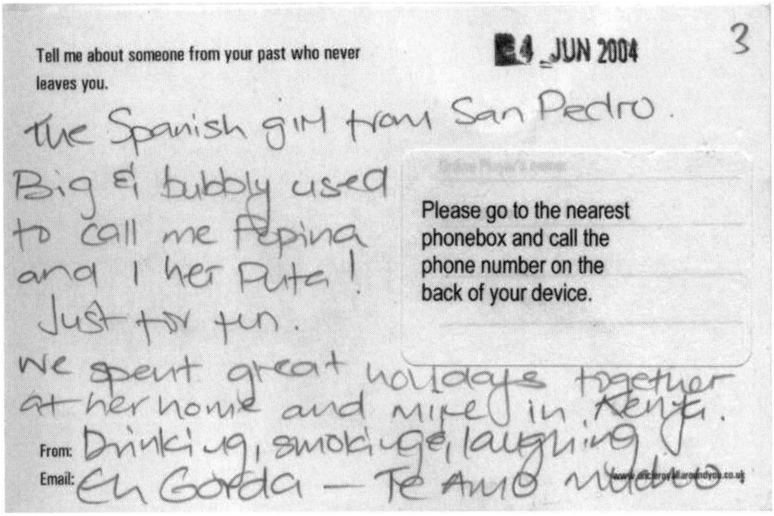

Figure 1.8
Uncle Roy All Around You (2004). West Brom Postcard Scan.
Copyright Blast Theory.

seat of the car and asked them the same question the online player had already been asked. Participants could then finish the game in their own time.

In the words of Matt Adams, the game played on a contrast or "disparity between the city as a place of quotidian banality that is based around drudgery and servicing our various needs" and "the city as a fantastic place for otherness and endless possibilities where multiple worlds are nested in one another" (2005). Described as an "arena where the unfamiliar flourishes" and a "zone of possibility" (Blast Theory 2005), the city constituted the somewhat hyperreal stage of this game. Street players, who were at once "inside and outside the game" (Adams 2005), were required to interpret clues, wayfaring through urban spaces that—seen through the lens of the game—often acquired unexpected, uncanny qualities. Instead of presenting the global city as a site of "progressive dematerialisation" (Crang, Crang, and May 1999, 120), no longer connected to local geographies (Sorkin 1992, xi), Blast Theory adopted surveillance technology to present the city as a navigable object. Here, the simulation did not operate in substitution to the city's materiality, but rather was ambiguously overlaid with it. Likewise, the game did not ignore local geographies, but rather built on them, so that street players were directed to look at, in the case of the Manchester game, for example, what has been described as "grand, redbrick Victoriana, a solitary, minaret-like chimney, manky flags flattering outside faded hotels" (Dodson 2004). This was particularly evident when *Uncle Roy All Around You* was performed in London

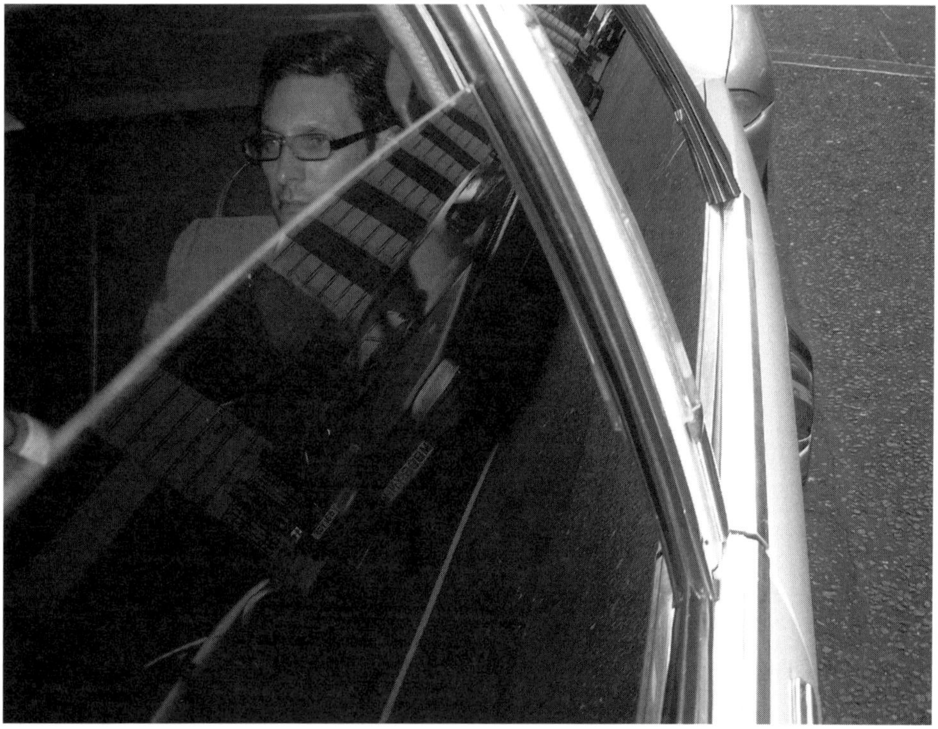

Figure 1.9
Uncle Roy All Around You, London (2003). Performer in the limousine.

at the ICA (2003). As Adams notes, the site here was not only "charged with personal history" (2005), but had further cultural, political, and social ramifications. Apart from the historic quality of the built environment, the game had taken place at the time of the Queen's birthday. The site, which consisted of around one square kilometer of London streets, had been crowded with police and was surrounded by helicopter units. It was also the known location of a number of documentaries and films, such as the Harry Palmer films, in which Michael Caine played the anonymous secret agent. Finally, the site was charged with political implications, as the barracks nearest to Buckingham Palace, for instance, are located just round the corner from the hosting venue (Adams 2005). These factors contributed in creating an intertextual context for the game, which prompted some street players to feel "rather like the protagonist in a film" (Adams 2006).

Seemingly, *Uncle Roy All Around You* just charged participants with the responsibility of fulfilling a mission. However, the piece framed players within what has been described as a complex "set of internal relationships" (Adams 2005). The dramaturgical strategy of the game, explains Adams, had been that by "not announcing a concept or theme; clearly, [people were invited] to inhabit these spaces and then be implicated much more directly in the relationships that emerge and the ways that technology is mediating their relationships with other players and the artwork generally" (2005). Interestingly, these relationships were intended not only to last for the course of the event, but also to affect participants beyond it. Both the beginning and the ending of the piece required an element of trust and were intended to make participants rely on and feel dependent on the information received. Though the beginning intended to increase their sense of anticipation and dependence on Uncle Roy, it also isolated and disconnected them from their own means to communicate with their own friends and family (Benford, Flintham, and Drozd 2006) so that all they could rely on in the end was the information received through the PDA. Likewise, the ending aimed at expanding this reliance by encouraging participants to trust a complete stranger for a prolonged period of time. Thus London player Kate Adams, for instance, recalls how she suddenly realized that her agreement to stay in touch with another player would "have *real* consequences outside the game" (2006; emphasis added).

Previous studies of *Uncle Roy All Around You* identified three design strategies for such location-based games. These were to (1) "use the city as your canvas"; (2) "exploit ambiguity"; and (3) "encourage social game-play" (Benford, Flintham, and Drozd 2006). Unquestionably, the city had been used as a stage for the experience, and not only were real locations referred to during the chase for Uncle Roy, but physical locations like the limousine, a bench, and a phone box were also integrated within the game; others, like Uncle Roy's office, were staged. To facilitate collaboration, players were given distinct perspectives, so that they would be motivated to exchange information and work together while maintaining the feeling that they were on distinct journeys. Passers-by were often implicated in the game, and emergent live action and preprogrammed content were mixed, so that participants were deliberately left unsure of their status, wondering, often somewhat paranoically whom to trust, what exactly the online players could see, and whether what they themselves were witnessing had been planted by the company or was part of the occurrence of everyday life. Questionnaires revealed that participants variously "suspected everyone," "asked a bunch of strangers if they were Uncle Roy," felt "everyone in London passing being involved," and that they did not know "who at first was a performer and who was not a performer" (Benford, Flintham, and Drozd 2006). Typically, *Sunday Times* critic Stephen Armstrong confessed that he was "reduced to stopping passers-by and begging them for help, in the belief that they were Blast Theory stooges" (2003).

As part of these preceding studies, a framework was conceived that aimed to capture the spectator experience of this game. This framework, which we expand upon in chapter 3, distinguished between various forms of engagement within such location-based games. It defined a performer as "the primary user of an interface" and the spectators "as the secondary users who experience their interactions, either as part of a deliberate performance or accidentally as a side effect of being present in the same environment" (Benford, Crabtree, Reeves, et al. 2006, 433). It further distinguished between an audience, denoting "spectators who are within the frame of the performance" and bystanders who are "outside of the frame" and maybe observing interactions that belong to the frame of the game but are "unable to interpret them as a performance" (434). Adopting Gregory Bateson's theory of performance frames (1955), and its subsequent readings by Erwin Goffman (1974) and Richard Schechner (1993), *Uncle Roy All Around You* was found to have extended the apparent frame of the performance beyond the actual frame by "drawing on bystanders as content; implying that bystanders are involved; heightening the perceived or actual exposure of performers and audience to the scrutiny of bystanders." At the same time, the apparent frame of the performance was shrunk inside the actual frame of the performance by "implying that actors are bystanders" and "implying that props and controlled spaces are in fact external objects and spaces" (Benford, Crabtree, Reeves, et al. 2006, 435). At design level, the team aimed at "different, but connected, physical and virtual worlds, rather than a seamless augmented reality style experience" (435). This was achieved by utilizing what was identified as a "general trajectory" moving primarily from the "digital domain of text clues and messages delivered alongside a digital map of the city via a PDA to increasing involvement and introduction of live performance" (428). The beginning of *Uncle Roy All Around You* introduced participants to the game through a digital interface; during the course of the game, participants became increasingly implicated in a series of "local" physical environments whose clues, however, they could make sense of only through the information received digitally.

Having introduced our first two examples of mixed reality performance, the following section now turns attention to their underlying treatment of space and especially the hybrid spatial nature of the "stages" upon which they take place.

Hybrid Space

Can You See Me Now? and *Uncle Roy All Around You* are distinctive in the way they support performances that span "online" and "on the streets" participants. They simultaneously occupy multiple points on the mixed reality continuum that we discussed in the introduction and can be thought of as generating a hybrid rather than an augmented or virtual reality experience. In combining different kinds of spaces, these hybrid experiences can span multiple timeframes, and encourage participants to become aware of a multitude of spaces and adopt various roles within them. Here we discuss the intrinsic characteristics of hybrid spaces identified by related scholarship, focusing in particular on these spaces' tendency to act as folds, their disjunctive properties, and their emergence as the product of collaboration between dispersed communities.

There is a longstanding tradition of developing "virtual spaces" within computer science and its allied disciplines, dating from the first computer programs that used geometry to create computer graphics to contemporary notions of mixed and augmented reality. Although the "desktop" and "windows" metaphors that are embodied in the interfaces of personal computers constitute forms of virtual space, it was the use of interactive 3D computer graphics to establish the illusion of computer generated "virtual realities" (Sutherland 1970) that led to an explosion of interest in this topic, especially when coupled to the Internet to create shared virtual spaces. Over a period of more than twenty years, these ideas and their enabling technologies have given rise to a large market for computer games and social virtual worlds that immerse their users in computer-generated fantasy environments, mostly for the purposes of entertainment, although there have been many discussions of how such environments might also support training, learning, visualization and other forms of work (Kelly et al. 2007).

More recently, the advent of mobile computing, including location-based computing in which participants' positions can be tracked as they move through the real world, has led to the idea of augmented reality in which virtual worlds appear to be overlaid on the everyday physical world as we discussed in the introduction. In turn, Paul Milgram and Furnio Kishino have proposed the idea of the "mixed reality continuum," a spectrum of possibilities for combining real and virtual worlds ranging from physical reality at one extreme to fully immersive virtual reality at the other, but also including various intermediate points along the way such as augmented reality and its mirror, "augmented virtuality," in which virtual worlds are made live with data streams from the real world (1994). These largely mathematical and technology-centric notions of constructing virtual spaces and aligning them with real spaces have been complemented by a recognition of the socially relevant and constructed nature of space from within the fields of human-computer interaction (HCI) and computer-supported cooperative work. Drawing on earlier studies of media spaces (Gaver 1992), the use of persistent audio and video connections to reconfigure existing physical spaces (also discussed in our interview with Holger Schnädelbach, discussed shortly), Steve Harrison and Paul Dourish have argued for thinking of socially constructed notions of "place" to complement more technical notions of "space" (1996), and in subsequently revisiting their argument have suggested that both place and space are indeed complex social *and* technical constructions (Dourish 2006).

Of course, many other disciplines have much to add to our understanding of the nature of, and relationships between, real and virtual spaces. In further broadening our understanding of space, we now turn to Henri Lefebvre's thesis that space consists of an interaction between perceived, conceived and lived space. As it is in part the result of a social construction, it is in motion (1992, 26) and subject to processes of negotiation. In the hybrid spaces generated by mixed reality performance, this negotiation, we show, occurs at the level of trajectories. Before we discuss trajectories, however, further analysis of the concept and practice of hybrid space is necessary. As Assia Kraan, suggests, a hybrid space is not only formed by space's "materiality and social and political actions," as indicated by Lefebvre, but also by digital technology (2006, 39). A hybrid space therefore emerges out of the relationship between perceived, conceived, lived physical *and* digital spaces. As mixed reality performances also operate as cultural spectacles, they often entail an intertextual dimension. So the hybrid space of a mixed reality performance spans intertextually, connecting digital and physical worlds to a matrix of cultural references. The participant in a mixed reality experience travels through these interconnected physical, digital, and intertextual worlds, witnessing, participating or even generating new, unexpected, and highly subjective experiences. The paths, or journeys that lead through these experiences and that may be have been prescripted, or that could have been generated by participants, are what we call *trajectories*.

In her work on location-based mobile games, Adriana de Souza e Silva points out how mobile technologies "transform the physical environment in which we live into an unexplored territory" and notes how this creation of "imaginary spaces" may be related to the activity of travelers "who went to unknown places and mapped new territories" (2004). De Souza e Silva, who adopts the term "hybrid space" to discuss games generated by ubiquitous computing, notes that these spaces can become multiuser when mobility and communication are involved (2003; see also 2009). So she cites mobile phone use to show that "someone talking on a cell phone is part of the context of people who share the same spatial area, but they are also part of a distant context, because she is also talking to someone who is spatially remote for her area" (2003). This suggests that mixed reality performance spaces, which likewise tend to involve mobility and communication, form part of a network of further, distant, "invisible," and private spaces. To describe the relationship between hybrid spaces, she then cites Katherine Hayles, who introduces the idea that these spaces create contexts that are "enfolded" so that what we witness "is no longer a homogeneous context for a given spatial area, but rather pockets of different contexts in it" (in de Souza e Silva 2003). This echoes the words of the architect Stephen Perrella, who noted that the virtual does not merely add another dimension, but rather "has folded itself *into* the world" (in Zellner 1999, 46; emphasis in original). The idea of a folding space cannot but bring back Gilles Deleuze's theorization of the fold, as an in-betweenness of spaces, able to represent dialectical opposites such as organic and inorganic, inside and outside (1993, 13). This kind of space, which can no longer be represented in a two-dimensional drawing, is a hybrid space, which like Deleuze and Felix Guattari's rhizome is "always in the middle, between things, interbeing, *intermezzo*" (1988, 25;

emphasis in original). Thus hybrid space is composed of different, adjacent, "enfolding" spaces, simultaneously occupying different points on the mixed reality continuum, which remain, however, in a heterogeneous, discontinuous, unsynthesized, and changing relationship with one another.

In *The Rise of the Network Society*, Manuel Castells famously introduces a separation between a "space of places" which is localized, associated with local history, tradition and memory and a "space of flows" which is a-historical, location-free and continuous (1996). For him it is the space of flows that constitutes "a new spatial form characteristic of social practices that dominate and shape the network society" (442). Eric Kluitenberg, who adopts the term hybrid to refer to networked spaces, argues that quite differently from Castells's placeless and continuous space of flows, hybrid space is characterized by discontinuity and multiplicity, also because connectivity itself is discontinuous, because the space of electronic communication is rooted in local networks (1996, 10). Where Castells saw a separation between different types of space, we claim that these do not exist separately, but rather cohabit—not so much in conjunction, but rather in disjunction with on another. To understand the implications of a definition of these spaces as adjacent but operating through disjunction, we now draw on Bernard Tschumi's work on architectural disjunction.

Tschumi argues that the experience of architecture is defined in the fact that, by "its very nature," it is "about two mutually exclusive terms—space and its use or, in a more theoretical sense, the concept of space and the experience of space" (1996, 16). For Tschumi, in architecture disjunction implies "that at no moment can any part become a synthesis or self-sufficient totality"; that "each part leads to another, and every construction is off-balance, constituted by the traces of another construction." A disjunctive architecture or architectural method therefore rejects the notion of "'synthesis' in favor of the idea of disassociation, of disjunctive analysis" (212). Use and form are here not in opposition but rather juxtaposed. Methodologically, emphasis is placed on "disassociation, superimposition, and combination" (212). Tschumi contends, "The very heterogeneity of the definition of architecture—space, action, and movement—makes it into an *event*, that place of shock, or that place of the invention of ourselves" (258; emphasis added). Hybrid space, like cyberspace, or liquid architecture, to adopt Markos Novak's definition, is architectural because, like the latter, it entails not only the "object but the principles by which the object is generated *and varied* in time" (1993, 251). Where Tschumi refers to architecture as an event, Novak talks about a building's "*performance*" as a form of "dance and theater" (1993; emphasis in original). So as a "built" environment, hybrid space constitutes an event to be witnessed or experienced. As a form of liquid architecture, it also constitutes a performance that may be watched, practiced, or even generated. Crucially, hybrid space is both a space where *real* events occur and a space of *performance*. Characteristically, the two spheres contaminate each other, so that participants remain unsure as to what is real and what is performed. This disjunction, and the uncertainty it raises, constitutes one of the mechanisms by which hybrid space can be experienced as uncanny, that is, as something that is both familiar *and* estranging (in the Brechtian sense of *Verfremdung*).

Hybrid space entails other "architectural" qualities. Lev Manovich describes two kinds of artistic augmented spaces, namely Janet Cardiff's audio walks and Daniel Libeskind's Jewish Museum. Whereas the former overlaid an existing landscape with a data space, the latter connected a matrix of addresses through some lines, which then formed the structure for the Museum. Manovich then concludes by saying that augmented spaces should be approached architecturally (2006). Indeed, hybrid space entails an architectural dimension interconnecting built environments with digital and cultural spaces. The fact that hybrid space is both material and, at least in part, networked is crucial. Expanding from Manovich, de Souza e Silva defines hybrid spaces as "blurring the boundaries between digital and physical spaces . . . in opposition to augmented and mixed realities, concepts that also claim the blurring of borders between the physical and the digital" (2006, 5). She argues that the merging of mixed reality, augmented spaces, mobility and sociability create a "hybrid" rather than "augmented reality" generated out of the "mix of social practices that occur simultaneously in digital and in physical spaces, together with mobility" (5). Hybrid spaces, she concludes, are not constructed by technology but rather "built by the connection of mobility and communication, and materialised by social networks developed simultaneously in physical and digital spaces" (5). It is, for her, the fact that hybrid space is generated as a result of mobility and communication that distinguishes it from other forms on the mixed reality continuum. We argue that hybrid space is distinctive because as a result of this co-occurrence of mobility and communication, it generates the possibility but not the inevitability of a network. As a consequence of this, hybrid space is uneven. It throws its inhabitants off balance.

The kind of spaces we analyze here constitute environments which draw from different theatrical, performative, and ludic conventions and so establish trajectories that reposition the audience from participant to performer to witness or even bystander. What is presented here is not only, as in a theater, a self-contained world that is removed by an imaginary fourth wall. Neither is it only, as in a game, a "temporary world within the ordinary world" (Huizinga 1955, 10) so that, as in Katie Salen and Eric Zimmerman's well-known definition, "only when a player has entered into the magic circle of a game do game rules imbue game actions with meaning and consequence" (2004, 573). Rather, as in performance art, it contains aspects, either physical or digital, that are integrated within and undistinguishable from the fabric of everyday life so that there is a blurring of boundaries, which necessitates the continuous renegotiation of the performance frame. Moreover, the relationship between these spaces is often prescripted, established a priori. Crucially, these spaces can therefore never quite be experienced holistically from within and can often be explored only through the help and with the cooperation of others.

In talking about the wall paintings from the late Roman Republic depicted in the Second Style of Pompei in the Villa dei Misteri frieze, Oliver Grau mentions how by seemingly extending the wall surface beyond a single plane, "the room appears longer than its actual size and draws the visitor's gaze into the painting, blurring distinctions between real space and image space" (2003, 25). Grau describes this kind of space as a space that "addresses the observer from all sides" (27), a sort of virtual reality "which not only sought to involve the observer through its subject but also through the use of panoramic images, specific colors, and dramatic gestures, aimed at emotionally arousing the observer to ecstatic participation" (29). The hybrid spaces of mixed reality performance are likewise illusionary. In *Can You See Me Now?* and *Uncle Roy All Around You*, they at once extend and shrink the actual and apparent frames of the work, while also augmenting their temporal span by drawing materials from outside the world of the game and then pouring content back within the sphere of participants' everyday lives. These spaces are constructed not only culturally and socially, but also communally. They are the shifting and ephemeral product of an encounter between participants, expressing a temporary and in many ways emergent network of viewpoints. Because these works are not only grounded in specific locations but also mediated—as in the case of Tschumi's disjunctive architecture, both a mathematical abstraction and a built environment—they are unstable and, like in Libeskind's Jewish Museum, reduce the *flaneur* that strolls through them to continuously renegotiate their equilibrium. Because of this, not only do these hybrid spaces constitute new and ever-changing territories for the exploration of mixed reality environments, they do also constitute new means, lenses, or paths to explore the context of everyday life itself.

Interview 1: Designing Hybrid Space

Box 1.1

We ask the architect Holger Schnädelbach from the Mixed Reality Laboratory to describe how theoretical considerations of hybrid space are reflected in his work on mixed reality architecture.

My research revolves around adaptive architecture, that is, buildings that adapt to their environment and to their inhabitants in a number of different ways. This encompasses a wide variety of building types, from sustainable architecture to theater spaces, and it involves associated practical and theoretical concerns. Within this multidisciplinary field, I concentrate on those adaptations that can be created by extending building architecture with audiovisual communication media.

Box 1.1 (continued)

I have two main design aims. First, I am concerned with the incorporation of remote spaces into architectural configurations, going beyond mere communication links but instead considering the architectural integration of these types of media in a more fundamental way. By "remote," I typically mean spaces that are located in different cities, although spaces on different floors are interesting too, as they often appear just as remote when it comes to social interaction. Second, I aim to make building architecture more dynamic, so that it can better respond to organizational change and the changing needs of its inhabitants. This is particularly relevant in an environment where organizations have become very flexible and individuals frequently work on different projects in relatively quick succession, collaborating with a changing set of project team members who are then also often dispersed, for example through doing tele-work. Both of these aims are underpinned by a fundamental interest in how social interaction can be supported in these new types of architectural topologies. The concrete outcome of this research interest is mixed reality architecture or MRA, an architectural topology that spans virtual and physical spaces in a dynamic way.

How does mixed reality architecture work? What kind of spaces does it consist of?

MRA works as an extension of an ordinary office environment. The offices incorporated into MRA connect into a shared virtual environment, which is displayed on a large digital screen. This, for example, can be projected onto a wall and is designed to appear embedded into the office as much as possible. A camera facing away from the screen captures an overview of the particular office space. The physical installation is completed with an echo-canceled microphone and stereo speakers. (See figure 1.10.)

The 3D virtual environment displayed onscreen serves as communicative mediator between multiple physical spaces that are a represented within it as virtual offices. Each

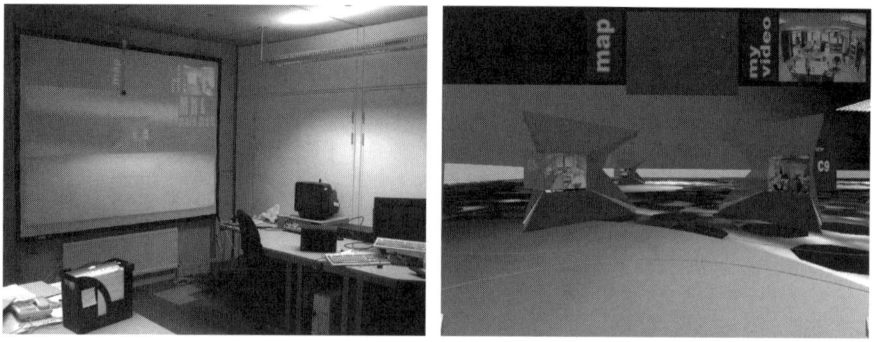

Figure 1.10
An office installation and the MRA.
Copyright MRL.

Box 1.1 (continued)

of these virtual offices is associated with its relevant stream of live audio and video. (See figure 1.11.)

Inhabitants of MRA virtually move their offices around in the shared environment, establishing spatial connections on the fly with whomever they feel like. All offices can be moved by their inhabitants in relation to all other offices, resulting in a dynamic architectural topology.

What kind of social spaces are constructed in mixed reality architecture and how do these spaces operate in relation to one another?

The social spaces created in MRA are fundamentally the result of the dynamic combination of digital and physical environments, both local and remote. The current work has focused on office environments analyzing the professional and social relationships of its inhabitants. The MRA interface is always on and often in the background of people's focused activity, operating like an open door (that is, if the inhabitant has configured it to be open). So MRA allows for spontaneous social interaction *and* provides people with an awareness of activities occurring in other spaces, making it possible, for instance, to understand the work habits of colleagues who are located in a different city, or providing information about which colleagues are frequently in contact with each other. In addition, verbal communication can be initiated by any of the MRA inhabitants by talking into their MRA node, if that is within audio range of another or multiple others. Once this virtual spatial closeness has been established, the video fills a suitable proportion of the screen and the audio level is sufficient for communication. Our analysis of MRA showed that people used this to exchange small pieces of information quickly, for example asking for relevant papers to cite but also made use of MRA for longer meetings. Most typically,

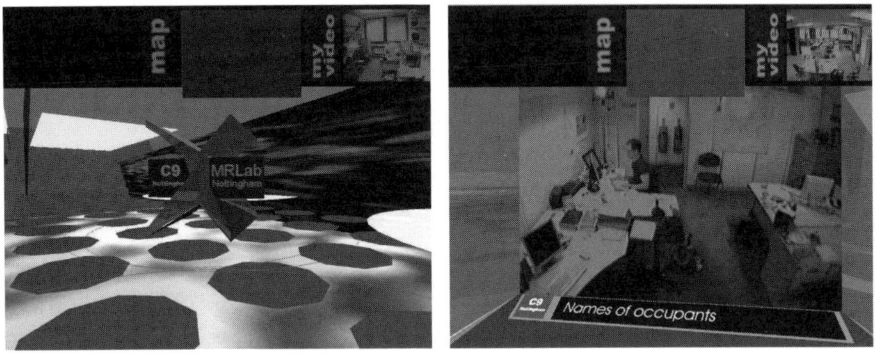

Figure 1.11
Two offices close to each other and the resulting view across.
Copyright MRL.

Box 1.1 (continued)

meetings were spontaneous, but there were also occasions when they were planned and regular (see Schnädelbach, Penn, et al. 2006).

In what ways are these spaces dynamic?

MRA creates a dynamic architectural topology, in which the relationship of spaces is not predetermined. This is impossible to achieve in physical architecture, at least at the speed at which it is possible here, though of course, there have been visionary design proposals in this area, such as Cedric Price's Generator Project (2003). For me, the critical issue here is the relationship between social life and architectural configuration. Architecture can be described as a physical manifestation of the rules and norms of a particular society. For example, Robin Evans ([1978] 1997) has shown how changing attitudes have lead to different types of architectural layout ranging from those that encourage encounters to those that are more preventative. In turn, the resulting architecture clearly structures physical space and this structure then has an influence on our movement patterns through that space, being partly responsible for determining who we encounter and who we avoid. In physical architecture, this two-way relationship is very stable and emerges over long periods of time.

Within MRA, exactly the same processes can be seen, but in much accelerated fashion (Schnädelbach et al. 2007). It is the social rules and norms of the office environments within which it has been installed that determine certain aspects of how each individual arranges their MRA node in relationship to the others around them. For example, remaining in someone's audio range for any length of time was not accepted by inhabitants in the same way that it is not acceptable to linger nearby someone's office door and listen in. The configurations were also the result of the particular preferences of its inhabitants. For instance, when colleagues knew each other well, they often remained within audio range, being able to generally hear what was going on without being able to pick out any details. Once set up in a particular way, MRA then encouraged or prevented certain types of encounters. One example would be the way that it enabled chance encounters between people who were located in a different city, as long as two or more nodes were already connected. Crucially, the architectural configurations and any social interaction taking place within them remained legible to bystanders as spatial relationships are clearly represented within the virtual environment.

What role do trajectories play within this context?

Bill Hillier and Julienne Hanson have shown how architectural configurations influence our movement patterns through space, whether inside buildings or in urban spaces (1984). It is important to emphasize that this is true for an aggregate of everyone's movement, and that this is indeed largely independent from whatever might be present on the ground—for instance, what kind of shop or a theater may be near by. Techniques analyzing the connectivity of architectural spaces and the visibility within them have been

Box 1.1 (continued)

successfully used to predict movement in a number of different scenarios, while other measures are often necessary to complete the picture and understand locations in detail. So in this way, the spatial configuration of architecture already shapes our trajectories through space.

Of course, architects also set out to design for specific trajectories through buildings and frequently these are linked to specific events or social conventions. A mundane example is the layout of out-of-town cinemas, with their front entrances and foyers, the cinema space itself, and the exit directly pointing from this space to the car park. A specific and much more celebrated example is Daniel Libeskind's Jewish Museum in Berlin, which takes visitors on a journey through the building and Jewish history along a particular, designed spatial trajectory. Of course visitors may then follow different paths for a number of reasons: the exhibition design makes the building trajectory unreadable, a part of the building is closed, wheelchair users access the building from a different entrance, or someone simply runs out of time and leaves via a different exit. More importantly, uses of buildings change over time, making trajectories anticipated for the original purpose superfluous or even counterproductive.

Overall, however, for people to adhere to very specific spatial trajectories, some form of orchestration or event is nearly always necessary, that is, some form of specific guidance to channel people down a particular path. This activity in turn might well be framed within architecture that specifically allows for such orchestration. Theater spaces are the prime example in this context, especially in the way that they are designed to be adaptable to a variety of events.

Expanding architecture through mixed reality technologies then creates the potential for trajectories to extend into virtual environments. In the first instance, the interface technology in MRA serves as a link between the physical and virtual environments, but it also clearly acts as a boundary. "Interface" here refers to the entire setup including the projected display, the speakers, the microphone, the camera and the joystick, which allow the spatial reconfigurations described previously. In the first instance, it is only through this technology that one gets access to the virtual environment and the mediated remote physical environments; that is, it is through this technology that inhabitants can hear and see events taking place in those spaces. This enabling technology has clear limits, resulting in the fact that it can also act as a boundary between physical and virtual. This is because it is a view into a virtual space with very particular properties, where movement is constrained to that which was programmed, the view is limited to the field of view set in a configuration file, and audio is transmitted from a particular range. Very much in the same way, the view into other physical offices is mediated by technology. The physical properties of camera and microphone, their specific location and orientation, determine what one can see of the connected physical spaces.

So although the technology links us to events taking place in the shared virtual space and in the connected physical environments, it does not actually allow us to physically

Box 1.1 (continued)

enter either of these. In this way, a journey that might take you toward an embedded interface technology for audiovisual communication like the MRA can only continue in a disembodied way beyond.

Vilem Flusser states that "the architect no longer designs objects, but relationships" (1992, 83)—how do you think this relates to mixed reality architecture?

One very important concern that architects deal with in the complex process of design is the establishment of spatial relationships within the constraints of the creation of an overall architectural object, that is, the building. These relationships are within the building in the way that individual spatial units relate to each other and outside, in the way the building relates to its surroundings. The spatial relationships chosen are a reflection of our social rules and norms, and one might simply compare the differences between traditional living and dining rooms and open-plan living in this context. By setting up spatial relationships, the architect can then aim to influence social interaction. In a typical courthouse, for example, spaces are laid out so that the defendant does not meet the plaintiff or witnesses except during the court proceedings. However this is a special case. Typically the influence of architectural configurations is more subtle than that, namely in the way that they impact on movement patterns of people and therefore the frequency of encounters between individuals. Encounters in physical space in turn are the prerequisites for social interaction (Hillier and Hanson 1984).

In architecture that is extended through embedded audiovisual communication media, the architect gives up the exclusive claim on the design of spatial relationships, as buildings become adaptive and are reconfigured by their inhabitants on the fly. They themselves decide which of the spaces connected through communication technologies appears next to theirs, at what particular time, and for how long. At the same time, it is clear that the physical placement of interface technologies requires considerable architectural expertise. This is related to the technology's relationship to the space it is placed in, the adjoining physical spaces and other communication technologies, and it needs to carefully consider the existing social networks and those that one might want to support with such an intervention. In this way, the architect's role is to enable dynamic spatial relationships within wider architectural configurations, which can then in turn enable a wider range of social relationships.

Pursuing Trajectories

A fundamental aspect of mixed reality performances is that participants follow individual trajectories through different spaces, finding routes and defining trails that link physical environments with virtual worlds. These trajectories form the fabric of mixed reality experiences. They cross, leading to encounters in both worlds that shape participants' spatiotemporal, social, and aesthetic experiences. Here we focus on the use of trajectories for spatial navigation. Each participant's trajectory may move through several kinds of space in sequence, for example, street players often became online players in *Uncle Roy All Around You* and some online players in *Can You See Me Now?* visited city streets and ran alongside the performers. Participants also shaped or followed each other's trajectories, chasing each other in *Can You See Me Now?* or remotely guiding one another in *Uncle Roy All Around You*. We analyze how participants' experiences of mixed reality performances are shaped by spatial trajectories and show how these generate a hybrid space that can be exploited through a process of orchestration. Moreover, we introduce a core distinction between canonical and participant trajectories that expresses the constant tension between the artists' and the participants' control of interactive performance. Finally, we observe that in *Uncle Roy All Around You*, self-reported positioning occurred, in that people declared their position to be ahead of their actual location. Conversely, in other events, there was a need to visualize actual locations where people had been in the past. For instance, in *Savannah* (2003), a strategy-based adventure game discussed in greater detail shortly, there were visualizations of trials in the Den so that participants could reflect after playing each level.

Trajectories define routes, or journeys across space. Spatial metaphors to do with navigation are common in game and new media theory, which can be seen from the introduction of terms such as strolling and flaneurism as means to explore a world or an interactive experience. For instance, talking about *Myst* (1993), Bernadette Flynn identifies strolling as salient feature of games in which the player appears to become a "flaneur." Here, she notes, "the player has to try and map the geographical relationship of the environment in order to understand where they are and how to proceed (or go back)" (2000). Likewise, Manovich identifies movement through space as a key feature of games like *Myst* and *Doom* that "present the user with space to be traversed, to be mapped out by moving through it" so that "narrative and time itself are equated with movement through 3-D space, progression through rooms, levels or words" (2001, 246–247). Manovich extends this line of argument to the entire sphere of new media arts by also including works such as Jeffrey Shaw's *Legible City* (1988–1991) and Char Davies's *Osmose* (1994–1995), in which the user controlled the environment by cycling and by breathing, respectively. Crucially, he notes that "new media spaces are always spaces of navigation" where "narrative becomes traveling through space" (252).

This is also the case in locative media, in which movement in the game world often occurs concurrently with movement through a physical location. In this process, trajectories are created between different points on the mixed reality continuum. These trajectories embody past, present, and future planned action and can be exploited through a process of orchestration. They can be visualized on maps, described mathematically, and analyzed as they develop and change over time. They can mark a potential rather than an actual development and so facilitate reflection and planning. Unlike conventional scenarios, based on dramatic action, they take into account the complexity of hybrid space, its folding between different points on the mixed reality continuum, its disjunctive nature, its coming together as the result of a collaboration between participants who may be spatially and temporally remote from each other. The importance of these trajectories and the maps they create is crucial. Tim Ingold describes how through cognitive maps the traveler does not plot their routes mechanically from A to B, as if executing a prescribed course, but rather "'feels his way' toward his goal, continuously adjusting his movements in response to an ongoing perceptual monitoring of his surroundings" (2000, 230). Knowledge about the environment, he notes, is determined while we are "on the move" within it. The traveler who "knows as he goes . . . is neither making a map nor using one. He is, quite simply, *mapping*" (231; emphasis in original). Trajectories, unlike routes or journeys, mark these embedded and emergent past, present, and future mapping possibilities, thus representing not only a direction, or path, but also, as we have discussed in our Introduction, a way of knowing, or—as we see in the case of *Savannah*—of learning.

To explain the relationship between the different types of routes that we may encounter in a mixed reality performance, we introduce a core distinction between *canonical trajectories*, which are prescripted and embedded into the original structure of the piece, and *participant trajectories*, which are defined by participants and are emergent and unpredictable. The relationship between them expresses the constant tension between the artists' and the participants' control of interactive performance. Two examples from *Uncle Roy All Around You* show how two participants' experiences were steered toward a canonical trajectory by a group of orchestrators and an online player. In the first example, derived from video footage from the West Bromwich performance, it is clear that one of the orchestrators is unsure as to whether a particular player had filled in their own postcard and suggests to another remote orchestrator that they might wish to ring the players who are in Uncle Roy's Office. The player is then seen answering a phone call, and immediately afterwards writing his postcard. In the second example, cited beneath, we see how a street player is steered through a tricky moment in the game by an online player called Dave who helps them to understand Uncle Roy's instructions. This example is from the Manchester game and captures the moment the street player realized that Uncle Roy gave them directions but was unsure as to how to interpret them:

[Reading the message out loud] "An ambulance stopped here. It looks like someone I know. I turned away towards the bank as it was then." Ah! So it used to be the bank. [Mumbling to himself] Eighteen minutes left. I think he's giving me directions to Chinatown. . . . Dave's just sent me a message. [He reads it out] "Go into the graffiti phone box by the railings." So I must send him a little message. Dave, can you direct me to it? I'm outside the red phone box outside Reyner Street. Do you want to direct me there? [He listens.] That would be wicked. Cheers mate.

Both examples show how processes of orchestration, either between orchestrators and players or among street and online players, steered players from a participant to a canonical trajectory from which they could proceed to a different level in the game. In *Uncle Roy All Around You*, as Adams discusses in the interview in the next section, the clue trail was to build around a small number of anticipated routes through an area of the city using a color map authoring tool. As mentioned before, because the game did not use GPS, players reported their own position by panning their view over the map and using a stylus to drag the "me" icon to a different position. The map then recentered itself around this new position. In order to declare their position, players placed the "me" icon and pressed the "I am here" button, which sent a declaration to the game server. Orchestrators and other players could then help players toward their goal by moving them between different trajectories. To this extent, they used outer region messages that guided participants back into the game by saying, for instance, "the policeman was firm but polite, not this way today" followed by "You are off track" and "I cannot guide you out here. You have got lost. Go back the way you came" followed by "Retrace your steps, you are too far away and in the wrong place."

Movement between trajectories was often orchestrated through messages. There were different categories of messages whose function was tied to where players were within the game:

1. The first category of messages indicated a situation in which the online players had a "precise enough fix on a street player's location to be able to give directions or tell the street player where they are." The game entailed 735 such messages, such as: "The big street in front of you," "and stay on that side of the road," "u r very close step back 5 feet," or "stop take a right NOW."
2. The second category of message indicated a situation in which the online player "is less confident, for example, questioning whether the street player is at a specific location." There were 112 of these messages, such as: "Are you near a piece of scaffolding?" and "My map shows you are near the bridge. Are you?"
3. The third category indicated a situation "where the online player gives general directions or makes geographical references that do not necessarily assume precise knowledge of the street player's location." There were 569 such messages, such as: "Go to 12 waterloo place," "Head for the big building with a flag on top."

4. The fourth category of messages intended to "cast doubt on the usefulness or validity of reported positions or appear to question the behavior of the positioning system in some way." There were 32 such messages, such as: "I can't pinpoint you" and "How did you get over there?"
5. The fifth category consisted of requests for location updates. There were 222 messages in this category in which online players appeared to be inquiring about the location of a street player.

The study found that players often declared to be at landmarks even when they were some distance from them and tended to position the map so they could see ahead rather than behind so that "planning ahead and deciding where to go before actually reaching the next major decision point." Other examples showed players "explicitly declaring themselves to be ahead of their actual position, almost anticipating a 'time delay.'" Some players also reported to be behind their actual position to retrigger clues that were no longer visible or, for the benefit of an online player declaring ahead, offered a sense of a player's trajectory through the streets (Benford, Seager, et al. 2004).

Interview 2: Designing Trajectories

Box 1.2

We ask Blast Theory members Matt Adams (MA) and Nick Tandavanitj (NT), "What is the importance of locality in works such as Can You See Me Now? *and* Uncle Roy All Around You?*"*

NT: Our starting point was to look at the individual and the individual in the city, that is, situations where you are out and about, and you are moving through the city. We were interested in what happens to your sense of yourself and your sense of presence, and the sense of the social space or the public domain that this occupies.
MA: While you are moving about in the city, you become connected to a network. This situates you in two different types of spaces at once. *Can You See Me Now?* is all about managing this proximity and distance. You know your game play is dependent on being far away from someone and yet the work itself plays around with proximity and presence—absence and distance.
NT: With *Uncle Roy All Around You*, we moved on to a space that operated through windows or boundaries.
MA: Being lost or getting lost was wired into the player experience. Participants felt lost, however well they played. They felt uncertain about where they were and whether they were going in the right direction. This threw back onto them an anxiety about place, which was a crucial part of the game experience.

Box 1.2 (continued)

What role do maps play in these works?

NT: Maps are a paradigm allowing participants to share and navigate a given space together. They are a way of structuring people's movements or navigation through an experience.

MA: In *Can You See Me Now?* we used a top-down approach based on how people might navigate through a city. In selecting the participant routes, we checked how wide these were, and how many points of entry and circulation they had. We were aware that wide, open spaces meant better GPS. We looked for prosaic things, like where it was going to be safe for us to run, where the busy roads were. In the early days, when we were setting up our own Wi-Fi networks, we also looked for good, high buildings where we could mount antennae and get public access. I remember that when we went to Oldenburg it was important that we could get to the top of the Church Tower and the multistory car park to mount a Wi-Fi antenna. We have always been interested in looking at how and why people moved across space. The first works we ever made—*Gunmen Kill Three, Chemical Wedding,* and *Stampede*—were promenade performances. We used to map how people would move as we inserted obstacles or performers in that space. That was during the 1990s, and I remember discussions about desire paths—how designers of urban space studied how people might move down certain side streets according to what they could see as they approached the neck of the street. We always had an interest in how space guides or drives people in certain directions. When we did *Uncle Roy All Around You* in Manchester we wanted to bring people down to the canal footpaths and make them walk right along the canal rather than have them stay up above on the road level. People came back to us and said, "I saw bits of the city I have never seen before—I have lived here for 20 years and I have never walked down that alley, that street, through that car park." That was really important to us because it meant that we were drawing people away from their habitual reference points.

NT: We used GPS predicate maps, which filter the position they are given. In *Can You See Me Now?* when a runner is moving around in the city, their GPS reports them to be roughly where they are, but because there could be an error in the GPS, they might appear to be in the middle of a building next their location. The predicate maps create zones that are out of bounds, so, if someone is running down a street, the map knows that they can't be inside someone's private house, and even if their GPS shows that they are inside a house, the map pushes them to the nearest available space, which will probably be on the street in front of the house. These maps are "invisible," so online players are not aware of these processes. There is also an equivalent for the online player, which is a collision map. This shows all the areas that they are allowed to run around in. We sometimes played with the way collision maps work, so that if there was a very steep hill, we put in obstacles in the online players' version of the map, so that they would be slowed down. These processes were invisible to the users but they formed an underlying structural map of the entire experience.

Box 1.2 (continued)

MA: These different kinds of maps are nested within one another. They have different properties for the people playing online and the people playing on the street. They tidy up the inherent entropy of the locative systems we use, which are always approximate, moving between functional, marginally functional and dysfunctional. We use a number of tools, including these maps, to make sense of these disparities.

What is the relationship between these maps and participants' experience?

MA: One of the first things we did when we made touring work in the1990s was to think of the smallest stage where we were likely to perform. That would then become our space and provide the context in which we created our work. This is also how our maps function for the online players in *Can You See Me Now?* and *Uncle Roy All Around You*. They prescribe their space and set their boundaries. Players tend to head towards the margins of the space that is available to them and explore doors and exits to see where they can and cannot go. During this process, they build up a spatial grammar that helps them to navigate the environment. We inserted barriers, chevrons, or indicators in these maps that specified where people could and couldn't go. The other crucial factor is the position of the camera in the 3D space. The very first version of *Can You See Me Now?* was a 2D top-down map, but by the time we performed it in Rotterdam, we used a 3D space with a camera, and the position of the camera was critical in terms of limiting what players could and couldn't see. Even if players zoomed out to have a of helicopter's view, they could only ever see part of the space. We deliberately did not allow players to see everything and created a space in which they had to move in order to explore the game.

NT: In *Uncle Roy All Around You* the map didn't necessarily show where you were, but where you said you were. There was no GPS, so the map didn't track you. It was about filtering who was around you and who might be able to help you. The map served as a kind of filter.

MA: *Can You See Me Now?* offers a Cartesian view of space. It really matters who is near you. In these online worlds, even though there is nothing there, space maintains a social meaning. We are interested in performance and that is about the here and the now, and the very relationship between the performer and the audience at a specific point in time and place. A lot of our work can be seen as explorations of how you might reconfigure these dynamics in a networked digital age, an age where things are fragmented and multilayered. In *Can You See Me Now?* we were interested in exploring how technology brings you into a shared space with other people around the world and whether it truncates or possibly even cauterizes your relationships with these other people. I remember the audio recording of the Oldenburg game and the first thing you hear as it starts is the sound of church bells and then you hear Paul Dungworth's voice saying "the bells are striking 8 o'clock—welcome to tonight's game of *Can You See Me Now?*". It's instantly evocative of a small German town on a Sunday evening in which the church bells are ringing "right now." This is the imaginative space in which the online players are invited to site themselves.

Box 1.2 (continued)

In Uncle Roy All Around You*, participants follow a number of anticipated routes through the city. What were your aims in designing these particular routes?*

MA: Martin Flintham from the Mixed Reality Laboratory devised a system of color maps that allowed us to create routes and reflect about them. There is no GPS in *Uncle Roy All Around You*. So in designing routes, we had to head off degenerate game strategies. Theoretically, someone could have stood outside the starting point and done the entire experience without ever moving. So we wrote clues and content for moving that was very location-specific, like "Look for the name of the person who dedicated that bench and find their statue." That meant that people really needed to be at that place for that direction to make any sense.

NT: We were trying to get everyone to arrive at a single location, but we didn't want to create a single path for everyone.

MA: Everyone has different route-finding styles and we had to gradually manage the confusion that emerged from this diversity. We designed a teardrop of content pointing at "A" and then branching out into a pear-shaped circle around "B," on the assumption that people could choose perhaps two different ways as they came out of the door of the venue. Within a hundred yards, they could have chosen four or eight different ways. Within another hundred yards, they could have chosen sixteen different ways. So the possible ways in which they could get lost multiplied as they move from "A" to "B." It is no coincidence that in *Uncle Roy All Around You* the actual physical distance from "A" to "B" was probably as little as 200m and could be walked in 90 seconds for a one-hour experience. This says a lot about how much tolerance we needed to add. Clues were very much about guiding people. As you walk from the ICA towards Uncle Roy's office, you cross Pall Mall with all the gentlemen's clubs on your left side, so you are moving through very politically charged, highly guarded, very heavily socially filtered spaces. We wanted the clues to reflect that to some degree. At the end, you were invited to walk up to a building and press on the door. When the door magically opened, you were invited to go into a deserted office. That felt like a very transgressive thing to do. We wanted people to be shocked and uncertain about whether the game was really inviting them to go inside a deserted office. The fluidity and anxiety about what the boundary of the game is, was really important here. It mattered to us that people would not be sure where the game ended and the real world began. Almost all of the most powerful experiences in this piece were unplanned by us. They were accidental and had to do with the chaos and the entropy of the city that one cannot control. People came back and said that they had been amazed by the acting of the tramp. They didn't actually believe us when we said that there was no actor playing a tramp. People just folded everyday experiences back into the fictional experience and intermeshed them.

The Educational Game: *Savannah*

The visualization of trajectories and their locations is a crucial design tool for interactive experiences that require a moment of explicit reflection. This is the case for educational experiences, but also for environments that allow players to progress between levels of growing complexity. Such was the case of *Savannah*, a strategy-based adventure game developed by the Mixed Reality Laboratory in collaboration with Hewlett-Packard Laboratories and NESTA Futurelab. The game, which intended to facilitate children's learning about the ecology of the Savannah, foregrounded a virtual Savannah that was overlaid on an open playing field of about ninety by sixty meters, in which groups of children hunted together as lions. Equipped with iPAQ PDAs with Wi-Fi and GPS capabilities, the children explored the terrain and the resources the lions need to survive in the Savannah by moving around the open playing field. The virtual Savannah comprised areas of long grass, short grass, gully, kopje, springs, and trees, and was populated by local wildlife. Using the lion's senses, hearing, seeing, and smelling the world of the Savannah, and remembering what they found in various locations within the area, the children mapped the virtual terrain while navigating the outdoor space.

The game consisted of three levels: in the first level, the pride had to explore and scent mark its territory. In the second and third levels, the pride hunted for food, first in the bountiful wet season and then in the harsher dry season. Whereas the first level was about gathering and mapping information, the second and third were about survival. Participants needed to maximize their health, and gained health points by eating and drinking, or lost them by starving, getting dehydrated, and being attacked by other animals. Participants could also die, in which case they had to return to the starting point before being allowed back into the game after a penalty interruption of a few minutes. Points were awarded according to each lion's health levels and at the end of each of the three levels of the game. The children had to avoid a number of threats, such as an angry elephant, a bush fire and the Masai hunters, a competing pride of lions, whose cubs they had to kill. Each region also presented a number of resources, such as shelter, prey, shade, and water. Finally, the children had to collaborate and negotiate with each other to ensure the achievement of the game's objectives (Facer et al. 2004, 400–401).

An early study of the game focused on how several colocated participants coordinated their movements. The design vision was that just as a pride of lions has to work together to survive, the children also had to work together to win the game by deciding which animals to attack and how many of them needed to attack together in order to succeed (Benford et al. 2005, 722). The children were briefed about this before the game started, and then again reminded of this during the interval session in the den. From the videos of *Savannah*, it is clear that even while playing, the children collaborated with each other by directing each other to go to specific destinations, trying out different strategies, and advising each other on their status in the game—for instance, by telling each other whether they were hungry or thirsty, whether they were in a dangerous area, like a fire or near an elephant, or whether they were close to an area in which they had found food in the previous layer of the game. A number of significant strategic collaborative behaviors were identified, which included "rapid movement and dynamic group formations; a tendency to halt on encountering new information; encouraging others to gather by shouting and gesturing; often attacking systematically" and sometimes "opportunistically on the move; counting in order to synchronise attacks," "remembering the locations of targets and, in one session, even marking them with physical objects" such as a map (727).

A den was included in the game, which consisted of an area in the classroom where the children were briefed about the game's missions and offered access to further research materials, including books, videos, and websites. Here, they could plan their game strategy and reflect about their past game experience. This was supported by an interface for replaying a system recording of each completed level that offered "a birds' eye view of the virtual Savannah across which recorded movements and actions can be replayed, scrolling forward and backward through time." This was displayed on an interactive whiteboard (Benford et al. 2005, 722). After each initial exploration, the children discussed what they found with their teachers in the den, where they used the flip-chart paper to create a map of their experience of the territory and the whiteboard to "revisit their movements within the environment, examine where they had not searched and discuss how they could improve their search techniques" (Facer et al. 2004, 402). While the children were in the den, the whole mission was replayed for them "as if live" so that they could "see their progress across the virtual savannah displayed as a series of trails, with icons marking the locations of their actions" (Benford, Rowland, et al. 2004).

Locale maps were designed for each of the levels in the game (see figure 1.12). These were created by coloring in different virtual locales within a rectangle that represented the field and could be overlaid with the positions of players, of key events such as attacks and movement trails for selected players, including movement through time and movement between significant events (Benford et al. 2005, 722). These maps played a crucial part in the children's experience of the game and were primarily used for orientation, but also for the evaluation of past experiences. In watching the videos that were recorded at the time of the trial, it is clear that the children had memorized the map from the first level and used their recollections as a basis to engage with the game at subsequent levels. For instance, children memorized the precise location of food, and then reentered the game knowing where to find specific resources. Children would often move between the interactive whiteboard and a flip chart, assigning each other tasks such as where to spray and where to hunt. One group of children even

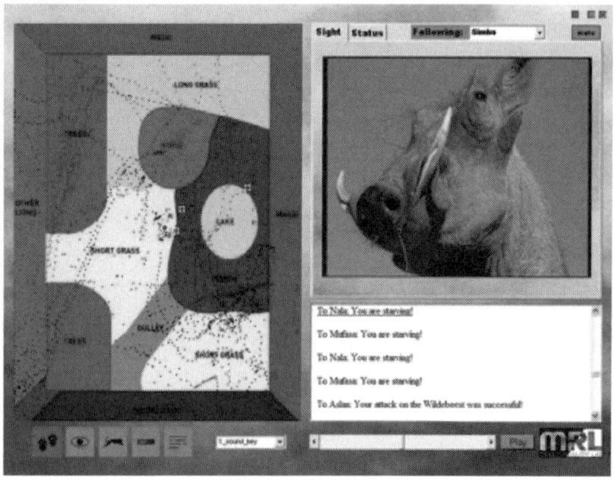

Figure 1.12
Savannah. Locale map.

drew their own maps and organized their strategy around it. When asked during the feedback session with the team, what they would have done differently, they often suggested that they would "map stuff out" more before playing the game again so that they could "trace them [the animals] down" and "put markers down" to remember where to go. Finally, the den's interface for reviewing offered sufficient entertainment for the team, which was following the game on the board from the den to cheer the children who were playing in the field, as if they were present in front of them.

In the Grain of Seams

So far we have explored different understandings of how hybrid space emerges from the mixing of real and virtual worlds. For this final part of our discussion, we consider the impact of the underlying technologies that are used to knit together the real and virtual on the nature of hybridity. Mixed reality performances rely on a "ubiquitous infrastructure" of sensing and communications technologies to connect the real and the virtual. Sensing technologies, especially positioning technologies, track participants' movements through physical space, while wireless communications technologies relay these to remote online participants, often via intermediate servers, and in turn relay the actions of these online participants back to "street players" in the physical world. A wide variety of positioning technologies are available, ranging from global navigation and satellite systems such as GPS and Galileo to approaches that triangulate position by comparing signal strengths from nearby mobile phone masts or Wi-Fi access points, or more local solutions based upon proximity to Bluetooth beacons or radio frequency ID (RFID) readers, or "human approaches" in which participants report their own positions. Similarly, there are multiple wireless communication technologies ranging from mobile telephony services (GSM, GPRS, and 3G) to multiple forms of Wi-Fi, or localized channels such as Bluetooth. Different performances mix these according to their specific needs and local availability. For example, *Can You See Me Now?* adopted GPS for positioning, though it initially used Wi-Fi for communications, but subsequently switched over to GPRS, and *Uncle Roy All Around You* employed a combination of self-reported positioning and GPRS communications.

This ubiquitous infrastructure is largely invisible to participants. Remote satellites, masts, beacons, and the paraphernalia of wireless communications in general cannot directly be seen. Furthermore, it is often assumed to be universally available. Indeed, Mark Weiser's original vision of ubiquitous computing stressed that the embedding of technology into the everyday world would render computing largely invisible while also being universally available, leading to computing experiences that would be *seamlessly* transparent to participants, yet available anywhere and at any time. He states, "The most profound technologies are those that disappear. They weave themselves into the fabric of everyday life until they are indistinguishable from it," and "we are therefore trying to conceive a new way of thinking about computers in the world, one that takes into account the human world and allows the computers themselves to vanish into the background" (1991, 19). The current situation, however, is very different, as the limited coverage and accuracy of both sensing and wireless communications have a profound impact on our experience of hybrid spaces. The idea of "seams" is a useful metaphor here. One can think of the fabric of an experience as being stitched together from many different parts. For example, a hybrid space involves the stitching together of initially disjoint physical and virtual spaces using combinations of sensing and communications technologies and various computer interfaces as the threads that join them. Rather than being seamless, however, these threads all too often become visible to participants, as the following examples reveal.

As noted earlier in this chapter, a study of the performance of *Can You See Me Now?* at the DEAF festival in Rotterdam in 2002 highlighted the impact of limited GPS and Wi-Fi coverage on both online and street players (Benford, Crabtree, Flintham, et al. 2006). Figure 1.13 reveals the nature of the problem. This visualization of combined GPS and Wi-Fi coverage adopts a bird's-eye perspective, looking down on the peninsular where the game was played; the surrounding black area is water, and the superimposed black rectangles show the positions of major buildings. Each blob of light represents a location where a street player managed to transmit a GPS update to the game server over Wi-Fi, that is, where both GPS and Wi-Fi were available to a player. Small blue blobs represent relatively high accuracy GPS with just a few meters' error, at least according to GPS's own self-reporting mechanism, and larger green blobs show

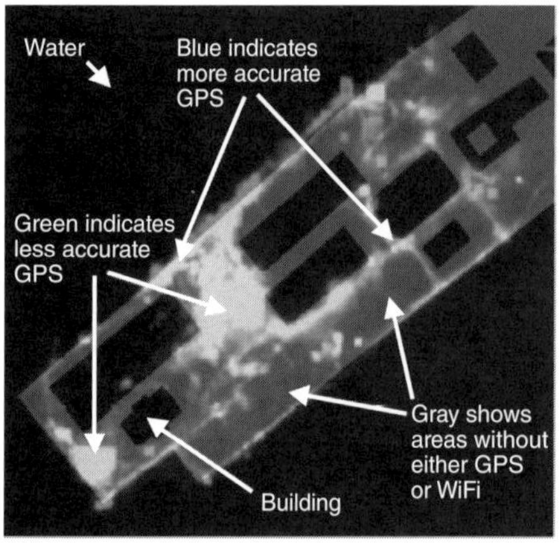

Figure 1.13
Can You See Me Now? Limited GPS and Wi-Fi coverage.
Copyright MRL.

larger estimated errors (in the region of 10 meters or more). The visualization shows the combined data from several street players over two hours of play. What is really striking about this image, however, are the areas where there is no color; either our street players never ventured here (but this is generally not the case, as we observed them covering most of the peninsular during this two hours of play, especially the central street running between the buildings) or there were significant areas in which there was no coverage, which was indeed the case. GPS relies on having line of sight to at least three orbiting satellites, which is often not possible in built-up urban areas, and Wi-Fi signals are easily blocked by buildings and other structures. In short, whole areas of the game space were unplayable, and the available hybrid spaces, where the virtual successfully connected to the real, were patchy and dispersed across the game zone. The seams in the ubiquitous infrastructure are all too apparent when one looks at this image.

This study also revealed that these seams had varied impacts on the different participants in the performance. Street players were obviously and profoundly affected. It was very clear to them when they could not play due to lack of one or both of GPS or Wi-Fi coverage, and they spent much of their time trying to locate playable areas and attempting to connect to the game. Over the course of several days of play, they gradually built up a "working knowledge" of the hybrid space from their experience, usually in dialog with the technical support team and with other players, including though formal briefing sessions before each session of play. Street runners had to become relatively expert in the behavior of GPS and Wi-Fi in order to play the game, although this could be especially challenging as the nature of coverage would change dramatically over time—for example, due to shifting configurations of the overhead satellites; indeed, some members of the control team went as far as to look at publicly available data on satellite positions to try to predict good and bad times for play during a session as well as good and bad places. In contrast to the street players, the impact of seams on online players was more varied. Some clearly noticed them, as revealed in their chat to others; some wove them into the structure of the experience (e.g., commenting on runners having an "invisibility power-up"), and a few actually exploited them, encouraging others to hide in the "GPS shadows."

Studies of *Uncle Roy All Around You* and *Savannah* also highlighted the impact of seams. In *Uncle Roy All Around You*, the key seam was limited GPRS network coverage, with frequent drop-outs breaking the connection between street and online players (Benford, Flintham, et al. 2004). Although the performance was designed so that street players could continue through short periods of disconnection by relying on clues stored on their local handheld computers, frequent disconnections had a major impact on control room staff, who spent a great deal of their time trying to predict where they might be and even sending street performers to try and locate them in the city as a part of orchestrating the experience (as we discuss in chapter 4 in greater detail).

The choice of an open school playing field as the location for *Savannah* was intended to increase reliability by minimizing obstacles to GPS and Wi-Fi reception; however, even here seams revealed themselves. A study of *Savannah* showed how players struggled to coordinate their actions, especially with regard to the requirement to gather together in a "virtual locale" and simultaneously press a button in order to attack prey (Benford et al. 2005). This requirement was often problematic, in that players who were standing directly next to one another were at times unable to see the same material on their handheld computers. Figure 1.14 presents a typical example from the study. The top part of the figure (taken from a video recording) shows three lionesses (Nala, Dandelion, and Elsa) gathered closely together trying to initiate an attack on a gazelle. A transcription of their discussion reveals that this apparently simple act of coordination is in fact extremely problematic, even though they are standing shoulder to shoulder in the real world and directly comparing handheld computers that are just inches away from each other.

Elsa: Ohh look! OK ready? One . . .
Nala: [indistinct] We haven't got it.
Dandelion: We haven't.
Elsa: . . . two . . .
Dandelion: I haven't got it.
Elsa: One . . .
Dandelion: Ready?

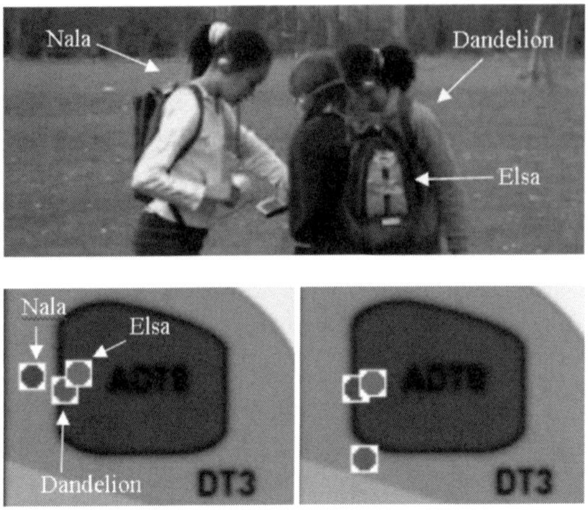

Figure 1.14
Savannah. Problems with seams and boundaries.
Copyright MRL.

Nala: Wait, wait, wait, wait, wait, wait, wait!
Nala: I'm going to wait until it just changes. It'll change in a sec.
[then to herself] Please change.
Dandelion: No mine's changed back again.
Elsa: Err, one . . .
Nala: Hold on wait wait wait.
Nala: [Holds her PDA out from her body and reorients it in a searching gesture] Please wait. Come on. It's got to work.
Dandelion: Mine's not worked.
Elsa: Mine is.
Dandelion: [Looking at Elsa's PDA] Yeah 'cos you're standing . . .
Elsa: One . . .
Dandelion: I can't even see now.
Dandelion: Oh no, mine's not . . .
Dandelion: Don't do it. Don't do it!
Elsa: I've attacked.
Dandelion: Ahhh flipping hell . . . go [indistinct].
Elsa: I've attacked. I can't help it.
Nala: Sorry!
Elsa: Well I'll do it again.
Dandelion: Who had it? Attack?
[They pause for a few seconds before being notified of success.]

Elsa: I can't actually help it.
Nala: Mine was successful.
Elsa: Mine was successful.
Dandelion: No. Why couldn't you wait for me for me, you guys?

The bottom part of figure 1.14 reveals the cause of their difficulties. The group is in fact standing on the edge of the virtual locale (labeled "ADT8") that contains the gazelle. At the beginning of the sequence, Nala is just outside of the locale and the others are inside. By the end, a small amount of "GPS drift" has carried her inside the locale, but has now placed Dandelion outside. At no point can all three lions simultaneously see the gazelle, so, very frustratingly, they are unable to initiate their attack. The causes for such problems (which were frequent) are complex and interleaved. First there is a human tendency to stop and act as soon as there is a visible change in the content; in other words, the players would tend to physically stop upon first entering the boundary. Second, the virtual locale boundary is invisible in the real world, so the players were unaware that they had stopped on the boundary. Third, small technical seams—in this case, shifting positions due to small GPS fluctuations—exacerbated the problem by shifting the players back and forth over the boundary even though they were physically stationary.

Such problems are not limited to *Savannah*, but can also be found in everyday situations. When people try to make mobile phone calls while on trains and get cut off, they often try to reconnect as soon as they see a signal strength indicator on their phone—that is, as soon as they have crossed the boundary of a seam of (dis)connection. The result is that they are often cut off again very quickly if this turns out to be just a temporary rise in signal strength. Additional complications might arise due to network congestion if several hundred people tried to reconnect at the same time. Problems such as these reveal complex interactions between human behavior and the all-too-often-invisible characteristics of the underlying sensing and communications infrastructure, that is, in how people experience and react to seams.

Previous research on seams proposed five different strategies for how designers and participants might deal with these seams in the ubiquitous infrastructure (Benford, Crabtree, Flintham, et al. 2006). These are:

• *Remove seams* Develop improved sensing and communications technologies or deploy more resources (e.g., more masts, access points, satellites and so forth). Although it is likely that the infrastructure will improve over time, this strategy is rarely an option for specific short-term projects, and it is doubtful whether the infrastructure will ever provide complete coverage or accuracy for both technical and economic reasons. Another option is to carefully choose the location and time of the experience to fit the technologies. However, we saw with *Savannah* (where this was indeed the strategy) that this may be insufficient to produce a smooth experience.

• *Hide seams* Create performances that hide the impact of seams from key participants. This is the case with *Can You See Me Now?*, in which online players have only limited and fuzzy connections to the physical world and so often remain largely unaware of the full extent of disconnections and inaccuracies that tend to be at least partially hidden from them.
• *Manage seams* Adopt various fall-back strategies, such as providing some minimum level of experience that will continue to work even when disconnected (as with *Uncle Roy All Around You*) or engaging in extensive behind-the-scenes orchestration to react to the effects of seams as they arise (a strategy that was used by all three of our experiences).
• *Reveal seams* Reveal the presence, magnitude and scope of seams to some participants. Examples include providing visualizations of areas of good and bad connectivity and position through dynamically created color maps. We wondered at the time whether we could have enhanced the ability of the street players in *Can You See Me Now?* to build a working knowledge of seams by showing them images such as that of figure 1.13.
• *Exploit seams* Some participants may be able to exploit seams as part of the experience, as we saw with a few online players in *Can You See Me Now?* who hid in the "GPS shadows." A more extreme form of this idea has been explored by Matthew Chalmers and his colleagues in their work on "seamful games," in which they have created and studied a series of mobile games that deliberately use the seams in the underlying technical infrastructure as resources for game play, requiring players to locate, map, and play with the boundaries of coverage and connectivity (Chalmers and Galani 2004; Barkhuus et al. 2005). Interestingly, not only do seams provide resources for the game, but their games also map the presence of seams as a side effect of play, potentially producing useful information to support other applications.

We have argued that mixed reality performance involves the mixing of real and virtual spaces to create a hybrid space, such as overlaying a virtual model of a city on the space of the real city or the virtual space of a simulated savannah on the real space of a school playing field. Recognizing the central importance of technological seams now further complicates this picture. If we reconsider the spatial structure of *Can You See Me Now?*, we note that the ideal of overlaying virtual upon real actually results in a series of zones in which real and virtual are overlaid (where there is both GPS and Wi-Fi coverage) interspersed with a series of zones where they are not due to lack of coverage. The resulting spatial structure is a complex tapestry of real and virtual spaces that are connected in multiple and constantly shifting ways.

Such a hybrid tapestry is constructed from two key spatial relationships. The first is *adjacency*, in which one space is *connected* to the other so that it appears to be next to it, enabling a participant to look from one into the other or possibly move between the two. Real spaces can be adjacent to other real spaces, being connected by doors or windows, and the same is true of virtual spaces. Computer interfaces also establish adjacency relationships between real and virtual spaces by enabling participants to look from one into the other, exemplified by our earlier discussion of mixed reality architecture and its underlying idea of mixed reality boundaries that establish permanent bidirectional windows between real and virtual worlds. Indeed, mixed reality architecture emerged from a previous theoretical discussion of mixed reality boundaries that proposed a taxonomy of boundary properties including transparency, symmetry, and permeability (Benford et al. 1998). The second is *overlaying,* in which one space appears to be *superimposed* on the other. As a participant moves through one, so they automatically move through the other. Virtual spaces can clearly be overlaid on real spaces. However, real spaces can also be overlaid on other real spaces, such as a theatrical set that superimposes the fictional setting for a play on a physical stage. In the same way, virtual spaces can be overlaid on other virtual spaces. The hybrid space of a mixed reality performance derives from both relationships, with various technologies being used to establish a fabric of many adjacent and overlaid real and virtual spaces. Participants then follow their own trajectories through this hybrid structure. For example, an online player in *Can You See Me Now?* employs a computer within his or her local physical spaces to establish a window into what then appears to be an adjacent virtual space; he or she then moves through this virtual space, passing from one adjacent (sub)space to the next. In turn, some of these virtual spaces appear to be overlaid on remote physical spaces. This unfolding trajectory includes several key transitions, moments of passage from one space to its adjacent neighbor, or into and out of overlaid regions, which require special attention from designers if they are to achieve a coherent overall experience—a subject that we return to in later chapters.

Conclusion

This chapter has explored the spatial structure that defines the stage upon which a mixed reality performance takes place. Analyses of landmark performances, most notably of Blast Theory's *Can You See Me Now?* and *Uncle Roy All Around You,* have shown how complex this structure can become. Conventional notions of virtual reality, augmented reality, and mixed reality that involve the construction of virtual worlds or the seamless overlaying of one virtual world onto one real world are not rich enough to capture this complexity. Instead, we need to work with the idea of complex *hybrid realities* in which computer technologies connect together many real and virtual spaces into complex spatial tapestries. A mixed reality performance then takes its participants on a journey—following a trajectory—through such a hybrid reality, moving from one space to another and constantly seeing the spaces and their participants in interesting new alignments. Indeed, the underlying configuration of the hybrid space may itself be constantly shifting during the performance, perhaps due to changing coverage and accuracy of the underlying ubiquitous technologies, for example. This core idea of a trajectory through hybrid space can also be found in more conventional forms of performance and entertainment, from the traditional theater in which a set imposes a virtual space onto the physical space of the stage, to journeys through museums and even theme parks in which participants encounter various interactive technologies, including virtual worlds. However, the notion of hybrid space is a truly essential component of the new kinds of mixed reality performance that we have begun to consider in this chapter and so understanding its structure is key to its analysis and design. Now that we've considered the hybrid nature of space in mixed reality performance, the next chapter turns attention to its key counterpart —time—exploring the equally complex hybrid temporal structures of mixed reality performances.

2 Synchronizing Time: Past, Present, Future, Replay

This chapter investigates the temporal structure of mixed reality performance, introducing the ideas of "hybrid time" and "temporal trajectories." The first part of the chapter presents our case study, *Day of the Figurines*, a deliberately slow mixed reality performance, driven by an underlying narrative unfolding over twenty-four hours in the life of a fictional town that is mapped onto twenty-four days of the players' actual lives. We present the design of *Day of the Figurines*, alongside findings from various studies that highlighted the episodic nature of players' engagement with the game as they struggled to match its rhythm to the patterns of their daily lives (Benford and Giannachi 2008). We include an interview with its creators, Blast Theory (see box 2.15), about the game's temporal characteristics. The second part of the chapter develops a new theoretical account of time in mixed reality performance, motivated and illustrated by *Day of the Figurines*. We begin by reflecting on findings in sociology and philosophy of media claiming that we are witnessing the introduction of new forms of temporal organization that coexist alongside other models and allow for fluidity between previously separate fields of social existence (Castells et al. 2007; Attali 1982; Hassan and Purser 2007). The impact of these changes on entertainment is already noticeable in the way people increasingly consume entertainment in "between time," while waiting or on the move. We then propose a general framework for describing the hybrid temporal structure of mixed reality performance in terms of five distinct layers of time—story time, plot time, schedule time, interaction time, and perceived time. We conclude the chapter with an exploration of recording and replaying mixed reality performances, considering how system logs of events and messages offer novel ways to capture and even recreate performances "as if live." An interview with the ethnographer Andy Crabtree from the Mixed Reality Laboratory reveals some of the challenges involved in using record and replay to support ethnographic studies, and a second case study, *Avatar Farm*, demonstrates a variety of creative uses for record and replay alongside some of the techniques that can support these.

Day of the Figurines

Something distinctive is occurring in terms of the temporal organization of entertainment. This is particularly noticeable in multiplatform works, which span different types of information and communication technologies (ICT) application and encourage diverse forms of temporal organization and social cooperation. One such work is Blast Theory's *Day of the Figurines*, a massively multiplayer board game in which players interact remotely by using their mobile phones to send and receive SMS text messages from anywhere in the world. The premiere took place in Berlin at Hebbel am Ufer, as part of Trampoline, from September 28 to October 21, 2006. On this occasion, the game was run for twenty-four days for 141 players. The game was then played from December 6–30, 2006, in Singapore at the National Museum, where it was again run for 146 players. In 2007, while on tour in the United Kingdom, it received an honorary mention at Prix Ars Electronica.

Day of the Figurines was developed in collaboration with the Mixed Reality Laboratory as part of a larger research project, IPerG, funded by the European Commission's IST Programme, whose objective was the investigation of pervasive games. A core aim for the game was to explore how the mobile phone that enables us to communicate with others at many times and in many places could allow a long-term gaming experience to be more finely interwoven with the patterns of daily life, building on the agenda set by previous games such as *Mogi Mogi* and *Feeding Yoshii*. Here we analyze the nature of the different temporal conventions utilized within the game and include an interview with Nick Tandavanitj and Matt Adams from Blast Theory in which they discuss the design of time in this work.

Although *Day of the Figurines* was primarily a text messaging experience, each player's journey began at a physical venue where they registered for and entered into the game. This made use of a series of tabletop interfaces that provided a concrete physical manifestation and overview of an experience that would otherwise have been fragmented and invisible. These displays subverted the conventions established by previous location-based games in that a physical space was constructed as a display, an output device in human-computer interaction (HCI) terms, rather than as an input.

One of these displays was a large-scale white metal model of an imaginary town. On this board, there were representations of fifty destinations, based on a typical British town including, for instance, a 24 Hour Garage, Big Chef, the Blue Cross, a Boarded up Shop, a Hospital, an Internet Café, a Level Crossing, an Underpass, the Locarno Club, and a Nuclear Bunker. Each destination was cut out of the surface of the table and bent up vertically to form a white silhouette with a bare metal shadow revealed behind it (see figure 2.1). Two video projectors beneath the surface of the board shone through holes in the table and reflected off mirrors mounted horizontally above it, enabling the surface of the table to be augmented with projections of infor-

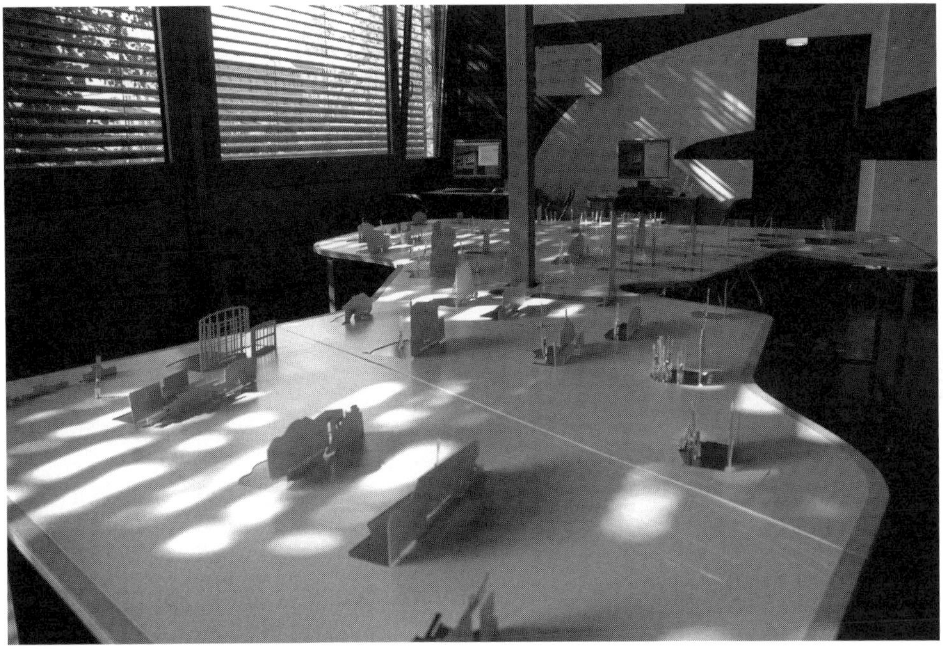

Figure 2.1
Day of the Figurines. The board displayed at Hebbel am Ufer, Berlin.
Copyright Gabriella Giannachi.

mation from the game (see figure 2.2). This augmentation system was turned on periodically (normally once an hour) to show the game operators where to move each figurine as they updated the physical game board. For each figurine in turn, the augmentation system projected a line from the figurine's position on the board to its new position as a result its recent play. This interface supported the task of the operators, but also enhanced the public spectacle offered by the board.

The board was baroquely shaped to act as a "fold," continuously repositioning the inside of the game as outside. By establishing a level of theatricality, it turned participants into spectators, seemingly sharing its spatiotemporal coordinates. But although the board offered a site for viewing, the action or drama was located elsewhere. Through the augmentation system, the board enfolded the liveness or presentness of the game into its history. Because of its relatively large size, as well as its unfolding appearance, spectators remained unable to view it in its entirety without physically circumnavigating it. Despite the presence of a message display allowing them a fleeting view of players' SMS exchanges at a given point in time, they, however, remained deprived of the possibility of an overview or metanarrative.

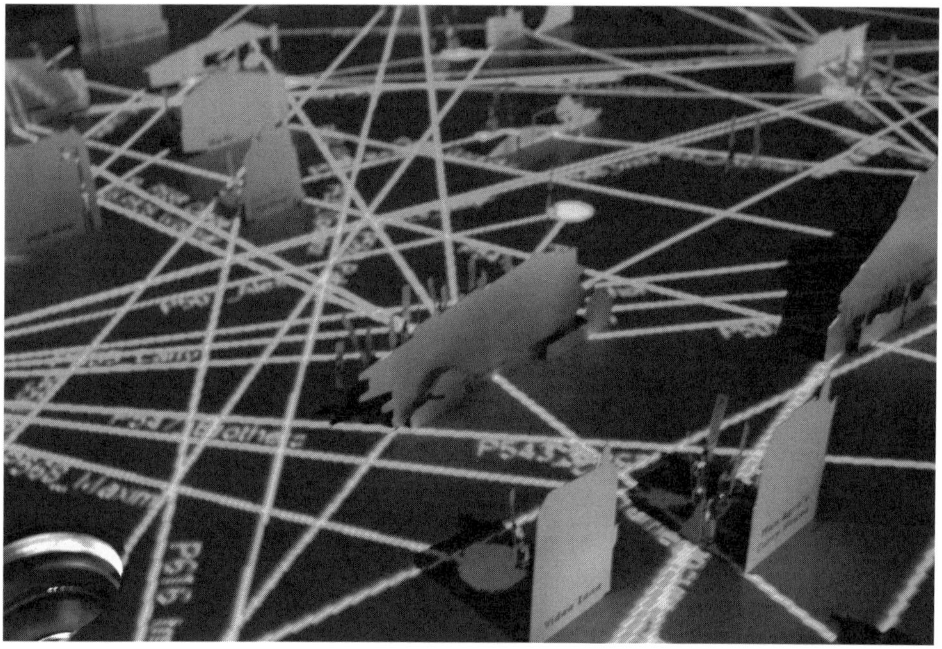

Figure 2.2
Day of the Figurines. The augmented board showing all recent figurine movements at once. Sonar, Barcelona.
Copyright Blast Theory.

To enter the game, participants were asked to select a figurine from a display of one hundred figurines neatly arranged on a second, smaller square table (see figure 2.3). The figurines were cartoon-like, the size of a thumbprint, made of plastic, and brightly colored (see figure 2.4). Assisted by an operator, they gave their figurine a name, answered a few questions that defined the figurine's role, and then watched as it was placed on the edge of the board. At this point, their mobile phone number was also registered with the system. They could then start to perform in *Day of the Figurines*. Before leaving the space, they were given some basic instructions about the game, including the fact that the goal of the game was to help others, which explained the text messages that they needed to send in order to move, speak, pick up and use objects, find other players, receive help, or even leave the game.

After leaving the hosting venue, the game continued to contact the player through the medium of SMS. The game commands were deliberately simplified in order to suit the constrained size and interactivity of text messages and consisted of the following:

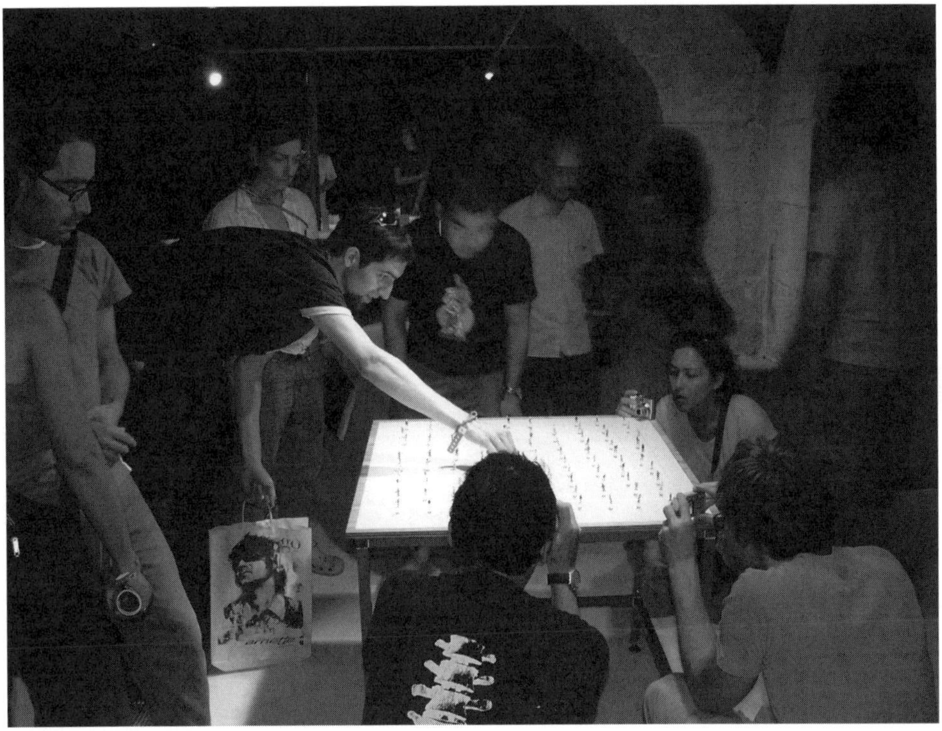

Figure 2.3
Day of the Figurines. A player choosing a figurine at Sonar, Barcelona. Photo: Mauricio Capra. Copyright MRL.

GO <destination> moves this player to the named destination
SAY <message> sends this message to other players nearby
FIND <player> checks whether the named player is at the current destination, and if they are, moves this player to be within talking distance of them
PICK <object> picks up the named object
DROP drops the currently held object
USE uses the currently held object, triggering its particular effect
UPDATE tells the player which other players and objects they can currently see nearby and reminds them of their current health status
HELP returns a message directing players where to find online help and also logs a help request in the system for operators to deal with later on
LEAVE TOWN quits the game for this player. (Benford 2007)

The first message was received soon after registering with the game, as can be seen in box 2.1 in a set of examples drawn from the Geneva game at Version Beta, which took

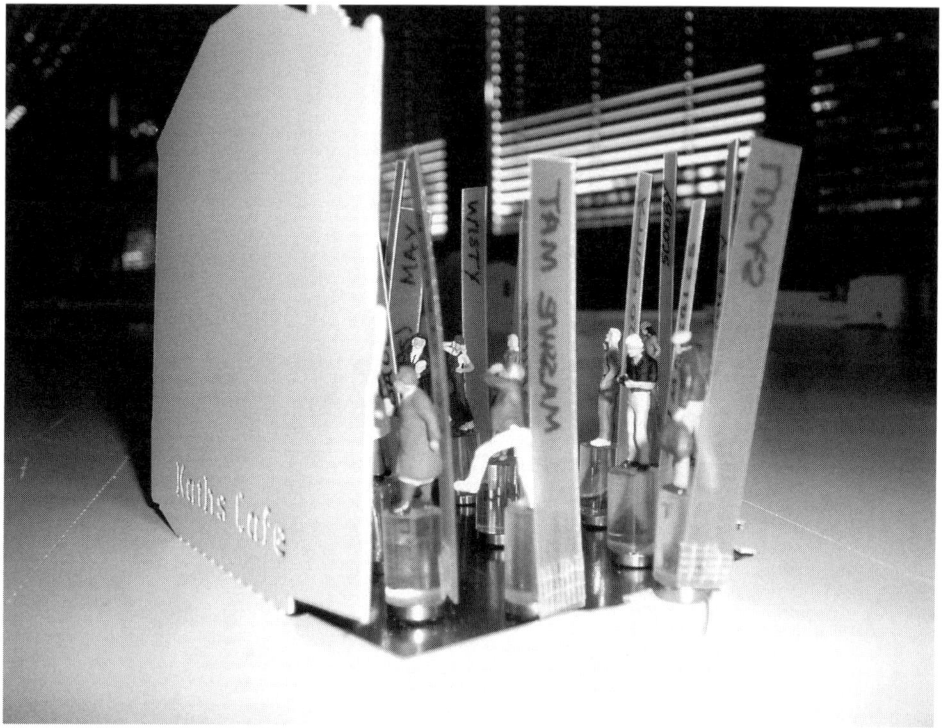

Figure 2.4
Day of the Figurines. Kath's Café displayed at Hebbel am Ufer, Berlin.
Copyright Gabriella Giannachi.

Box 2.1

Received **17:06** GMT Fri 31 Oct	06:13am, welcome to Day Of The Figurines. BANKER has been dropped by a truck at the edge of town. You are feeling OK. Where do you want to go?

place in October–November 2008. Each example message is shown as a separate row in a box. The first column of this table shows the time and date at which each message was actually received or sent by the player. The second shows the message, which begins with the current fictional time in the game and in which the names of players (e.g., "BANKER"); the objects that can be manipulated in the game are also shown in uppercase.

At this stage, the game asked for directions. If participants chose a destination, the figurine was moved toward it. Once the new destination was reached, they could encounter other players with whom they could exchange text messages that allowed them to converse with each other—an essential element of a game that relied heavily on social interaction. The game was also driven by an underlying narrative that took the form of a series of carefully crafted prescripted "event" messages that were sent to players at set times. From time to time players would also receive dilemmas, that is, multiple-choice questions that required them to make a decision within the game. The sequence of messages shown in box 2.2 begins with an event, which is followed by a conversation and then ends with a dilemma.

Box 2.2

Received **14:21** GMT Sat 22 Nov	04:22am, outside the steady thud of a helicopter passing overhead. Someone tries the handle of the front door, shouting and then quiet
Sent **14:23** GMT Sat 22 Nov	Say i've being watching you, bio
Received **14:40** GMT Sat 22 Nov	04:23am, BIOVIRGO said: "what's your problem banker? Did u lose your job hehe? We all know that you're a criminal anyway"
Sent **14:42** GMT Sat 22 Nov	Say i find that my salary goes a long way to drowning out your whining.
Received **14:57** GMT Sat 22 Nov	04:25am, BIOVIRGO said: "Hahaha! so u still didn't get it did u? Money has no power here and your hours are counted! Zai jian!"
Sent **14:59** GMT Sat 22 Nov	Say on the contrary—I already have a seat reserved on the helicopter.
Received **15:40** GMT Sat 22 Nov	04:30am, a soldier grabs your elbow hard, "Will you help us?" in a heavy accent. Do you A: readily agree B: make your excuses C: twist free and run.
Sent **15:55** GMT Sat 22 Nov	A
Received **16:00** GMT Sat 22 Nov	04:32am, OK, there's a helicopter coming to The Rec in an hour. Be on it. And keep away from trouble makers. Your so-called friends are endangering you.

Destinations, events, objects, and dilemmas could all be combined into missions, the most complex structure within the game. The fragment in box 2.3 shows an example of part of a mission in which a player is asked to free the sick dogs from the Rat Research Institute, which involved finding a stepladder at the canal, bringing it to the Institute, using it to scale the walls, and then successfully solving a dilemma.

Finally, in terms of the underlying gameplay, each player had a health score that ranged between 0 percent and 100 percent. Successfully completing missions, answering dilemmas, and using certain objects (e.g., sandwiches and beer) could increase one's health. Conversely, failing missions and dilemmas and using some objects served to damage one's health. Players could also use objects on one another, such as beating someone with the pool cue to hurt them or applying the defibrillator to restore their health. If health decreased to 0, the player died and was removed from the game. However, before that point they first become incapacitated. This meant that they could not move or use objects, but could still talk. At this point, they could beg other players for help, asking them to find and apply a suitable health-restoring object. In one of the most interesting social dynamics of the game, the system could automatically allocate a player a mission to help another player who had become incapacitated.

Together, the game board interface and SMS-based gameplay defined the core structure of *Day of the Figurines* as created by Blast Theory. We now consider how players

Box 2.3

Received **09:01** GMT Sun 10 Dec	10:36am, the fence is high. A passing workman gazes up at that high fence: Gor blimey, guvnor, you ain't getting over that without a step ladder, so you isn't.
Sent **09:05** GMT Sun 10 Dec	Say hey everyone, i found a load of stepladders at the lock. Let's see if they get me in.
Sent **09:06** GMT Sun 10 Dec	Use stepladder
Received **09:08** GMT Sun 10 Dec	10:36am, You are feeling OK.
Received **09:11** GMT Sun 10 Dec	10:37am, you nip up the steps and jump down inside the yard. Fantastic work, liberator! Wait for a second to catch your breath.
Received **09:36** GMT Sun 10 Dec	10:39am, now do you A: Run across the car park in a crouch to reception B: Creep around the perimeter to a fire exit C: Smash a slot window at basement level?
Sent **10:01** GMT Sun 10 Dec	A
Received **10:06** GMT Sun 10 Dec	10:42am, you stumble on a patch of greasy substance, alerting a guard in reception. Task failed. You head for the exit and come across a SICK DOG. Pick it up.

actually experienced this structure, drawing on further recorded sequences of messages to illustrate the typical nature of the experience as it unfolded. As time went by, with each day of actual time corresponding to one hour of game time, the town underwent a series of subtle changes, which gave the sense of the passing of time within an overarching narrative. Participants, who were refugees in this alienating town, learned that by eating and drinking certain foods, or advising others on how to do so, their health could be restored and even improved. They also discovered that objects had more than one function, and they learned that in order to survive, they had to share objects as well as the knowledge embedded within them. Although the game published some basic instructions, which were available to players as cards and on the web, it was only by engaging with the game that players could gain knowledge on how to survive. The game did not entail a conventional dramatic or game conflict, or result in a clear quantifiable outcome—players did not clearly win or lose (unless they died). Rather, the game's pace was more lifelike. For instance, it remained unclear whether by following the goal of the game, which was to help others, players were meant to support the army or the rebels in the town. So, despite the presence of missions, dilemmas, and even a goal, the piece followed ambiguous and less formal play activities, which created the possibility of interaction and emergent behavior. This variable aspect of the game, which allowed players to weave in and out of role-play over more or less extended periods of time, was a fundamental characteristic of this work, as illustrated by the fragment in box 2.4.

Another feature of the game was that it was a slow pervasive game that unfolded over a month through the exchange of "just a few text messages each day" (Benford 2006). As suggested by Blast Theory founding member Matt Adams, this work was developed "in diametric opposition to the high speed, adrenaline fuelled world of "'twitch' console games in which time is measured in 60ths of a second" (Adams, Benford, and Giannachi 2008, 226). Although participants were often required to engage in missions, which—through their own action-grounded logic—tended to turn them into players, the majority of game time was spent simply surviving, working out what to do, seeking advice from others, and providing for them—"being" in the game. Distinctively, the slow pace, and the fact that nothing much happened to its participants, especially in the early Berlin version, prompted groups of players to "gang up" with each other to produce more substantially "dramatic" action or even generate bespoke missions and happenings. So, for instance, in the example beneath drawn from the Berlin game, Hassan, twenty days into the game, doubled up his role-play by acting as a doctor in some kind of impromptu subplot (see box 2.5).

To survive, players often relied on the information they passed on to each other. This reliance, especially in the Singapore game, which had a higher number of dilemmas and missions, drove participants to circulate warnings about a handful of dangerous players who behaved, literally, like killers on the loose (see box 2.6).

Box 2.4

Received **15:56** GMT Fri 07 Nov	01:27pm, PANGUR said: "hi! Every1, i'm journalist."
Received **16:04** GMT Fri 07 Nov	01:28pm, ANNLEE said: "hello Pangua"
Received **16:49** GMT Fri 07 Nov	01:33pm, PANGUR said: "i'm pangur but not pangua or panda ;! Nis 2 mit u here. Mebi c u later in sauna. I gues i shd wash my badi cos pasin a dirty plas."
Received **18:27** GMT Fri 07 Nov	01:42pm, ANNLEE said: "ok i see you in sauna later" CITÉ, FIREFLASH and ANNLEE are here.
Received **13:03** GMT Sun 09 Nov	03:10pm, JANINE said: "whats going on here?" JANINE, IL PAPARAZZI, FIREFLASH and CITÉ are here. There are many mugs of TEA and some GOLDFISHES here.
Received **13:17** GMT Sun 09 Nov	03:12pm, IL PAPARAZZI said: "It's always tea time here. Will you be pleased to have a cup of tea? And by the way, I will take some photos;-)"
Received **13:24** GMT Sun 09 Nov	03:12pm, JANINE said: "oh yes. Photos of me? Il paparazzi."
Received **13:29** GMT Sun 09 Nov	03:13pm, IL PAPARAZZI said: "Salut Romeo et Juliette comment ca va? Rien a signaler au niveau du lard contemporain?"
Received **13:31** GMT Sun 09 Nov	03:13pm, IL PAPARAZZI said: "to Janine Clic Clac Kodak! That's it, You're in the box! Are you a celeb?"

Box 2.5

Sent **18:52** GMT Tue 17 Oct	Say Hello Paul. I'm a doctor. Now what seems to be the trouble?
Received **19:07** GMT Tue 17 Oct	14:05pm, PAUL said: "Hi I'm feeling bad. Can't figure why."
Sent **19:12** GMT Tue 17 Oct	Say I see. Tell me, do you think you might have eaten something that has disagreed with you recently?
Received **19:23** GMT Tue 17 Oct	14:06pm, PAUL said: "Probably the opposit. Haven't found a decent place to eat at since this morning."
Sent **19:27** GMT Tue 17 Oct	Say Hmmm, that could be the problem. Still it's best to be careful. Do you mind if I examine you?

Box 2.6

Received **08:43** GMT Sat 23 Dec	11:36pm, MIDNITE said: "floss no din hear abt it. Who killed who?"
Sent **09:00** GMT Sat 23 Dec	Say It was DJ Raj and Dr No. They killed five people at kaths cafe earlier today. They beat them to death with planks of wood. They're still on the loose!

Box 2.7

Sent **16:37** GMT Wed 04 Oct	Say this is a strange town. A man who I know nothing about just slapped me!

Box 2.8

Sent **13:48** GMT Mon 09 Oct	Say is it not getting strangely dark around here?
Received **13:56** GMT Mon 09 Oct	05:22pm, HASSAN said: "It certainly is. Weird isn't it? Any idea what's going on?"

Box 2.9

Sent **10:40** GMT Wed 11 Oct	Say There is a lot of military around? Do you have any idea about what is going on?

Although players had no metaview of the game, they often discussed the game with each other, particularly in the Berlin version, in which fewer missions and dilemmas meant participants were often unsure as to what they were required to achieve in order to survive (see boxes 2.7–2.9).

For some players, "their figurine's behavior reflected their own actions and mood in the real world" (Benford 2006, 12)—so much so that "aspects of players' personalities, real world activities and situations" often "[bled] through" into the world of the game (43). This contamination between life and game, art and technology, "real" and representation was a fundamental characteristic of the piece. The Berlin and Singapore versions of the game presented numerous instances of this kind of "contamination." Players recurrently abandoned their role-play to identify themselves to fellow players, as in the case of Constance's (Berlin game) sudden query in German

"Rich, Bist du's? [is it you?]" or Tin Man's (Singapore) attempts to catch out Miss Biscuit (box 2.10).

And then, two days later in a similar conversation with another player (boxes 2.11–2.14).

One the most complex and distinctive features of *Day of the Figurines* is its temporal structure. This can best be described as being "episodic," engaging players in short burst or episodes of play that were then often separated by relatively long intervals. This fundamentally episodic nature arose from a series of interactions between three different aspects of the experience: narrative, schedule, and use of mobile phones.

The narrative structure of *Day of the Figurines* was defined around a series of "narrative arcs," or episodes of the story that were scheduled by Blast Theory to take place at set times and destinations. In particular, the structures that defined the game—objects, destinations, events, dilemmas, and missions—could all be associated with temporal scopes that defined when they would become visible, and dilemmas and missions could also be associated with "timeouts," after which they would be auto-

Box 2.10

Sent **04:38** GMT Sun 10 Dec	Say MISS BISCUIT hello. Are you a volunteer at the museum?

Box 2.11

Sent **08:03** GMT Tue 12 Dec	Say gel i say you today at the museum.
Received **08:07** GMT Tue 12 Dec	12:30pm, through pursed teeth, you force the chemically enhanced brew towards your stomach. You feel a little more warmed and alert.
Received **08:07** GMT Tue 12 Dec	12:30pm, GEL said: "tinman u saw me at d museum?" You are feeling extremely well.
Sent **08:08** GMT Tue 12 Dec	Use coffee
Sent **08:09** GMT Tue 12 Dec	Say gel yah, You were with amaranta at the rotunda
Received **08:12** GMT Tue 12 Dec	12:30pm, through pursed teeth, you force the chemically enhanced brew towards your stomach. You feel a little more warmed and alert.
Received **08:13** GMT Tue 12 Dec	12:31pm, You are feeling hot to trot.
Received **08:14** GMT Tue 12 Dec	12:31pm, GEL said: "tinman yeah but no idea who r u:p"
Sent **08:16** GMT Tue 12 Dec	Say gel i am the guy in black polo t. Dont know if you rem

Box 2.12

Sent **17:34** GMT Sun 08 Apr	Say to dwight what is going on here?
Received **17:39** GMT Sun 08 Apr	10:39am, GEOFFREY said: "well i know its early, but i was just about 2 open my bottle of wine. Anyone fancy a glass?"

Box 2.13

Sent **11:19** GMT Tue 10 Apr	Pick up sleeping bag. Say to chaos does anyone know how to help the people stuck in the boarded up shop.

Box 2.14

Sent **18:44** GMT Thu 26 Apr	Say anyone around knows what going on? Am i supposed to be helping the soldiers? Anyone there?
Received **11:14** GMT Fri 27 Apr	05:00am, the rumour is getting stronger: get to the Rec by 5.45am to catch a ride out of this town before it's too late. You are feeling very ill.
Received **12:20** GMT Fri 27 Apr	05:06am, LITTLE ANGEL said: "RALPH are u ok? We should try 2 go 2 the rec b4 its 2 late!"

matically resolved so that the narrative could move on even if an individual player has not responded. This underlying temporal and spatial structure was created using the online authoring tool (see figure 2.5) that enabled Blast Theory to associate each element of the game with a particular combination of destinations and (fictional) times. All players in the game shared the same game time, meaning that time in the fictional town unfolded linearly no matter how much or little each individual played. Even if a player switched off his or her phone or otherwise refused to play, his or her figurine would continue to exist within the game and be subject to events and the actions of others as fictional time marched forward.

Another feature of the temporal structure of *Day of the Figurines* was its schedule. The experience was delivered as an event-based touring performance. Each performance was scheduled for a particular twenty-four days and furthermore was open for only ten hours each day while the hosting venue was open. As a result, players could engage with the experience only during set times on set days. Even when *Day of the*

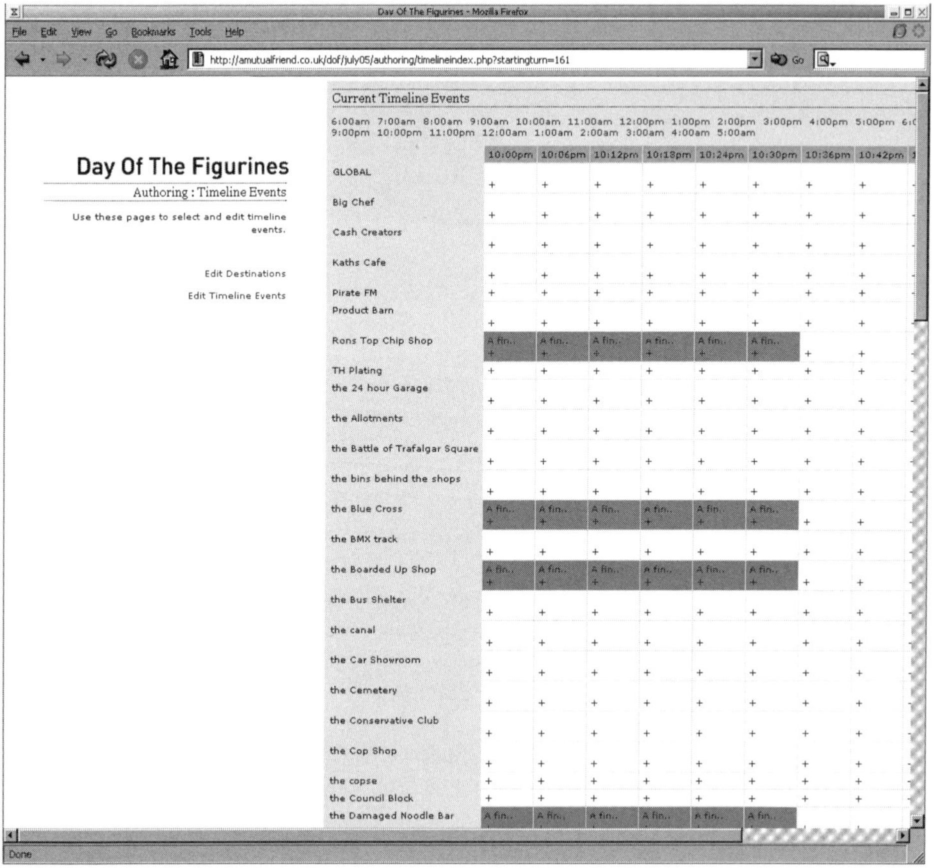

Figure 2.5
Day of the Figurines authoring tool used to create and schedule episodes.
Copyright MRL.

Figurines was actually available to them, players still interacted with it in an episodic manner due to a combination of personal preferences and technical constraints arising from to the use of mobile phones. Questionnaires and interviews reported that most people felt that their style of play became episodic as they attempted to fit the game to their varied patterns of daily life; some preferred to play on weekdays, and others preferred weekends; some enjoyed playing during office hours, and others could not. Patterns of play were as varied, as were the circumstances of people's lives. Beyond this, players would move in and out of mobile coverage, batteries would run down, or players might lose their phones for several days before finding them again.

As a result of a combination of all of these various factors—the structure of the narrative, its scheduling, and players' individual preferences and constraints—it was common for players to be inactive in the game for several days at a time before appearing to wake up again and reengage. This is revealed in figure 2.6, a visualization of patterns of play drawing on system logs of text messages from the initial London test of the game. Each of the 85 rows represents a different player who took part, and the 24 columns represent the 24 days over which the game was played. A black-shaded cell represents that this player actively sent a message to the game on this particular day, whereas a gray-shaded cells represents when they were inactive. By manually inspecting each row, we have roughly classified each players pattern of play as being episodic, continuous, or mixed, or that they disengaged early or joined too late for us to see a pattern. The point here is that the typical pattern of play can best be described as episodic, with the player frequently dipping in and out of the experience.

This visualization's suggestion of episodic engagement was confirmed by feedback from players. More than half of respondents to questionnaires following the Singapore and Berlin games reported that they played "occasionally" as opposed to "regularly" or "seldomly." Patterns of engagement also varied greatly among players due to variations in their preferences for where and when to play, different patterns of phone use, and shifting personal circumstances over nearly a month of play. Several players also observed that they would have liked to be able to explicitly suspend and resume the game.

As a consequence of spotting this episodic pattern of engagement from the London test, the structure and technology of *Day of the Figurines* was deliberately revised to better accommodate episodic play. The most notable difference was to the spatial structure of the town and the way in which players moved through this. In the initial (London) version of the game, the board was divided into squares, and figurines would travel from destination to destination one square at a time (as they might with a traditional board game), a process that would frequently take many hours or even days. Given that players would often initiate a new episode of play with an instruction to move to a new destination, this resulted in a lack of quick responses. Put another way, the request to "go" to a new destination could be seen as often trying to trigger a new episode of play and thus demanded some kind of rapid payoff for the player.

The spatiotemporal structure of the game was subsequently significantly revised through the introduction of a "hub" model of movement. In this new model, when journeying from one destination to another, figurines would metaphorically step out into the "street," represented by a central meeting point called "the hub." Here, they were immediately randomly allocated a new interaction, either a prescripted game event message, an encounter with another player passing through the hub, or a dilemma that required a response to a multiple-choice problem. Once this step was complete, they then moved onto their destination, where they would receive further content. The result was to give an immediate response to movement while still preserving the feeling of stepping outside destinations to move through the streets to other destinations. Consequently, and in direct contrast to the impression given by

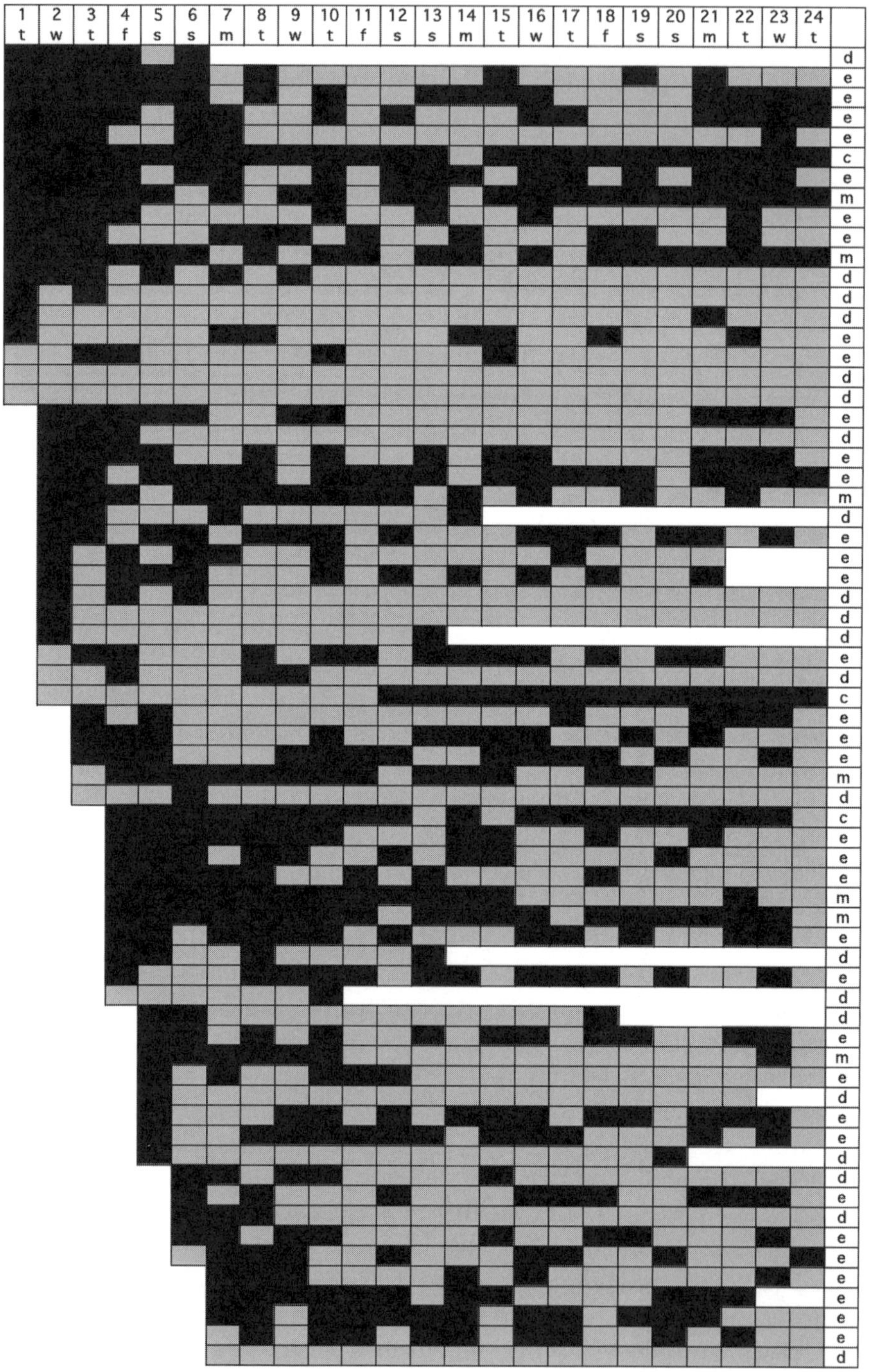
1 2 3 4 5 6 7 8 9 10 11 12 13 14 15 16 17 18 19 20 21 22 23 24
t w t f s s m t w t f s s m t w t f s s m t w t
d e e e e c e m e e m d d d e e d d e d e e m d e e e d d d e d c e e e m d c e e e m m e d e d d e m e d e e d d e d e e e e e e d

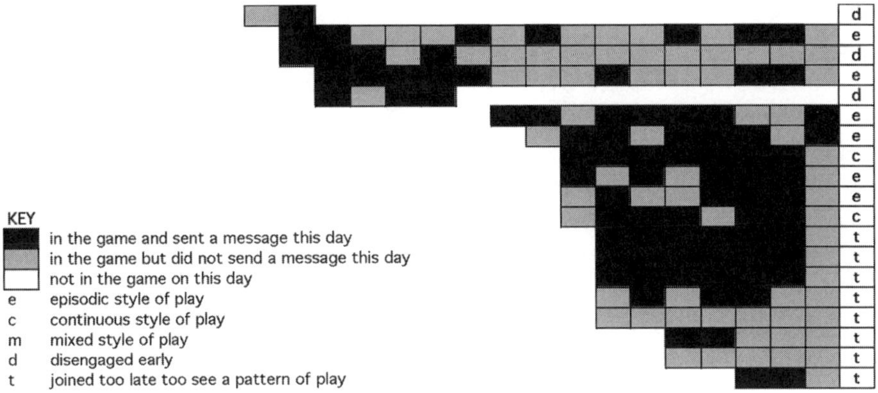

Figure 2.6
Visualizing episodic patterns of engagement in *Day of the Figurines*.
Copyright MRL.

the game board, all destinations in *Day of the Figurines* were equidistant, being two hops away from each other. The physical board contained several hub regions on the city streets into which figurines were moved while they were in the central game hub. So there was a deliberate difference between the geography of the board and the actual structure of the game. Interestingly, though, this difference was not perceived by the majority of players.

In spite of this revision to movement across the fictional world, the episodic nature of engagement could still cause problems at times. Feedback from players revealed that text messages were occasionally delayed for hours before being delivered to players due to network congestion, lack of coverage, or phones being switched off. This might cause them to miss important events or to respond to out-of-date events when phones were able to be used again. Others reported feeling flooded by messages from the game when they switched on after a delay. In extreme cases, these messages informed players that they had died while their phone had been inactive—for example, if another player had repeatedly hit them with a weapon during their absence. A few players reported frustration with playing across time zones, as this led to a mismatch between the game's scheduled opening hours and their own daily routine. For example, UK players in the Singapore game tended to miss the first half of each day's game and then became very active toward the end. This combination of delays, episodic engagement, and multiple time zones could make it difficult for players to engage in meaningful conversation and maintain social relationships within the game (Benford 2007).

A subsequent experiment based on of *Day of the Figurines* concluded that it may be possible to infer players' levels of engagement from the patterns of them sending and receiving messages by utilizing a model that uses *elapsed time* and *response time* in system logs (Fisher and Benford 2009). The study drew inspiration from conversation analysis, which describes how conversational styles are characterized by lapses between "turns of sentences" or "sequences of turns that occur when participants disengage and re-engage." Elapsed time, which was described as "the time interval between two player activities" or "the time interval since the player last sent a message," was here defined as the "property of a message the player sends to the game" or "the time period since they last *sent* a message to the game"; response time was defined "as the time interval since the player last *received* a message." The study showed that short elapsed and response time intervals indicated "high engagement" and pointed out that if a system was able to use these measures to infer a player's level of engagement, it could hold back messages if the player was assumed to be disengaged and inform other players of his or her temporary unavailability.

Interview 3: The Design of Time in *Day of the Figurines*

Box 2.15

We ask Blast Theory members Matt Adams (MA) and Nick Tandavanitj (NT), "What was the function of time in Day of the Figurines?*"*

MA: *Day of the Figurines* is a very slow game, which runs for twenty-four days. We wanted it to have a performative structure, so we decided that it should operate for a certain number of hours each day, typically, ten hours a day in clock time over twenty-four consecutive days, including weekdays and weekends, from about midday until 10:00 p.m. This allowed people to employ SMS in the evening, when they were out with friends, which gave the game a social dimension. Each ten-hour daily session covered sixty minutes of game time, so essentially one hour of clock time was equivalent to six minutes of game time. We deliberately slowed down the passage of messages through the game to reflect this overall slowing of time. Clearly this is something that is directly opposed to the way in which most "twitch" games, which are all about the highest possible speed, are structured. When it comes to these console games, it is critical that your screen and processor update at least sixty times a second. People who play online games are very interested in how quick their network connection is and how fast it can respond. In games like online Quake, this could mean the difference between life and death. We were aware that because we were using SMS we were running very directly counter to the prevailing way in which these games are designed.

NT: Theoretically, we could offer an immediate reply to the message or command that was sent via SMS. However, except when players were interacting with each other, we put pauses in. These were definable within an orchestration interface that would tweak the amount of time it took for players to do any particular action. When players decided to

Box 2.15 (continued)

move from one area of town to another, we had to consider the passage of time in the fictional town, while also allowing for activities that fitted within patterns of people's behavior in using SMS. Ideally, participants were able to have a session of play that lasted less than five minutes if they were to pick up an object and try and use it. The session would last longer if they tried to do anything more dramatic, like move from one place to another, in which case the game forced them to wait. In other words, players had to wait for the world to move on, in order to move in the game.

MA: During the first period of testing, we learned that when people communicate via SMS there are inevitable time delays, which means that the conversation is very fragmentary and rarely moves in a regular, frequent, sort of metronomic backwards and forwards way. However, when players communicated with each other within the game, the inevitable slowness of their communication was something that fitted neatly with the overall pattern and rhythm of the game. In the first three or four test versions of *Day of the Figurines*, we used a game board with a Cartesian model of space. When players set off to go from one place to another, we moved the player's figurine several squares at a time towards their destination, every ten minutes or every hour, depending on different versions and different tests. If a player had chosen to go to a place at the opposite end of town, it would have taken them several days of game time and several hours of clock time to reach their destination. But within the world of SMS, players' sense of space was sufficiently tenuous that they did not register where things were in relation to each other.

In what way did each element, including objects, have a temporal scope?

NT: The *Day of the Figurines* software used a number of different elements to structure the game. We had destinations, such as the locations of the town, that were defined by a default description, so when players arrived at it, it would tell them something about that place. Each destination also had other descriptions, which were only applied at given times of the day. A description would have a certain scope. For example, there was a place called the Product Barn, which was like a superstore in the middle of closing down. From 6:00 a.m. to 9:00 a.m., just before it opened, there were people queuing outside. The description then changed to create a sense of the progression through the day. Places opened and closed, and so we created two parallel sets of descriptions for each destination, interior descriptions and exterior descriptions, which we were able to change over the course of the day. When people arrived, we were able to define whether they were allowed into a destination or they had to wait outside.

Objects—that is, things that people could use and pick up—also had a temporal scope. They did not have changing definitions but could be used for different purposes at different times of day. They were either placed inside or outside the destinations. For example, certain objects were located inside the shops, and players could only access them when the shops were open. Finally, we had events, dilemmas and missions, which were all defined temporally. Events generally took place at specific moments and could happen in

Box 2.15 (continued)

many places at once. No single player could witness the same event twice. We had the flexibility to reuse content across the day, but also sharply define when things happened. If an event took place, like a helicopter flew overhead across the town, sightings could unfold like a wave and people would see it at slightly different times of the day across the whole town. We also had a total eclipse of the sun, which was synchronized across the town so everyone saw that at the same time unless they were indoors and then they only had an oblique awareness of it.

Why did you slow down time? What was the importance of waiting?

MA: In some ways, *Day of the Figurines* is a conventional, massively multiplayer text adventure game, but in many respects it is also an antigame that refuses most traditional modes of activity and pleasure that rational games afford. We wanted to invert the kind of Nietzscheian superpower-type function of traditional games in which you are given enormous power and the ability to be at the centre of events. The function of most games is structured round your agency and the way you control your own destiny. Entire environments depend on you and you know that you are interacting with other agents or software algorithms, which in some way constrain your universal power. In *Day of the Figurines*, we wanted to create a different type of experience. Not only did we adopt this anti-Nietzscheian position, but also we wanted to create a game that was in keeping with the way in which we live our lives. So we aimed to construct a slightly degraded daily experience, in which time passes slowly, events are fairly banal, and outcomes are unpredictable. In most games you are taught right at the beginning what you need for your character not to get harmed and so you know exactly what to do to succeed. In Grand Theft Auto, for instance, the running down of pedestrians is a complete side effect of the game. You do not even pay any attention to it. In *Day of the Figurines*, because of the brevity of SMS, you were put in a position in which you had to think about what you did. Your agency was limited to 160 characters. So you had time to think carefully about how you might respond to a message and you had time think about the malleability, the plasticity of language and what that might enable you to do.

What were the roles of missions and dilemmas in determining changes of tempo-rhythm?

NT: It was a bit of a problem to ensure that people maintained a sense of purpose in this town, so we used missions to create contexts that would take place in real time over one, two, or even three days of actual time, like giving a goldfish to an old lady, finding a cop's uniform to dress up, or locating some clothing to get warm. Missions could vary from very simple things like finding an object through to things that were multistaged and involved finding an object, getting it to a destination and then taking it elsewhere or meeting up with other people. This gave us a period of time in which people had more of a sense of what they were doing, were exchanging messages more frequently and were not trying to understand the purpose of the game as a whole.

Box 2.15 (continued)

How did the authoring tool operate with respect to time?

NT: All content was defined in a database with a generic day-to-day web-based interface to the database. One of the problems we had initially with trying to construct stories and develop the content for *Day of the Figurines* was managing the fifty destinations and their parallel, ongoing, and interweaving stories, when all we had was a number of discreet web pages that were defining individual objects. So in the course of working on *Day of the Figurines*, we helped in specifying an authoring tool, which gave us an overview of what the content was and where it was missing. We could then look at any particular day, look down at any particular hour, and see what was going on. The authoring tool was essentially a large grid with destinations down the left hand side and a clock, which ran from 6:00 a.m. at the beginning of the day through to 6:00 a.m. the following morning [see figure 2.5]. The grid would show whether there were descriptions attached to each of the destinations. If there were events, dilemmas, or missions associated with each of the destinations and at any given hour of the day we could click on a particular hour and zoom in on that hour and then we could click on a particular object within a location within a five-minute period and learn more about it or add and assign scopes to it. So if there was a fight at the Product Barn at 11:00 a.m. in the morning, for instance, you could click on the Product Barn at 11:00 a.m., find all the events and missions that had been assigned and edit the text of the fight. You could also assign that fight to take place across a different scope of time, so you could assign it to take place at a different location.

MA: We had fifty destinations and twenty-four hours of game time. Each hour was cut into six-minute slots, so we had 240 time slots for each of the fifty destinations. This means we had several thousand game slots. The question for us then was: how could we see fifty places at once for twenty-four hours continuously? This proved to be an extremely difficult problem. So we created enormous spreadsheets in which we used color photos as icons to represent the different destinations. We put in all the text and hung them on the wall because a large physical display was one of the ways we could get to understand what we were doing. Finally, we built half a dozen narrative arcs, which linked things across time and space, and created narrative threads that drew players through a certain event. For instance, the dead lovers are a romantic couple that go to the cemetery, take poison together and kill themselves. When their bodies are discovered, the authorities secure the scene and then remove the evidence from the cemetery. Ju [Row Farr] took on the responsibility of authoring this narrative arc and she then wrote events that happened across multiple places and times, and offered tangential references to this event. So you might witness a police car going past the pub to the cemetery to secure the scene. Or you might be at the cemetery and see the lovers in the distance, or, at a different time, see the white tent erected by the forensic team over the scene or even, at yet another point in time, you might find the bottle of poison and the lovers' suicide notes.

Box 2.15 (continued)

How did you structure the piece narratively through SMS to facilitate engagement and disengagement with the work?

NT: We used the arcs. These constituted chains of events or stories of particular characters, normally nonplayer characters, like the couple who commit suicide but also a closing-down sale at the Product Barn which turns into a riot, a gig at the Locarno where players were invited to be the drummer in the band. We used these as a basis from which to write more detailed pieces of narrative and more detailed messages, even individual messages, which expressed how the story would become apparent. To facilitate engagement with the work, there were different types of messages. There were Event Messages, which usually did not invite interaction but told people the story at the beginning of each day just to remind players that the game was there. Then we had Messages, which actively invited players to reply. Dilemmas, for instance, invited players to make a choice about how they responded to a situation, and Missions invited them to act, to pick up objects, to go and speak to people, to go and find things at different destinations. We had a whole range of messages that did not explicitly need a reply, but generated a sense of failure. Finally, we had Pointer Messages, which guided people. To keep players engaged in the game we tried to get them to gather around some of the spikes of activity in the town. So we had different locations that would become active at different points in time and become the focus of a particular story or a particular arc at different times of the day. We used these Pointer Messages, which we scattered liberally through the town, to indicate what was happening where. They opened a window for players who wanted to engage in the game to know where to go and where to find things going on.

Hybrid Time

Having presented the design and experience of *Day of the Figurines* as a motivating case study, the second part of this chapter uses this to illustrate a new theoretical account of the nature of time in mixed reality performance. This begins by considering the temporal structure of *Day of the Figurines* from the standpoint of the existing literature on time in performance practice and computer games, before introducing a new approach based on five distinct layers of time. In chapter 5 we present an exposition of *temporal trajectories* that express different paths through this layered structure.

Day of the Figurines adopted temporal conventions that seemingly aligned it with naturalist theatrical traditions—for example, the chronological unfolding of the story allowed for progressive development and change—yet performance time was a slowed-down version of the fictional time span, in the sense that the story's twenty-four hours occurred over a period of twenty-four days, such that its progressive development was continuously interrupted if not disrupted by everyday life. Alternatively, considered as a game, *Day of the Figurines* operated within a set time (games played for a fixed period of time after which a winner is declared), in the sense that as a performance the game lasted ten hours a day, for twenty-four days, and players, via the allocation of missions and dilemmas, which had to be completed within a given time span, were able to control smaller units of set time within the overall time the game put forward. There were also timeouts associated with missions and dilemmas so they involved an element of set time as well as result time (games played until someone wins). Additionally, the piece operated through result time in the sense that if players died, for instance, the game stopped for them and when missions were completed before the set time, the game moved on (see Thomson 1970, 64–65). By requiring participants to move between these different types of times, the game created a tension that displaced them from a more passive, theatrical mode of spectating and instead prompted them to choose between different forms of engagement, so directly affecting the length and intensity of their experience. Finally, as a game, *Day of the Figurines* also utilized play time (see Juul 2004, 131–132, 134) and this was of course highly subjective, with players adopting their own episodic mode of play, often affected by events in their own life. Although in this case play time could be interpreted as the time the game was accessible for play (usually from 12:00 a.m. to 10:00 p.m.), it would be more accurate to describe it as the relationship between this time (which had a specific real-time duration) and the time the player was engaged with the game (which varied from day to day, and player to player). Just as players were continuously relocated between the aesthetically charged narrative descriptions of the game's destinations, and their real-life locations, so they were also constantly repositioned between different temporal conventions, which in turn affected their engagement and disengagement with the game.

One of the most important capabilities of the mobile phone is the way in which it enables us to interweave different activities in an increasingly fine-grained way. People could rapidly switch between multiple tasks, and move between leisure, work and entertainment. As we see with *Day of the Figurines*, this raises new opportunities for creating artwork that can be experienced while dealing with other tasks, and be accessed while being on the move. Structurally, this means constructing work that allows for the juxtaposition of an ongoing performance with different activities, dynamically interrupting participants, and utilizing flexible temporal structures that allow them to engage and disengage with a given aesthetic experience according to the circumstances of their everyday lives. This temporal interweaving raises significant new challenges, especially with regard to managing frequent disengagements and reengagements with an ongoing narrative.

As *Day of the Figurines* is available at almost all times, it needs to be playable at different paces and accommodate for different and often highly subjective types of engagement. For this reason, *Day of the Figurines* was constructed through what

Castells would have described as "flexible compartments of time" (2007, 176), playable in more or less prolonged bursts of engagement (Benford 2006, 90), which were designed to fold into one another in such ways that a temporally "hybrid" form of engagement would became possible. We have seen that *Day of the Figurines* offered a passive spectating mode, which allowed for a slowed-down unfolding of events in chronological order. This was occasionally interrupted by a series of missions and dilemmas that operated through a combination of set and result times, which turned passive spectators into active participants. Players could also enter into conversation with each other and devise their own subplots and missions.

Crucially, the game adopted waiting as a means through which to control engagement and steer participants in and out of play time. Hence waiting was used to allow players to interweave the game with aspects of their everyday lives, thus creating an equation between the figurine's day and participants' own lives. Additionally, the game adopted slow time as a technique to prevent a full immersion within the game world. In the theater, this technique has often been employed by director Robert Wilson to capture the collapse of representational forms, and is used again here to generate *Verfremdung* and thereby alienate participants from engaging too strongly with any one given set of spatiotemporal coordinates. Adams explains:

> The choice of slowness in *Day of the Figurines* is so accentuated that it violates almost all game design rules because it is centered on and causes complete disruption to play. Theatrically, even in Robert Wilson the extension of time is through elaboration, repetition and slowed action: it never actually stops. In *Day of the Figurines* we insert gaps lasting minutes purely to maintain this pace of slowness: a sent message may be held back for some time for no reason other than to prevent a rhythm of speed to establish itself. These gaps allow players to conduct their daily life or, more, they force daily life to assert itself in the interstices between each game event. At one level this constantly breaks game immersion but it also intertwines the two states in an unusual way. Your experience of "now" is therefore always contingent and in some sense removed. There isn't really any immediacy in *Day of the Figurines*, which is a rarity for any work that has a performative element. (2007)

Unlike naturalist theater, and unlike a typical computer game, *Day of the Figurines* neither required the voyeuristic viewing of a spectacle nor the full immersion of the participant within the imagined word, but rather asked that they engaged, and then indeed disengaged with it intermittently over a prolonged period of time. To facilitate this varying tempo-rhythm—a slowing down, or even halting, and then, occasionally, a speeding up of the game—was introduced so that missions and dilemmas could be engaged with and different temporal "worlds" occupied. These were constructed so they appeared adjunct to the game narrative while also being superimposed with clock time. Interestingly, the compact nature of the tasks required by these missions and dilemmas was suitable for periods when players were "between times," or during work breaks. For longer periods of availability, on the other hand, an augmented form of "being in" the game, was encouraged, which meant that players could engage with the game as long, as actively, and as interactively as they wished.

Day of the Figurines probably represented the first artistic work that realized Jacques Attali's "time of codes" (1982, 247–248), in that not only did it consist of autonomous compartments of time, responsible for the delivery of the game's emergent narratives, but also of a collective and integrating time, through which the embedded narrative proceeded and the relationship to clock time could be managed and maintained throughout twenty-four days. The most important theoretical implication of these various uses of time is the way that the relationship between them not only constructed the "now" for the player in the game world, but also did so in response to the actual "now" of their everyday life by facilitating their continuous engagement and disengagement with the game itself according to their circumstances. Three fundamental concerns emerge from these considerations: first, this hybrid use of game time had to coexist and be managed asynchronously alongside linear industrial models dependent on a "universal" clock time and relative cyclical times; second, for the participants in *Day of the Figurines* there was no longer a separation between work time and social time, so the game's hybrid use of time had to be flexible yet system-specific; third, despite this specificity, a convergence between these semiautonomous systems was necessary, which means that some kind of integrative framework between fairly independent subject-specific temporal structures and an overarching collective framework had to occur.

Five Layers of Time in Mixed Reality Performances

As with the spatial structure of mixed reality performances that we discussed in the previous chapter, it appears that their temporal nature is also essentially hybrid, involving multiple time scales that rub up against one another. The hybrid temporal universe created by these kind of experiences not only accommodates embedded and emergent temporal narrative constructions, each with their own varying and occasionally even contrasting tempo-rhythms, but also manages its inhabitants' relationship to clock time and therefore their ability to inhabit and operate within digital and physical worlds simultaneously. In this section, we present a framework to guide the analysis and design of hybrid time in mediated interactive narratives (see figure 2.7). This comprises five layers, each of which addresses a different aspect of temporal structure, ranging from the mapping of time in the fictional universe created by the author through to the way in which time is ultimately perceived by participants. Between lie three intermediate layers that address the temporal aspects of narration, scheduling, and interaction.

The first layer is constituted by *story time*. We adapted the term from dramatic literature (Pfister 1998) to express a time determined by an "author" that describes

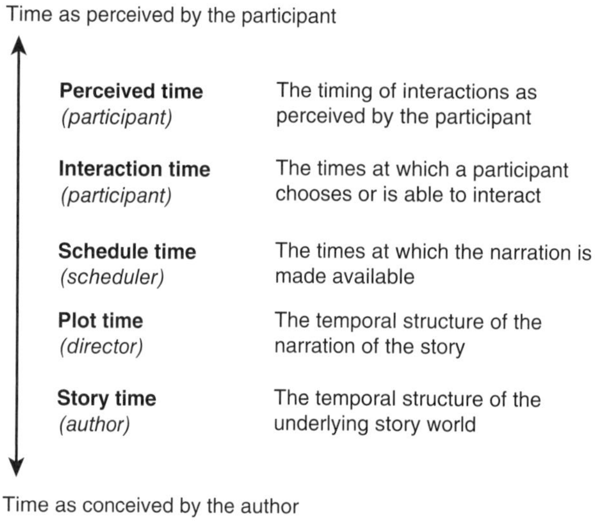

Figure 2.7
The five layers of time in interactive narrative.
Copyright MRL.

the time span defining the narrative outline of a story, in chronological order, that is, the span, timing, and order of the underlying events in the implied story universe. Important characteristics of story time include the historic epoch in which the story is set and its subdivision into primary, secondary, and tertiary time (Pfister 1998). Games involve their own distinct narrative subdivision, including the distinction between "result time" (games played until someone wins) versus "set time" (games played for a fixed period of time, after which a winner is declared) (Thomson 1970). *Day of the Figurines'* story time, which encapsulates the life of a contemporary town over a period of twenty-four fictional hours, operates according to an overall set time, though some of its missions and dilemmas, and the narratives they summarize, are structured around result time.

The second layer consists of *plot time*, which describes the temporal structure of the narration of the story, that is, the timing and ordering of events in their representation. This need not be the same as their timing and order of the story. For example, dramatic texts may adopt "open" structures compressing story time into a shorter plot time, which then refers to events outside of plot time that influence the course of the plot's events; others assume "closed" structures in which the story is self-contained, with no background events influencing the beginning, and the ending being final. Plots may contain subplots defined through different temporal narrative orders that may vary according to given set and result times. Film and television narrative structures also compress time (e.g., "ellipsis") and alter the ordering of events as they are narrated (e.g., "flashbacks") (Allen 1992). In turn, interactive media have introduced their own distinctive structures in the form of multithreaded hypertext plots and the looping structures of computer games, which may be combined with more traditional filmic elements. Adopting film terminology (Allen 1992), the structure of plot time is determined by the director (who may be the same person as the author or even the performer). The more interactive the work, the more the participant will be able to author their own plot, determining its temporal construction and influencing its perception by other players. In *Day of the Figurines*, unconventionally, plot time expands story time, mapping twenty-four hours of the former onto twenty-four days of the latter. This allows participants to author their own plots and subplots within the overall narrative framework according to a number of variable factors, such as how much free time they have in their everyday lives and what kind of pace or tempo-rhythm (e.g., set or result time-based) they may wish to experience.

The third layer consists of *schedule time*, which is controlled by the producer, curator, or publisher, and describes the times at which the narration is made available to participants, be they readers, viewers, or players. All media involve a schedule time (plays and films are shown at set times), but it is in television that schedule time, through its relationship to channels and advertising sponsorship, takes on a particular significance, to the point where it strongly influences the form of the underlying story and plot, as seen by the rise of TV series and serials. As an example, *Day of the Figurines* is scheduled to be performed for ten hours a day beginning on set "opening days," although this can vary due to local circumstances such as a venue being closed.

The fourth layer consists of *interaction time*, which describes the times at which participants engage with the story once it has been made available, either as a matter of choice (playing at times that suit them) or as a result of technical constraints (such as network availability and delay). Interaction time is primarily controlled by the participant. Research in the field of HCI has produced various accounts of interaction time in narrative experiences including studies of how players' engagement with long-term mobile games adapts to the ongoing patterns of their daily lives, such as their commuting (Bell et al. 2006). Interaction time in *Day of the Figurines* is characterized by largely episodic patterns of play, with players frequently disengaging and reengaging over a prolonged period of time.

Finally, *perceived time*, which, building on Alan Dix's work on user perception and action within an HCI context (1987), refers to the way in which the timing of events may be perceived by individual participants. For this, it is useful to refer to Francisco Varela's study of the specious present. Inspired by Edmund Husserl, Varela talks about perceived time as having a three-part structure, based on now, retention, and protention (1999). Retention is described as belonging to the past even though it is happening now; protention is portrayed as the expectation of the construction of the future

(1999). Studies of computer gaming have noted that players may enter a flow state in which their perception of clock time appears to be altered (Chen 2007). Whereas "flow" indicates that the present moment can be perceived as duration, though not necessarily one that is adhesive to clock time, the "now, retention, and protention" structure points to the possibility that the experience of perceived time could be based on tenses or trajectories.

We offer three general observations about this layered framework. First, we propose that a holistic analysis or design of time in an interactive narrative experience requires recognizing or constructing appropriate structures for plot, schedule, and interaction time, and the ways in which they interact with one another, so as to establish a particular mapping between story time and perceived time. For instance, the distinctive temporal qualities of *Day of the Figurines* emerge from the way in which story time is mapped onto plot time, further shaped by a schedule of performances, which are in turn subject to the temporal patterns of episodic play and finally experienced by participants. In other words, a powerful interactive narrative experience requires an understanding of how story time can be related through plot time, which in turn is affected by a schedule, and then by patterns of interaction, and finally by the ways in which participants perceive time. Second, we suggest that there is longer-term "back-pressure" between these five layers in the sense that our emerging understandings of higher layers ultimately shape the nature of the lower ones. As a concrete example, television theorists (Allen 1992) attribute the rise of new story and plot forms such as series and serials to the impact of TV schedules, showing how the nature of schedule time has exerted a back-pressure on the structure of plot time. Looking to the future, we predict that a growing understanding of interaction and perception time will ultimately lead to new structures for schedule and plot time that are adapted to the demands of highly episodic play. Indeed, the design of *Day of the Figurines* already shows some evidence of this in the way that it deliberately accommodated episodic play through small "bite-sized" scripted events and dilemmas that were responsively allocated to players whenever they chose to engage. Finally, this framework relates to notions of the divergence and (re)convergence of media over longer timeframes. It is now commonplace for a story to be retold through different media forms that are often interleaved, remediating earlier narratives that were possibly in some other form or medium. Although medium-specific structures are unable to address these complex layers of intertextual reference, and the degree by which participants continuously engage, disengage and reengage with these works, our framework is able to map multiple temporal structures flexibly onto one another.

Record and Replay

We now turn our attention to a second major facet of time in mixed reality performance: the idea of recording and replaying experiences. The ability for the underlying computer system to capture logs of all of the interactions that it sees and messages that it sends and receives offers a new approach to recording interactive performances that might potentially enable richer and more interactive forms of study and reflection and also generate materials to be used in further artistic works. There are multiple audiences for this kind of record and replay, ranging from researchers who wish to more effectively study what took place during to a performance to participants who wish to reflect on and compare their experiences to artists and curators who may wish to create legacy installations that enable the public to review a work after it has been performed. We consider each of these in turn.

Researchers constitute the first kind of audience for recording and replaying mixed reality performances. There is a longstanding tradition of using ethnomethodologically informed ethnography as a research method within the field of human computer interaction (Crabtree 2003). Originally applied to study technology within the workplace, this involves immersion of a field worker in natural settings (rather than controlled conditions in laboratories) to identify the real-world, real-time practices that provide for the actual use of interactive technologies. These studies yield "thick descriptions" of the situated use and collaborative organization of interactive systems that can then be input into the design process. This approach has been adapted to the study of mixed reality performances, including many of the examples presented in this book, contributing to a series of publications since the mid 1990s. Ethnographers have also documented the challenges of studying mixed reality performance, especially the documentation of multiple, distributed and frequently mobile participants as they use personal or even wearable interfaces (Crabtree et al. 2006). Responses to these challenges have included developing new technologies to combine recorded views of interaction in the real world as well as system logs of software events, system messages, and sensor data, and to replay these alongside each other in a synchronized way to develop thick descriptions and detailed analysis (Crabtree et al. 2006).

Researchers at the Mixed Reality Laboratory have recently incorporated these mechanisms into a tool called the Digital Replay System (DRS) that is freely available as open source software for Macs and PCs and is beginning to be used by other researchers from the social sciences and the humanities. Figure 2.8 shows an example screenshot from DRS being used to analyze recorded data from *Day of the Figurines*, which in this case includes a video recording of a participant using a mobile phone (top right), an annotated transcription of text messages (left), and a map of the virtual town that displays the locations and movements of the players (bottom right). These views are automatically synchronized so that interacting with one (e.g., editing an annotation, selecting a destination on the map, or scrubbing the video) updates the others to display the same moment in time. Further insights into the nature and challenges of ethnography in relation to mixed reality performance are offered by Andy Crabtree in the following interview (box 2.16).

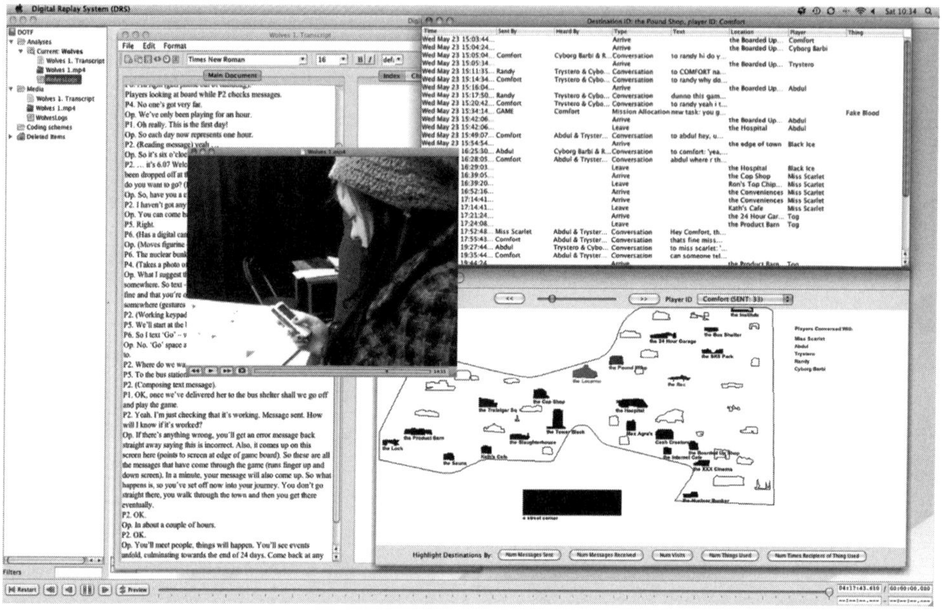

Figure 2.8
Image from the Digital Replay System (DRS).
Copyright MRL.

Interview 4: Recording and Replaying Mixed Reality Performance

Box 2.16

We ask Andy Crabtree of the Mixed Reality Laboratory about his ethnographic studies of mixed reality performances, including Day of the Figurines, *and the challenges of recording and replaying mixed reality performance to support research analyses. We start by inviting him to give us an introduction to ethnographic studies of interactive systems design.*

Ethnographic studies, as I practice it, comes from ethnomethodology. It is a means of looking at the world and, in particular, looking at how people *perform* human actions, not in any dramaturgical or theatrical sense, but rather by focusing purely on the mundane details of the practical arts, skills, and competences required to perform action. For me, ethnography is very much about going out into the world, immersing yourself into what we call the "work" of the setting, or the interactional work, looking at that closely, and trying to produce detailed accounts of the naturally organized ways in which human actions are performed and structured by those who do them in the actual course of doing them.

Box 2.16 (continued)

What has been the role of ethnographic studies in projects such as Day of the Figurines*? How would you say these studies have contributed to our understanding of this experience?*

Ethnography bridges two distinct topics within design. One of them consists of the evaluation of a system and the other feeds into conceptual understandings of new design domains. With respect to *Day of the Figurines,* Peter Tolmie, another ethnographer at the Mixed Reality Laboratory, and I looked at ordinary, mundane human actions and interactions involved in playing it. What emerged very clearly from some of the studies were the ways in which the game was made accountable to social settings and the everyday situations people already found themselves in. A good example is that of a family sat round watching TV one night, where one of the people who was playing *Day of the Figurines* started pulling a mobile phone out of their pocket because they were getting messages. The wife turned round and said, "Are you watching this film or what?" So he was very clearly being called to account here and being made answerable to the things that were going on around him there and then.

It's not that you just play the game in some isolated vacuum, but rather the game is accountable to all the other things that occur alongside it. At times, of course, the game can run quite happily alongside everyday life without interrupting it. It may, on occasion, become remarkable—a source of fun or stories to tell. At other times, it can be completely ignored. There was an example of a teenager who came into a kitchen and said something to his mum. He said someone had just died, and that was not remarked upon by his mother. It was not remarked upon because he knew, and his mother knew, that the was "just" playing a game. If it was really somebody who had died, it would have been an entirely different order of account.

So there is a kind of assimilation of the game into daily life.

Yes, absolutely. So much so that you don't even have to talk about it any more, at least to those who have become familiar with and know what it is that you are doing. When you are offering accounts about it as it becomes more embedded in everyday life, it's often to do with moral accountabilities. Asking the question "Are you watching this film or what?" makes the game accountable and subservient to the moral order of the household and the activities its members are currently engaged in. So, what is interesting is how the game finds an organized way into everyday life, an organized set of rhythms and routines in which you can play it. There are set times as it were, or set places, and there certainly are set places when you shouldn't do it.

By observing people playing the game in the settings and situations in which they are, you are able to pull out some of these issues about accountability, interruption, and time. So, what does that observation actually involve in Day of the Figurines*—in other words, what do you need to capture and what is your method for capturing?*

It's a matter of being there to some extent. So it's about immersion, getting inside what people are doing. That does require a sustained amount of engagement with the players

Box 2.16 (continued)

of the game. It's not something you can do via telephone interviews or questionnaires. You have to be there yourself. You can, of course, use questions, though I would never call it interviewing because we don't really do interviews, rather we tend to have conversations. It's about opening up people's *reasoning* about the game, how they think about it and how they thought about weaving it into their own and others' lives.

In *Day of the Figurines*, we also used systems logs. The interesting thing about those is not that they're a source of data in themselves, but that they provide a resource for engaging in conversation with players. So with some of the players we talked to, we started with the logs and said, for instance, "I see you were playing with such and such a person, and you were doing this kind of thing, and this happened, can you tell me about it?" So the logs functioned as an aide-mémoire for the person you're asking the questions of, whereas for us they gave us an index into the kind of things that players had been engaged in. It gave a good starting point to open up something that's clearly relevant to understanding game play.

Can you tell us about your work in developing the Digital Replay System (DRS)?

The very first experience of having systems logs was in *Can You See Me Now?* in 2003–2004. Originally, we just had text files that had thousands of entries in them, lots of numerical characters and occasionally a little bit of sensible, legible text. Wading through those logs took weeks, even months. So we needed tools that allowed us to get these down into intelligible units that we could interrogate. Simply put, there was a log that had the records of, say, 50 people in them over a month. We needed to be able to break it down into constituents to look at the person, the days, the things they did, so that one could much more easily see what actually happened. Then we developed a way to synchronize these with video, audio transcriptions, field notes, and photographs. The problem with a log is that it's just an index to something that happened in the real world, so we needed to put as much material, real-world material, around that as we could to flesh out the log and to make it more real.

How does this system make use of record and replay techniques?

The idea is that you could take these logs and you can take the various resources such as video and audio recordings, put them together and replay them. This allows us to reinspect the action and interaction that is indexed in the logs and marry it to any other recordings that we have detailing interaction outside the system that is going on at the same time, and other sources such as conversational feedback from users or field notes, so that we can build up a rich picture of gameplay for analysis.

Could you use this technique for archiving?

I could see how these mechanisms could be exploited as part of an archiving tool. I think the real challenge is yet to come out in terms of what archiving is really going to be all about. This is something that is going to be fraught with interesting tensions. As a matter

Box 2.16 (continued)

of professional practice, I wouldn't want to make my data widely available via an archive because I need to respect and protect the participants' confidentiality. So the question is: who are you archiving for? If you want to share archives between analysts then all sorts of ethical issues present themselves. If you want to do it for the participants themselves, I think the issue is one of producing a high-quality and engaging archive that adds value to the experience.

What does this tell us about time?

Time is something that clearly runs throughout every kind of human activity. So for me it's always an issue of teasing out these particularities of time, the way in which time is relevant within any set of activities for the people who are doing it. And it's going to be different from situation to situation. So coming out with any general statements on time is enormously difficult, because time is always situated and occasioned by action itself.

Creative Uses of Record and Replay

Looking beyond researchers who wish to study mixed reality performances, a second and important audience for record and replay is the participants themselves, who often wish to reflect on and compare their experiences, especially as these become increasingly personal and subjective. *Uncle Roy All Around You* and *Day of the Figurines* are highly personalized experiences with participants following their own individual trajectories. Feedback from participants has repeatedly highlighted a need to be able to better reflect on these experiences and to discuss and compare them with others. Indeed, some participants created their own public records of their experiences in the form of personal blogs. For example, a group of friends documented and shared their experience of the Brighton performance of *Day of the Figurines* by blogging game events alongside records and images of where they were in the real world as these events occurred. We suggest that the individual nature of these experiences, especially when compared to more traditional forms of theater in which a performance takes place in front of a co-present audience who share a relatively objective view of the events that are occurring on stage, demands new ways of being able to document, reflect, and discuss them. In *Day of the Figurines*, each player could review his or her own history of play, either partially, through records on their phones during the experience (although these tended to be incomplete, as participants had to continually delete messages to make space for new ones), or in its entirety through the web, but only after the performance had finished. We saw in the previous chapter how this idea of replaying experience was taken a step further in the educational experience *Savannah*, with participants grouping together in the classroom after playing each level and using a shared interface displayed on an interactive whiteboard to debrief, replaying trails of where they had been and what they had done, discussing tactics and learning from their mistakes (see figure 2.9a).

A third audience for record and replay is artists and curators. All of the case studies presented so far have been documented on video, which has usually involved recording footage of participants using various interfaces in the "real world" and editing together views of the media and virtual worlds that they were experiencing, sometimes recreated from system logs after the event. There is also some demand to create legacy experiences that give some sense of how an experience unfolded after the event. For example, rather than staging a live version of *Can You See Me Now?* at the Ars Electronica Festival in 2003, the team created an installation that enabled delegates to be able to replay a recording of a previous performance from Oldenburg in Germany. In this case the recording consisted a system log file that contained a time-stamped list of all online and street players' movements, game events, and text and audio messages. These recorded events ware injected back into the 3D model of Oldenburg as if they were live events coming from actual players (the recorded events were indistinguishable from live ones from the system's point of view). Three different viewpoints were then projected onto a wall (see figure 2.9b); the central was one controlled by the system to show key events of interest such as players being captured. The two views to the side of this were controlled by visitors who could freely explore the action or latch their viewpoint onto particular recorded players.

The DRS, *Savannah*, and *Can You See Me Now?* examples that we have discussed demonstrate the potential of record and replay to support different audiences for mixed reality performance: scholars, participants, and artists/curators. However, their

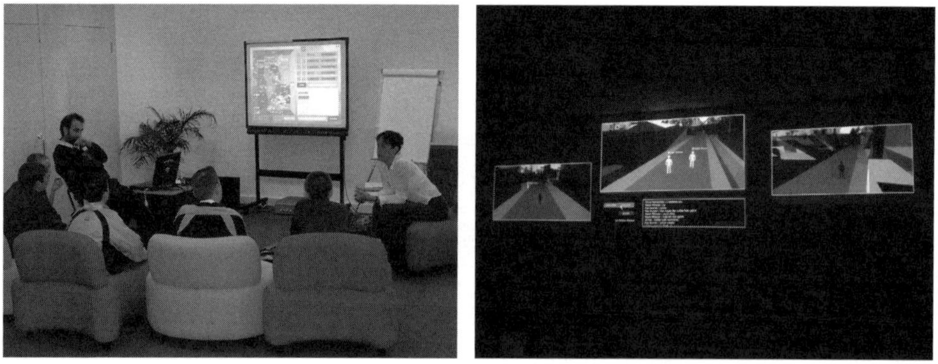

Figure 2.9
Savannah replay interface (left) and *Can You See Me Now?* replay interface (right). Copyright MRL.

technical approaches to recording and replaying mixed reality performances have been relatively straightforward, involving capturing a global system log of events and replaying this through a bespoke separate interface at a later time. To further explore the possibilities of record and replay, we now turn to an additional case study that demonstrates more technically sophisticated mechanisms for, and hence a wider range potential uses of, record and replay.

Avatar Farm

Our second case study in this chapter describes the use of record and replay techniques to create an experimental "inhabited television" show, that is, to make TV broadcast material from the improvised performances of actors and public participants in an online virtual world (Benford, Greenhalgh, Craven, et al. 2000). *Avatar Farm* was the second major experiment in inhabited TV that was conducted by the European Union–funded eRENA research project. Whereas the first, *Out of this World*, had focused on the virtual camera control and mixing facilities that were required to support live broadcasting from virtual worlds (Greenhalgh et al. 1999), the focus of *Avatar Farm* was on how to record the action within a shared virtual world so that it could be replayed in various forms at a later time. To this end, *Avatar Farm* was constructed on top of a virtual world platform called MASSIVE-3 that provided a sophisticated 3D record and replay mechanism. MASSIVE-3 virtual worlds were constructed as sets of locales that could be linked together in different ways to create an overall virtual environment, such as being placed adjacent to one another (e.g., tiled), but also nested within one another. This linking mechanism provided great flexibility for manipulating the relative geometrical relationships between two related locales, such as making one appear as a world in miniature within the other or perhaps dynamically move through the other. MASSIVE-3 also provided a mechanism to log and time-stamp every action that occurred within a particular locale, including every movement of each avatar, every manipulation of a virtual object, and crucially, also the live audio streams (e.g., speech) passing between avatars (MASSIVE-3 incorporated an integrated "in-world" audio streaming facility that could support in the region of ten to fifteen avatars talking to each other within a given locale). A log file could then be linked back into a live locale at a later time and replayed so that the recorded action appeared to be recreated as if live from the perspective of a current (live) avatar. Unlike conventional video recordings, live avatars could fly around the replayed material, viewing it from any angle or choosing to follow particular characters, effectively immersing themselves within the replay that would then appear to take place around them. This record and replay facility was then wrapped up in a mechanism called "temporal links" (Greenhalgh, Purbrick, et al. 2000) that gave users and developers a great deal of control over the replay of recorded material within a live virtual world. In particular:

• The recordings could run forward or backward relative to live time.
• They could also be slowed down or speeded up relative to live time.
• There could be controls in the virtual world to enable live avatars to trigger a replay and control its direction and speed.
• Exploiting the flexibility of spatial relationships between locales, recorded material could be replayed in many spatial relationships to a live locale—for example, appearing as a small world in miniature.
• The presentation of the replayed material could be altered to make it visually distinct from live material—for example, using translucence to give the appearance of ghostlike figures appearing from the past.
• A temporal link could be set up as a delay line so that a live avatar could automatically see a recording of itself (and others) in a locale from the past.
• The resulting combination of live and recorded material could itself be recorded and then replayed again in another live environment so that live avatars could watch recordings of themselves (or others) watching other recordings. This could be done recursively enabling the nesting of recordings within recordings within recordings and so forth.

In short, though temporal links, MASSIVE-3 provided a highly flexible and recursive facility for recording and replaying virtual worlds, and the goal of *Avatar Farm* was therefore to explore its potential for generating new narrative structures in virtual worlds. The creative lead for *Avatar Farm* was writer Alex Butterworth, working through the company Illuminations Television. His brief was to script a nonlinear drama in a virtual world that would involve improvised dialog between members of the public and professional actors. *Avatar Farm* drew its inspiration and world designs from an online community called the Ages of Avatar that had been created by the project several months previously as a way to engage the public in creating virtual characters for the show. The team recreated the four virtual worlds of the Ages of Avatar in the MASSIVE-3 system and then invited four particularly active members of this community to join seven professional actors and a production crew in a dedicated studio for a weekend in order to record the show. The resulting drama was staged as four separate chapters, each with a duration of twenty to thirty minutes.

In chapter 1, the four members of the public—the players—were reawakened in the familiar worlds from the Ages of Avatar to find that the original creators of these worlds—the feuding gods Virbius, Egeria, and Attis—had resumed residence, along with various sidekicks. The players were split up, taken to different worlds, and were recruited or forced into the service of these gods. Chapter 2 involved the players learning about the nature of the worlds, especially how to gain special powers such as flying, changing appearance, and becoming invisible. They also learned how to trigger a "time rift"—a ghostlike playback of a scene from the past (part of a backstory that had been recorded using MASSIVE-3's temporal links mechanism by the actors on previous days). In chapter 3, the players' loyalties to one another were tested and they began to rebel. Further time-rifts revealed more of the history of the feud between the gods. Finally, in chapter 4 the players rose up to overthrow the villains of the piece and restore harmony to the worlds.

In terms of the production infrastructure, the four public players used standard desktop PCs, as did five of the seven actors. The remaining two actors used immersive interfaces with head-mounted displays so as to give them more expressive avatars. Members of a production crew were also present in the worlds, although invisible. Each player was followed by an invisible stagehand who could invoke special effects and grant them powers. One of these stagehands was also responsible for triggering the replay of the recorded backstories within the worlds. The author and the dramatic director, assisted by an artistic director, were provided with an interface to monitor the action in the worlds and to pass instructions to the actors and production crew over a separate (out of world) audio channel. In this way, he could adapt the story on the fly, sending the actors into the world with appropriate instructions. There was also time between chapters to adapt the story and to rehearse actors for the next installment.

Uses of Record and Replay in *Avatar Farm*

Avatar Farm exercised the temporal links record and replay mechanism in multiple ways. The first was to create the flashbacks ("time rifts") that were triggered during the actual improvisation of the story, as was done several times during the story. Figure 2.10 shows an example where several live avatars are watching a prerecorded scene in which Virbius destroys a forest in a fit of temper. In this flashback, the recorded material is rendered with a semitransparent, ghostlike appearance.

However, the main use of record and replay was in enabling viewers to explore the story of *Avatar Farm* after it has been staged. This was particularly important and also challenging due to the nonlinear nature of the narrative. The core of the story was based upon the four players' experiences and for much of the time they were separated and involved in parallel scenes, often taking place in different worlds. In order to follow the overall story, a viewer would therefore need to watch these parallel scenes, including the five prerecorded backstory sequences that were replayed as time-rifts. Given this corpus of dramatic material (in the form of 3D recordings), the eRENA project wanted to explore the different ways in which viewers might be able to experience *Avatar Farm* and make sense of its nonlinear structure. They therefore developed four deliberately contrasting replay interfaces by which an audience could experience the recorded material: an online promenade performance, a form of immersive cinema with multiple simultaneous viewpoints, a tabletop projection system, and a more conventional linear postproduced television-style broadcast.

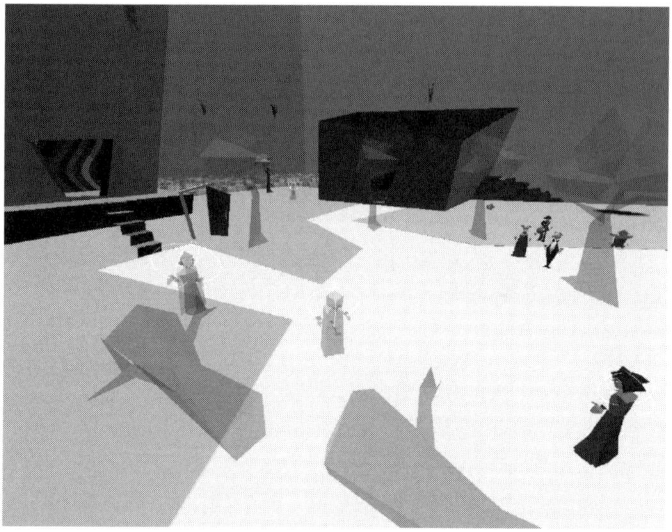

Figure 2.10
Live players watch a ghostly flashback during the recording of *Avatar Farm*.

In a promenade performance in theater, the action takes place among the audience, who move around an extended stage in order to view it. The team developed an online promenade showing of the *Avatar Farm* recordings. Using temporal links, the recorded chapters and backstory segments could be replayed within a live virtual world. Members of a viewing audience could then enter this world over a network and move around within the recordings, following particular characters or perhaps waiting at key locations for the action to unfold. These "viewers" were themselves represented as avatars so that they were aware of one another's presence and could directly communicate. In order to ease the challenge of navigating through the virtual world, viewers could choose to select a character or object from the recording (or even another viewer) and to automatically track them through the recording. Figure 2.11 presents a screenshot from a promenade showing taken from one viewer's perspective in which we see two actresses and another viewer (embodied in this case as a virtual camera so as to make this visually distinct from the recorded material). This interface provided one further navigation facility: the ability for an external director to shepherd groups of viewers to particular locations at particular moments in order to witness key scenes.

In July 2000, the eRENA project took the *Avatar Farm* recordings to the EVE Dome, an immersive cinema facility in Karlsruhe, Germany (see figures 2.12 and 2.13). The

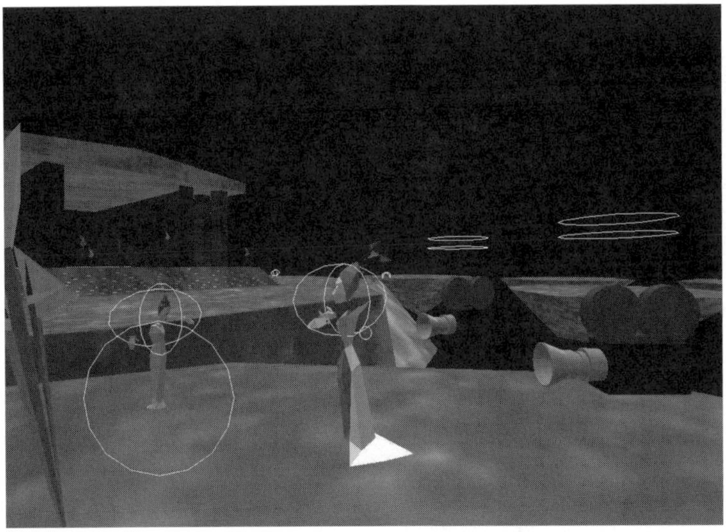

Figure 2.11
Viewers attend a promenade showing of the *Avatar Farm* recording. Copyright MRL.

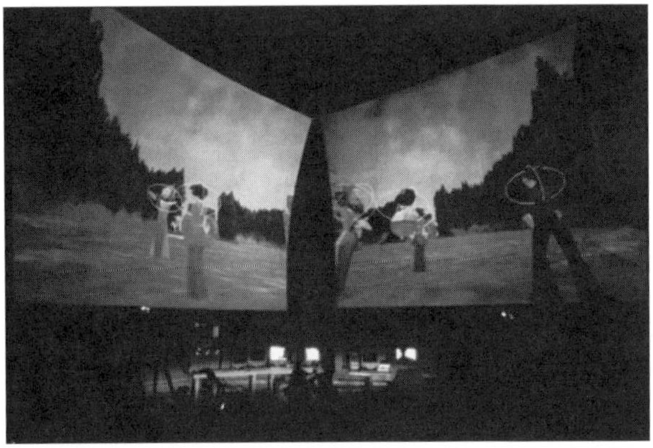

Figure 2.12
Replaying the *Avatar Farm* recording in the immersive EVE dome. Copyright MRL.

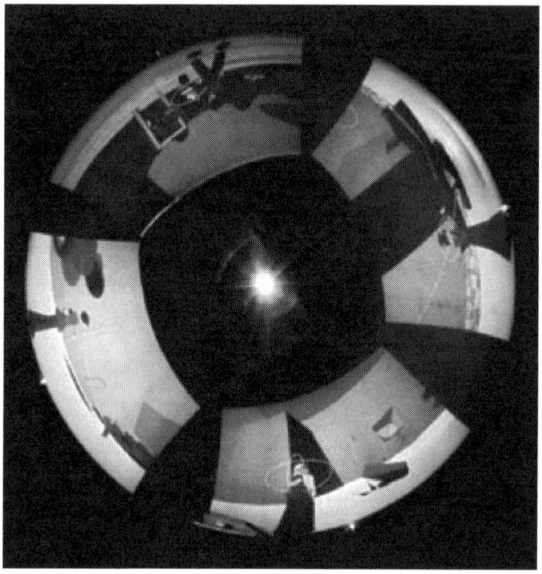

Figure 2.13
Wide-angle shot of the four simultaneous viewpoints in the EVE dome.
Copyright MRL.

EVE Dome is a large dome environment that can hold an audience of approximately ten people. Four projectors and an eight-channel audio system project film or computer graphics and sound onto the inside of the dome. The team constructed a local network of computers, one running the *Avatar Farm* recordings within a live virtual world and four more running virtual cameras within this world. Each camera machine was connected to a different projector so that four independent views could simultaneously project four independent views from the same recording. Most of the time, these viewpoints were set to track the four players in the *Avatar Farm* story (using the character-tracking interface described previously). Viewers inside the dome could therefore follow what each of the major characters was doing by physically moving about the dome to look at different viewpoints. As they were sharing the same local physical space, these viewers would naturally be aware of where other viewers were looking. However, whenever the four players met within the virtual world, the four cameras would pull back and up to offer a single panoramic view of the scene. In other words, the interface would switch between showing a single viewpoint or multiple viewpoints according to the current content of the recordings.

In the third experimental replay interface, the table, a parallel rendering of the recordings was projected onto a horizontal tabletop to produce a live map that showed the positions of the actors and players as they moved around. Viewers gathered round the table and interacted with the map to select particular scenes. These were then displayed as detailed in-world views (with associated audio) on an adjacent vertical screen. In this way, a group of viewers can watch an individual scene while maintaining an awareness of where other potentially interesting action is taking place within the virtual world. A single viewer interacted with the table using a mouse or trackball in one of two modes. The first mode positioned the virtual camera that captured the detailed in-world view. By clicking on the map, the viewer can directly specify both the position of the camera and the point at which it is looking. The second mode scaled and positioned the map, zooming in and out and panning horizontally. Figure 2.14 shows a group of viewers using the table. The white triangle on the tabletop display shows the view frustrum of the virtual camera.

The final exploration of how to experience the *Avatar Farm* recordings was as a conventional linear television broadcast. In this case, an experienced director or editor established a mapping from the highly parallel action in the virtual world to a linear

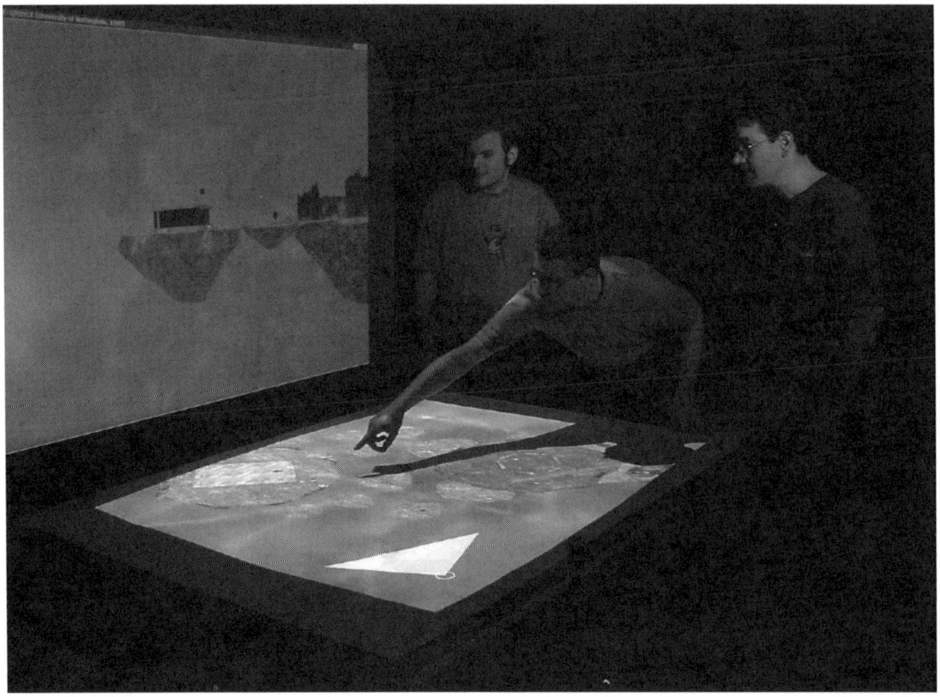

Figure 2.14
Replaying *Avatar Farm* recording on the table.

timeline. The team explored two ways of broadcasting *Avatar Farm*. The first was as a live webcast during the actual recording of the four chapters. The production team included two virtual camera operators and a professional television director. Each camera operator controlled four virtual viewpoints looking into the four worlds. They could control each camera individually, guiding it into position and marking positions for later use. The director's interface allowed her to select one broadcast viewpoint from those available. This viewpoint was passed to a final rendering machine that was connected to a video scan converter, a video streamer, and finally to the Internet. It proved difficult to produce a coherent live webcast of *Avatar Farm*, in part due to the highly improvised and nonlinear nature of the drama. It was difficult for the director to follow the action and predict where it might go next. Then, there was always the problem of having to choose between two interesting and relevant parallel scenes. Live broadcasting from complex real-world situations—for example, sports events—is of course, possible, but the environment is usually well known and highly constrained. The second approach was to postproduce a non-real-time animation for broadcast after the event. The director could then manipulate the timeline of the story at will, interleaving scenes and reordering events, in order to collapse it onto a linear form. As a result, the team implemented the ability to export 3D recordings from MASSIVE-3 into industry-standard animation packages (Lightwave) so that an experienced animator can create an offline rendering. Camera work can then be carefully controlled—for example, following traditional film conventions—and the final rendering can be made to professional animation standards (with smooth movement, enhanced lighting, shadows, and so forth). Figure 2.15 shows a still from one of the first short animated sequences to be produced from *Avatar Farm*.

In summary, *Avatar Farm* provides an example of a sophisticated approach to recording performances within virtual environments and then replaying these recordings in various ways. Although *Avatar Farm* was itself restricted to recording and replaying virtual environments, the variety of replay interfaces that were developed in this project, from projection in immersive domes to replay on an enhanced tabletop, hinted at wider possibilities for embedding the replay of virtual worlds into the physical world as part of a mixed reality experience. One follow-on from this project was the development of the Augurscope, a location-based mobile augmented reality display that could be used to review MASSIVE-3 recordings in such a way that they appeared to be overlaid on a physical site, transforming what was a virtual reality experience into more of a mixed reality experience.

Conclusion

Drawing on *Day of the Figurines* as a case study, this chapter has explored the nature of time within mixed reality performance. Mirroring our earlier discussion of hybrid

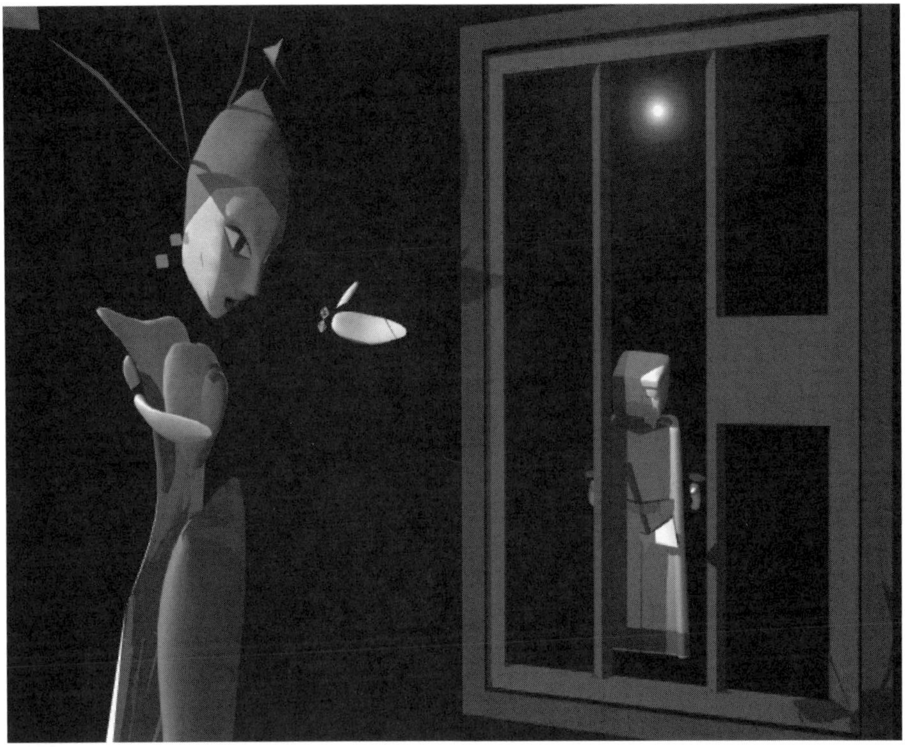

Figure 2.15
Viewing the *Avatar Farm* recordings as a postrendered animation.
Copyright MRL.

space, we have uncovered the complex and hybrid nature of time in these experiences, most notably the ways in which they combine multiple timeframes. We have suggested that the temporal structure of mixed reality performance can be considered in terms of five key layers—story time, plot time, schedule time, interaction time, and perceived time—and have shown how interactions between these may naturally lead to episodic modes of engagement with an experiencc. We have also considered the importance of being able to record and replay mixed reality performances to the benefit of scholars, participants, and artists/curators, and, through the further case study of *Avatar Farm*, have explored some of the detailed mechanisms for doing this in a principled and flexible manner.

The next chapter analyzes the role of the computer interface in creating hybrid structures, and explores how participants' interactions with them can be described in terms of trajectories.

3 Assembling Interaction: Ecologies of Tangible and Traversable Interfaces

This chapter explores how mixed reality performances involve the assembly of diverse computer interfaces into complex ecologies. It focuses in particular on the role of tangible and traversable interfaces in establishing "interactional trajectories" through such ecologies. We begin by revisiting *Day of the Figurines*, but this time concentrate on the design of its "spectator interface" in the form of a carefully constructed and arranged suite of tangible interfaces. A second case study, *Desert Rain*, focuses on the embedding of an immersive virtual environment into a theatrical performance through the use of the "rain curtain," a projection screen made of a fine water spray through which participants and performers could physically pass. This leads us to a broad discussion of traversable interfaces that establish the illusion of physical passage between real and virtual spaces. Our third and fourth case studies, *Flypad* and the *Shape Living Exhibition*, demonstrate in different ways how diverse collections of interfaces, including spectator, tangible, and traversable interfaces, may be assembled to fit within specific public settings—the atrium of a contemporary public gallery and an ancient historic castle, respectively. We include interviews with Matt Adams and Nick Tandavanitj of Blast Theory (see box 3.1), and Boriana Koleva of the Mixed Reality Laboratory (see box 3.2), who have been involved in these various works and who have explored the role of tangible and traversable interfaces in mixed reality performance and museum installations. We then introduce a taxonomy of spectator interfaces based on the four strategies of designing secretive, expressive, magical, and suspenseful interfaces. Finally, we conclude with the observation that the structures of interfaces in mixed reality performance form complex and hybrid ecologies that can be best understood in terms of interactional trajectories.

The *Day of the Figurines* Spectator Interface

For our first case study in this chapter, we return to *Day of the Figurines*, but now focus on the design and experience of its spectator interface—that is, of the two table top interfaces that framed the experience and openly revealed the progress of the game to a watching audience. As we saw previously, the *Day of the Figurines* spectator interface consisted of a small white "figurines table" standing near the "game board," a larger scale model of the fictional town. The former enabled participants to choose their figurines, and the latter provided a public representation of the unfolding game, with the positions of the figurines being periodically updated by operator/performers employed by Blast Theory, who followed a series of arrows that were projected onto its surface. In software terms—that is, in terms of the computation and projection of the arrow augmentations—the design of this interface was relatively simple. However, there was far more to the design of the interface than the software. An ethnographic study conducted by Andy Crabtree and colleagues at the Mixed Reality Laboratory uncovered the detailed rationale for Blast Theory's design of the spectator interface in this game alongside the manner in which it was experienced by participants (in Capra and Benford 2007).

The town where the action of *Day of the Figurines* took place was purely fictional and very abstract in nature, being formed by textual fragments received via SMS on a mobile phone interface. For Blast Theory this constituted "the most hostile environment you can go to. No picture. No sound. No font even" (in Capra and Benford 2007, 13). The challenge for them was how to create a world that was still "meaningful, and resonant, and immersive while using this very narrow information channel" (13). The spectator interface that was specifically devised for this piece thus constituted the artistic response to this challenge, and not only made an invisible fictional place visible, available, and tangible to the audience, but also—as suggested by Crabtree and his colleagues—it quite literally "framed" the participants' experience from the outset (14). In this sense, the two tables constituted a key *theatrical* device.

The team found that creating something that "invites you to consider and look at it" (in Capra and Benford 2007, 14). involved attention to physical detail that does not normally occupy the design of more conventional computer interfaces. First there was the shape of the board itself. This was irregular, in order to attract interest from the outset, and invite participants to consider what it was and take a closer look. Its surface, made from plain, white, painted metal from which cut up shapes were folded upward, was white in order to "highlight the figurines very dramatically" (14), in Blast Theory's words. Likewise, the buildings were designed to capture the spectator's attention. For Blast Theory,

> The idea is that the detail in the table, in the buildings, is enough to give people a powerful sense of what kind of building it is. So some of them have very intricate detail. In the traffic island, for example, you have got the exact shape of the traffic sign. The same is true for the Gasometer. They invite your gaze. Others, like Trafalgar Square, are more abstract and have a simpler silhouette. Nevertheless, there should still be enough detail to pull people in and make

them *feel* that they can imagine what they're looking at. (in Capra and Benford 2007, 14; emphasis in original)

The buildings were oriented so that, when lit by theatrical lighting, shadows always fell in the same direction to define the front and back of the interface. This was echoed in the irregular shape of the game board, which had a central opening point at the front and provided a privileged viewpoint from which spectators could obtain a panoramic picture of the town. The physical definition of front and back was not intended to confine the spectator to the front of the interface, but rather to create different perspective views onto it. This offered "a privileged sense of going around the back" (in Capra and Benford 2007, 15) so that one could see, in Blast Theory's words, "figurines inside the buildings, inside the silhouettes, inside the shadows" (15).

The irregular design of the game board and arrangement of buildings to display front and back articulated different points of engagement with the spectator interface. Crabtree's study found that the height of the interface was particularly important. As the design of the buildings and placement of the figurines invited the spectators' gaze, the spectator was obliged to crouch down to get a closer look—an action that became highly visible to others, thus encouraging the formation of secondary audiences or bystanders. Thus the very height of the table immersed participants more deeply in the life of the town (see figure 3.1). Moreover, the edge of the interface was clearly delineated by a wooden beading that not only circumscribed the interface itself, but also demarcated the tangible boundary between the gallery space and the artwork, framing the spectacle and further focusing the spectators' gaze while drawing people in and anchoring them to the experience.

The final built facet of the interface was the augmentation of the game board in which digital arrows showing individual figurines' names displayed alongside them marked out the paths along which the figurines were moved. The shape of the arrows, the color, and even the font generated a precise aesthetic. This was enhanced by a small computer display built on the edge of the table that showed all the SMS messages coming into the game. The augmentation created and articulated a very tangible connection between the distributed participants who were involved in an utterly fictional experience and the spectators in the room. This aesthetic, Crabtree found, generated an *interactional framing* of the experience (in Capra and Benford 2007, 16). Thus the board framed and directed the spectator's interaction with the interface by inviting participants' interest at a glance, capturing their gaze, inducing them to crouch down and take a close look, allowing for them to adopt different perspectives, and making it possible for them to witness the dynamics of the experience as it unfolded. The work involved in situating the spectator interface was therefore an essential part of framing the spectator experience, reaching out into the physical space and attracting their gaze from afar. The lighting of the interface to "pull the gaze" and

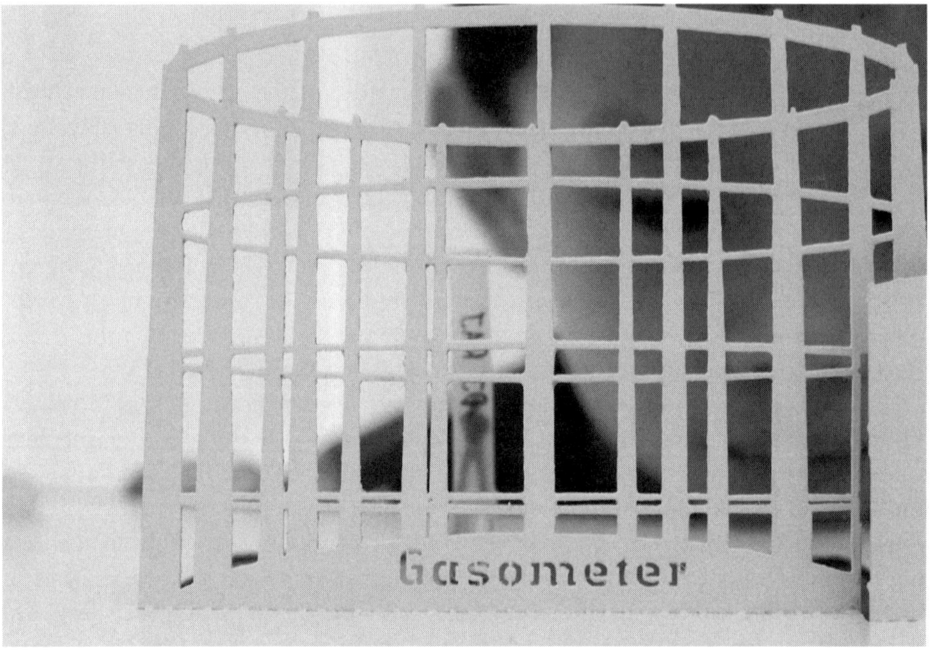

Figure 3.1
Day of the Figurines. Inviting the spectator's gaze.
Copyright Blast Theory.

its positioning to enable the ready access and flow of people also shaped the spectator's journey to and through the interface, leading them from passing doorways and walkways to the boundary of an imaginary experience whose dynamics unfolded in very tangible ways before their eyes.

So far we have considered Blast Theory's goals in creating the spectator interface and the ways in which these were reflected in the interface's physical design. We now draw on observations of use to reflect on how it was experienced by participants. Crabtree's study (in Capra and Benford 2007) revealed that passers-by noticed the installation, and many of them approached it to take a closer look. What initially caught people's attention was the figurines table. This provided the game's operators—that is, the performers who were waiting nearby—with the opportunity to approach them and explain what the figurines were about. Attending to them thus created the opportunity to invite players into the game and the game board beyond the figurines table was invoked as a means of articulating a potential experience. The act of choosing a figurine was quite often negotiated between participants. Whether individual choices were made or players operated as a pair or in groups, they usually sought to find a figurine that they felt some affinity with, one that, according to the findings of the questionnaires, was "cool," or "different," or "interesting." Players would also often move around the table, point out figurines to one another, bend down to look closely at them, discuss the relevant merits of different selections, pick them up to take a much closer look, turn them around in their fingers, and discuss their perceived merits in further detail. The tangibility of the figurines was an essential factor not only in choosing a figurine, but also—once the game started—in creating the character that would allow them to *become* one.

The tangible character of the figurines permeated the work of registration, as participants made the transition from potential to actual player of the game. In order to start the game, participants had to give the figurine an identity by answering six questions, the answers to which were used to shape subsequent gameplay. These were:

What is your figurine's name?
What is a special name from his or her childhood?
How would he or she like to be remembered?
Who is someone she feels safe with?
What is her most distinctive feature?
What kind of shoes is she wearing? (in Capra and Benford 2007, 18)

In the course of formulating answers to these questions, the tangible properties of the figurine came into play again, as the following fragment of conversation demonstrates:

Operator: Think about her (lifts figurine up). What do you think *she's* called?
Player 1: She looks like maybe she's come from Latin America.
Player 4: She's got a story behind her man. She killed her pimp.
Operator: I'm liking that.
Player 6: Do you think she's going somewhere or coming from somewhere?
Player 2: She's going somewhere, definitely going somewhere. She's on her travels.
Player 6: Yeah.
Player 1: What about, she could be called Comfort.
Player 6: Comfort! (Group members laugh).
Player 6: She's not a fabric softener. (in Capra and Benford 2007, 18)

Even in situations where operators were not involved in the formulation of answers, players drew on the physical characteristics of the figurines to develop concrete answers, such as: they have black hair, they have no shoes, or they are barefoot.

Crabtree's study points out that operators invoked the game board to articulate how the game was played. They gave the players two items: a small piece of card with text commands on one side and locations on the other, and a piece of A4 paper that described the game's workings in detail. The operators offered a gloss on the content of these items rather than a detailed account—"because it's about you exploring and finding out and seeing what goes on" (in Capra and Benford 2007, 19)—and then turn players' attention to the game board:

Operator: So, we're going to put Comfort on the edge of the town now. Have you got your mobile phone with you?
Player 2: I have.
Operator: Do you want to see if you've got your first message?
Player 2: All right (gets phone out of handbag).
Operator: So it's six o'clock in the town.
Player 2: (Looking at phone) It's 6:07. Welcome to *Day of the Figurines*. Comfort has been dropped off at the edge of town. You are feeling OK. Where do you want to go? (Laughs).
Operator: What I suggest that you do now is that you actually go somewhere. So text—just to make sure that everything's working fine and that you're off—type in "go," space, and then choose somewhere (gestures at board) where you want to start off.
Player 2: (Working keypad on mobile phone.)
Player 5: (Looking around game board.) We'll start at the bus shelter.
Player 2: So I text "go"—was it capitals?
Operator: No, "go," space, and then somewhere in the town you want to go to.
Player 2: Where do we want to go to?
Player 5: To the bus station.
Player 2: (Composing text message.) (19–20)

Invoking the game board to instruct players in playing the game also consisted of using it to check that players understood the basics of play before they left the venue and that the game was working for them (i.e., that messages were being sent/received).

The game board had a strong influence in determining the performative character of the piece. This was particularly visible during its augmentation. Here movement was usually done through the concerted efforts of a couple of operators who worked together to move the figurines from one location to another, following the augmented arrows to do so. This augmentation both *enhanced* and *emphasized* the spectacle being performed. As one operator reported: "As soon as the augmentation system switched on, suddenly people would appear out of the gallery from other places and huddle round it because they were keen to watch the performance moment of the figurines being moved. It's not just a functional thing. It's the act of change taking place in the town, and that in itself kind of compels people to watch" (in Capra and Benford 2007, 21). However, it was not only the artists who were visibly performing the table at that point: the players who gathered around the tables were also drawn into performing for others (see figures 3.2 and 3.3). These findings are not themselves new to design. The sociality of interaction has previously been recognized by researchers in museum settings, where it has been observed that visitors frequently notice exhibits by attending closely to the actions of others around them (Hindmarsh et al. 2002). As these

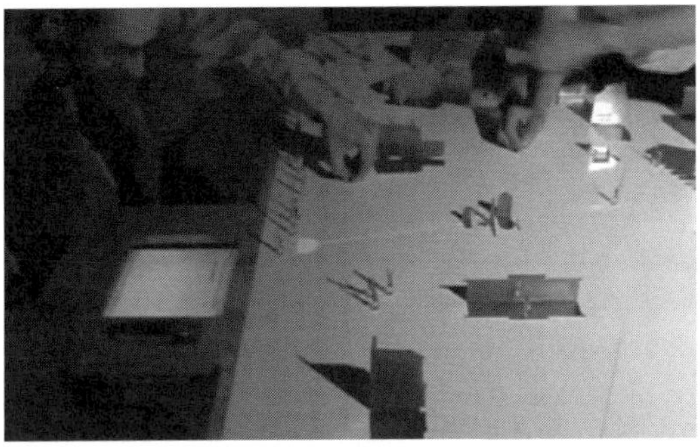

Figure 3.2
Day of the Figurines. Operators doing an artistic performance.
Copyright MRL.

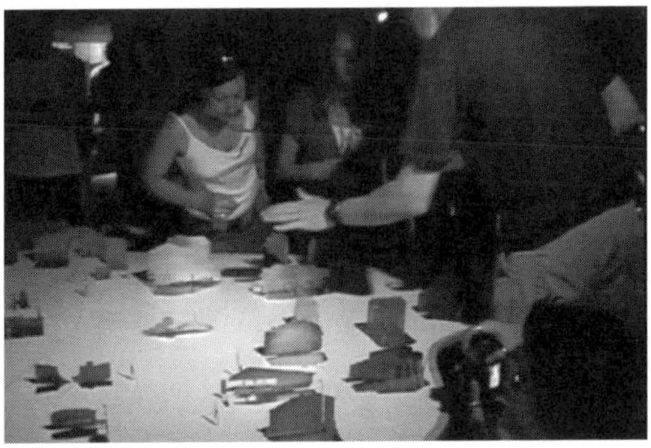

Figure 3.3
Day of the Figurines. Spectators working the game board.
Copyright MRL.

studies confirm, and as we shall discuss in our next section, social interaction begets interaction with exhibits, and recognition of this has fostered a call for the concept of interactivity at work in such public settings to be extended beyond individual participation and passive audience observation.

Tangible Interfaces and Interactional Trajectories

Perhaps the most striking aspect of the *Day of the Figurines* spectator interface is its tangibility, both in terms of the physical form and augmentation of tabletop interfaces and in relation to the nature and importance of the small plastic figurines. Consequently, our first conceptual discussion in this chapter centers around the nature of tangibility and its significance for establishing interactional trajectories.

It has long been recognized that the physical form of an interface determines its affordances, that is, the kinds of interactions that it communicates to its users (Norman 2002). The concept of affordance, originally developed by James J. Gibson, implies an object's potentiality for action (1979) and constitutes what has been described as "a three-way relationship between the environment, the organism, and an activity" (Dourish 2001, 118). Creating, in William Gaver's words, "a direct link between perception and action" (1991, 79) and connecting technologies to the people who use them (80), affordances are useful in drawing out possible trajectories of interaction, but also, if organized in sequences, creating situations in which acting on an affordance may reveal information leading to new affordances (82). More recently, the field of human computer interaction has begun to explore the concept of tangible interfaces, the embedding of digital information and computation into physical artifacts. This has resulted in the creation of hybrid artifacts in which digital information, organized tangibly, tries to adopt the affordances of the objects into which it is embedded.

During the 1990s, architectural experimentation with surface as a means to broadcast information led to the development of a number of innovative buildings, such as Nox's water pavilion at Waterland in Neeltje Jans (Netherlands), consisting of *FreshH20 eXPO*, built by Lars Spuybroek, and the adjoined Salt Water Pavilion built by Kas Oosterhuis (1994–1997), which "fused" (Schwartz 1997) architecture and media to such an extent that even the act of walking through the building triggered sensors converting the visitors' movements into weaves of virtual water. To explore the complexity of this meshing of real and virtual environments in architectural practices, Stephen Perrella elaborated the concept of the hypersurface. Overlaying the real and virtual, Perrella argued, the hypersurface "appear[s] in architecture where the copresence of both material and image upon an architectural surface/membrane/substrate is such that neither the materiality nor the image dominates the problematic" (1998, 13). Described by Perrella as an event (10) and by Markus Novak as a "portal between worlds through which subjectivity emerges" (in Perrella 1998, 88), the hypersurface implies binary relationships such as "image/form, inside/outside, structure/ornament, ground/edifice" (8). Just as hypersurfaces are places of exchange, flickering overlays of strata in which dialectical opposites interact and contaminate one another, tangible interfaces bridge between digital information and physical objects and so fold seemingly opposite worlds into one another. But whereas hypersurfaces remain a projection, caught "sur" or on the "face" of things, tangible interfaces—which, as in the case of the tabletop display in *Day of the Figurines*, may also be hypersurfaces—allow for a *tactile* and therefore *tangible* experience of the interweaving of physical and digital data.

Tangible interfaces extend some of the properties of hypersurfaces. Interestingly, the concept of tangible interfaces, which was presented to the human computer interaction community by Hiroshi Ishii and Brygg Ullmer in 1997, also drew inspiration from a number of interactive artworks in which virtual and physical elements were embedded into one another. These included Durrell Bishop's *Marble Answering Machine* (1992), in which users were able to grasp their messages as marbles and drop them into the answering machine to listen to them; Natalie Jeremijenko's *Livewire* (1995), a 3D real-time network traffic indicator that consisted of a length of plastic string hanging from a ceiling at the end of a corridor connected to a stepper motor; and Anthony Dunne and Fiona Raby's *Fields and Thresholds* (1995), which blurred the boundaries between telematic and physical spaces through the use of non-visual media. The distinctive feature of tangible interfaces is that, as noted by Ishii and Ullmer, they allow users to "grasp and manipulate" bits "by coupling the bits with everyday physical objects and architectural surfaces" (Ishii and Ullmer 1997). This act of "touching" one world (of information) through another (the object) generates a disjunctive "transformative" experience through which, as in the case of *Marble Answering Machine,* a message becomes a marble ball or, as in the case of *Day of the Figurines,* a user is turned into a miniature figurine (see figure 3.4).

Inspired by Mark Weiser's vision of ubiquitous computing (1991), which we discussed in the introduction, Ishii and Ullmer pointed out that to make "computers truly ubiquitous and invisible" a new type of HCI, "Tangible User Interfaces," had to be established, which would "augment the real physical world by coupling digital information with everyday physical objects and environments" and so shift "the locus of computation" onto our skins/bodies and into the physical environments we inhabit (Ishii and Ullmer 1997, 2). Whereas the transition to bodies constituted the subject of the field of wearable computing, the transition to the environment represented the subject of tangible user interfaces. With respect to the latter, Ishii and Ullmer suggested three ways to make information accessible to users: interactive surfaces (such as walls, desktops, or doors) that would connect physical and virtual worlds: seamless coupling of everyday graspable objects (such as cards, books, or models) with the digital information that pertains to them and ambient media which indicates the use of sound, light, or water, among others, "for background interfaces with cyberspace at the periphery of human perception" (2). These "ways" are evident in *Day of the Figurines* through the inclusion of an interactive surface in the form of the game board and the everyday graspable nature of the figurines themselves. This double focus on grasping and manipulation as well the insistence on the generation of a peripheral world was crucial for the design of the tangible interface in *Day of the Figurines.*

There are parallels between this concept of tangible interaction and the overlay of physical and fictional spaces in theater and performance practice. In the theater, by convention, a core dramatic action or plot is structured within and around a series of

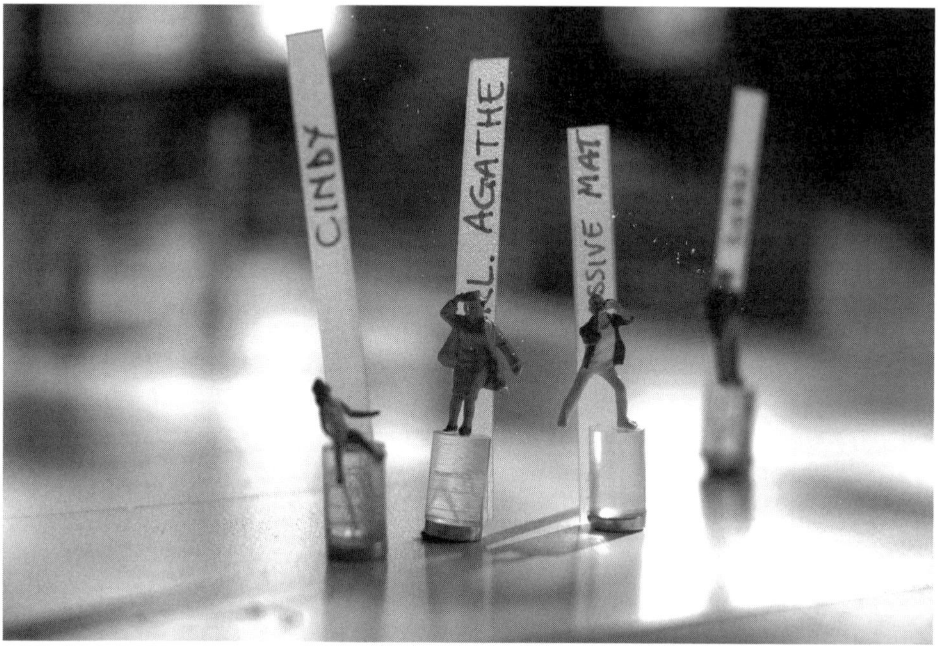

Figure 3.4
Day of the Figurines. The figurines.
Copyright Blast Theory.

peripheral events that are derived from the story and generate subplots. In other words, a central dramatic event is intertwined with a number of peripheral events offering contextual information and creating perspectival points through which to view the central event. However, whereas in theater practices these are usually kept separate from the world of the auditorium by an invisible fourth wall, so that spectators may become voyeurs of a world that is presented as relatively distinct from the one they inhabit, in experimental performance these frames are often overlaid or even intertwined. So, in *Roberta Breitmore* (1974–1978), for instance, Lynn Hershman created a semiautobiographical persona whose existence over a period of four years could be traced through actual correspondences, newspaper announcements, dental records, receipts of financial transactions, and even a psychiatric evaluation. Whereas in theater practice, these spheres of action (both the central and the peripheral) are usually kept separate from the audience, in performance practice, they are frequently overlaid, thus implying the spectator much more directly within the fictional world. Through the use of tangible user interfaces, however, the spheres of action are not only overlaid with the user's environment, but are also juxtaposed against a digital world.

This interlocking of data, objects, and environments implies the possibility of not only designing paths that interconnect physical and digital data, but also of designing physical environments which prompt specific sequences of affordances that establish trajectories through a collection of interfaces. So Eva Hornecker and Jacob Buur suggest that the creation of tangible interfaces "requires not only designing the digital but also the physical, and their interrelations writing hybrid ensembles" (2006, 437). In their framework on tangible interaction, they identify four interrelated themes: tangible interaction, which is said to refer to "the material representations with distinct tactile qualities"; spatial interaction, which points to "the fact that tangible interaction is embedded in real space and interaction therefore occurs by movement in space"; embodied facilitation, which "highlights how the configuration of material objects and space affects and directs merging group behavior"; and expressive representation, which "focuses on the material and digital representations employed by tangible interaction systems, their expressiveness and legibility" (239). As they note, the "interrelations" of materiality, data, and environment—which, following Paul Dourish (2001), also include their social, cultural, and historical background—constitute this form of mixed reality experience. It is also known that the design of objects evokes certain behaviors (Williams, Kabisch, and Dourish 2005, 215), thus providing opportunities for sustained interaction both with and around a certain exhibit, between users implied in the exhibit and those watching them (Hindmarsh et al. 2002). As the design of an interface can steer a user's experience of an artifact, its environment and their relationship with other visitors, it can also be utilized toward the generation of a mixed reality experience. Thus Hornecker and Buur suggest that tangible interfaces establish "interactional trajectories" in which people are drawn into and through a sequence of actions. This idea mirrors previous ethnographic studies of interactive museum exhibits by Dirk vom Lehn and colleagues (2001), which revealed how one visitor's interactions would help establish a trajectory for the next, and so on, and Ernest Edmonds's study of the interactive artwork *Iamascope*, which also raised the notion of establishing a "trajectory of interaction" that included four states of embodiment as well as "the interrelation between those states, the progression and regression from one to another and the key moments that mark the transition between states" (in Costello et al. 2005, 49). Interestingly, the authors note, this also marked the shift between "investigative exploration (what can the object do?) and diverse exploration (what can I do with the object?)" in the work (49). Here, we suggest that interactional trajectories are transformative precisely because they constitute the mechanism through which information shapes action. In other words, interactional trajectories not only afford sequences of actions, marking crucially different stages in interacting with a work, but they also literally inform that action, thus turning a visitor into the actor of their own performance(s) (see also Dinkla 1997 and Giannachi 2004).

It is this relationship between tangibility and an interactional trajectory that lies at the heart of the *Day of the Figurines* spectator interface. Crabtree's previously cited ethnographic study of the *Day of the Figurines* interface revealed how, through detailed attention to factors such as shape, size, height, material, surface, digital augmentation, position, orientation, and lighting, Blast Theory was able to create a series of "distinct interactional trajectories" (in Capra and Benford 2007, 9) that framed participants' behavior and extended the work's design "far beyond the traditional boundaries of conventional interfaces" (9). These interactional trajectories fostered engagement, supported performance, and afforded the social interaction that is key to the production of public spectacle. Crabtree and his coauthors already noted the extension of the interactional trajectory beyond the interface itself "to reach out into the physical space and attract the spectator's gaze from afar" (17). Here, the interface was not merely a functional input or output device but both, in Crabtree's analysis, a "*framing device*" (17; emphasis in original) and a transactional device, creating sequences of movements, affordances, and interactions between people, objects, and spaces, thus framing and shaping the spectator experience as well as their ability to reflect about it not only at the time of the encounter with the work, but also performatively and pervasively, for the subsequent period of game play.

Desert Rain

Our second case study, *Desert Rain* (1998), sent six players at a time on a mission into a virtual world that was embedded into an extensive physical set via six "rain curtains," screens composed of a fine water spray through which the players and actors could physically pass, appearing to step into and out of a projected image of a virtual world. Developed by Blast Theory in collaboration with the Mixed Reality Laboratory as part if the eRENA project, *Desert Rain* aimed to exploit the concept of an electronic arena and adopted mixed reality technologies "to create environments for potentially large-scale real-time participation in media-rich cultural events" (Bowers 1999, 2). The piece, which was described as "an intermeshing of computer game, installation, live performance and cultural polemic" (Armstrong 1999), was inspired by Jean Baudrillard's controversial text *The Gulf War Did Not Take Place* (1991) and, in the words of Blast Theory's Matt Adams, articulated "the ways in which the real, the virtual, the fictional and the imaginary have become increasingly entwined" (Blast Theory 2002).

Desert Rain began with a performer leading six participants at a time into a semidark antechamber, where they were asked to give up their coats and bags, which were then placed in a box under their chairs. In return, participants received a hooded black jacket and a magnetic swipe card with a picture of a person, their "target," that they had to find. This moment marked their transition from being spectators, passively waiting for something to happen, to players (Rinman 2002, 65), actively engaging with the virtual environment. After listening to their instructions, they were led through darkness, one at a time, into another chamber, which was divided into six fabric cubicles, one for each participant. Here, they stood on a footpad. Wearing a headset with a microphone, they faced a fine water spray or rain curtain upon which a virtual world was projected. This rain curtain was turned on only after they had taken their position on the footpad, yielding a dramatic visual and audible effect as the water suddenly began to fall and the projected image appeared. By moving their weight on the footpads, which acted as "large joysticks" (Blast Theory 2002), they could move through the virtual environment. This moment marked the beginning of a game-like search during which the participants, who could visualize themselves and each other only as avatars, had to locate their targets. Rachel Clarke describes this phase as follows: "Working largely with computer game logic of find, retrieve, kill or rescue, the target to find is a virtual person recognizable by both name and face within the virtual environment. The goal is to find this target and escape with the other five participants to a hotel room in the virtual environment within an allotted time of 20 minutes" (2001, 44).

The first projected image was a motel room with a chair, a double bed, a lamp, and a TV set showing CNN coverage of the first Gulf War (see figure 3.5). Upon leaving

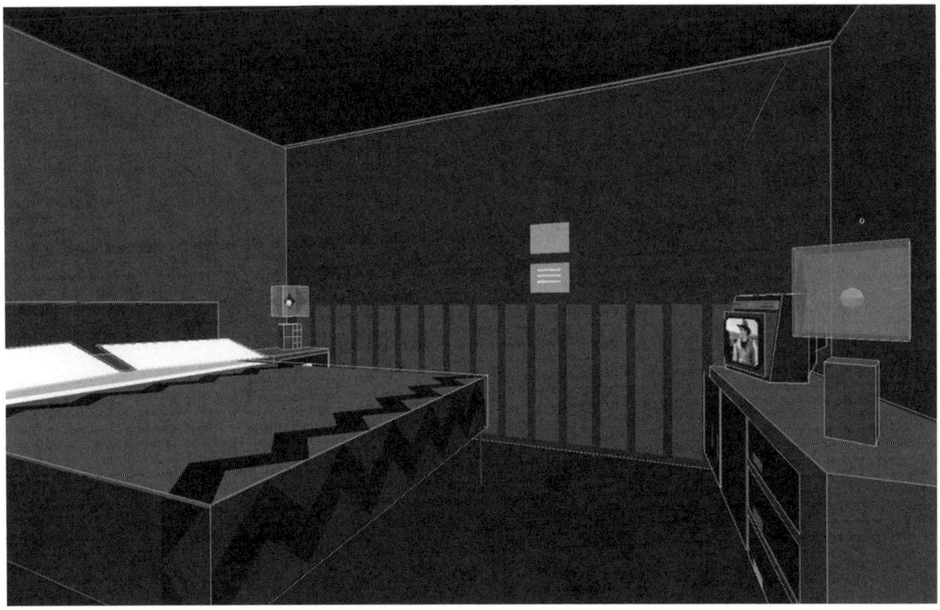

Figure 3.5
Desert Rain. The virtual motel room.
Copyright Blast Theory.

the motel room, participants were relocated to a desert, which, like the motel, had been created as a projection on the rain screen and consisted of geometrical forms scattered with flags that represented their objectives. When participants approached their targets, a voice stated the target's name and a picture of the target appeared next to their name (see figure 3.6). If participants walked through these pictures, they could proceed in their journey toward the exit. Participants had not been told what the aim of this "game" was, so although they were actively playing what clearly felt and looked like a game, they did not know what the consequences of their actions were. Clarke summed up her uncertainty as follows: "What are my targets for? Am I saving them? Are they annihilated when I find them? . . . If they are white, what are they being targeted for?" (2001). Players did not know that they were in a very controlled environment in which they were constantly monitored by two members of the company who, without being seen, watched over them from behind the rain curtain (exploiting its asymmetric nature that was similar to that of a one-way mirror) and from a bank of six monitors in a control room, each of which was slaved to the viewpoint of a particular player's avatar (Blast Theory 2002). These orchestrators could influence participants to move in particular ways, either by giving encouragement over a live

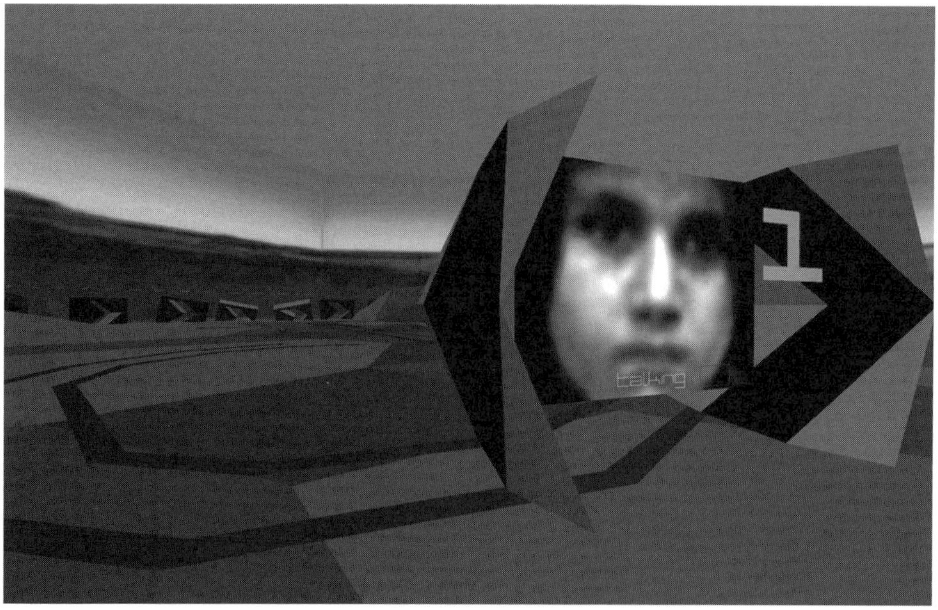

Figure 3.6
Desert Rain. A player's avatar seen against the desert landscape.
Copyright Blast Theory.

audio link or by directly steering their avatars, in order to influence their journey through and experience of the game, sometimes helping them along the way if they were stuck and sometimes deliberately slowing them down to maintain the tension of racing against the clock.

The deserted landscape contained three buildings. The first building held a map of the area; the second was a cylinder with six doors leading to images of each of the visitors on their respective platforms—an environment that thus created a reverse link from the virtual back into the physical world within which the players were located (Adams and Row Farr 2001, 745–746); and finally the third building seemed empty but in fact contained the players' targets. The game could be successfully completed only if all participants reached the end of a final corridor together, so players often had to work collaboratively, and were frequently helped by the orchestrators, to exit this phase of the game. When they located their target, the virtual environment was suddenly and unexpectedly penetrated by a Blast Theory performer who physically emerged, in a *coup de théâtre*, through the rain screen and collected the magnetic swipe card received at the beginning of the game and handed over a second card that marked a new phase in the piece (see figure 3.7). This disturbing contamination between real and virtual marked the collapse of the digital and physical worlds into one another. Clarke sums up this dramatic moment as follows: "This momentary interruption of the game disrupts the telepresence experienced by the participant, for it fractures their solipsistic virtual engagement with the screen and points to the potential of something existing beyond the realms of the image. . . . It is therefore the performing live presence existing alongside the vitriol world that enables a critique of virtual technologies to be considered" (qtd. in Blast Theory 2002).

During the third phase of *Desert Rain*, participants were themselves led through the water curtain, in a ritual act of symbolic purification, to find that the narrow exit corridor leading to the subsequent performance environment had been blocked by a large mountain of sand (see figure 3.8).

Having climbed up and come down the other side of the mountain of sand, participants reached the final room. This physical space, like the first virtual one, staged a motel room and contained a television that could be activated by swiping the card obtained from the performers during the game (see figure 3.9). For those players who had successfully found their targets, this meant that they could listen to their experience of the war. The targets proved to be: Glenn Fitzpatrick, who drove an Armoured Personnel Carrier in the first Gulf War that collected Iraqi casualties and was now studying fine art; Shona Cambell, who had suffered from colic during the conflict, but had served in the Army for three years and was now a captain in the territorial army; Richard Kilgour, a peace worker on the Iraqi-Saudi border, who had helped to establish a peace camp in December 1990; Sam Halfpenny, an actor who played a soldier in a television drama about the first Gulf War; Eamonn Matthews, a BBC journalist who

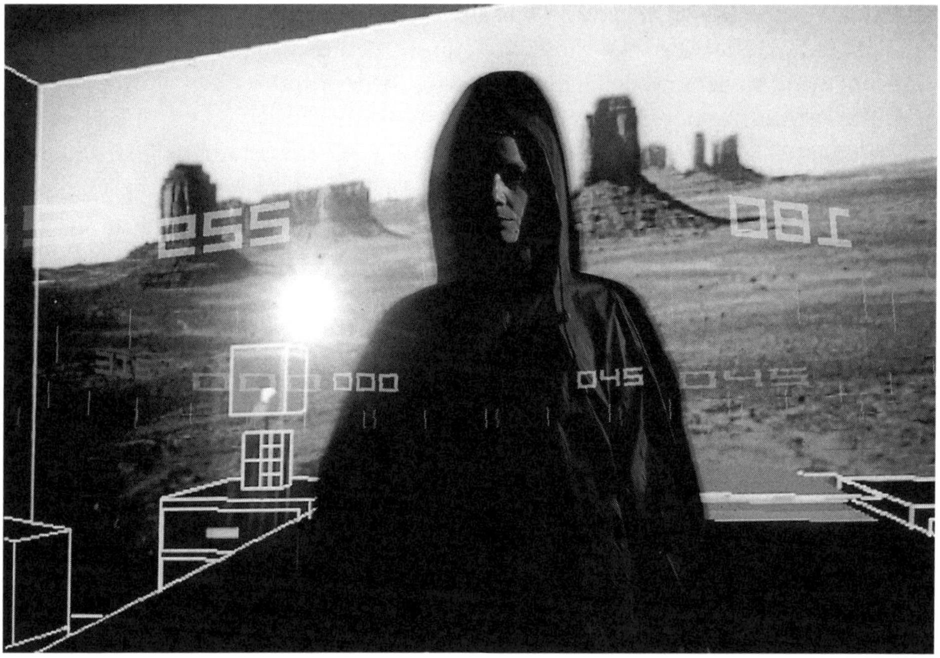

Figure 3.7
Desert Rain. Blast Theory member Ju Row Farr emerging from behind the rain screen. Copyright Blast Theory.

was in Baghdad when the air raids started and was now deputy editor of *Newsnight*; and Tony Taras, an actor who was on holiday in Egypt at the time of the conflict. All targets talked about their relationship to the events during the conflict and how "real" it all felt (Blast Theory 2000). Upon leaving the room, participants finally changed back into their original clothing and then left, usually unaware of something that had been placed in their pockets—a small box of 100,000 sand grains reporting a quotation from a speech by General Colin Powell, published in the *New York Times* on March 23, 1991, which referred to the possible number of Iraqis killed during the war as follows: "It's really not a number I'm terribly interested in" (Tyler 1991).

Artistically, *Desert Rain* constituted a powerful response to the philosophical debates prompted by Baudrillard's writings about the Gulf War and exposed the complexity, "fragility and interconnectedness" of the relationship between the "physical and the virtual, the fictional and the factual" (Clarke 2001, 44). The performance was structured, like other works by Blast Theory, around complex contaminations between genres (performance, installation, theater, game), physical and digital environments,

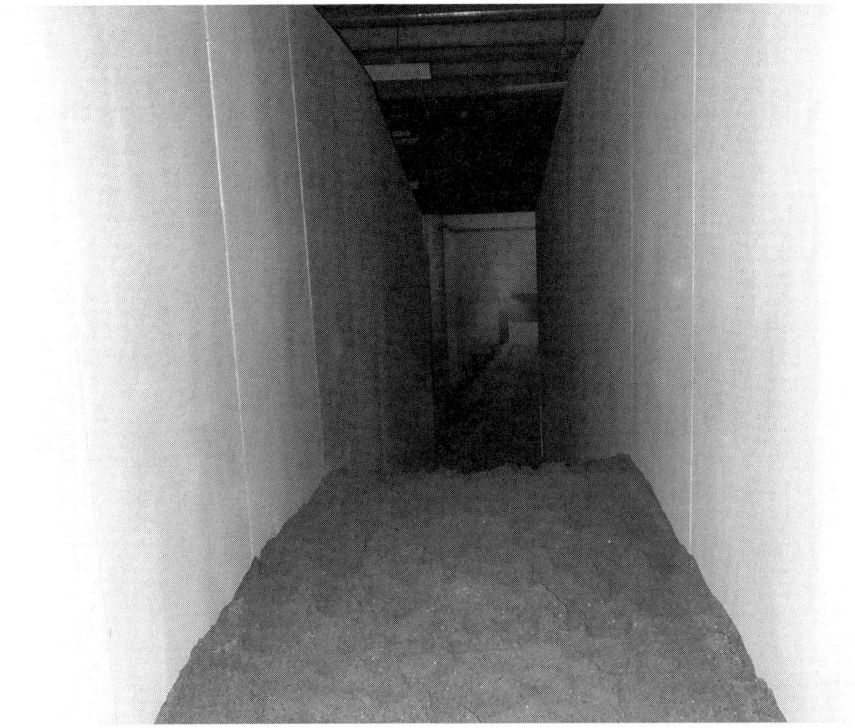

Figure 3.8
Desert Rain. The mountain of sand.
Copyright Blast Theory.

and forms of perception. Material and virtual objects often doubled up throughout the piece: the desert of the title, alluding to the first Gulf War, was also an environment in the virtual game, as well an implicit reference to the sand that participants had to cross over to proceed toward the end of the piece and the box of sand that they found after the end of the performance containing a citation referring to the number of casualties during the first Gulf War. Predating Slavoj Žižek's work, here the virtual world became a horizontal plane extending in all directions without features (2002). Moreover, the spray of water that allowed for the virtual projection, constituting a "fully permeable mixed reality boundary" (Shaw, Staff, and Row Farr 2000, 17), often drenched participants, but was also an explicit reference to the rain of the title of the piece while implicitly referring to the falling of the bombs that caused the casualties referred to by the citation. The motel room and the targets were part of both digital and physical environments, though the targets never appeared in the flesh, and the participants never appeared figuratively in the virtual.

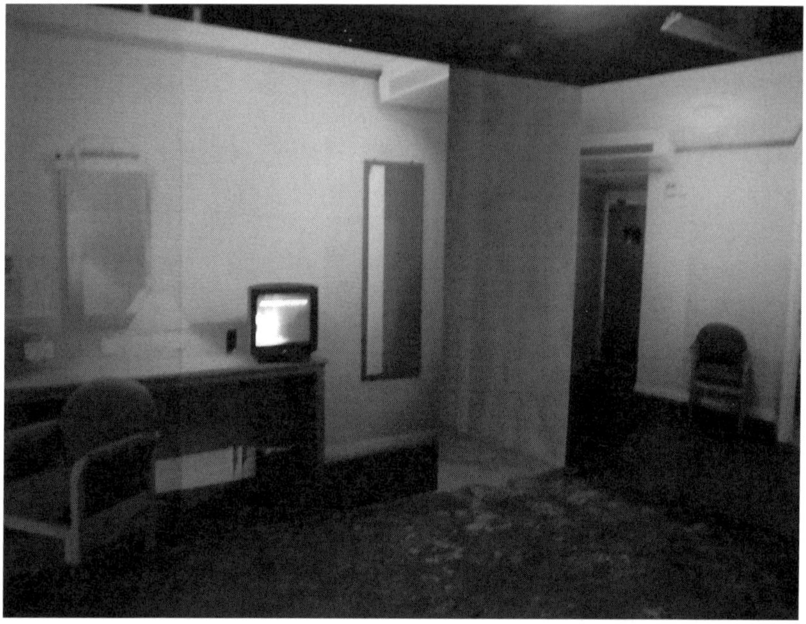

Figure 3.9
Desert Rain. The motel room.
Copyright Blast Theory.

Not only did the set constitute a complex combination of "the real and the virtual, each mirroring the design of the other" (Blast Theory 2002), but it also intertwined physical and virtual environments intertextually with an absent and remote place of conflict (the desert) *and* the texts that analyzed the social and philosophical repercussions of the conflict for western society's world view. Within this "contaminated" hybrid space, in which participants were constantly repositioned between real and virtual, fact and fiction, present and history, the interface of the rain-curtain operated as a liminal gateway or boundary superimposing distinct worlds that were in friction with one another and creating trajectories between them. So the rain curtain, providing "a continuously shifting and blurred view of the virtual world," actively disoriented participants by offering ambivalent information and distorting the projected image (Gaver, Beaver, and Benford 2003). Moreover, the rain curtain was tangible, and the fine spray of water that constituted it spilled onto the participants, who were so literally stained by the technology that created the world they were in. At this level, *Desert Rain* deliberately utilized ambiguity as a design strategy to blur the boundaries between real and virtual. It also merged the portrayal of warfare in television news, Hollywood films, and computer games to blur the boundaries between fact and fiction. Elements of theater, installation, and computer game were thus juxtaposed to create a dramaturgically hybrid work in which genres, such as the 3D gamelike graphics and the video clips describing people's real experiences of the war, and materials, such as the sand and the water, were overlaid onto one another so as to destabilize participants between seemingly dichotomous fictional and actual physical and virtual environments.

Traversable Interfaces

Like *Day of the Figurines*, the interfaces to *Desert Rain* involved a degree of tangibility, from the graspable swipe cards to the materiality of the rain curtain. However, *Desert Rain* also embodied a further key interface concept in the way that it related physical and virtual spaces and provided the illusion of passage between the two. The field of virtual reality has long been concerned with finding new ways to immerse its users in virtual worlds. From head-mounted displays to Powerwalls™ and CAVEs™ (Cruz-Neira et al. 1992), engineers have created multiple ways of engaging the user with the virtual world of 3D graphics, sound, and haptics, while simultaneously trying to block out as much of the existing physical world as possible. A key goal of this physical immersion is to foster a sense of presence, that important feeling of being there that many argue is the central defining feature of virtual reality (Steuer 1992; Barfield and Weghorst 1993; Barfield et al. 1995; Slater and Usoh 1994; Sheridan 1992a, 1992b). Under this view, immersion is a physical characteristic of an interface that may contribute to the psychological state that is presence (Slater 2003), as may various other factors, including the design of the virtual environment and one's avatar within it. A well-known early example of an interactive VR CAVE installation was the cartoon-like *Crayoland* (1995), built by David Pape at the Electronic Visualization Laboratory at the University of Illinois, which allowed users to travel through a child-drawn landscape complete with forest, flowers, buzzing bees, and randomly flying butterflies. *Crayoland*, consisting of the drawings of flat, two-dimensional objects that were encountered in a three-dimensional world, showed that the most effective environments were not necessarily the ones displaying the highest degree of realism and that the construction and perception of presence were in this case more dependent on behavioral or performative features than photorealism. Another well-known work was Maurice Benayoun and Jean-Baptiste Barrière's *World Skin* (1998), which immersed users into a war-ravaged area that they could photograph, though each image taken resulted in a fragment disappearing from the CAVE screen. The work—which, again, did not draw on photorealism—suggested that photography had become "a weapon of erasure" (Benayoun in Wilson 2002, 707) and reminded users that actions taken in virtual reality could affect their lives by giving them, upon leaving the installation, reproductions of the pictures they had taken inside CAVE. Although *Desert Rain* also pursued the idea of immersing the user in a virtual world that was not based on photorealism, it differed in one important respect: it focused on the actual moment of passage between the physical and virtual by having people quite literally step into and through a projected image. The rain curtain was not only—quite literally—an immersive interface, but it also provided a specific example of a more general class of "traversable interfaces" (Koleva et al. 2000) that sought to establish the illusion that physical and virtual worlds were joined together and that people could physically cross from one to the other.

A central goal of a traversable interface is to establish an appropriate sense of crossing between the real and the virtual. This might involve trying to sustain the illusion of physical transition, or it might mark a more symbolic moment of transition. Traversal might be a key dramatic moment within a performance, as in *Desert Rain*, or might potentially be a more everyday occurrence in which a user repeatedly changes the locus of their activity from real to virtual and vice versa. At their core, traversable interfaces require a mechanism for "crossing the screen," and there are various ways in which this might be achieved. One is to employ a permeable screen made of water spray (as in *Desert Rain*), smoke, or some similar material that can hold a projected image but also allows easy physical passage. Another possibility for the future might be the use of holographic projection. As part of its initial research into traversable interfaces, the Mixed Reality Laboratory explored several more everyday mechanical possibilities including strips of fabric through which the user could push, sliding doors, and hinged screens that could be lifted, all of which aimed enabling integration with the structures of buildings (see figure 3.10). Another possibility might be to follow a more topological approach, folding a projection screen to create a structure that has a distinct inside and outside, both of which can hold an image, and enabling the user

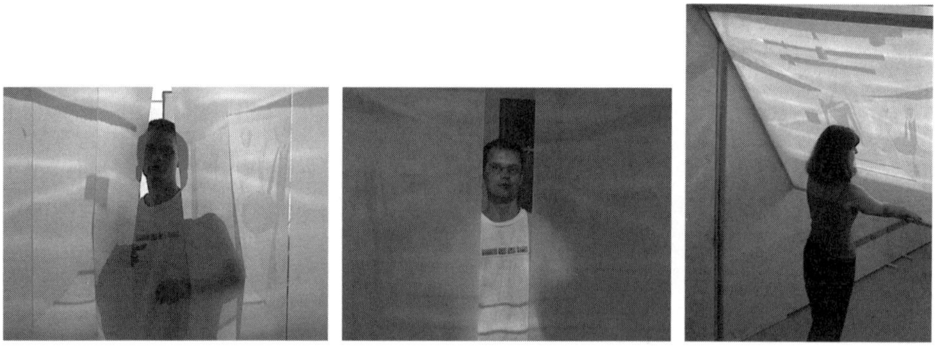

Figure 3.10
Traversable interfaces: fabric curtain, sliding doors, and titling screen.
Copyright MRL.

to pass from the a public outside view to an immersed inside view from which they can interact with the world. The Storytent discussed later in this chapter provides an example of this approach.

Establishing a clear sense of traversal is important not only for the participant who is crossing the boundary, but also for onlookers on either side. Traversal should make sense to those who remain on one side of the boundary and watch someone depart, and also to those who await on the other and watch them arrive, and should be integrated into their interactional trajectories. In other words, watching someone cross a traversable boundary forms a coherent part of an observer's own experience, giving them the expectation that they too might step from physical to virtual and vice versa and affording them the action(s) that they could subsequently perform. Traversable interfaces might even enhance onlookers' experience by providing them with a specialist public view of a remote environment. Consider the example of immersive interfaces to virtual environments such as a CAVE: often, one side of the interface is left open, enabling participants to step in and out and also providing an opportunity for onlookers to watch them. However, watching someone else use such an interface can be difficult, as the projected stereo graphics are designed to make sense to the immersed user from their particular viewpoint, typically while wearing a stereo display such as shutter glasses; they may be unintelligible to observers who are positioned outside without the benefit of such equipment. In response to such problems, Anthony Steed and colleagues describe how they added a traversable doorway to the open public side of their ReaCTor, a CAVE-like immersive facility (2002) (see figure 3.11). This consisted of a curtain of strips of fabric onto which was projected a public view of the

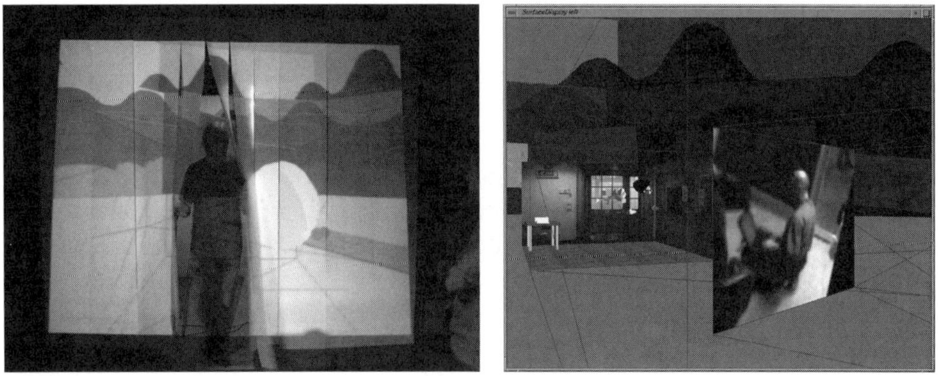

Figure 3.11
Crossing into the ReaCTor (left) and the view inside the virtual environment, including the video window looking back out (right).
Copyright Anthony Steed.

activities that were taking place inside the environment. A "cave door" such as this might help frame the experience for the direct user, helping establish their sense of presence; it might also help shield them from distractions due to onlookers, which might potentially disrupt their sense of presence; and finally, it might provide a more intelligible public view of events inside. The team also provided a live view inside the virtual environment so that immersed users could look back into the public space outside if they wished.

A true traversable interface between real and virtual worlds would also allow traversal from virtual to physical. Though this could simply mean stepping back through the screen from being immersed in a virtual world to being a public observer once again, a more extended interpretation is also possible. A traversable interface might enable the inhabitants of a virtual world—represented by avatars—to project their presence into a remote physical environment, crossing a boundary from virtual to real to become mobile within the remote environment and potentially even interact with it. One possibility is to take charge of a remote robot or vehicle that then becomes this participant's physical avatar. The field of telerobotics, driven by applications such as space and underwater exploration, in which humans need to work in inaccessible or inhospitable environments, can provide a range of techniques for achieving such remote forms of physical telepresence (see Goldberg 2000). There have also been experiments with technologies to support mobile physical telepresence within more social settings, including robots that can gesture as part of giving instructions during remote training (Kuzova, Ishimoda, and Nishimura 1995), and small social proxy robots called Personal Roving Presences (PROPS) (Paulos and Canny 1998). Another, quite different approach is to project "shadow avatars" into the remote physical environment that give fleeting impressions of ghostlike figures from a parallel world. Previous work has demonstrated the idea that when an avatar passes by a specific location in the virtual world, its shadowy image (with associated sound) can be projected onto the wall or floor of the equivalent physical location (Benford et al. 2001). This might even be extended through the use of steerable projectors to create moving avatar shadows within the physical environment (Pinhanez 2001).

Figure 3.12 draws together these various threads of discussion—physical traversal, the observer's view, and physical telepresence—to present a conceptual design for a generalized traversable interface. The top part of this figure summarizes the overall effect that we wish to create which should work coherently for four distinct kinds of participant: A, an observer in a physical environment; B, an observer (avatar) in a virtual environment that is connected to this; C, a participant who traverses from physical to virtual; and D, a participant who traverses in the reverse direction. The lower part of the figure proposes one technical arrangement that might support this effect. The physical and virtual environments become linked through a mixed reality boundary. The physical environment now contains a physically traversable projection

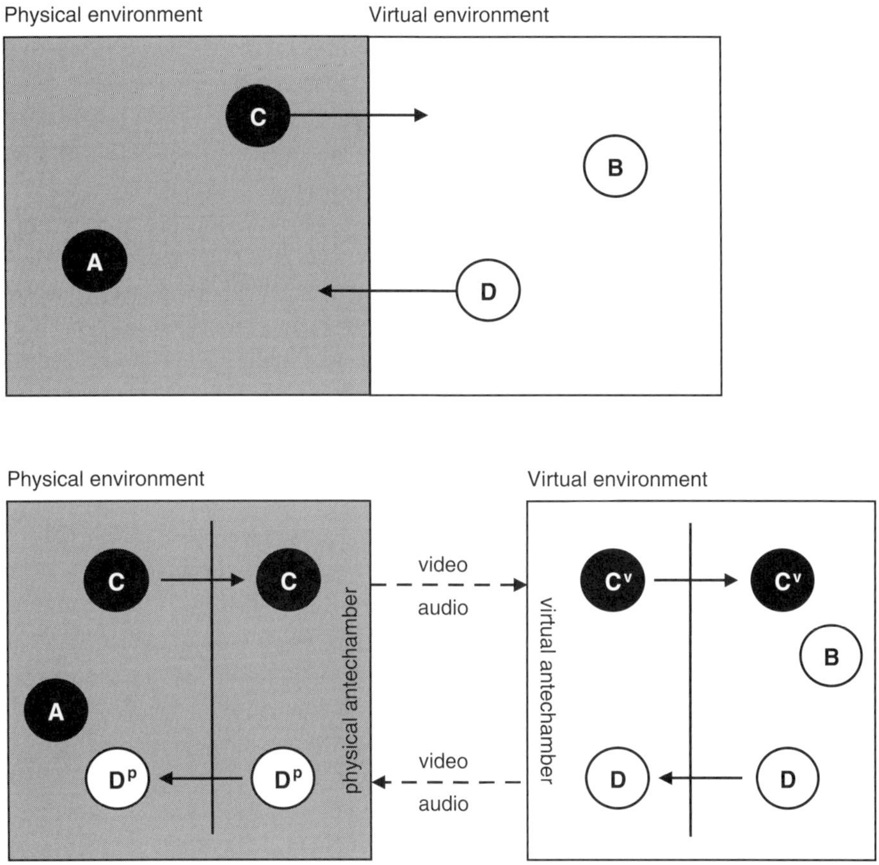

Figure 3.12
Design of a generalized traversable interface.
Copyright MRL.

screen that presents an image of the remote virtual world and through which participant C can move, entering into a private antechamber in which they find the immersive technology required to control an avatar in the virtual world (C^v). Conversely, the virtual environment now contains live video texture that looks back into the physical environment, through which the avatar D can move, at which point they enter a virtual antechamber in which they find the (virtual) controls for a remote physical telepresence, such as a mobile robot (D^p). This arrangement enables C and D to step through their respective ends of the mixed reality boundary to enter a private space in which they can control their remote proxy. It also provides observers A and B with an appropriate view of these traversals. A sees C step through the physical screen and sometime later sees C^v appear in the virtual world. They may also see avatar D approach them in the projecte3d view and then disappear to be replaced by D^p that emerges through the physical screen sometime later. Observer B sees a converse set of effects that give a sense of D's traversal out of his or her local space and C's arrival in it. This arrangement is the most complicated general case of a traversable interface that supports the illusion of full two-way traversal, and in practice, many actual traversable interfaces employ only part of these designs, for the rain curtain focuses only on providing the illusion of an actor (D) emerging from a virtual world and then disappearing again from the point of view of a participant C. The Storytent that we encounter in our final case study provides an illusion of traversal into and out of a virtual world for participants C and A in a physical space, but does not involve remote avatars or physical proxies.

Flypad

Our third case study in this chapter, *Flypad* (2008–), also developed by Blast Theory in collaboration with the Mixed Reality Laboratory, was an augmented reality game in which up to twelve players at a time engaged in midair wrestling, jumping on footpads so as to steer their avatars as they appeared to fall through a large physical space. The work was designed to operate as a permanent installation within a purpose-built arts center. More specifically, *Flypad* was designed to occupy a three-sided balcony space overlooking a large open atrium within this building. It was also required to integrate with other exhibits by utilizing and adding to a visitor's evolving "data body," a set of data that captured their preferences and history of interactions, and that was shared over a common technical backbone. The visitor carried an RFID card that identified them to each exhibit they encountered and enabled it to access their data body in order to configure itself. As described in an early design report, the idea was to create a narrative thread running throughout the entire exhibition: "as part of the exhibit area, there will be a sense of narrative throughout the visit. There are to be large scale trans-exhibit structures that support this continuous thread, such as networked data backbone in which ongoing information about the visit is stored, shared and fed into later exhibits" (Reeves 2005).

Figure 3.13 shows how *Flypad* was structured to fit the balcony and atrium. Twelve player terminals were arranged in groups of four on the three sides of the atrium. Each consisted of a monitor, a footpad, and a motorized pan-tilt video camera that was mounted behind the screen looking out into the atrium. The monitor displayed the image from the steerable camera, giving the illusion that the player was looking through a window out into the atrium. The game began when the player stepped onto a footpad (figure 3.14, left), which had five directional controls moving backward, forward, upward, and sideways. Their RFID card was read by the

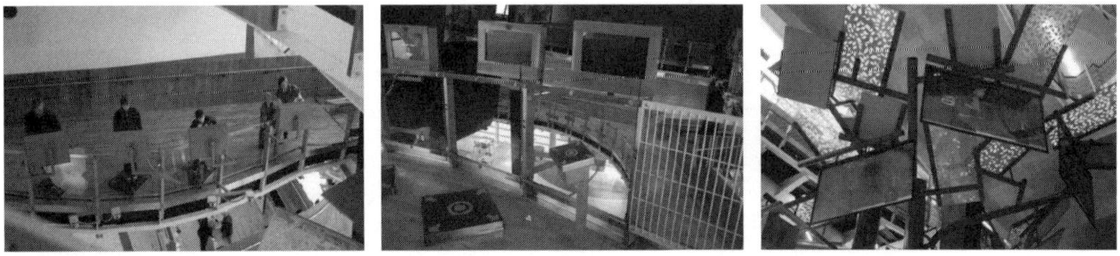

Figure 3.13
The spatial design of *Flypad*.
Copyright MRL.

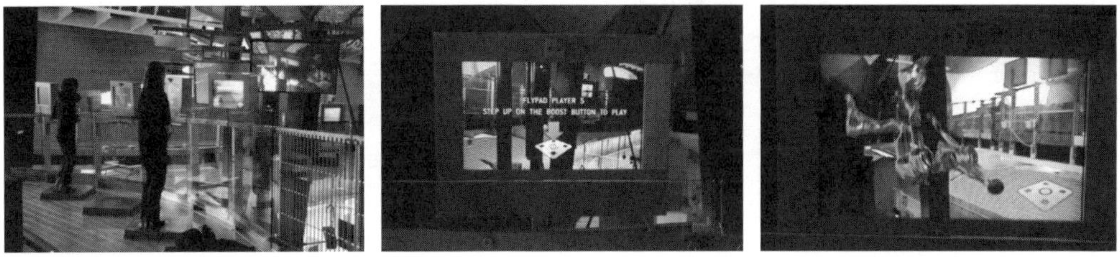

Figure 3.14
Flypad. Interactions.
Copyright MRL.

display, causing their avatar to be generated from their particular data body and appear to them on the screen so as to instruct them on how to play the "game" (figure 3.14, center and right). The player could see this personalized avatar overlaid on the video feed so that it appeared to be floating over the atrium (see figures 3.14, right, 3.15, and 3.16). Due to the effects of virtual gravity, the avatar would gradually fall to the floor if left to its own devices. However, jumping on the center circle in the footpad would thrust the avatar upward toward the ceiling, and the arrows could be used to steer its direction. As the avatar moved, so would the motorized camera, panning and tilting so as to maintain the virtual avatar in shot. By steering their avatars into one another, players could wrestle in midair. Colliding arms and legs would trigger various wrestling holds, which in turn led players to exchange body parts, mutating their avatars over the course of the game. As the minutes passed, so avatars would become increasingly heavy, eventually falling to the ground, at which point their owner's game would be over.

The twelve terminals were carefully arranged to foster collaboration among groups of players, both within each local group of four, but also by being able to look across the atrium at players on the other side. By being slightly raised up, the players' screens

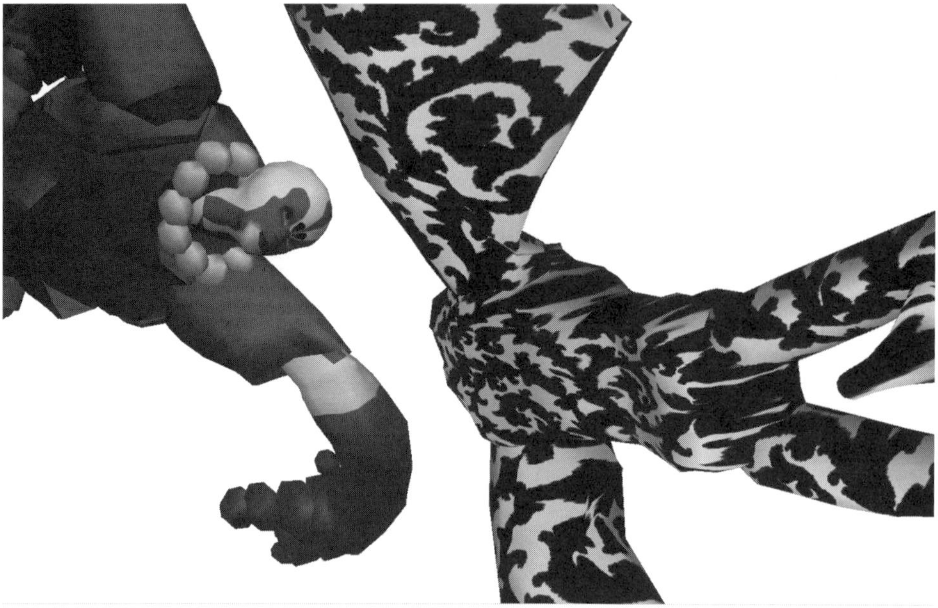

Figure 3.15
Flypad. Personalized avatars.
Copyright Blast Theory.

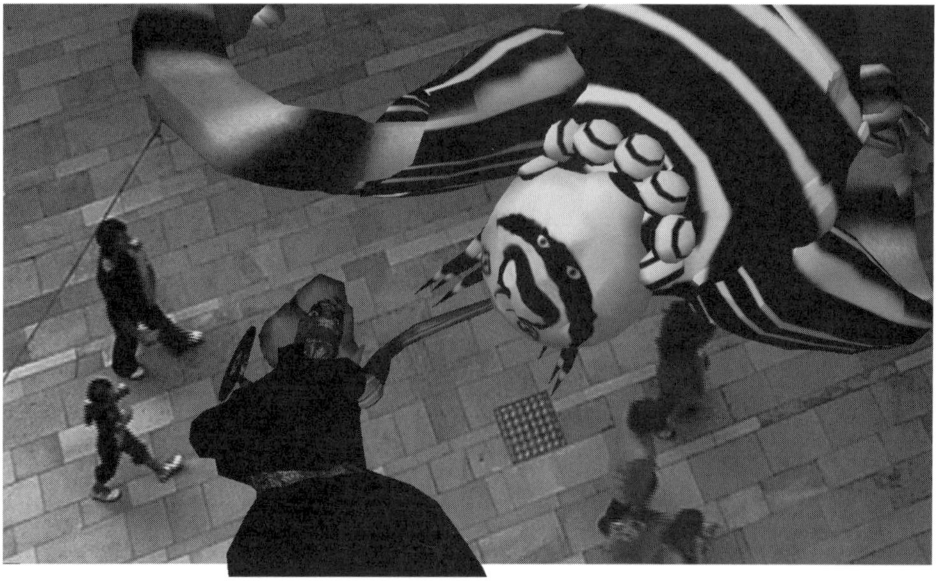

Figure 3.16
Flypad. Avatars overlaid on a video view of the atrium.
Copyright Blast Theory.

and their movements on the footpads also become visible to visitors standing behind them on the balcony. Finally, *Flypad* provided an additional spectator interface in the form of the "tall trees," an arrangement of three large screens in the center of the atrium. These would display video segments advertising the game and replaying highlights from selected players in order to attract passing visitors to the game and encourage them to join in.

For Blast Theory, *Flypad* was a "site-specific" work combining "game play with interaction, joyful goofing about with a visceral sense of the blur between real and virtual experience" (2008). The design of the installation, which intended to turn visitors into a spectators and participants (Reeves 2005), was illustrated through the use of trajectories that marked how a visitor could enter the exhibition, flow into the playing area, and became participants, while another could spend more time as an audience to someone else's interactive play (Reeves 2005). Interfaces were formed that, for Blast Theory, were aimed at not getting "physically in-between you and the experience" (Reeves 2005). Camera-wise, as the movements of the avatars were relatively unpredictable, paths or way-pointed motions were created so that the cameras could follow the avatars through given trajectories. Finally, *Flypad* operated by extracting information from the visitors and reembodying it within the avatars so that visitors could see and experience themselves as part of an "other."

Interview 5: Designing Tangible Interfaces

Box 3.1

We ask Blast Theory members Matt Adams (MA) and Nick Tandavanitj (NT), "What role do spectator interfaces play in Flypad *and* Day of the Figurines*?"*

NT: *Flypad* was a multiplayer game and participants played in a shared space. We designed it with a whole range of audiences in mind, from 5 to 70 years old. One of our goals was to make it really engaging and fun. The piece itself was based around a number of terminals facing out into an atrium. Each player was able to control an avatar, which flew around this augmented reality space. The spectator interface consisted of three projection screens that overlooked this space, which all of the players and anyone who happened to be walking around the atrium could see. The idea was that the work would try to get people to relate to each other across the space and across the terminals. It was about facilitating that kind of physical link between players and getting people to recognize each other and themselves on that big screen, and for that moment of recognition to be a real cause of excitement.

MA: *Flypad* was about an interplay between the virtual space, the real space, and the spectator-client. There were a number of interrelationships between the physical body of

Box 3.1 (continued)

the player, their personal screen in front of them, which gave them their virtual view, their augmented reality view, the real space in which their avatar was flying, and the spectator-client, the tall trees, which were the shared reference points. We tried to create a productive interrelationship between these four spaces, so that people looked between one and the other, or jumped from one to the other. The motivation for players to do that varied at different times. Sometimes they looked up at the shared screen for information. They also looked at their neighbor's screen, just out of curiosity. We deliberately clustered the screens in groups so that people shared a space. This was aimed at setting up productive inter-relationships between the real, the virtual, and the augmented reality spaces. I suppose in a sense there wasn't a virtual space, but in my mind the augmented reality space still had some sort of virtual property. All of these interrelationships were designed to move players energetically across these different spaces. They were not just strategies of play, or ways of using the system, but rather aimed at letting people do things in a playful and socially engaged way.

NT: The spectator interface for *Day of the Figurines* was the table or the board, which was a scaled model of the town within which the game took place. The board was used to visualize the positions of all the players who were taking part in the game, or their locations within the town. On one side of the board was a screen, which scrolled through the most recent messages that had been sent into the game. The players themselves were represented by these small plastic figurines. Each hour the operators repositioned the figurines around the town to reflect the movements of the players as they journeyed around town using text messages. The game itself was distributed and its audience dispersed. Some players may have registered two, three weeks before others. Some may have been playing remotely, while others might have been standing right by the board. The interface had two roles: the first was aimed at the players who were playing the game, and the second was for the people who were curious about what was going on and for whom it operated as a kind of window into the space. Players often came back to the table to look at the world. It gave them a "god" view of the town that wasn't really afforded through text messaging.

MA: Although they're superficially quite different, the spectator interfaces in *Flypad* and *Day of the Figurines* did a number of things in common. They both attracted people to the work, as they were designed to be seen from a distance and draw people towards themselves. The positioning, or angle of the table in *Day of the Figurines* is crucial. The buildings on the table are folded bits of metal coming up to 90 degrees. Looked at from the side, they're almost invisible, but looked at from front they appear in the most dramatic way. The nature of the lighting also makes a big difference because of the shadows that are cast by these two-dimensional buildings. As people make that journey towards the interface, they build up a picture and assemble a model in their mind as to what's going on. And that's partly to pull them towards the work and seduce them into engaging with it. But it's also for them to start building a conceptual model of what the work is doing and what it's about.

Box 3.1 (continued)

NT: *Day of the Figurines* was focused on the social structures at the heart of the work. You have up to 1,000 players who are playing from anywhere in the world. They are dispersed, but they are also moving around this virtual town, and they're communicating with each other in nested clusters within fifty locations. Some of these clusters are technologically driven by silos and others are socially constructed. The board is one way of giving a representation to the social complexity of the game and enabling people to playfully engage with it. Through it, people can see the game as a set of clustered individuals. And then they can see the projection of the arrows onto the table. These enable the invigilators to move the figurines. Each of the arrows represents a virtual trajectory through space, but it's also a social trajectory, as it often shows people coming together or moving together, and that enables people to read who's meeting whom in a particular destination. Combined with the built-in screen on the side of the table, it enables people to get a skim across the current interaction of the game.

What is the function of tangibility, the fact that something may be touched?

NT: We felt that having a physical figurine, which allowed participants to pick it up, hold it in their hands, see all the detail of their clothing, their expression, was an amazingly productive way of allowing someone to implant all their hopes or feelings about what this avatar, character, or person was going to be, bringing in a lot of themselves and their sense of who that person might be, in a very short period of time.

MA: We found that people had very emotive responses to their figurines. For instance, it was very common for people to bend down at the table and have their portrait taken with their figurine. People also put up pictures of their figurines online. I talked before about the role of the table in pulling in participants. The figurines acted in exactly the same way. Because they are so tiny, they invite you to squat down at the table. The fact that they're magnetic and that they have this kind of sticky relationship to the metal table on which they're sitting invites you to pull them off or slide them around. We noticed that people find it almost irresistible to touch them. People steal them as well. Their tangibility is crucial.

Coming from a background as theater makers and performance makers, we've always been interested in how the real insinuates itself into the virtual. These small plastic figurines in *Day of the Figurines* are a really good example of that dynamic. One of the most important things to start off in this context is the relationship between the real and not just the virtual, but the real and the fictional, by which I also mean the performative and the theatrical. We might think, for instance, of the relationship between theater as a kind of fictional spectacle based around a fourth wall and performance art as a form that asserts its presence within a real landscape in all directions: it refuses the existence of the fourth wall. All of our work has some kind of theatrical and performative frame. When materiality rears its head then, you're talking about something that rubs up against that. The figurines are undeniably real and tangible, but they are also representational and theatrical. They

Box 3.1 (continued)

are actors on the stage, props for the player (who performs the figurine and constructs the character they assign to it), and game tokens.

In our early work, the performers would be among the audience dressed in the same way as the audience, and would step into the performance space just by what they did, purely through their action. There might be an uncertainty in the minds of the audience around them as to whether they were watching a performer beginning an action or a member of the audience taking it upon themselves to cross the boundary and do something that announced itself performatively. That was about the proximity of the performer to the public and their indistinguishability. We still use the material world in this way. For instance, the corridor that features in *Desert Rain,* which is 17 meters long, about 3½ meters high at its highest point, has several tons of sand in it. Every participant in *Desert Rain* walks or runs down it, and they have to climb up the large pile of sand, and comes down over the other side. It's not actually a 2-meter-high pile of sand, but rather it's a sort of 2-meter-high ramp with 30 or 40 centimeters of sand on top of it. I use the word "ramp" quite deliberately. So it's both a pile of sand and a fictional representation of sand. The sand is metaphorical in relation to the work—I am thinking about the grains of sand and the numerical uncertainty around the casualties in the first Gulf War that they represent—and it is metaphorical of the desert, and it is real sand, in the sense that it is something that has to be negotiated by the members of the public.

Another example of the role of materiality in *Desert Rain* is the rain curtain itself. Originally we started working on this project in 1994–1995 as part of a residency at the Institute of Contemporary Art in London, where we sprayed a garden sprayer onto each other's faces in front of the audience to simulate sweat. This gave our skins some sort of glistening effect, and at the same time we noticed that it caught the slide projections that we were using very beautifully. In fact, the rain curtain has very particular material properties: it has a swirling nature, it moves, it has depth and wetness. These are intriguing properties when you're dealing with a work that is about reality and fictionality, the real and the imaginary, and that asserts that these categories are interpenetrated with one another. It's interesting how people relate themselves to it. For some people it is an obstacle, a definite barrier, and they prefer not to cross it; they duck and run through it because they do not want to get wet and cold. And so that sense that when you are crossing the screen you are penetrating the skin of the virtual environment in a very tangible and material way is a very important part of how we set up this transition in the work.

How did you design the interfaces in Flypad*? What is the relationship between visitors and their avatars?*

MA: The interface in *Flypad* originates in *Desert Rain,* where we first used a rockable platform on which to stand. The initial idea came out of a very long process of develop-

Box 3.1 (continued)

ment. We were looking for an interface that removed as many barriers as possible between a member of the public, the work itself, and the screen. We wanted people not to be protected by their interface. When you sit at a desk in front of a computer, you are inherently protected by its interface. We considered a tank operator–style interface where you'd have two levers coming out of the floor and you could move forward by pushing them both forward, backward by pulling them both backward, and turn by pushing one forward and one backward. One of the reasons we moved away from this idea was to remove the sense that you had something to hold on to which gave you a safety zone. We wanted people to feel unanchored and were drawn to the idea that your body is your mode of orientation within a virtual space. Your agency is expressed through choreography as you move your body around the platform.

Flypad is about flying. We started by looking at skydiving and Mexican wrestling, people escaping gravity, astronauts. The idea that by shifting your body weight you negotiate a space felt very liberating—leveling even. It removes traditional hierarchies of expertise with technology to a great degree. The work is also informed by the nature of the technological systems that we employ. What comes with that is a whole bunch of social, political, and, most important, ideological inscriptions into the technology. These are classically hierarchical: "I am better than you, I have done this more than you, this is something I feel more at home with or more at ease with than you." We, however, wanted to make a work that didn't entirely render itself into these existing structures. We wanted to set up a situation where someone who never engaged with technology might still have tremendous skill. This was a political choice.

In terms of the relationship between visitors and their avatars in *Flypad*, there's a clear separation between the player and their avatar. The avatar is fantastical-looking, distorted, multicolored, with unfeasible body shapes that tend to violate humanoid limits. Apart from Mexican wrestling, key reference points were Peking Opera and the performance artist Leigh Bowery. We deliberately looked at things that were highly stylized and based on the concealment of identity. Bowery uses the most outrageously self-aggrandizing, over-the-top and noisy, colorful, highly taboo violations, but then conceals himself to the point that he's completely hidden within these things that scream for attention. So in terms of how an avatar functions, we found this was a very interesting idea in that it gives you tremendous freedom to identify with the avatar. This reminds me of Scott McCloud's writing about understanding comics (1993) where he talks about why comics are so great for identification, because as you move away from naturalism, your ability to identify increases, and that's definitely one of the things that are at work in *Flypad.*

Flypad is also about mutation and miscegenation. Your aim is to go into holds with other people. Your avatar grapples with others, sometimes in ways that look very much like wrestling, sometimes almost sexually. Your aim is to stay together, and as you do this, your ability to fly is increased, but it's very hard to do that without breaking apart, and

Box 3.1 (continued)

as you break apart, one of your limbs is being exchanged with the other avatar. Running the whole way through *Flypad* is the interlocking and interlinking of people, the fact that your identity gets diluted almost to extinction.

How do interfaces shape participants' interactions in your work?

MA: Installation artists, from Alan Kaprow to Fluxus, violated the boundary of the traditional artwork and extended it into real space, ultimately making "immersive" artworks, which participants inhabited. You could almost see this as a correlating history to interface design, moving away from two-dimensional screens to interfaces that get larger, or grander, or more immersive, such as the CAVE and VR interfaces, or get fragmented into mobile devices, where instead of any single interface we've got two, three, four, or five interfaces perhaps even working simultaneously.

There's an interesting tension around our relationships with computer science. HCI is about the user-centered nature of design and how it functions, and we're very interested in some divergence from supposed good practice. Traditional virtues of interface design assume they're clean, simple, easy, quick, and adaptive to multiple styles. But there's also an important part of interface design that introduces ambiguity and uncertainty, putting people into a position where the rules are not necessarily quite as clear. And that's partly an artistic impulse and partly a given of making works that are unprecedented in some way or form. So pieces like *Uncle Roy All Around You* were the first mixed reality games or location based games of their kind. People who came to play, by definition, were negotiating interfaces that they were unused to, or that were functioning in ways that they had not seen before. Consequently, people are often uncertain or apprehensive when they are in our work, as they're in a position where it may not be entirely clear to them what their inputs into the system are doing in relation to the outputs. In *Desert Rain* when players find their target, a performer walks through the screen. It's not really clear that what they have just done has triggered a performer to walk through the screen. So in that respect it's very unlike traditional interfaces, where the relationship between your action and a response from the system is normally readily readable before you begin that action, which means that when you click on a button that says "print" you know before you click that a document may emerge from a nearby printer. Generally interfaces are about use, value and a set of utilitarian outcomes, and so once you bring these things into an artistic environment, you've got to negotiate what that means. The history of interface design has been so heavily governed by these presumptions, with the obvious antecedents being military and commercial, they're the two big strands of almost all interface development. It's a very recent idea that you might design a phone that is as much about play as it is about work.

The *Shape Living Exhibition*

Like *Savannah* from chapter 1, our final case study in this chapter focuses on the use of mixed reality to support learning, in this case as part of a family museum visiting experience. The Shape (Situated Hybrid Assemblies for Public Experiences) project, part of the European Union's Disappearing Computer initiative, undertook a three-year-long exploration of new interfaces for public settings (Bannon et al. 2005). Like many of the examples in this book, Shape combined technical innovation with ethnographic studies of new technologies deployed "in the wild," in this case through two "living exhibitions" in partner museums that directly engaged the public in the design and experience of novel interfaces. Our case study focuses on the first of these, the *Shape Living Exhibition*, which was created at Nottingham's historic castle in the summer of 2001 (see figure 3.17). Nottingham Castle has witnessed over one thousand years of British history, as the backdrop for the exploits of the mythical Robin Hood and his followers and the location at which King Charles I raised his standard at the opening of the English Civil War, and having been burned down in public rioting over the Corn Laws. The heart of the modern castle, which is now a public museum, was built in more recent times, and is set on top of a sandstone outcrop overlooking Nottingham. Although the more ancient castle walls persist and the ruins of some of

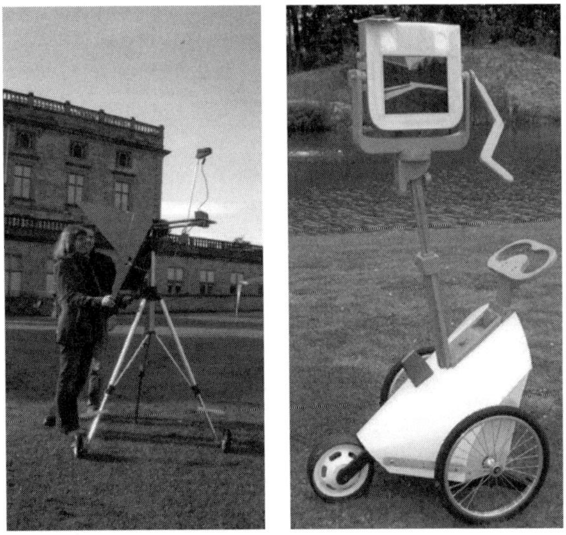

Figure 3.17
Shape Living Exhibition. Augurscope I (left) and Augurscope II (right).
Copyright MRL.

medieval buildings can still be found on site, most of the earlier castle structures have long since disappeared and been replaced by a public park. Under the surface, the sandstone is riddled with caves and passageways that were used as storerooms and dungeons, and that provided the setting for various gruesome stories from the castle's history. Nottingham Castle therefore presents a challenge to visitors and curators alike: there is a complex mixture of timeframes and events to understand; these are associated with diverse locations around the site, inside, outside, and even underground; and many interesting features can no longer be directly seen. The challenge for Shape was to create an engaging and informative mixed reality experience that would enable families to explore and make sense of this complex and interleaved mixture of events and locations. Its approach was to create a diverse set of interfaces appropriate to different locations—indoors, outdoors, and underground—and then to find ways of assembling these into a coherent overall experience.

The Augurscope was created to enable visitors to explore 3D graphical reconstructions of ancient castle buildings that would have once occupied its now open grassy spaces, including the Great Hall that had once been the centerpiece of castle life (Schnädelbach et al. 2002). Visitors would approach a distinctive display in the form of a screen mounted at head height above a wheeled base. They could then push this device around the grass and rotate and tilt its top so as to be able to adopt different perspectives on the 3D model that was displayed on the screen. Through the use of an onboard GPS receiver, a potentiometer, and tilt sensors, the physical location and orientation of the display were matched to a corresponding viewpoint in the 3D model, producing an augmented reality–style experience in which the virtual world appeared to be overlaid on the physical one. In other words, visitors would wheel the display across the grass and tilt and turn its top to see how the castle might one have appeared from different viewpoints. The physical form of the Augurscope was designed to enable groups of visitors to be able to quickly engage and disengage (e.g., avoiding having to don and remove head-mounted displays), to easily share the display, and also (like the *Day of the Figurines* tables) to be highly visible from a distance so as to attract new visitors and also enable them to learn what to do by watching others. Experience from initial trials at the Living Exhibition informed the subsequent design of the Augurscope II, including the construction of a lighter, smaller, and far more mobile design (Schnädelbach et al. 2006).

To support exploration of the caves underneath Nottingham Castle, the team developed their interactive flashlights technology (Ghali et al. 2003). Visitors shone beams of light onto a surface such as cave wall; a camera mounted nearby captured video images of the resulting pools of light as they played across the surface; computer software used bespoke algorithms to analyze these images in real time, detecting when flashlight beams were present, tracking their positions as they moved, and identifying different flashlights from the distinctive (to the software) patterns of their beams (see figure 3.18). Additional software detected when the beams of light from particular flashlights entered predetermined hotspots in the image (that may or may not have correlated with visible features on the wall) and triggered the playback of audio clips. This technology enabled groups of visitors to explore the caves with flashlights, triggering audio commentary as they illuminated particular features. A child's flashlight would trigger material for children; an adult-size flashlight controlled a separate layer of commentary for grown-ups, with the aim of supporting families to explore the history of the caves together. This technology was subsequently refined and deployed commercially within several museums and science centers in the United Kingdom, with interfaces ranging from handheld flashlights up to large, stand-mounted swiveling searchlights.

These two outdoor and underground interfaces were complemented by two indoor installations that enabled visitors to interact with various digital materials, including images, sounds, and 3D virtual worlds. The first of these, the Storytent, was a mini immersive projection environment in the shape of a classic A-frame tent (made of a projection screen folded over and stretched to a frame) (Green et al. 2003). Two synchronized images of a virtual world (a reconstruction of Nottingham Castle from the Middle Ages) were projected onto its sides, while sound was played from the outside, so that visitors could sit inside the tent to immerse themselves in the virtual world. Although viewing projected images this close up is less than ideal in many ways, the Storytent compensated for this issue through the excitement and intimacy of sitting together inside a tent in a darkened room, which was especially appealing to young

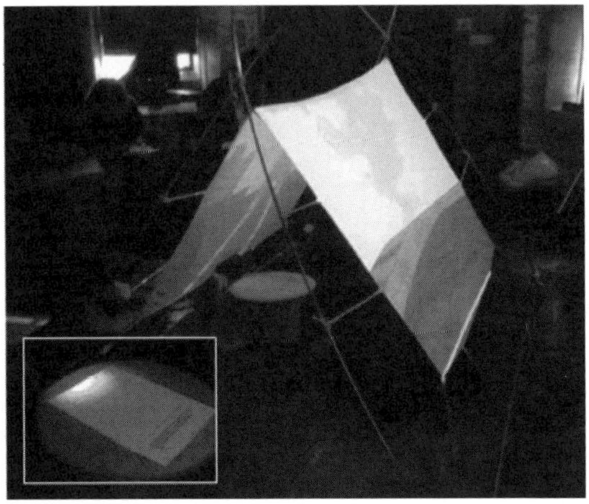

Figure 3.18
Shape Living Exhibition. The Storytent with the turntable inset.
Copyright MRL.

children. Interaction involved revolving a small turntable inside the tent in order to "look around" the virtual world. The Storytent constituted a further example of a traversable interface, as discussed earlier. In this case, audience members could see the projected images when standing outside of the tent, but actually needed to enter the tent—crossing over to the other side of the screen—in order to be able interact with them, at which point they were also shielded from outside interference. Thus, participants stepped backward and forward through the screen as they moved into and out of the tent structure.

The second indoor installation was the Sandpit, which consisted of an image of sand projected onto the floor from above. Visitors could shine flashlights at this image (using the same interactive flashlight technology that was deployed in the caves) in order to agitate the virtual sand and thereby dig for images of Nottingham Castle and the historic events that had taken place there, causing them to gradually appear, grow, and then break up and fade away (see figure 3.19).

These four interfaces—the Augurscope, flashlights in the caves, the Storytent, and the Sandpit—were clearly quite disparate in form and function, with each being tailored to a particular use and setting around the castle, from outdoors on the open grassy area to the underground caves and indoors in the museum galleries. However, they were also connected in various ways so that each contributed to the wider overall experience of visiting and learning about the castle and its history. One such connection was through the sharing of media; for example, the same 3D graphical reconstruction of the castle could be explored from both the Augurscope and the Storytent. A second connection was through the use of common interaction devices, such as the

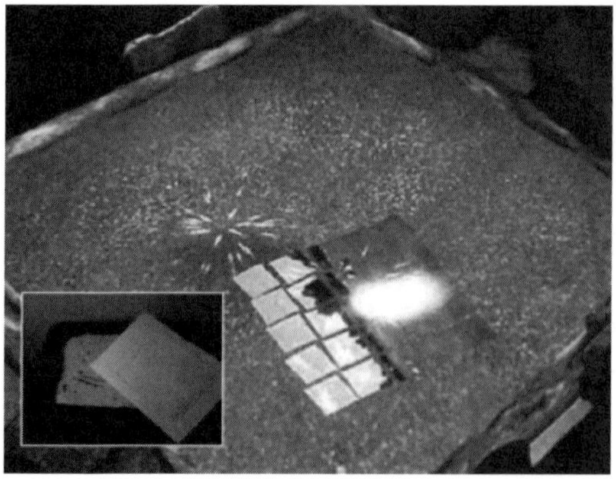

Figure 3.19
Shape Living Exhibition. Digging in the Sandpit.
Copyright MRL.

use of flashlights in both the caves and with the Sandpit. Beyond these, the *Shape Living Exhibition* introduced a further innovation as a quite deliberate attempt to more explicitly connect different aspects of the visit, assembling these diverse displays into a larger overall experience (Fraser et al. 2003). On arrival, each visitor could collect a set of sheets of paper with instructions about places to visit within the grounds and with questions to answer or activities to complete there, such as making a drawing or a rubbing. Such activity sheets are of course common within museums and similar attractions, and are also a familiar feature of school field trips. The Shape activity sheets, however, were also electronically tagged with RFID tags taped onto their backs, and the code generated by each tag identified a particular location around the castle. These tagged sheets of paper could then be used in the Storytent and at the Sandpit to instruct them to reveal content associated with a particular location. In the Storytent, the tagged paper would be placed on top of the turntable that contained an embedded RFID reader, with the effect of transporting the tent to a particular location around the castle. For example, an activity sheet might ask a participant to make a drawing of the Castle Gatehouse (see figure 3.20); placing this sheet on the turntable would transport the Storytent to a reconstruction of the gatehouse as it might have appeared in medieval times and would replay audio associated with King Richard's arrival there on his return from the Crusades. In a similar way, placing an activity sheet on a box of sand near the Sandpit installation (which also contained an embedded RFID reader) would load images associated with the gatehouse and King Richard into the Sandpit ready to be discovered. The project described this idea as "paper as glue," meaning that the pieces of paper served to glue the whole experience together,

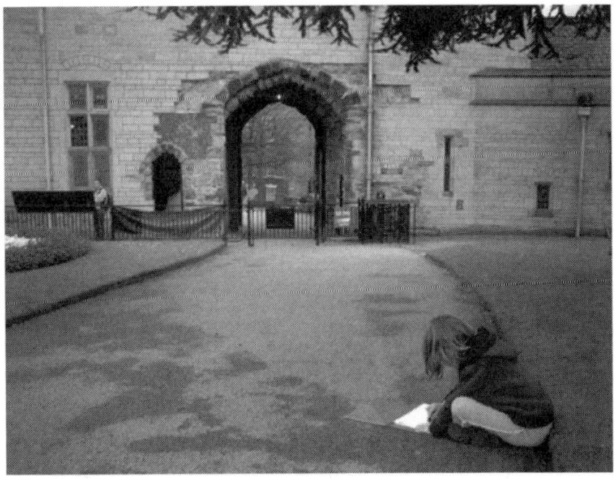

Figure 3.20
Shape Living Exhibition. Making a drawing of the Castle Gatehouse.
Copyright MRL.

making connections between different locations around the Castle grounds, diverse displays and installations, and also between the present and the past. Interestingly, the pieces of paper were also annotated and personalized by the participants and could be taken away afterwards as souvenirs and possibly even reused, such as to reconstruct a wall display back in the classroom.

Interview 6: Interface Design

Box 3.2

We ask Boriana Koleva from the Mixed Reality Laboratory: what role do interfaces play in establishing a trajectory or journey for the user?

We see more and more computing interfaces situated in public spaces such as museums, amusement parks, city centers, and shopping malls. In some cases these interfaces are purposefully and carefully designed to function as a thematic ecology; in others placement is more ad hoc and their purpose disparate. I think that, however, in all of these environments the interfaces could become points of interest for the user along their journey and thus be the key factor in shaping their trajectory through space and time. At one extreme, visitors may plan in advance an entire experience based on their interest in the available installations and interfaces, for example, in an environment such as a museum or amusement park. On the other hand, the design of interfaces and their physical arrangement in space may be such as to entice visitors to approach and lead them from interface to interface through a designed interactional trajectory. Interfaces can then play different roles along a particular trajectory. For example, in a museum setting, an interface at the start of the visiting experience could provide an introduction and allow users to register. Subsequent interfaces could then offer information and interaction with each building upon what the user has experienced already.

How can interfaces and affordances be used in the design of museum visiting?

Interfaces can serve a variety of roles during a museum visit to make the experience more informative, interactive, and fun. Interfaces can be used to augment museum artifacts and sites with digital information such as interpretations and background materials in order to educate, entertain, and engage visitors. An example here is the Augurscope, a sharable mobile augmented reality (AR) interface that makes use of a variety of positioning technologies to visualize a medieval castle as it used to appear in relation to its current, quite different site. Interfaces can also enable interactivity with artifacts and content. For this purpose, tangible interfaces are very effective, as they allow visitors to physically manipulate and explore objects while at the same time triggering the display of relevant annotations. To achieve this, physical artifacts are usually tagged in order to associate them with digital content. Interfaces can also be used to guide visitors through the museum environment and thus shape their trajectory through space. For example, mobile devices can lead

Box 3.2 (continued)

visitors through a selection of displays and artifacts to create a thematic journey. It is desirable that through the physical design of the interfaces used in museums (such as larger screens, multiple input options) collaboration and discussion among visitors is supported. Similarly, through the design of an interface, such as making interaction legible at a distance, we can support varying degrees of visitor engagement and allow visitors to learn how to interact with an interface while observing others.

How do you design ecologies of hybrid interfaces?

As ecologies of hybrid interfaces are designed to be situated in specific environments, often in public spaces, it is very important that they are appropriate to their setting. Initial qualitative studies (e.g., those based on the ethnographic tradition) of the target environment can help us to understand its specific social and interactional context and thus sensitize the overall design. We then follow a process of iterative prototyping through participatory design sessions and focused deployments in the particular setting in order to develop a series of increasingly robust prototypes that both function as an ecology of interfaces and fit to their setting.

It is not always about seamlessly fitting into the environment. Another approach that we often follow in the lab involves collaboration with artists. Here the aim sometimes is to encourage people to see a particular space or subject matter in a new way and so the ecology of interfaces is purposefully designed to stand out and possibly even seem at odds with the environment in which it is situated. An iterative design process, however, is still the means through which the desired interfaces are developed.

What is the role of tangibility or materiality within this context?

The museum setting is usually oriented around artifacts and their physicality and materiality is key to the user experience. By using tangible interfaces in this setting and enabling visitors to physically touch and explore objects, we can enhance their curiosity and allow them to make discoveries. When such interfaces are designed for this context, we have to be sensitive to the physical characteristics of the space and artifacts they augment. This can be done through the choice of materials for building the interface, its size, its input and output capabilities, as well as its placement. Also, as I mentioned before, through the physical affordances and constraints of an interface we can encourage collaboration among visitors and offer different levels of engagement.

How can you use mobile phones to relate to installations in museums?

By using mobile phones in tandem with museum installations, we can link currently isolated situated installations into a coherent experience for the visitor. We can also build upon multiple visits, thus extending the user experience in time as well as space. The approach allows us to take advantage of the personalization and data storage provided by mobile phones. When visitors are carrying mobile devices, they can be used to maintain an interaction history and user profile, and the interaction with installations can then be

Box 3.2 (continued)

configured based on these. For example, when a visitor places his or her mobile phone on a table installation displaying a map of a historical site and slides it across, it can reveal places of interest based on his or her profile. The mobile phone can also be used to capture information for later inspection by the visitor, such as slides and sound clips from an installation providing information about museum artifacts. At the same time, the mobile phone can allow visitors to leave information for other users, such as photos and comments on a discussion display board. A mobile phone can also be a useful means of interacting with an installation, that is, act as a remote control/pointing device that allows a user to select options and browse through information.

What are the differences between mobile and fixed interfaces?

Mobile interfaces are now widely used as many people own devices such as mobile phones and PDAs. These enable "anywhere, anytime" computing and are usually optimized for mobility and general tasks (e.g., calendar events, web browsing). Fixed interfaces, on the other hand, are usually designed for a specific task, are often shared by groups of users, and are owned and maintained by the location in which they are situated. Although mobile devices are increasingly computationally more powerful, they usually have more limited display sizes and their input capabilities differ from those that are available with fixed interfaces. As indicated previously, it can, therefore, be beneficial to combine mobile and fixed interfaces to take advantage of their different characteristics.

What role did traversable interfaces and boundaries play in Desert Rain*?*

Desert Rain took place in the late 1990s and played a significant role in shaping our notion of traversable interfaces and boundaries. In the performance, each participant viewed the virtual world projected onto a "rain curtain," a screen composed of a fine water spray. This permeable and physically traversable display allowed objects and people to pass through, which was used to great effect as part of the performance. When a participant accomplished their main objective in the virtual world, finding their target, an actor would step through the rain curtain, appearing to emerge from the virtual world, and hand them a swipe card. Later on, the participants themselves would step through their curtains when they successfully completed their mission in the virtual world. These traversals were very dramatic, key moments in the participants' journey through the *Desert Rain* environment, creating the illusion of crossing between physical and virtual space and blurring the boundary between them. Our understandings from *Desert Rain* then shaped our further elaboration of traversable interfaces and boundaries in terms of managing participants' transitions between different spaces.

How did your work in this area develop after the Shape Living Exhibition*?*

The *Shape Living Exhibition* featured another traversable interface—the Storytent. It was in the shape of an A-frame tent with two projectors throwing different but synchronized images onto its surface and surrounding speakers playing sounds. This interface provided

Box 3.2 (continued)

a shared immersive experience of a virtual world for those visitors who entered the environment of the tent. At the same time the space outside the screens was also part of the experience, providing those standing in the vicinity or passing by with a view of what was happening inside. The experience of utilizing this interface, as well as others such as the Augurscope, led me to consider the specific design challenges for situated public interfaces such as the getting the physical form factor right through a series of low-tech physical prototypes, allowing for learnability at a distance so that visitors can gain a good sense of how to interact with an interface while observing others and providing different means of engagement for users including hands-on, overseeing, passing by.

The *Shape Living Exhibition* was also a starting point in addressing the issue of how to support a continuous experience across multiple interactive installations. It explored the use of tagged paper as a simple linking mechanism. This then led to considering how mobile devices may be used across situated installations in order to take advantage of the personalization and data storage that they offer.

How did you develop toolkits for authoring experiences such as the ARTECT work?

The ARTECT toolkit was designed to support the rapid prototyping of hybrid museum experiences by domain professionals. The toolkit uses visual markers to associate digital resources with physical artifacts. As ARTECT was developed for use by museum staff, I believe it is essential that toolkits aimed at creative professionals promote quick and easy experimentation with ideas. To achieve this aim we followed an iterative user-centered development process. Specifically, the ARTECT toolkit evolved through three iterations, from a proof of concept demonstrator to a fully featured tool, based on feedback from museum experts. As well as the meetings and design workshops with museum professionals, there was also regular testing by researchers not involved in the technical implementation of ARTECT in order to receive frequent feedback on the basic usability of the tool's interface. This iterative process of design and refinement of the toolkit highlighted the need to adopt experience-oriented representations in the user interface, allowing authors to think in terms of the physical and digital "things" that constitute a hybrid experience (such as museum artifacts, webcams, sensors, images, sound files) rather than in terms of the underlying technical components.

Designing for Spectating

A common thread running through the case studies in this chapter is the idea of addressing spectators to, as well as direct participants in, an interactive experience. *Day of the Figurines*, *Flypad*, and the *Shape Living Exhibition* include dedicated interfaces in the form of the Table, the Tall Trees, and the Storytent, respectively, deliberately targeting spectators and providing them with an overview of an unfolding experience. Moreover, displays such as the Augurscope, flashlights, the Sandpit, and *Flypad*'s footpads appear to emphasize their users' interactions, rendering them unusually visible to onlookers. On the other hand, the footpad in *Desert Rain* was located in a personal fabric cubicle that served to isolate its user from other people. We shall return to the distinction between participants and spectators (and indeed, other performance roles) in chapter 4, but for now our key point is that the form of an interface shapes the experience of onlookers as well as of its direct users, either addressing them explicitly (a deliberate spectator interface) or perhaps more indirectly. This is a relatively unexplored aspect of interface design in HCI, which has tended to focus on the details of the dialog between a user and their interface. The closely related field of computer-supported cooperative work has explored the topic of mutual awareness among the users of colocated interfaces, both in terms of ethnographic studies of control rooms and similar workplace settings (Heath et al. 2002) as well as technically through work on shared projected displays and other forms of "Single Display Groupware" (Stewart, Bederson, and Druin 1999). However, this work has tended to focus on relatively symmetrical situations in which users with similar roles or statuses engage in a collaborative task. Our focus on spectating, on the other hand, considers a more asymmetric relationship in which one person is driving an interface in the presence of others. Our key point is that it is important to also address the needs of these others so as to attract them to the experience, frame their sense of what it is, and even help them learn what to do when their turn comes by watching others. Indeed, it can be argued that it is the very presence of these spectators that transforms an interaction with a computer into a performance.

Stuart Reeves and colleagues introduced a taxonomy of spectator interfaces that captures in a simple and yet surprisingly subtle way various common approaches to their design (Reeves et al. 2005). This taxonomy defines and then compares two dimensions in order to chart out an overall design space for spectator interfaces. The first dimension is that of *manipulations*, the actions carried out by the primary user of the interface, henceforth referred to as the performer. The performer's actions may include manipulations of physical controls (mice, buttons, sliders, joysticks, and so forth) and we as physical movements that are sensed by the interface (e.g., through GPS, RFID, video tracking or all manner of sensing techniques). Manipulations can also include movements that do not result in any input to the interface, that is, performative gestures that occur around the interface without directly controlling it. Such gestures may be an important aspect of expressing emotion and virtuosity, or may arise from physical preparation before and follow through after the actual moment of interaction. These gestures can often be seen in traditional performance settings such as musicians playing conventional instruments or in sports (think of a virtuosi piano player or golfer with his or her swing). As examples, Charles Rosen describes how pianists gestures at the piano shape audience's appreciation of their skill (2002), and David Sudnow also discusses how seemingly extraneous gestures become integrated with the practice of playing a piano keyboard (1978). Some previous work in HCI has considered the role of performative gestures in playing electronic instruments, employing the term "expressive latitude" for gestures that are not directly sensed by the interface (Bowers and Hellström 2000). Having a region for making gestures that do not make input also enables performers to temporarily disengage from the interface in order to rest or reposition themselves before subsequent reengagement. It may also support the handing over of an interface from one person to another without causing unwanted input while not properly connected to either. This discussion is related to Victoria Bellotti and colleagues' framework for the design of sensing-based interfaces in which they raise key issues for interface designers to ponder including "how not to address the system" and "how to disambiguate signal-to-noise" (2002). The form of an interface may serve to hide, reveal, partially reveal, or even amplify manipulations from a spectator's point of view. Trivially, small interfaces may hide manipulations, whereas very large ones may reveal them. The positioning, shielding, size, shape, and lighting of the interface may have a similar effect, as we saw with the *Day of the Figurines* table, which emphasized the action of inspecting figurines. Some issues partially reveal manipulations (one can easily see that someone is using a mobile phone from a distance, but cannot so easily see specific key presses or overhear what is being said) or may even amplify them, requiring unusually visible actions such as jumping up and down on a footpad.

The second dimension in the taxonomy is that of *effects*, defined to be display of graphics and sounds or the movement or other actuation of physical devices. These may represent the primary output of the display (e.g., playing music or rendering a virtual world), but might also include the appearance of menus, icons, and other widgets that provide the performer with feedback about the ongoing use of the interface. Effects may also include the apparent impact of the interaction on the performer themselves, either directly in that it is somehow controlling the movement or other response of their body, or indirectly in terms of their visible emotional response to the interface. As with manipulations, the design of the interface may serve to hide, partially reveal, reveal, or even amplify these effects from a spectator's point of view.

We are now in a position to classify how different performance interfaces address spectators by comparing the extent to which they hide, reveal, partially reveal, or even amplify manipulations against the extent to which they hide, reveal, partially reveal, or amplify the resulting effects of these manipulations. The resulting two-dimensional taxonomy is shown in figure 3.21, populated with examples of interfaces from the case studies in this book as well as with some examples from other works that we will describe shortly. At the bottom left, we find what are traditionally considered to be private interfaces in which both manipulations and effects tend to be hidden from spectators. *Desert Rain*'s cubicles provide a good example of this. The handheld computers and mobile phones used in *Can You See Me Now?*, *Uncle Roy All Around You*, and *Day of the Figurines* also lie in this corner of the taxonomy, as it is difficult for spectators to see their screens or overhear their audio unless they are very close by. Although it is difficult to see which keys someone is pressing from a distance, it is relatively easy

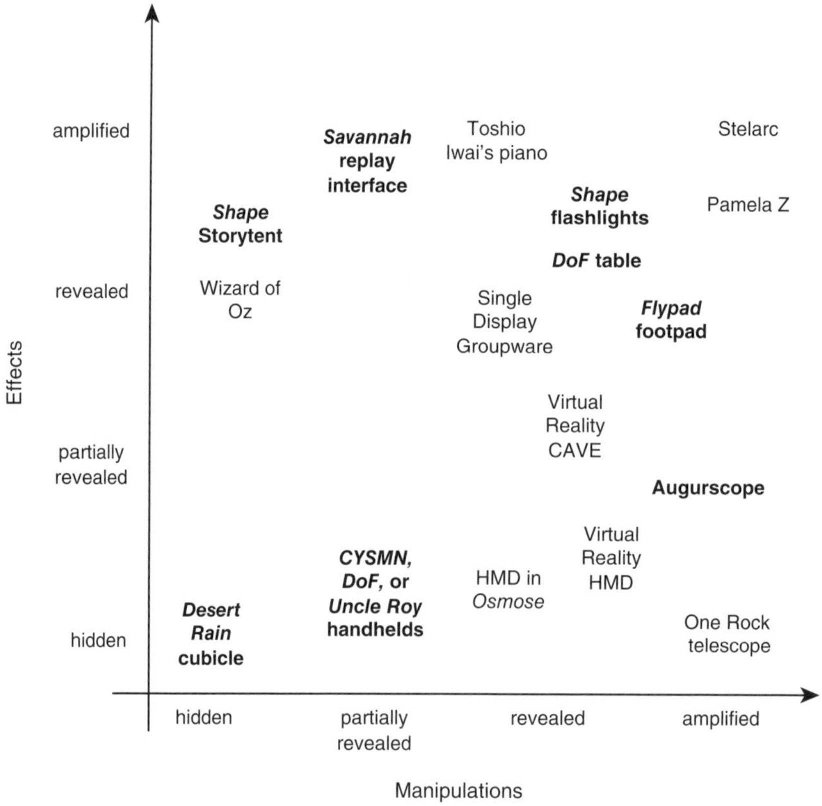

Figure 3.21
Classifying spectator interfaces according to manipulations and effects (*Day of the Figurines* [*DoF*] *and Can You See Me Now?* [*CYSMN*]).
Copyright MRL.

to see that someone is using a phone or handheld—they do partially reveal manipulations. *Shape's* Augurscope is somewhat more revealing of effects (one can see its larger screen more easily) and far more revealing of manipulations, as its large and distinctive physical form makes it apparent whenever someone is pushing or tilting it. *Flypad*'s footpad, the interactive flashlights, and the *Day of the Figurines* table all occupy a similar space in which manipulations (bending over the table, jumping on the footpad, and shining beams of light) and effects (graphics displayed in large screens and audio played over public speakers) both tend to be revealed, or even amplified. *Savannah*'s replay interface involves a public projection of effects, but with manipulation through a keyboard and pointer. Finally, the fabric screen of the Storytent mostly hides the manipulations of those inside, while revealing their effects through a public projection of graphics and sound.

We have also located some other interfaces on the taxonomy. Virtual reality head-mounted displays (HMDs) tend toward revealing manipulations (spectators can easily see where people are looking and gesturing) while hiding effects. Char Davies's virtual reality work *Osmose* (1995) was interesting in this regard, as the participant wearing the HMD was placed behind a screen and backlighting was used to cast a shadow of them interacting, further hiding manipulations (Davies and Harrison 1996). Virtual Reality CAVEs, on the other hand, tend to reveal effects to spectators, as they can see the projected graphics to some degree. Other performance interfaces adopt a strategy or amplifying both manipulations and effects in order to reveal as much of the interaction as possible to an audience. Musician Pamela Z uses gesture controllers in her performances in order to manipulate electronic instruments alongside her voice (Lewis 2007); Toshio Iwai's pianos (Wilson 2002) are enhanced with lighting effects that greatly amplify his manipulations of the keyboard; and some of Stelarc's performances such as *Stimbod* use muscle stimulators to directly stimulate the performer's body as a highly visible effect. An alternative approach can be found in the Telescope, a device created for a performance called *One Rock*, in which participants would visibly stand on a step, turn and tilt, peer into an eyepiece in order to see an augmented reality display (Reeves et al. 2005). Turning to more conventional interfaces, Single Display Groupware interfaces tend to encourage equal sharing among participants by revealing both manipulations and effects to one another, and the "Wizard of Oz" prototyping technique involves a human who is hidden behind the scenes pretending to be the computer (manipulations are hidden, but effects are revealed).

The wide distribution of interfaces across this taxonomy reveal that there are very many different approaches to revealing (or otherwise) manipulations and effects within performance interfaces. However, this is not to say that there are not broader underlying strategies at play. In reflecting on their taxonomy, Reeves and colleagues suggest that there are in fact four broad strategies for designing a spectator interface, each pointing toward a different corner of the taxonomy, as shown in figure 3.22.

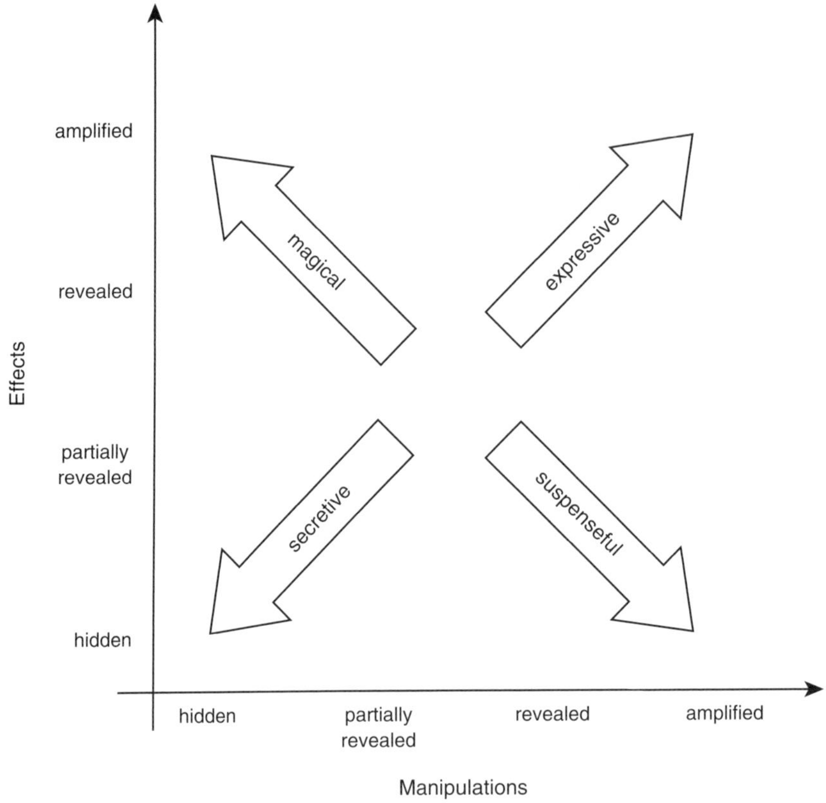

Figure 3.22
Four design strategies for spectator interfaces.
Copyright MRL.

Interfaces that tend toward hiding both manipulations and effects might be thought of as secretive, a strategy that might be employed to prevent spectators from knowing about an experience or to protect the performers using the interfaces from interference from spectators. At the other extreme are expressive interfaces that deliberately amplify manipulations and effects in order to engage spectators and enable them to appreciate the virtuosity of how the interface is used. A third strategy is to create magical interfaces that reveal effects while hiding effects. Peter Lamont and Richard Wiseman analyze the nature of performing magic in terms of the application of "methods" (akin to manipulations) that lead to "effects," emphasizing that the magician's skill lies in creating the effects without revealing the methods (1999). The fourth, and perhaps most counterintuitive strategy at first sight, is to create suspenseful interfaces (which might equally be called intriguing interfaces in our view). These interfaces reveal or even amplify manipulations in order to attract the attention of spectators and implicitly train them in how to use the interface, but without revealing the "payoff" of the effects until it is actually their turn to use the interface (e.g., when they actually put their eye to the eyepiece of the telescope). Although much of our focus has been on interfaces for performances that are deliberately staged, this taxonomy might also be applied to the more implicit kinds of performance that are occasioned by the everyday use of technology in public settings, from making mobile phone calls to using laptops or working in open plan environments. These uses of these interfaces also engage spectators, albeit often unintentionally, and it is important to consider how they may achieve this. What is especially interesting about this taxonomy, first developed by Reeves and his colleagues, is the way in which it challenges the traditional distinction between "public" and "private" uses of technology. Here we see that the single dimension of public-private (that would run as a diagonal line from bottom left to top right of the taxonomy) is replaced by more complex considerations of which aspects of interaction (manipulations and/or effects) are made public, or even turned into spectacles, or otherwise, which in turn have a more subtle impact on the performative nature of interaction. As already noted, this taxonomy also suggest that there is no one right way to create a performance interface and that all four design strategies can be appropriate. Moreover, rather than there being a single "true" way to create a performance interface, nearly all of the case studies that we have described combine multiple interfaces that adopt differing strategies. *Uncle Roy All Around You* and *Day of the Figurines*, for example, both combine mobile phones (secretive) with public displays (expressive). Perhaps then it is the way that these different interfaces—and their underlying approaches to spectating—come together that is the important issue here, which leads us to our final discussion in this chapter: the idea of there being ecologies of interfaces.

Ecologies of Hybrid Interfaces

What the *Shape Living Exhibition* demonstrates above all is the idea that a single mixed reality experience can involve a diverse collection of interfaces. Rather than relying on a single interface or interaction style, this experience works because different interfaces are provided for different purposes and settings, yet are also linked into a larger structure. Moreover, this tendency can be seen in the other two case studies in this chapter, and beyond this, in all of the examples that we have seen to date. Indeed, it will also be evident in all of the case studies that we introduce throughout the remainder of this book. Thus, *Can You See Me Now?* mixes personal computers displaying virtual worlds with wearable and handheld technologies; *Uncle Roy All Around You* did the same, but extended this with a public display on a large screen; *Savannah* combined handheld devices in the field with a shared smartboard back in the classroom; *Day of the Figurines* mixes mobile phones with augmented tabletop displays; and *Desert Rain* combines a traversable projected interface with swipe cards and video screens. As with the structures of space and time that we discussed in previous chapters, it seems that the nature of interfaces in mixed reality performances is essentially hybrid, combining different techniques and devices into a complex whole. Paradigms such as wearable computing, mobile computing, tangible interfaces, virtual reality, and augmented reality are here mashed up to create a far richer and more complex structure.

If existing paradigms are insufficient, then how we might describe such a structure? One possibility is to think of there being an *ecology* of interfaces in which diverse interface forms coexist and support one another through interactional trajectories. Each individual interface is specialized to a particular use, setting, or perspective (for example, navigating outdoors, reflecting in the classroom, immersing oneself in a virtual world) and through this contributes to the overall experience. Each individual interface within the overall ecology may itself be hybrid, consisting of a local ecology of devices and components. For example, the *Day of the Figurines* table combines a projector, and small computer display with the physical tables and figurines; the *Can You See Me Now?* runner interface combines a handheld computer with a GPS unit and walkie-talkie; the Storytent combines two projectors with an RFID reader embedded into a turntable. We have chosen to use the term "ecology" to implicitly refer, as pointed out by Matthew Fuller's study of media ecologies, to "the massive and dynamic interrelation of processes and objects, beings and things, patterns and matter" (2005, 3). We, however, use the term though not so much to indicate a "natural" or even "environmental" structuring or order of things, but rather to focus, still in Fuller's words, on "how information flows are routed within an organization" and so refer to "an inter-relationship with knowledge and time processes, intellectual property regimes, database and software design, content control, access structuring, metadata archiving, and the use and generation of new document and information types" (3). This ecology, as Blast Theory explain in the context of their work in the interview reproduced previously, creates aesthetic and political dynamics that afford determinate actions and reactions through a series of interactional trajectories. There is therefore here, as again noted by Fuller's analysis of Felix Guattari's use of the term, a "cross-fertilisation" between mental, natural, and social "modes" (in Fuller 2005, 5, and Guattari 2000), which suggests the possibility of a rhizomatic interconnectivity between human subjectivity, the environment, *and* social relations.

In adopting this term, we also refer to Crabtree and Tom Rodden's specific use of the expression "hybrid ecology" with respect to environments that combine mixed reality environments with ubiquitous computing infrastructures. These environments, the authors suggest, are both "geographically distributed and merge interaction across physical and digital environments that form *hybrid ecologies*." Here, the word ecology then refers to "the space or environment that cooperation takes place within and to the socially organized ways in which the environment affords collaboration" (2007, 483; emphasis in original). So, as we have seen, a number of the works described previously are formed as the result of collaborative ecologies whose parameters change alongside the nature of the cooperation that constitutes them. Interestingly, Crabtree and Rodden also identify the "fragmented nature of interaction brought about through different and differentially distributed mechanisms of interaction" (483). This again shows that the ecologies we discuss are not only hybrid, but also fragmented, distributed, nonhomogeneous, ambiguous, and inherently unstable.

The *ecology* of interfaces in a mixed reality performance extends beyond those interfaces that are directly used by the participants to also include those used to orchestrate the experience from "behind the scenes." We have seen how *Desert Rain* involved a bank of six displays that were used to monitor individual avatars. Similarly, each of the other experiences employed its own set of interfaces for monitoring participants and underlying systems, as well as further interfaces for communicating and coordinating (e.g., walkie-talkies). Chapter 4 gives a more detailed account of the importance and nature of orchestration, but for now it suffices to note that the ecology of interfaces covers these technologies too. Indeed, it might be argued that it also covers the interfaces that are used to author, document, and replay an experience.

Just as we spoke of a mixed reality performance involving trajectories through hybrid space and hybrid time, so too does it involve interactional trajectories through its ecology of interfaces. For example, a participant in *Day of the Figurines* begins at the tables, uses a registration interface on a nearby PC, and ends up using their mobile phone, whereas a participant in *Savannah* alternates between using a handheld computer in the field and a whiteboard during the debriefing sessions back in the classroom. We have seen how the design of an interface and its arrangement in an ecology shapes such a trajectory. Various researchers as well as our own studies have shown how interfaces can be created and aligned to "catch the eye" and draw participants in and through them as part of an "interactional trajectory." They have also shown how one participant's trajectory shapes that of a subsequent participant who is drawn by the spectacle of use and then learns what to do by watching the other. Finally, we suggest that the kinds of tangible and traversable interfaces employed by *Day of the Figurines* and *Desert Rain* respectively play particularly significant roles within such interactional trajectories by transforming information into action. Tangible tabletops and other shared surfaces provide a big canvas on which to reveal interactions to others, as we discuss in detail in the following chapter, in which we present a spectator interface taxonomy, in which tangible objects (e.g., figurines, swipe cards, and sheets of paper) that can be carried from one interface to the next enable participants to make a thread of connections between interfaces, effectively gluing them together into the larger experience. Traversable interfaces, on the other hand, support key transitions on an interactional trajectory as participants move between from a public space into a more secluded immersive environment.

Conclusion

Building on our previous discussions of space and time, this chapter has focused on the third of our four key facets of mixed reality performance—the computer interfaces that make them interactive. Once again, we have seen that mixed reality performance is essentially hybrid in form, in this case with diverse interfaces being assembled into hybrid ecologies, in which each interface may itself be a hybrid ecology of further devices and components. Our study of the *Day of The Figurines* spectator interface revealed that great attention to detail goes into the creation of such an ecology, covering both the physical form of each interface or component and also the manner in which they are arranged within a local setting. This study also affirmed the idea of there being interactional trajectories toward and through public interfaces, which has been raised by previous studies of museum exhibits, interactive artworks, and tangible interfaces. Our second case study, *Desert Rain*, focused on the inclusion of immersive interfaces within an ecology of mixed reality interfaces. In this case, we saw how a virtual world was embedded into a surrounding physical set through the use of the rain curtain, a physically traversable interface that supports the illusion of physical passage from real to virtual. Our third case study, *Flypad*, showed how an ecology of interfaces was integrated into a particular physical space, with various strategies being used to engage spectators and establish a trajectory of interaction through the experience. Our fourth case study, the *Shape Living Exhibition*, brought many of these ideas together within the context of a museum visiting experience, showing how a diverse set of interfaces, including both tangible and traversable interfaces, was assembled into an ecology at the site of an ancient castle, and how electronically tagged sheets of paper acted as physical tokens to connect these together. The next chapter now turns attention to our fourth key aspect of mixed reality performance: the various performance roles that may be involved, where once again we see notions of hybrid structure and trajectories at play.

4 The Experience of Mixed Reality: Spectating, Authoring, and Orchestrating

This chapter analyzes the construction of theatrical, performative, and participatory roles in mixed reality performance. So far, we have considered the structure of mixed reality performance in terms of space, time, and interfaces. In this chapter, we turn to a fourth and final aspect of mixed reality performance: the people that take part in its production and performance, considering the various roles that they assume and the trajectories that they follow through these roles. Our first case study, *Fairground: Thrill Laboratory* encompasses a series of events that employed a personal and wearable telemetry system to transform fairground rides into performances, capturing video and biosensing data from riders and displaying these to watching audiences, either live or after the event. This case study reveals a triangle of core roles—performers, spectators, and orchestrators—that are involved in mixed reality performances. Our second case study, *Rider Spoke*, takes place on the city streets. Participants explore a city on bicycles, recording personal stories and hiding them at different locations for others to find, before going on to discover and listen to the recordings of previous players. *Rider Spoke* highlights subtle distinctions in the nature of spectating in public spaces, leading us to refine the idea of spectators by considering how the frame of a performance separates the audience from unwitting bystanders and how this can become blurred in highly public settings. Our third case study, *Ulrike and Eamon Compliant*, is a highly subjective work in which participants are guided through urban spaces by unseen orchestrators who shadow them and issue instructions remotely as they go. Combined with the others, reflection on this case study leads us to further develop the performer role and also to unpack in some detail the nature of orchestration work, an essential component of all of the experiences described in this book. Building on previous studies analyzing interactive installations, we discuss the changing nature of participation, with the public increasingly taking on the role of performer. In turn, we see how artists are encouraging them to perform in the work by taking on the role of orchestrator. We conclude by proposing that mixed reality performances involve complex ecologies of roles (as they did spaces, times, and interfaces) and discuss how various transitions, transactions, or journeys between and through multiple roles in a performance can once again be explained in terms of trajectories.

Fairground: Thrill Laboratory

Our first case study is *Fairground: Thrill Laboratory* (2006–). This performance used a wearable telemetry system to capture various combinations of live video and audio, heart rate, galvanic skin response, the movements of key facial muscles, and acceleration data from the riders of roller coasters and other amusement park rides. These data were then used to enhance the experience of watching the ride by being displayed live on large public displays, supporting television broadcasts, or enabling the generation of souvenirs of the experience. *Fairground: Thrill Laboratory* took the form of a series of events created by artist Brendan Walker in collaboration with a series of artists, scientists, and technologists including the Mixed Reality Laboratory. These formed part of Walker's ongoing exploration of the nature of thrill, building on his previous publication of a "taxonomy of thrill" in which he analyzed how factors such as fear, pleasure, and arousal combine to create thrilling experiences (2005). More broadly, *Fairground: Thrill Laboratory* drew its inspiration from the long history of the fairground and amusement park as drivers of technical innovation in public entertainment, from the earliest manually operated roundabouts to modern rides that are substantially dependent on computing technology. For him, theme parks are increasingly exploring the "merger between the technologies of the amusement ride and those of the computer game," as in the case of virtual reality simulation rides such as Disney's Aladdin, which provides the experience of "flying a magic carpet through a virtual world" (Walker et al. 2007). Given their combination of real and virtual spaces, diverse interfaces, and even live actors, modern rides constitute a form of mixed reality performance, albeit one focused on large-scale mass entertainment. In *Fairground: Thrill Laboratory*, the aim was to explore the use of technology to not only design and control rides, but also augment the experience by producing views and souvenirs that could offer further entertainment to family and friends who had been on the "original" ride. This, in turn, revealed that in amusement parks, like in computer games, the documentation and subsequent replay of the original ride could constitute an additional source of entertainment and reflection.

The first *Fairground: Thrill Laboratory* event was staged at the Dana Centre, which forms part of the Science Museum in London, and aimed to provide "both an educational and an entertaining experience" (Walker et al. 2007, 116). The event comprised three separate performances, each employing a different fairground ride, in order to offer a distinct kind of thrilling experience. The first ride, the Miami Trip (see figure 4.1), aimed to provide a "thrilling but pleasurable experience" (116). It consisted of a horizontal bench of sixteen seats slung between two powered rotating arms. The bench

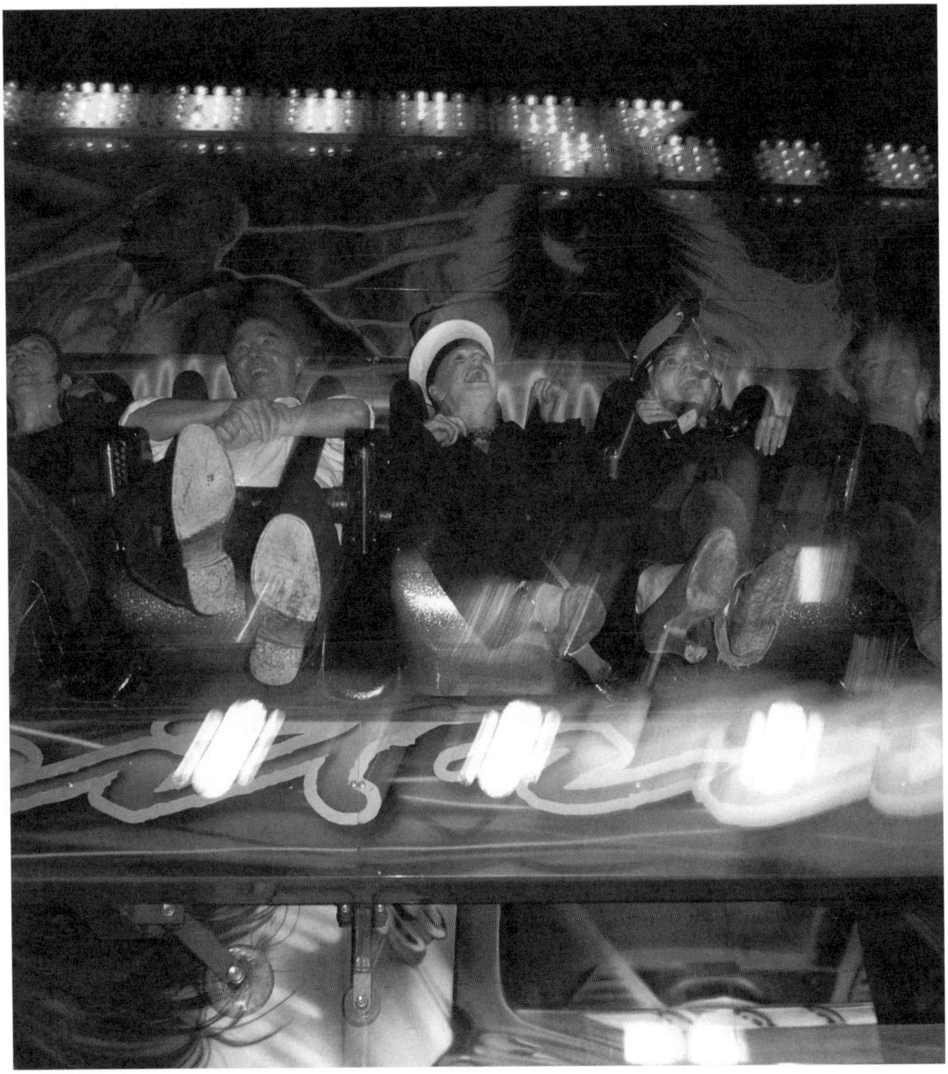

Figure 4.1
Audience members accompanying a Thrill-Lab-Lotto winner (fitted with Telemetry equipment) riding the Miami Trip during an experiment in the first week of Thrill Laboratory exploring ideas of Pleasure.
Copyright Brendan Walker.

was arranged so that the riders faced the spectators. This was a deliberate choice that was intended "to encourage interaction between riders and spectators" (116). The operator of the ride was able to control speed and direction.

The second performance, the Ghost Train (see figure 4.2), was intended to "provide an experience containing elements of anxiety" (Walker et al. 2007, 116). This ride utilized several carriages to carry two riders up an incline, and then down again through a series of tunnels. Additionally on this ride, darkness, actors, and props were used to startle riders and generate thrill.

The third and final ride was the Booster (see figure 4.3), a white-knuckle ride relying primarily on fear and extreme acceleration. Here, a central tower supported a 40-meter-long rotating arm, at the end of which were two pairs of riders seated back to back. Again, the speed and direction of the ride could be controlled by the operator. The key technical innovation at the heart of *Fairground: Thrill Laboratory* was the use of a personal wearable telemetry system to capture data from riders that could be transmitted to nearby public displays to be shown to a watching audience of spectators. This telemetry system used a helmet-mounted camera and microphone to capture close-up video

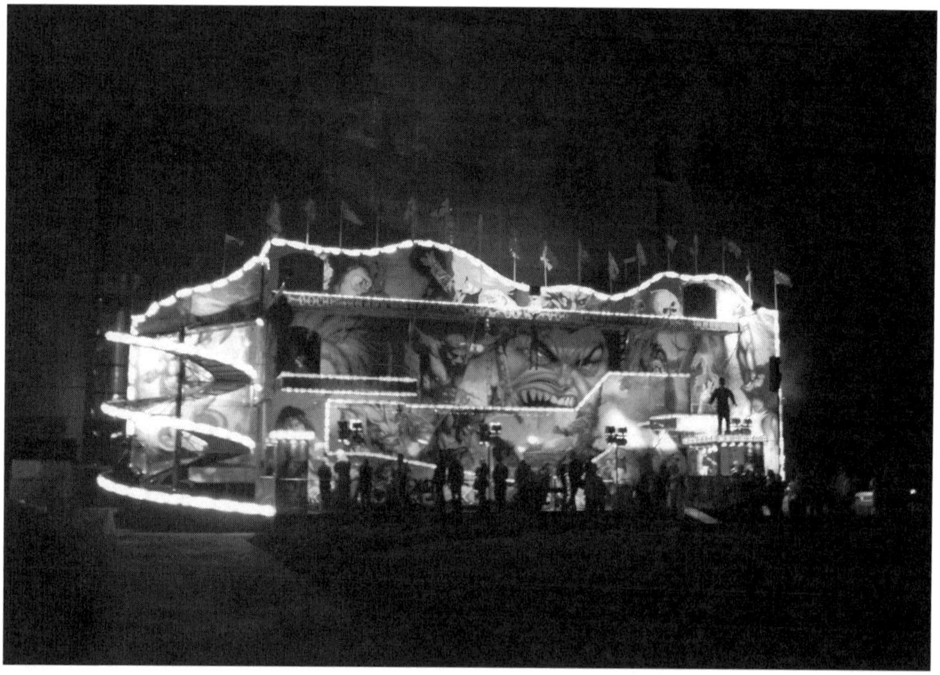

Figure 4.2
The Ghost Train.
Copyright Brendan Walker.

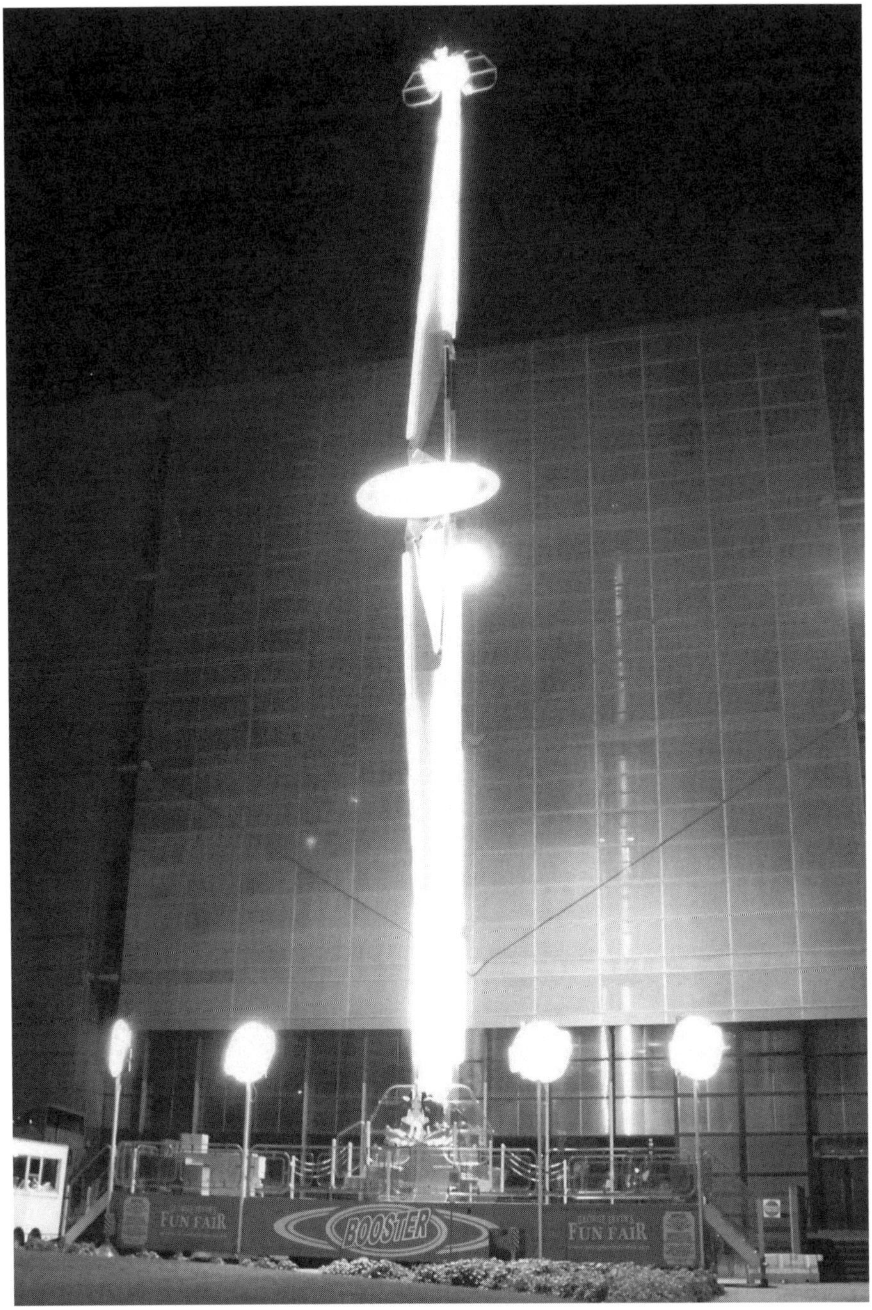

Figure 4.3
The Booster outside the Dana Centre.
Copyright MRL.

of riders' faces and audio recordings of their commentary and/or screams; a sensor attached to a chest strap to capture their heart rates; and an accelerometer to measure their moment-by-moment acceleration. A lightweight computer housed in a small rucksack transmitted these various data streams over a wireless network so that they could be shown live on three different public displays. The first display adopted "the style of a scientific analysis tool" and consisted of plots of heart rate and acceleration over time shown alongside the video and audio. These were projected onto a large display and explained by various experts to a watching audience. The second was a "simpler visualization that gave an overall impression of a rider's experience" that was displayed in a nearby bar. The third was a "large impressionistic image that was projected onto the outside surface of the building itself" (Walker et al. 2007, 117).

These various technologies, including the ride itself, were carefully embedded into a performance structure. The ride was first demonstrated by a "professional rider" and the nature of the equipment and visualizations explained to the audience by the host, the "showman." Several audience members were then selected by lottery to wear the telemetry system (aided by various "thrill technicians," who wore distinctive boiler suits) and then take the ride (see figures 4.5 and 4.6), during which their data would be on public display. The scientific visualization was explained to the audience by an expert in biosensing (see figure 4.4) and the evening also involved talks by scientists and ride designers, performances, videos, music and food (Walker et al. 2007, 117). Toward the end of the evening, more members of the audience could try the ride without the telemetry system.

The structure of this performance was crucial and carefully designed because, as Walker asserts, "the most important thing to remember when creating a roller coaster is the choreography. It's not just about loops and drops, but about theater, tempo and understanding your audience" (in Iseard 2009). So "spectacularity," timing, and careful audience construction, together with the trajectories between experiencing thrill and witnessing its production in three very different types of ride, constituted a fundamental aspect of the design of the work. Indeed, for Walker, each of the rides represented the center of a "theatrical event in which riding became a live performance that was deliberately staged for a watching audience" (Walker et al. 2007, 117). Thus juxtaposition of video, the rider's own reporting voice, and scientific data created the context within which participants could read one form of documentation against the other and draw their own conclusions about how thrill was being generated and experienced.

The second major thrill laboratory event, *Oblivion: Thrill Laboratory*, assumed a different form and focused on the capture of data from a preselected group of riders who experienced one ride only, Oblivion, during a day at the Alton Towers Resort, a major UK amusement park. The aim was to generate a unique scientific dataset in order to aid researchers (including experts in data mining) to systematically explore the rela-

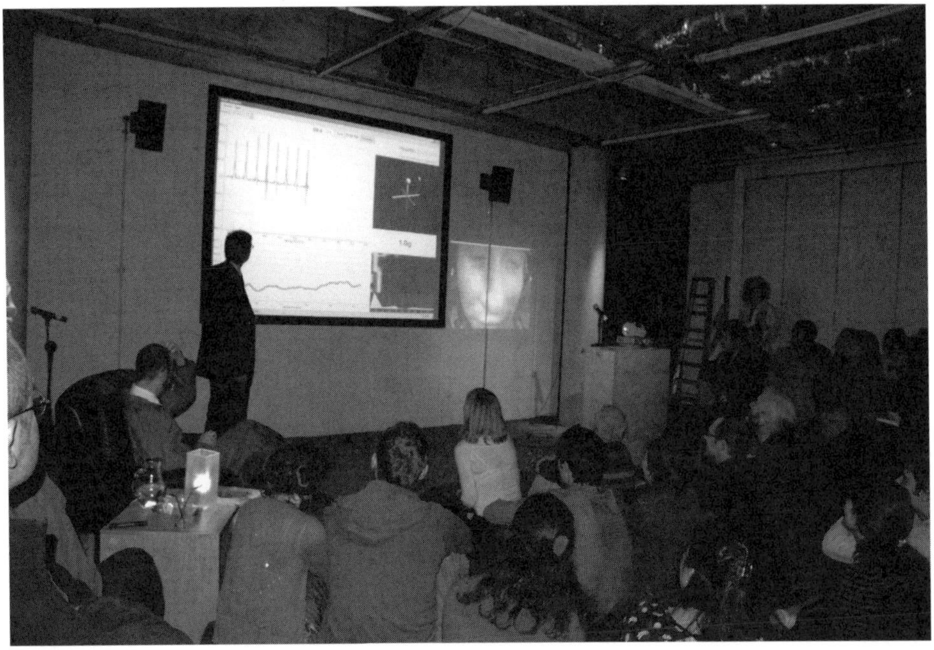

Figure 4.4
An expert explains the visualization to the audience.
Copyright MRL.

tionship between the experience of thrill and physiological responses gathered through biosensing.

The structure of the performance was adapted to reflect this more experimental approach, with the selected riders first completing a questionnaire that used Marvin Zuckerman's "sensation seeking scale" (1979), to assess their thrill-seeking tendencies before experiencing various rides. The riders also took part in a debriefing session in which they were shown their own videos and data and had the opportunity to discuss this with experts and also compare it with other riders (see figure 4.7). After the performance, each rider was sent a personal "data souvenir" consisting of his or her own video and data (see figure 4.8). Some riders were also engaged in a follow-up project to generate souvenirs in which images and measurements from the data were combined with their own captions to create a short comic strip.

Two subsequent *Fairground: Thrill Laboratory* events focused on the use of the wearable telemetry system as part of television broadcasts in which presenters tried out the rides and their data was analyzed and discussed for the benefit of the viewers. The first program, for the Discovery Channel, featured Walker himself as the presenter,

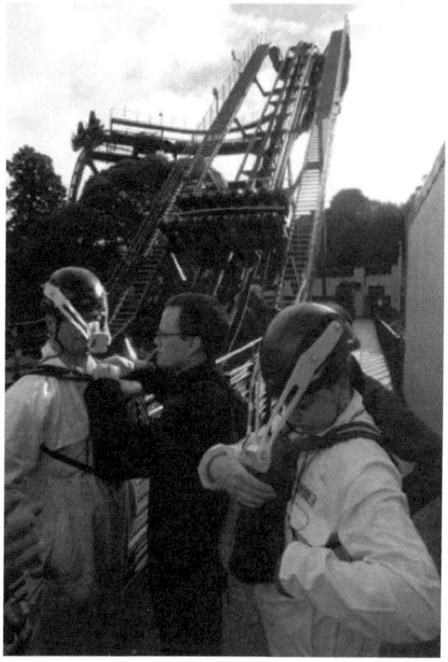

Figure 4.5
Preparing to ride Oblivion at Alton Towers. The wearable telemetry systems are being fitted in the foreground and the ride can be seen in the background.
Copyright MRL.

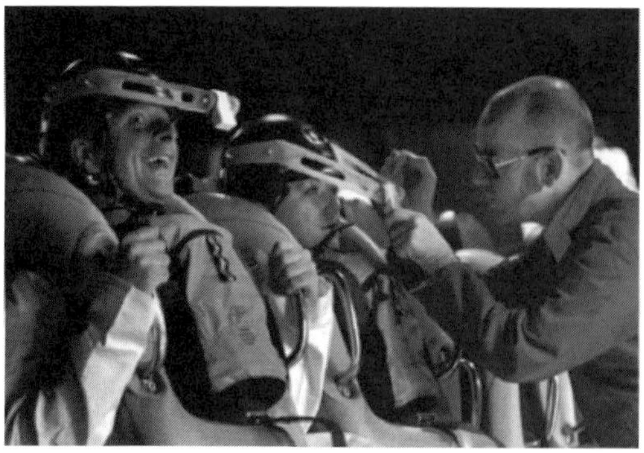

Figure 4.6
Close-up of the wearable telemetry systems on the ride.
Copyright Newsteam and the Alton Towers Resort.

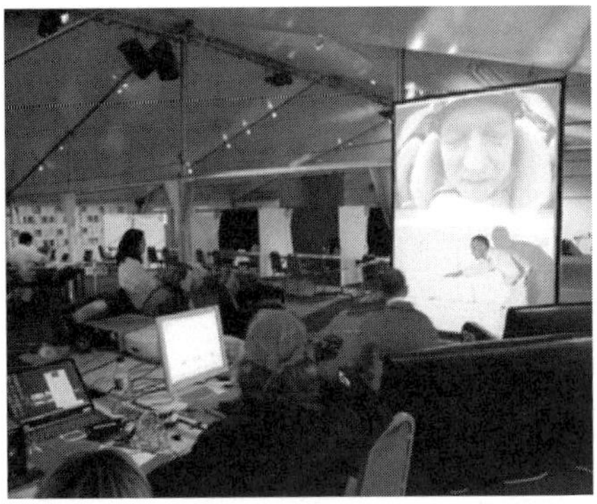

Figure 4.7
A debriefing session in which riders are shown their data and videos while members of the technical team look on.
Copyright MRL.

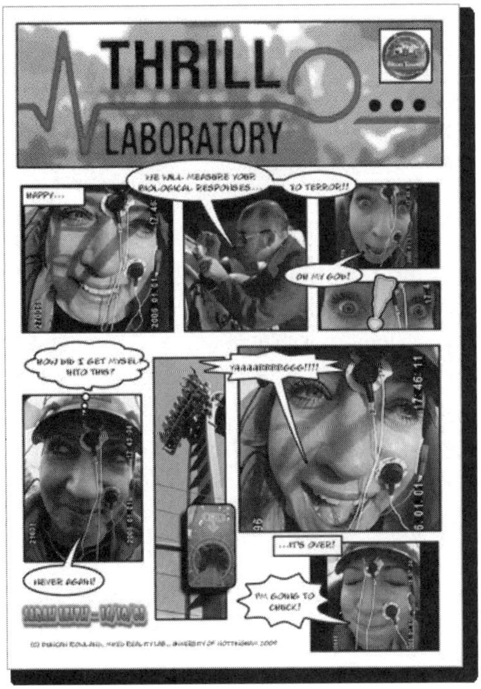

Figure 4.8
An example "data souvenir" in the form of a comic strip.
Copyright MRL.

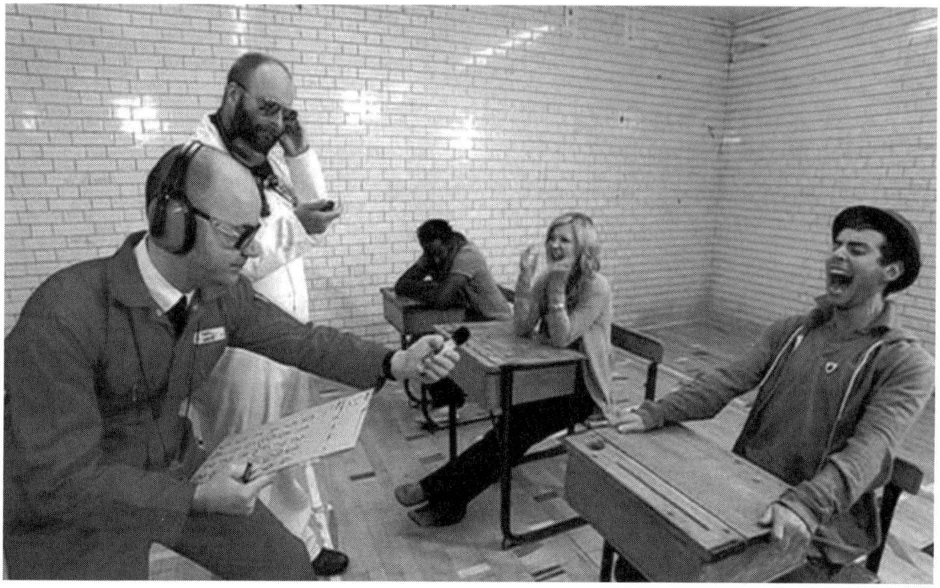

Figure 4.9
Testing the presenters to see who can scream the loudest as part of the rider selection process for the BBC *Blue Peter* article.
Copyright BBC.

whereas a second program, this time for the long-running BBC children's show *Blue Peter*, employed one of the show's regular presenters as the rider (see figure 4.9).

In each case, the telemetry system was extended to capture a further data stream, the movements of two key facial muscles, the zygomaticus major and corrugator supercilii, which are strongly associated with smiling and frowning, respectively, and could therefore give further insights into a rider's emotional response to the ride.

Finally, one subsequent Thrill Laboratory event involved a more radical shift in the performance structure. In an event created for a national UK science exhibition called Pioneers 09 (sponsored by the Engineering and Physical Sciences Research Council, EPSRC), members of the public were selected from a watching audience and invited to operate a ride based on information captured and transmitted from a professional rider, an actor (see figure 4.10).

In this case, the ride was a Bucking Bronco of the kind that can easily be hired for parties and similar events, and which can be quickly assembled and easily and safely operated. The selected audience member would be located behind a medical screen so that they could see only the telemetry data displayed on a screen, but could not directly see the ride or the rider. The "showman" then asked them to try to create

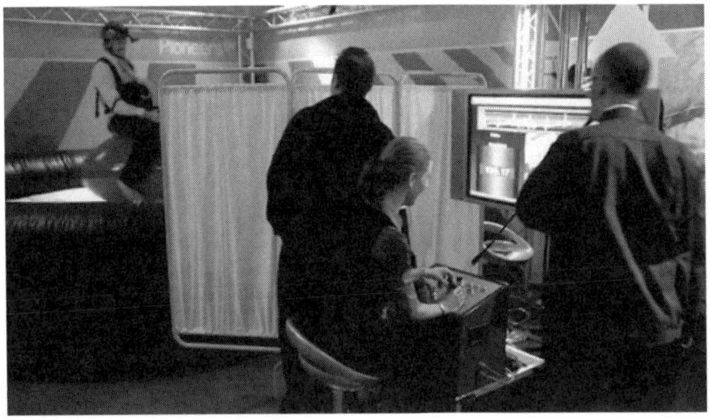

Figure 4.10
A member of the public controls the Bucking Bronco while the "showman" and a thrill technician look on.
Copyright MRL.

various kinds of thrill for the rider, including pleasure and anxiety, by interpreting the data and operating the controls (see figure 4.11). The rest of the audience could see both the rider/ride and the public operator during the event.

Performers, Spectators, and Orchestrators

These various Thrill Laboratory events involved collaboration among a variety of participants who were cast into a diverse range of roles. These included the selected riders who wore the telemetry system; audiences who watched the presentation of their telemetry data (both live and on television); the hosting "showman" and expert presenters; thrill technicians who marshalled the riders and managed the wearable hardware; ride operators who controlled the rides; additional technicians who managed the telemetry system from behind the scenes; other supporting roles concerned with admissions and management of the venue; and in some cases, visitors to the venue who happened to be in the vicinity, some of whom might have watched or ridden even though they were not directly involved in the event. Like the spaces, time scales, and interfaces that were discussed in the previous chapters, these multiple roles, and the ways in which they are structured and related, are core to the nature of the performance. This complex structure of roles is therefore a fourth fundamental aspect of mixed reality performance that needs to be considered alongside space, time, and interfaces.

As a launch point for this discussion, a second study proposed that *Fairground: Thrill Laboratory* could be described in terms of the relationships between three broad classes

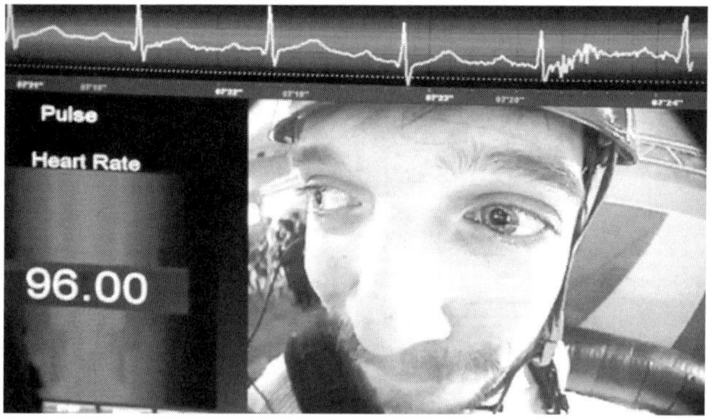

Figure 4.11
The visualization seen by the controller showing the rider's face, heart rate, and pulse. Copyright MRL.

of role: performers, spectators, and orchestrators (Schnädelbach et al. 2008). The riders who wore the telemetry system were described as performers; the spectators were those who had become engaged in watching them, either because they were part of the audience gathered in the auditorium to watch the visualization, or because they were watching the ride itself. Orchestrators were the professionals who operated the ride. This also included the technicians that managed the telemetry system, the host, and the front-of-house staff. These three core roles are also evident in our previous case studies. The street and online players of *Uncle Roy All Around You* are *performers*; its actors and technicians are *orchestrators*; and passing members of the public on the city streets or at the hosting venue are (possibly accidental) *spectators*. *Day of the Figurines* transforms its players into performers, while engaging spectators through the augmented table and employing orchestrators to manage the game from behind the scenes and to move figurines across the table. There is an important difference among conventional theatrical performances here that runs throughout this chapter and indeed this book. The performers are members of the "public," who are the primary users of the technology (as we discussed in the previous chapter when defining different kinds of spectator interface), whereas professional actors, even though they may be performing, typically feature as part of the orchestration team whose task it is to sustain the engagement of the public performers. There is a sense here in which theatrical actors need to at least partially vacate the stage in order to make space for this new class of public performers whose interactions form the core theatrical spectacle in mixed reality performances.

Schnadelbäch and his colleagues' study of *Fairground: Thrill Laboratory* found that the telemetry system not only modified each of these particular roles but also perturbed "the relationship between them." Transcriptions of riders' audio streams revealed that the combination of the ride experience and telemetry system tended to give them a license to perform, that is, to express themselves freely and sometimes extremely. This "urge to perform," however, depended on which phase of the ride the participants were experiencing, so that when the ride was slow, they were often lucidly explaining what they thought, but when the ride was fast, they tended to lose control, "shouting and screaming, but being unable to commentate" (Schnadelbäch et al. 2008, 0000). This loss of control appears to have been involuntary for many riders and was a cause of concern for a few, who worried about what they might have said over a public channel. From the spectator's point of view, the telemetry offered a level of detail that was not normally available simply by observing the rides from a distance and thus greatly enhanced their experience. The telemetry system also perturbed orchestration work by enabling the ride operators to tune directly into the experience of their riders. In one example, a rider used the audio channel to plead for the ride to be stopped on behalf of the person sitting next to them who was scared. The use of a public channel for this purpose is intriguing, as it may perturb the normal ability of operators to selectively "ignore" scared riders under the assumption that that this is a normal state of affairs (within limits) and that it is a less painful outcome for all concerned to let the ride continue rather than to stop it and try to get this person off, which might leave them suspended in the air for a long time. This provides a particularly compelling example of how new mixed reality technologies may alter the traditional nature of and balance between performance roles.

In chapter 3, we discussed how interfaces could be designed with spectators in mind, hiding, revealing, or even amplifying different combinations of manipulations and subsequent effects to deliver different styles of spectator experience from secretive to expressive, but also encompassing magical and intriguing. *Fairground: Thrill Laboratory* goes beyond this by creating networked interfaces whose primary purpose is to enhance the experience of distant spectators, in this case by enabling them to tune in to the personal experience of a rider, perhaps as part of a live performance or through a subsequent TV broadcast. The Bucking Bronco event introduces a further twist by transforming the role of ride operator (rather than rider) into a public performance. Similar remote spectator interfaces have also been used to reveal activities within online virtual worlds. The *Out of This World* (1998) "inhabited television" show created a series of dedicated virtual cameras to follow different avatars who were taking part in an online game show in a virtual world and capture their activity so that it could be broadcast to a watching theater audience. Similarly, *Uncle Roy All Around You* provided a public display of its online virtual world that would follow different online players and that was situated within the hosting venue. All of these interfaces serve to transform our three core roles of performer, spectator, and orchestrator and to (re)connect them in new ways. However, although these three core roles provide a good starting point for a general exploration of roles in mixed reality performance, they are too coarse to express all of the subtleties that are involved. Consequently, informed by further case studies, the remainder of this chapter explores the nature of these roles in greater depth, uncovering important distinctions and new relationships among them, including the way in which the framing of a performance establishes different classes of spectators as well as revealing the complex but essential nature of orchestration work.

Interview 7: Designing Thrill

Box 4.1

We ask Brendan Walker, "Why thrill 'laboratory'?"

The phrase *thrill laboratory* was inspired by a description of a fairground I had read, which was written by ethnocriminologist Mike Presdee. I was excited about how he described the fairground as a stage for so many forms of experimentation: social, cultural, technological, physiological, psychological, financial, chemical, sexual, and, sometimes, moral and ethical. The fairground is a place that has long been associated with dangerous experimentation both at the edges of physical possibility and social acceptability. I was interested in how all these factors contributed to a form of emotional experimentation in what I felt was a *thrill laboratory*.

The idea of a thrill laboratory quickly outgrew the fairground it originally described, as it began to symbolize a much broader idea of creation and experimentation. The phrase *thrill laboratory* also defines a space between subjectivity and objectivity, where factors pertaining both are considered.

What is the importance of the juxtaposition of art/science in your work?

The fairground fuses together different forms of art and science, from the science of freakish sideshow spectacles and amazing ride technology, to the art of performance and graphic illustration. Art and science are just two elements that the "showman" has at his disposal when creating an engaging entertainment experience. I see both elements being inextricably linked, operating in unity rather than as separate entities that can be divorced and viewed in juxtaposition. In the context of the fairground, and *Thrill Laboratory*, neither takes precedence, and either would become meaningless in the absence of the other.

How did you structure the first event? What was the importance of experiencing the rides in the particular order in which you placed them?

Performances were staged from 17:30 until 21:45 on Tuesday, and repeated on Wednesday, over three weeks. Each evening featured "an international team of scientists, artists, performers; and a carnival of live experimentation, performance and discussion." The format of each week remained the same, though the content changed. My aim was to create three distinctly different evenings, each exploring a different aspect of thrill—Pleasure, Frisson,

Box 4.1 (continued)

and Visceral Delights (previously titled Arousal)—each exemplified by a different fairground ride—the Miami Trip, Ghost Train, and Booster, respectively. I ordered the rides in the same way they would be experienced at the fairground, building up to the white-knuckle showstopper at the end. My intention was to give a sense of climaxing over three weeks, while making each week a self-contained event itself (a mixture of marketing strategy and care for the entertainment experience).

Did you design particular trajectories that took participants from one place to another, both spatially and experientially?

I was initially inspired by the architecture of the space in and around the Dana Centre in London, and thought of how members of the audience might experience different content in each space. I was keen to replicate the idea of the *tober* found at the fairground, which describes the relationship between the spatial and experiential journey of a visitor to the showground, or *gaff*. The showman takes great care to arrange smaller rides, shows, and games of chance—the *sidestuff*—to offer visitors a glimpse of the larger showstopper rides at the back of the gaff. This is to increase anticipation, but then create a journey through increasingly extreme *sidestuff* in a build up to the larger white-knuckle rides.

As I planned to feature only one ride each evening, I decided that each evening should build up to climax with the audience actually physically experiencing the ride for themselves. The evening would offer increasingly intense glimpses and engagement with the ride and the emotional experience it might deliver, from the spectacle of initially being switched on at the start of the evening set against an autumn night sky, to observing an expert riding the ride, to taking part in a lottery (the Thrill-Lab-Lott) for the chance to be the subject of a live ride experiment, to empathizing with a fellow audience member being experimented upon, to finally being allowed to take their own ride.

I used a multisensory approach in developing the tober; commissioning unusual fairground food and cocktails, and employing an artist to recreate smells as the *essence of the fairground*—each of which I utilized throughout the evening. I structured the evening to flow from an opening cocktail party in *The Observatory* (on the ground floor, to a backdrop of commissioned films contextualizing the evening, and an awkward mix of ad hoc faux psychological profiling from Thrill Technicians adding both excitement and apprehension) to a dangerous live experiment "where anything could go wrong," which was conducted from *Operations* (on the top floor, to a backdrop of scientific talks and hubbub of live production), before members of the audience broke free to experience the ride outside, or watch others from the Observatory. The spaces themselves also transformed over the evening—from tranquil lecture halls to a raucous night club—with music being mixed live by DJs for both the Observatory, Operations, and the ride, alongside live medical data streaming from numerous members of the public keen to be experimented upon.

Box 4.1 (continued)

What was the function of the actor, and what was your own role, within the context of this work?

Thrill Technicians—experienced performance artists predominantly from the theater company Shunt—played vital roles as entertainers. The trajectory of the audience throughout the evening was untested, and was essentially a work in progress. Thrill Technicians provided a flexible element to the event, which we developed together, in discussion at the end of each evening, to maintain engagement and the sense of tober, rather than allowing the audience to drift outside the performance. As well as providing the crucial role of setting context for each evening and maintaining audience engagement, Thrill Technicians performed functional roles—from receptionists to ushers—complementing a Science Museum team. This practical role helped to blur the boundaries between reality and fantasy, which added to the audience's bewilderment and engagement with the performance.

In their "job description," Technicians were "encouraged to define individual research domains within the larger context being explored, while also developing their own experimental methods and techniques." This gave each Technician scope to develop individual characters and mechanisms to interact with the audience in different ways. After a year of intense development, I primarily saw myself as the curator of the event, which was to play host to sixty contributors and over a thousand audience members. However, as the reality of the event dawned, and the idea of Thrill Laboratory evolved, I realized that someone was needed to present and pull together a growing collection of seemingly disparate elements. I initially passed this role to the Thrill Technicians—who were, after all, trained entertainers. My only appearance was to be in an enigmatic introductory video to the event, in the character of the Thrill Engineer. It was only after the opening night that I quickly reworked the performance, and I took forestage as Director of Thrill Laboratory, performing the role of the Showman to *compère* the evening from front of house. My role seemed to help an audience make sense of the event as a whole, seeing that at the center of all this content was one man, the Thrill Engineer, with his vision to pursue the perfect formula for thrill, seeing no boundaries between the different disciplines. I also took my place as the more sober leader of the Thrill Technicians.

How did you design the relationships between performers, spectators and orchestrators in Thrill Laboratory?

The computer scientists who conducted the live experiments played quite a different role than the performers and I, who engaged directly with members of the public. The scientists' primary focus was to technically produce a single ride experiment. This was built up to during the evening, and was an important moment of live theater. The entire audience waited with baited breath to witness a member of the public being chosen, kitted out with helmet cam and medical monitoring equipment—the unique *telemetry system*—to take their inaugural "flight," with data being broadcast live back for "audience analysis

Box 4.1 (continued)

and delectation." The scientists were housed in Operations, with all equipment and procedures on show. This was like being in NASA Control, with scientists going about their work, too focused to care that they were on display as performers in a public spectacle. However, at the end of each evening, as the event dissolved into a free form party, the scientists' role shifted naturally to engage directly with members of the public, entertaining them with impromptu ride experiments, and reviews of scientific data. I've since evolved this important role of "the scientist" into the character of the Thrill Technologist.

Is thrill the result of a combination of factors that require staging?

I often talk about the construction of thrill in reference to choreography, film direction, or composing. I feel particularly inspired by the scores written by John Cage, and hearing David Mamet talk about directing films. I was reminded of their work during a conversation I had with Jack Katz—a criminologist from UCLA—a few years ago (studying the recordings of human disasters, traumas, misdemeanors, and taboos is a major source of inspiration for me). He told me that while he was studying motivations for "petty crimes of thrill," he realized that he first needed to understand the moment-by-moment microdynamics of the situation, the layering of subtle causes and effects, and their interrelationships. Jack was effectively talking about how the perpetrator constructed their emotional trajectory.

After studying personal accounts from diverse thrilling experiences, in a multitude of contexts, I began to build up my own language for describing the fundamental building blocks for thrill, and how they might be applied. These building blocks for thrill fall into five main categories: *spectacle*, *sensation*, *efficacy*, *value*, and *immortality*. I've found that factors from these categories can be layered and applied to affect the conscious and subconscious mind, as well as experienced by the body. They can exist as ideas of fantasy or in reality, and can be experienced over many different time frames spanning from microseconds to years. At one end of the spectrum, the staging of popular forms of thrilling entertainment have often relied on applying clichéd superlatives, such as higher, faster, scarier, and sexier. At the other end of the spectrum, richer thrilling experiences have evolved either naturally, or by applying tacit knowledge or personal intuition. I'm trying to develop a language to bridge the gap between these worlds of crude objective construction and more delicate subjective evolution.

What is the relationship between the formula that you devised that is at the heart of the engineering of thrill and the production of thrill in an actual fairground, say, like the UK-based Alton Towers theme park. How do you translate the formula into an experience?

The original formula for thrill—the Walker Thrill Factor—evolved from a common feature I observed between all thrilling experiences, whether they were accounts of cross-dressing in the woods to white-water rafting in the Rockies. I spotted that the climax of a thrilling

Box 4.1 (continued)

episode was experienced when there was a sudden, rapid, and large increase in a sense of euphoria (elation, well-being, or excitement). I also observed that even though factors could be choreographed to create the context and conditions necessary for a thrilling experience, there still needed to be a trigger to create the necessary explosion in euphoria; otherwise, the conditions could quickly evaporate as the conditions for naturally occurring thrill can often be transient. This *thrill trigger* often takes the form of a sudden visceral spark.

As I thought more about the phenomenon of thrill, I wondered if it could be measured. I began to draw analogies between thrill and the engineering principles of work, power, and efficiency. I developed my definition of euphoria to become the product of pleasure and arousal, and to also take into account variations between individuals. The resulting relationship between variations is arousal and pleasure over time, and thrill was always intended to stand as a rule of thumb to help while choreographing different factors to create a thrilling experience, such as new fairground rides. In practice, the formula—and other factors discussed in my book *The Taxonomy of Thrill*—has worked best as a tool for reflection during the creative process, to compliment tacit knowledge and intuition and to serve as a resource for inspiration.

What is an adaptive ride and what do you envisage to be the relationship between different forms of spectatorship within this context?

Classic thrill rides can be thought of as industrial production lines that deliver standardized repeatable thrilling experiences to a conveyor belt of human riders. "Successful" thrill rides (i.e., the ones that net the highest return on investment) have to appeal to a broad demographic, and therefore often rely on the lowest common denominator of factors—for example, higher, faster, scarier, sexier—to create the necessary conditions for thrill. An adaptive ride breaks with this production line model to provide individual, or group experiences that can be automatically (a) tailored to employ a broader set of thrill factors peculiar to the rider, and (b) tuned to exactly meet the rider's own taste for thrill. Adaptive rides already exist, which inadvertently offer varying degrees of tuning and tailoring. Even the highest-tech prescriptive rides can deliver vastly different experiences depending on whom you chose to sit next to, a form of social adaptation. Some rides also offer an element of physical adaptation, for example by either controlling the ride speed locally—as in the Tea Cups—or by responding to the operator's instructions to "scream if you want to go faster," creating a real-time feedback system— as in the Waltzer.

When I think about the future of adaptive rides, I imagine machines that are able to build up a personal relationships with their riders, gathering data to allow them to tailor and tune multiple factors or ride features. Such rides would be capable to probing and monitoring to learn both their riders' irrational phobias, while refining standard palettes of possibilities. They would be able to automatically tailor, tune, choreograph, and experiment to hone techniques, which playfully tease its riders, ultimately bringing them to multiple points of

Box 4.1 (continued)

thrilling climax. The success of classic thrill rides relies in varying degrees on social interaction provided by the mechanisms of public performance and spectatorship, in which ideas of *efficacy* and *value* can be played with, to thrilling effect. However, I imagine complex future adaptive rides might be observed as an extension of their rider's psyche, and an expression of their desires and unusual quirks. In this sense, a spectator may no longer just be watching the performance of a rider responding to a machine, they may also be witnessing the performance of a machine as a refection of its rider's body and mind.

Rider Spoke

Our second case study is *Rider Spoke* (2007–), a location-based game for cyclists developed by Blast Theory in collaboration with the Mixed Reality Laboratory as part of the European research project IPerG. *Rider Spoke* encouraged players to cycle around London, as well as subsequent tours in Brighton, Budapest, Sidney, Adelaide, Athens, Copenhagen, Bristol, Liverpool, and Linz, to record personal memories and speculations to be associated with particular locations. The work, which has so far been experienced by over two thousand players, allowed participants to find and listen to the responses of preceding players, built over time; each day's recordings were loaded into the system overnight to appear in the work the following day so that the experience of the piece was always being counterpointed by its historicity (Chamberlain et al. 2010).

Rider Spoke was a mobile interactive work combining elements of performance, gameplay, and interactive technology. Participants arrived at the hosting venue, either on their own bicycle or to borrow one. They registered at the reception (see figure 4.12), where they signed a disclaimer and left a deposit. They then received a briefing that covered the nature of the experience, how to use the technology, and how to cycle safely, and also told them of an emergency paper map and phone number stored under their saddle. A receptionist logged them into the system and then sent them outside where a technician mounted their console onto the handlebar of the cycle and, for loaned cycles, adjusted their seating position so that they felt comfortable and safe. Riders then left the venue individually. The experience lasted approximately one hour.

After the first few minutes, music started playing, setting the tone for the experience, and a narrator, Ju Row Farr, begun giving instructions in a calm, slightly detached and melancholic voice:

This is one of those moments when you are on your own. You might feel a little odd at first, a bit self-conscious or a bit awkward. But you're alright and it's OK. You may feel invisible tonight

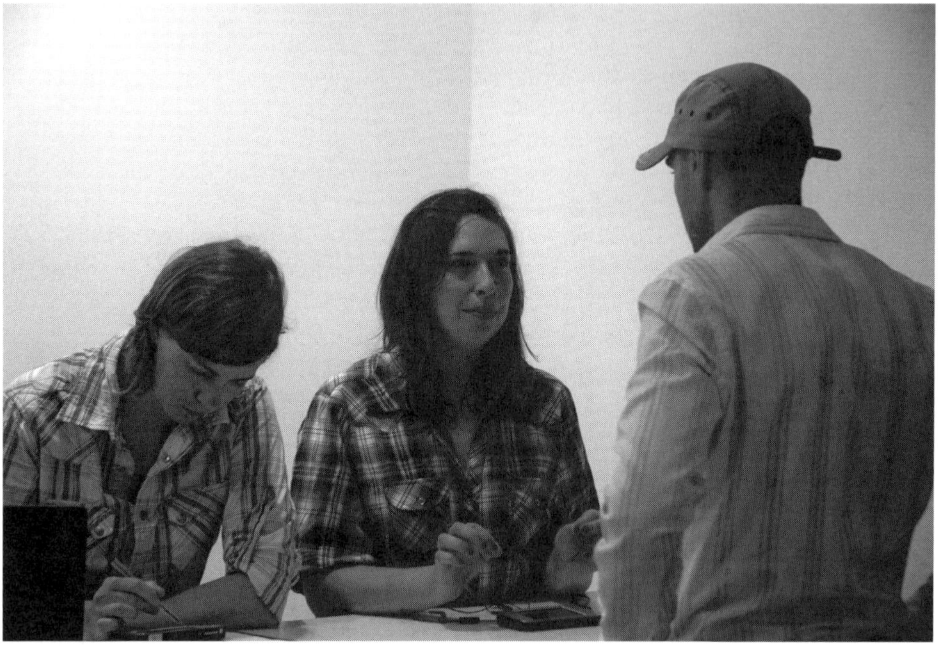

Figure 4.12
Blast Theory. *Rider Spoke*. The induction.
Copyright Blast Theory.

but as you ride this feeling will start to change. Relax, don't forget to breathe both in and out and find somewhere that you like, it might be near a particular building or road junction, it might be near a mark on a wall or a reflection in a window. When you have found somewhere you like, give yourself a name and describe yourself.

Riders could only record their description in "valid" locations, that is, sites that appealed to them, but that were also "empty," in the sense that they did not contain another message since every recorded message in *Rider Spoke* had to occupy a distinct location in the city. Following are some examples of how players replied to this instruction:

Hello my name is Kirsten; I am quite ordinary . . . a bit lonely at the moment, but that's ok.

My name is Emily and I can't describe myself because I don't know how.

Hello. I'm brunette. I'm Hispanic. I like riding bicycles. And I'm happy.

Participants then listened to a series of further questions asking them to look for hiding places in which to record their answers or listen to the stories of others (see figures 4.13 and 4.14). The questions, authored by the artists, asked them to reflect on significant, evocative, or hilarious moments of their life while engaging with the city through which they cycled. Typically, they might be told to look for a particular place: "I want you to look for a flat or a house and find a window that you would want to go through. I want you to stare into that window and tell me what you see and tell me why you want to go through that window." The following reply to this assignment shows how this particular participant projected himself or herself into the world inside the flat and beyond: "It's a window in somebody's flat and you can't see in it very well because the blinds are drawn, but there's little cracks, and I want to go in and I want to see what's on the other side." Or riders might be asked to identify meaningful locations, which often prompted them to reveal private details of their own lives: "This is roughly the spot where I should have split up with my first serious boyfriend but I chose not to. And it just made me think that perhaps you can never be really sure that you make the right choice at the time and you don't realize until later on that there are implications on any decisions you make." Although these kinds of instructions prompted participants to use details from the physical world around

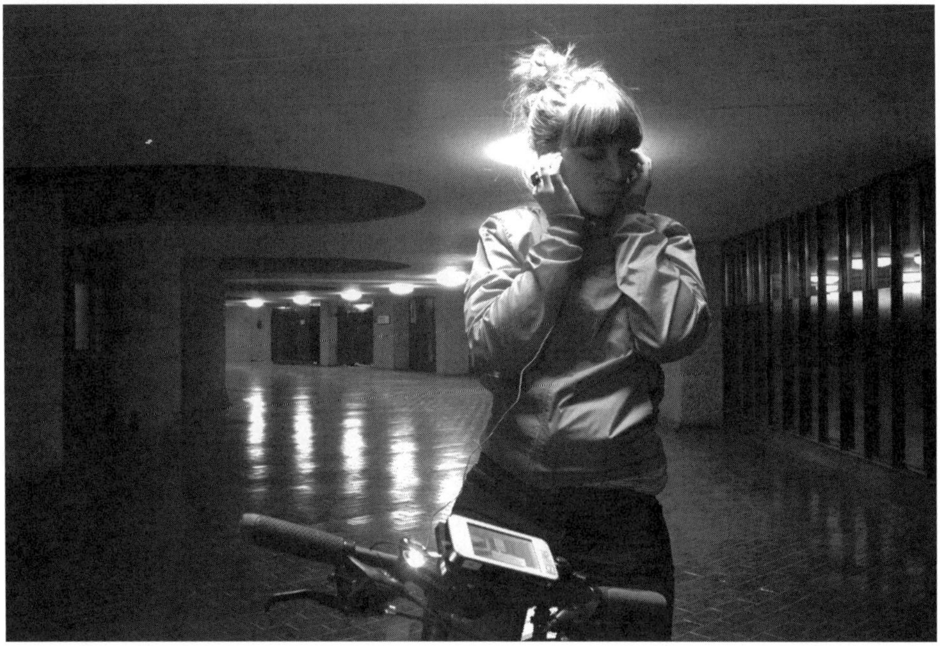

Figure 4.13
Blast Theory. *Rider Spoke.* Participant listening to audio content.
Copyright Blast Theory.

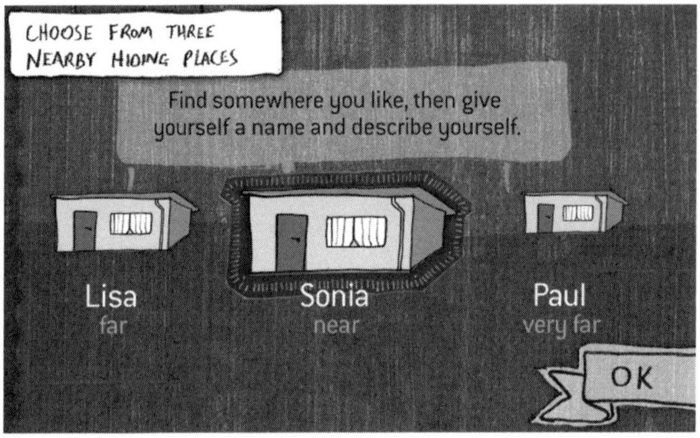

Figure 4.14
Blast Theory. *Rider Spoke*. Searching the interface for recordings.
Copyright Blast Theory.

them to start reflecting about themselves, others turned them into voyeurs—detectives, even—required to transform everyday life occurrences into spectacles for future participants. The instruction prompting this mode of observation said: "Will you be a voyeur for me? Please will you cycle back towards a busier place and look for someone who catches your eye. Stay back, don't intrude; just watch them and follow them. Think about who they might be and where they might be going as you track them. Don't be afraid to make it all up. Then, stop your bike, let them go and tell me about them."

Players often fictionalized or even identified with what they saw, as in these examples offered by the two players:

> I'm watching a man and his son and they are walking back and they are holding a toy and I think they are going home to play with it because I think it's that little boy's birthday.
> There's a girl. She doesn't look anything like me. She's got long brown hair and she's wearing a wavy white skirt. I think she might be the same age as me. I think she might be a lot like me. She is walking on her own, walking along the seafront. She looks like she really wanted to be with someone else. Maybe she tried to call people to come out for a walk with her and this is kind of like a slightly defiant "I am going for a walk on my own. To hell with everyone else!" feeling that she's got. I think she's got quite a soft character. She is quite blameless. She hasn't done much wrong in her life and she's probably got quite a lot of romantic ideals. It's just sort of the way her hair is quite floaty and her dress is quite floaty too. But I think she's quite down to earth kind of a creature.

Other questions were designed to elicit intimate, sometimes even confessional, stories, and encouraged riders to seek out locations that might have special meaning, and reflect on personal issues, for example:

> Please will you tell me about your father. You might want to pick a particular time in your father's life or in your life. Freeze that moment and tell me about your dad: what they looked like, how they spoke and what they meant to you. And while you think about this I want you to find a place in the city that your father would like. Once you've found it stop there and record your message about your father at that moment in time.

To which a player replied:

> I'm at St John's the Baptist church in Hoxton and I chose this place because I thought my father would like it, as it's a bit calm and relaxing and I admire my father because he's a very intelligent and wise person and he's very calm and in fact he's just had a birthday which I couldn't attend because of work commitments and I feel a bit sorry about that and I hope that I can make up for it by visiting him his next years birthday again, and hence I'm choosing this place in a kind off attempt to make up for it.

When the experience was near its end, riders were given one final task, to make and record a promise, which often prompted them to disclose a personal vulnerability, as in the case of the two riders cited here:

> My promise is going to be that I am going to let myself dream a bit more and I am going to let myself be a bit happier and I am going to pay a bit more attention to what's going on and that's my promise.
>
> I promise to tell people when something is wrong.

After the promise, players were asked to return to base, where the device was removed from their bike and their deposit returned.

Throughout *Rider Spoke*, interaction with the device was kept simple so as to be safe and not interfere with the distinctive subjective experience of cycling through the city at dusk. Riders interacted with the interface through a single-earpiece headphone with inbuilt microphone and a simple touch-screen interface. Interaction was through a touch-screen display that allowed them to choose what to do next. They could select and listen to messages, or record a message using an interface, based on the metaphor of houses as hiding places, that indicated whether the current location was available for leaving a recording or, if in searching mode, which recordings made by others were available to listen to from the current location (see figure 4.14). Like in *Day of the Figurines*, the cartoon-like quality of the interface design was intended to generate familiarity. Hiding places, in which memories were deposited, combined the properties of the physical location and the electronic location as reported by the handheld device, which used information about nearby Wi-Fi access points to determine the location of each participant (essentially, each valid location was associated with its own "Wi-Fi fingerprint," that is, a unique list of Wi-Fi access points that were visible at this location). Each city in which *Rider Spoke* took place thus became a mixed reality palimpsest, a user-generated repository of ephemeral memories in which a variety of individual voices, captured at specific locations, became, in the voice of one reviewer, "enmeshed in a suspended web of whispered secrets" (Williams 2009).

"Meandering" had constituted a significant design goal (Adams et al. 2007, 3), as it was assumed that a spatial meandering would afford a mental meandering leading participants to move from the present to the past and, toward the end of the piece, to the future. Like in Heiner Müller's play *Quartett* (1981), which takes place in a drawing room *before* the French revolution and an air raid shelter *after* World War III and where the characters play themselves, each other, and for each other, players in *Rider Spoke* were either projected toward the past or catapulted into the future, stepping in and out of a variety of different roles in order to "perform" their present. Unlike in other Blast Theory works, no background scenario or overarching metanarrative was offered. Rather, this piece exposed a tension between players' presence in space and their being in time. Whereas temporally, by asking them to remember, the piece relocated them to the past, spatially, by encouraging them to cycle forward, it projected them toward the future so that their "here and now," their present, was presented to them as being at stake both literally, in the busy traffic, and ontologically, over time. Their presence in the "here and now," in other words, their present, thus became a gift for others to listen to, which, to use Marcel Mauss's well-known analysis (2000), inevitably carried the "poisonous" obligation of reciprocation. By listening to the story of the first rider that spoke, other riders would also have to speak their "present," in turn creating more "affordances" for riders to come.

Most of these affordances would imply a change in role. As in other Blast Theory works, participants not only became the unwitting performers of the piece while bystanders were often framed as their spectators, but the opposite process was also encouraged, in that riders transformed bystanders into performers by presenting their story to future riders (Adams et al. 2007, 5). Whereas other Blast Theory works were based on the players' cooperation with each other, *Rider Spoke* sought to solicit "a sense of isolation in an otherwise crowded city," thus offering a "novel twist on the concept of social expansion" (Chamberlain and Benford 2008, 9). The work thus exploited social isolation "to create a deeply personal and sometimes emotionally moving experience" that gave participants license to turn their isolation into a spectacle for others to see (57).

A set of questionnaires developed by researchers from the Mixed Reality Laboratory, completed by seventy-one players and administered using the IPerG Polling Tool, showed that the majority of participants felt self-conscious while playing *Rider Spoke* because "they were seen to be on a cycle, covered in technology and talking to themselves" (Chamberlain and Benford 2008, 23). It was also noted that riders commented on elements of "self-reflection, vulnerability, feelings of self-consciousness, embarrassment and interestingly, isolation—even though they were in a very public setting" (23). One participant for instance stated that it was "As though I was leaving my diary open for someone else to read" (29); another noted, "I often made things and characters up to make it interesting, both for me and the other listeners" (25). But interestingly, the fact that players were "performing" did not necessarily mean that they felt they were performing within an artistic context. So, 100 percent players stated that their responses were truthful and 58 percent felt that they were in a therapy session, and although 35 percent felt like they were performing, 64 percent felt they were not. Moreover, the absence of direct cooperation did not prevent participants from feeling part of a public event, but the feeling of vulnerability developed not so much with respect to the urban landscape surrounding them as to the digital soundscape they were creating, so that, for instance, one participant felt a "*disconnected intimacy with a total stranger*" (55; emphasis in original), highlighting how the piece played with isolation, but at the same time brought absent, unknown individuals closer to each other.

Another design aim consisted of the exploration of how participants' surroundings, their location, and their place in a city affected what they felt and could do during an interactive experience and how the bicycle as a "low-tech device" enabling physical and mental roaming, created "both isolation and freedom," allowing "players to define their own geographic boundaries," while making it possible for "the existing culture of the street and climate to infiltrate and become a part of the experience" (Chamberlain and Benford 2008, 10). The questionnaires showed that 70 percent of riders believed that their "location affected the messages they left" and some riders attempted to identify "dramatic" locations in which to record their answers, as can be seen by the following feedback:

> I just found places that excited me to stand in, that would be seen in a film.
> When hiding in old alleys that reminded me of what Victorian London might have looked like, I think I romanticised the answers a bit more.
> Yes—sometimes the background noise or the atmosphere of a particular place really chimed or sometimes jarred with the words I was speaking. This added a layer of richness to the testimonials. (30)

Some locations also had a negative effect on the messages that riders left, so one player, for instance, commented, "I wasn't going to speak at length about my father while standing in a grimy back alley that stank of excrement" (30). Moreover, some participants "felt as though the experience had separated them from the environment to some extent" (32) and even that the event may leave an imprint on how they would experience the same urban space in the future, as in the example of the following player: "In some ways I think it will be more of a retrospective engagement, in that next time I go to that area I will associate it with this experience, my answers and the answers of others" (33). Finally, participants declared that taking part in the piece had changed their "perception of the world around them" and that after taking part in

Rider Spoke they conceived of the city in a more "*surreal*" or *magical*" way, with one player even suggesting they felt "*hyper-aware*" (31; emphasis in original).

In his writings about confession, Michel Foucault notes that "the confession has become one of the West's most highly valued techniques for producing truth" (1978, 59) and that "it seems to us that truth, lodged in our most secret nature, 'demands' only to surface; that if it fails to do so, this is because a constraint hold it in place . . . and it can finally be articulated only at the price of a kind of liberation" (60). For Foucault, the nineteenth century altered "the scope of the confession; it needed no longer to be concerned solely with what the subject wished to hide, but with what was hidden from himself, being incapable of coming to light except gradually and through the labor of a confession in which the questioneer and the questioned each had a part to play" (66). Here, the "questioneer" is mediated by technology, which acts as an affordance toward confession. The iconography of interface, which draws attention to a "home," or, in Freudian terms a *Heim*, a familiar context, makes it safe for participants to perform the confession *as* themselves. This, however, in a Freudian twist, then generates an uncanniness, or *Unheimlichkeit*, producing an unfamiliarity or, in Brechtian terms, *Verfremdung* or alienation toward what was once known, familiar and "present."

Framing the Spectacle: Audience and Bystanders

Having introduced *Rider Spoke*, we can now return to and expand upon our earlier discussion of the roles involved in mixed reality performance. By being staged in the highly public setting of the city streets, and by establishing a distinctive social dynamic with the inhabitants of these streets, *Rider Spoke* challenges canonical notions of spectatorship. More specifically, this enables us to draw a distinction between two kinds of spectator: those who are generally aware of the details of the performance, whom we might call its *audience*, and those who are not, whom we refer to as *bystanders*. Bystanders witness a performance but are not necessarily fully aware of what is happening. In the extreme, bystanders may be completely unwitting, that is, unaware that a performance is taking place even though they are affected by it or conversely may influence its course. This notion of unwittingness was explored in detail by Jennifer Sheridan in her PhD thesis, which described a series of performances such as the Schizophrenic Cyborg, a technically mediated performance work staged in nightclubs in which some participants could send messages to a display that was worn by another who (due to the placement of the display on their body) could not directly see their content (2006). In turn, *Rider Spoke* reveals the impact of bystanders and the importance of keeping them in mind when designing a performance. In this case, unwitting bystanders who are going about their own business in the city become a resource for the rider's stories, but also enhance the rider's own sense of vulnerability and of performing in public. Thus, the very presence of bystanders, even if they are unwitting, can enhance a performance. Other inhabitants of the city streets may themselves have previously taken part in *Rider Spoke* and may therefore well be fully aware of what is taking place. In our terms, these participants are a (witting) audience to events rather than (unwitting) bystanders and may chose to affect the course of events with a greater knowledge of what is occurring. *Uncle Roy All Around You* more consciously exploited the presence of bystanders, sometimes even deliberately implying that they were part of the experience without directly saying so (e.g., in a clue that asked people to follow someone wearing a white T-shirt). This distinction between audience and bystanders, drawing from Erwin Goffman's analysis of everyday social interactions (1974), arises from the framing of a performance through a set of structures, rules, and conventions, which establish that a performance is taking place and set the rules for what is acceptable within it. Here we also draw from Richard Schechner's notion of transactions (1968) to show how these frames are negotiated over by participants.

Mixed reality performances such as *Rider Spoke* and *Uncle Roy All Around You* operate by blurring the performance frame and challenging predicted participants' transactions around it. This may introduce risks for all concerned, but can also create new opportunities, as we see with the deliberately ambiguous framing of the spectator and the bystander in *Uncle Roy All Around You*. But *Fairground: Thrill Laboratory* and *Rider Spoke* also show that mixed reality performances are further transforming the roles of their primary participants—the performers. In *Fairground: Thrill Laboratory*, we see their transformation into "actors" who consciously perform the rider experience for the benefit of spectators. In *Rider Spoke*, we see elements of performance as riders cycle through city streets, but also of authoring, as these riders are able to create the content that other participants will listen to as the piece progresses. Interactive computer games and installations have already marked the transition from people being relatively passive consumers of media to more interactive participants and potentially to authors. We have already discussed in chapter 3 how spectator interfaces constitute an important part of these processes of negotiation, as they serve to attract spectators and enable them to learn about the performance by watching the conduct of others. Here we also see how mixed reality performances are taking us further along this route, transforming participants into performers and authors capable of contributing to the design of the trajectories of their own experience.

A framework was conceived that aimed to capture the spectator experience of these kinds of game. This framework, which was focused on *Uncle Roy All Around You*, distinguished between various forms of engagement within location-based games. It defined a performer as "the primary user of an interface" and the spectators "as the secondary users who experience their interactions, either as part of a deliberate performance or accidentally as a side effect of being present in the same environment"

(Benford, Crabtree, Reeves, et al. 2006, 433). The idea of a performer as a primary user and a spectator as secondary user of a performance frame was derived from Gregory Bateson's "A Theory of Play and Fantasy" (1955). The performance frame is presented, following Goffman's frame analysis but also Richard Schechner's theory of performance and ritual, as "a set of conventions and supporting structures, physical arrangements, rituals and technologies, through which performers and spectators come to understand that a performance is taking place." The frame, as seen here, then defines a "contract" between performers and spectators (Benford, Crabtree, Reeves, et al. 2006, 433–434). Within this context, audience become "those spectators who are within the frame of the performance. They are aware that a performance is taking place and are able to (try to) interpret the performers" actions as performance" while bystanders are those "spectators who are outside of the frame. Although they may observe the performers interactions, they are not able to interpret them as a performance" (434).

Typically, mixed reality performances, such as *Uncle Roy All Around You*, and also *Rider Spoke*, often blur the performance frame by implicating and involving bystanders and making the fictional world seem more extensive than it is or by making the "real" world appear to be more extensive than it is, thus shrinking the frame of the performance. *Uncle Roy All Around You* implicates bystanders in the performance, but also employs actors at various points (e.g., in the limousine) implying that they are part of the "real" world backdrop of the city. Consequently, *Uncle Roy All Around You* involves a highly ambiguous framing of the performance in which some participants who are not directly involved are implied to be, and others who are involved are implied not to be. This ambiguous framing enhances the experience by blurring the boundary between the fictional and real, leading players to question whether they are part of a much wider conspiracy. At the same time, it introduces risks that they will engage with people, places, and objects outside of the artists' control that may be disruptive or even dangerous—risks that are managed through a process of orchestration as we discuss shortly.

This blurring of the performance frame may also occur at the level of spatial conventions. So the study, which divides the performance frame into a front stage, occupied by performers who are visible to the audience, and a backstage that is home to orchestrators who are invisible, notes that in *Uncle Roy All Around You* the street performers step between these roles, moving between front stage and backstage (Benford, Crabtree, Reeves, et al. 2006, 436). We have seen in chapter 1 that at a design level, the team aimed at "different, but connected, physical and virtual worlds, rather than a seamless augmented reality style experience" (436) and that this had been achieved by utilizing what was identified as a "general trajectory" moving primarily from the "digital domain of text clues and messages delivered alongside a digital map of the city via a PDA to increasing involvement and introduction of live performance" (428). Though the beginning of *Uncle Roy All Around You* introduced participants to the game through a digital interface, during the course of the game, participants became increasingly implicated in a series of "local" physical environments whose clues they could make sense of, however, only through the information received digitally. What made this possible was a process of orchestration that continuously reframed the spectacle so that participants could experience it from different points on the mixed reality continuum.

The blurring over these frames occurs as part of a process of negotiation identified by Schechner as a transactional. In "Six Axioms for Environmental Theater" (1968), he suggests that "traditional distinctions between art and life no longer function at the root of aesthetics" and that a new aesthetics is emergent that is built on a "system of interaction and transformation, on the ability of coherent wholes to include contradictory parts" (151). Schechner implies not only that may competing independent systems form part of the same aesthetic frame, as we have already seen in our analysis of hybrid space and time, but also that there might be a variety of frames "depending on the perspective of the spectator and the performer" (151). He then presents a transactional model of the performance event formed by three primary exchanges:

1. among performers;
2. among members of the audience;
3. between performers and audience.

Schechner also introduces four secondary transactions, although he notes that they are secondary at the time of writing but may become primary at a subsequent point in time. These are

1. among production elements (i.e., scenery, costume, lighting, sound, makeup but also film, sound, projections, etc.);
2. between production elements and performers;
3. between production elements and audience;
4. between the total production and the space in which it takes space. (155)

Interestingly, Schechner highlights the role of technicians, whom he calls "performing technicians," and finds that the traditional separation between performers and technicians had started to erode so that technicians should be considered part of the "performing group" (1968, 156). Finally, he compares western theater in which performance "is trimmed to a space" to Balinese dance, in which the performance space "is organically defined by the action" and "creates its own space, moving where it must" (157). For Schechner, in this kind of performance, as well as in many intermedia performances, spectators actively participate so that the entirety of the space may be considered a performance space (159). He notes the distinction between the creation of an environment and its negotiation: whereas the former indicates an act of transformation of space, in which "the performance in some sense engineers the arrangement and behavior of the spectators," the latter indicates an engagement in a scenic dialog with it, in which "a more fluid situation leads sometimes to the performance being controlled by spectators" (159). In discussing intermedial forms, and his work with the New Orleans Group, he then notes that they were "not interested in sightlines or in the focused ordering of space," but rather in the presentation of a performance space in which all space was "designed," so in *Victims of Duty* (1967) there were "ridges" and "valleys" of "carpeted platforms" and spectators' viewing and subsequent understanding of the piece depended entirely on where they were seated. At the opposite extreme, Schechner places found space, indicating the kind of outdoor space "that cannot be transformed" (161).

Intermedia spaces and found spaces are opposite to each other, in that the former are entirely "designed" and the latter "cannot be transformed" (Schechner 1968, 161). However, when we encounter found spaces through mixed reality environments, the found spaces, which are by definition part of the mixed reality environment, are experienced as *if* they formed part of the design of the latter. We have already discussed how, from a spatiotemporal point of view, mixed reality performance constructs hybrid spaces and times that combine digital and physical properties and occupy different points on the mixed reality continuum. We have also seen how spectator interfaces often generate affordances that produce different types of interaction and modes of participation. And we have analyzed how these hybrid spaces, times, and interfaces are experienced through series of trajectories, some of which are embedded and preauthored by artists and technologists, and some emergent and authored by participants "on the go." Now we suggest that these trajectories may be occupied in performance through different roles and that these roles can be subject to transactions between different performance elements, which are defined by processes of orchestration.

Ulrike and Eamon Compliant

Ulrike and Eamon Compliant, commissioned by the De La Warr Pavilion, took place at Palazzo Zenobio, Fondamenta del Soccorso in Venice, on the occasion of the 53rd Venice Biennale in 2009. Described as an "ambulatory work exploring subjectivity in the heart of the streets, squares and churches of Venice" (Blast Theory 2009), *Ulrike and Eamon Compliant*, which lasted approximately thirty minutes, invited participants to inhabit the stories of either one of two internationally known terrorists, Ulrike Meinhof, who belonged to the Red Army Fraction that was active in Germany in the 1970s and committed suicide in prison in 1976, and Eamon Collins, an IRA member who was active in the 1970s and 1980s, and was murdered in the late 1990s. Participants were encouraged to embrace their characters, though they could also, as did the majority of players, perform as "themselves." In either case, they were frequently given the choice as to whether to continue in the piece, or give up and so cause the "game" to end for them.

For this particular event, no bookings were taken and no tickets were issued. Participants went to Palazzo Zenobio, and, after a brief induction, were encouraged to walk down a narrow corridor and enter a room (see figure 4.15). In the antechamber of this room, they could see, pinned up to the wall, two sheets of paper upon which the biographies of Meinhof and Collins were typed. Upon entering the room, which consisted of a temporary plywood structure within which tiny holes had been drilled, participants could see a plasma screen, and a shelf upon which a phone and a pair of sunglasses had been placed. Attached directly above the shelf was a set of instructions inviting participants to ring a number. Once contact had been made, participants were asked to remain on the line, stand in the middle of the room, wear the sunglasses, and look at the screen in front of them. A person, standing still, then appeared on the screen in a live video feed (see figure 4.16).

Right next to the person appearing on the plasma screen was an empty chair (see figure 4.16), which suggested not only that participants were under some kind of surveillance, but also that another presence was somehow going to become relevant for them in the course of the performance.

Following a slightly out-of-sequence conversation, participants were then asked whether they would like to be Eamon, described as "a Customs Agent from Northern Ireland with four children," or Ulrike, "a journalist and single mother based in Berlin." They were then told to leave the room, step out of the building, turn left, and wait for another call. Following that, they were required to walk onto a bridge and wait for the phone to ring.

Then the second call (see figure 4.17) was received: "Hello, it's me. You and I are going on a walk together but before we start let's take a minute. Now stand in the middle of the bridge and turn to look at the church towers. Can you see them? If you can see them nod your head slowly."

Subsequently, participants listened to the beginning of the chosen story and were told: "As everyone else moves past you as you stand on the bridge, I would like to know how would you describe your ability to make decisions. Are you a decisive or a hesitant person, Eamon? Now please record your answer. Start by saying "My name is Eamon" and then tell me, are you a decisive or hesitant person? When you have finished your recording, hang up. I'm going to start recording now."

Participants were then asked to walk along a canal, past a pharmacy, to a second bridge, where they were told to touch their head with their free hand if they could see "the grass in the distance." Once they sat down on the bench, they were asked to take their sunglasses off. These types of requests signaled to them that they were being watched and contributed to the creation of an atmosphere of surveillance. Participants were also required, twice, to record a message. The first time, on the first bridge, they

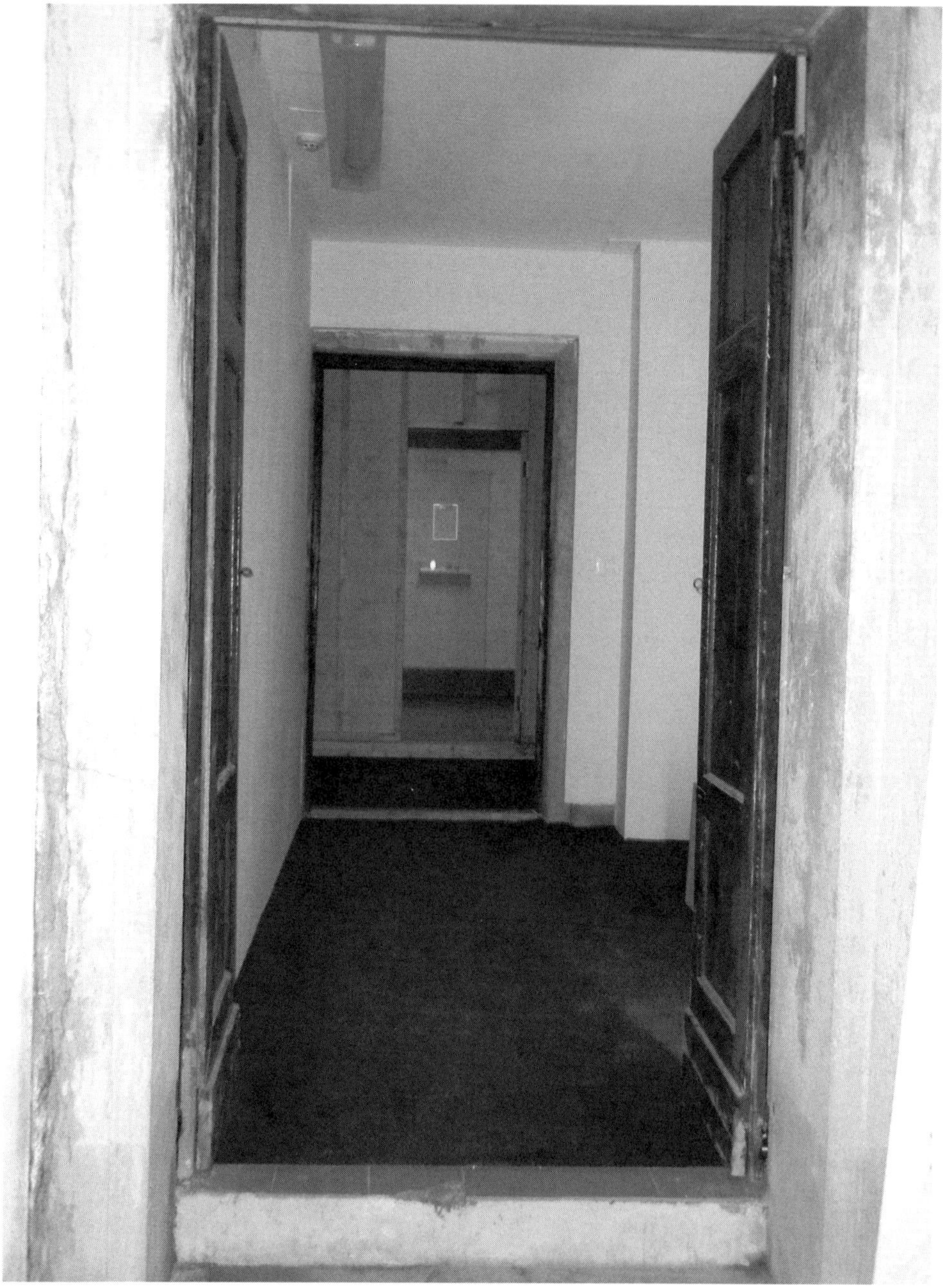

Figure 4.15
Blast Theory. *Ulrike and Eamon Compliant*. Entrance to room.
Copyright Gabriella Giannachi.

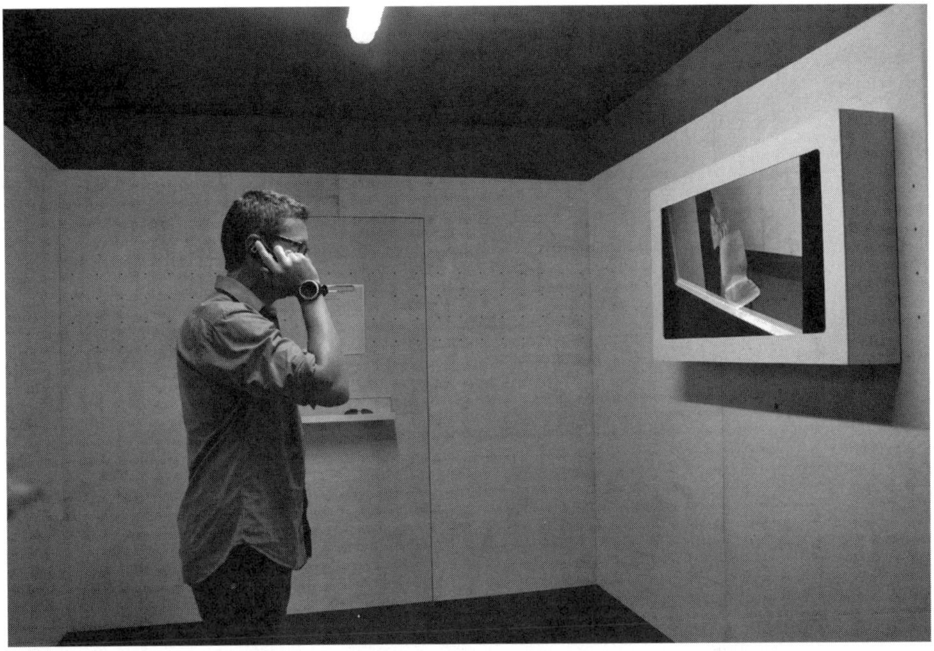

Figure 4.16
Blast Theory. *Ulrike and Eamon Compliant*. Person appearing on plasma screen in the live video feed.
Copyright Gabriella Giannachi.

were asked to say, "I am Ulrike [or Eamon, according to whichever story had been chosen]" and then indicate whether they were a decisive or hesitant person. The second time, while sitting on the bench, they were asked what they would do to help passers-by.

Participants then followed a trajectory that took them through neighboring streets, over two more bridges, down alleyways, and into a garden. During this journey, they were asked to listen to the unfolding story of Eamon's or Ulrike's life, and to learn more about their arrests, interrogations, and crimes, while also acquiring information about the disruption left behind, particularly in the lives of their own families. In the course of this process, participants' attention was twice drawn to bystanders. On one occasion, they were asked to select a passer-by and imagine following him or her home. This created a moment of potential intimacy with a complete stranger. On another occasion, they were asked to imagine how they could help passers-by: "Now you need to tell me this: as you sit looking at the windows and the alleys, what is it that you can do right now for the people around you? Don't be shy; it's a question

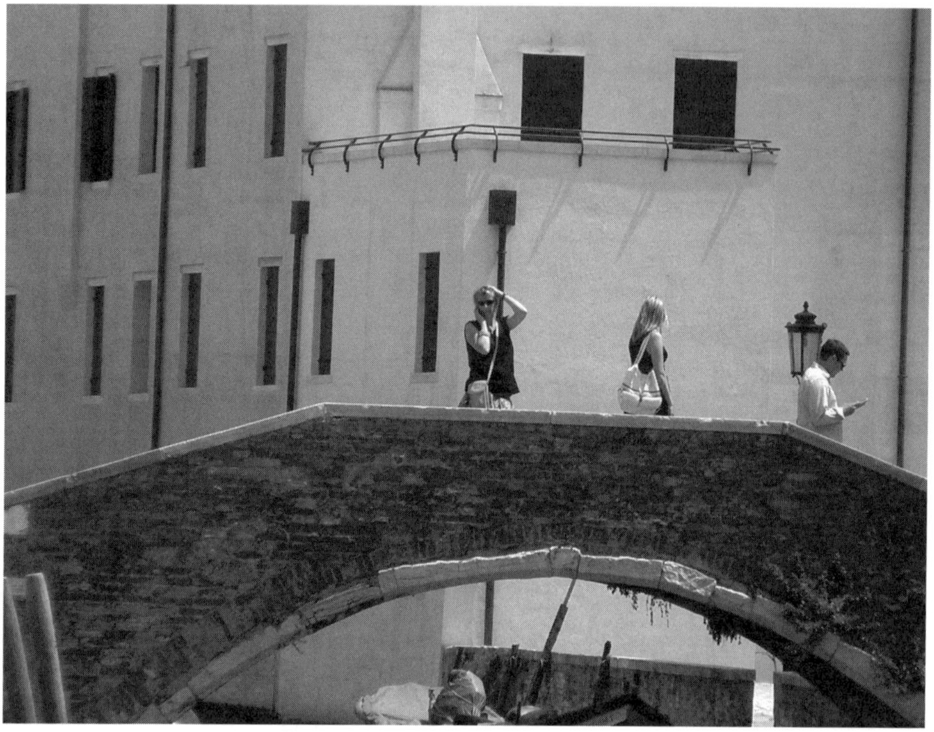

Figure 4.17
Blast Theory. *Ulrike and Eamon Compliant.* Participant standing on bridge and responding to instruction received via the phone call.
Copyright Gabriella Giannachi.

we all have to answer from time to time. And today, here on this bench, it's your turn. What can you do for the people around you? When you have finished your recording, hang up. There's no rush at all. I'm going to start recording now."

Participants were then taken past a square to a narrow, deserted, and dirty alleyway leading to a canal. Here they were asked whether they could make one final commitment. If they chose to continue in their game, they were guided to the abandoned Ludovico Church, where an actor was waiting for them (figure 4.18). If they didn't, the game would stop at this point and a final call would tell them how disappointing it was that they had failed to take responsibility for their actions. In the Ludovico Church, they were led to a room that was an exact replica of the first room in which the game had started. However, where there was a screen in the first room, here there was a mirror. And whereas the first room contained no furniture, this room contained two chairs facing each other. In fact, this was the space that participants had seen

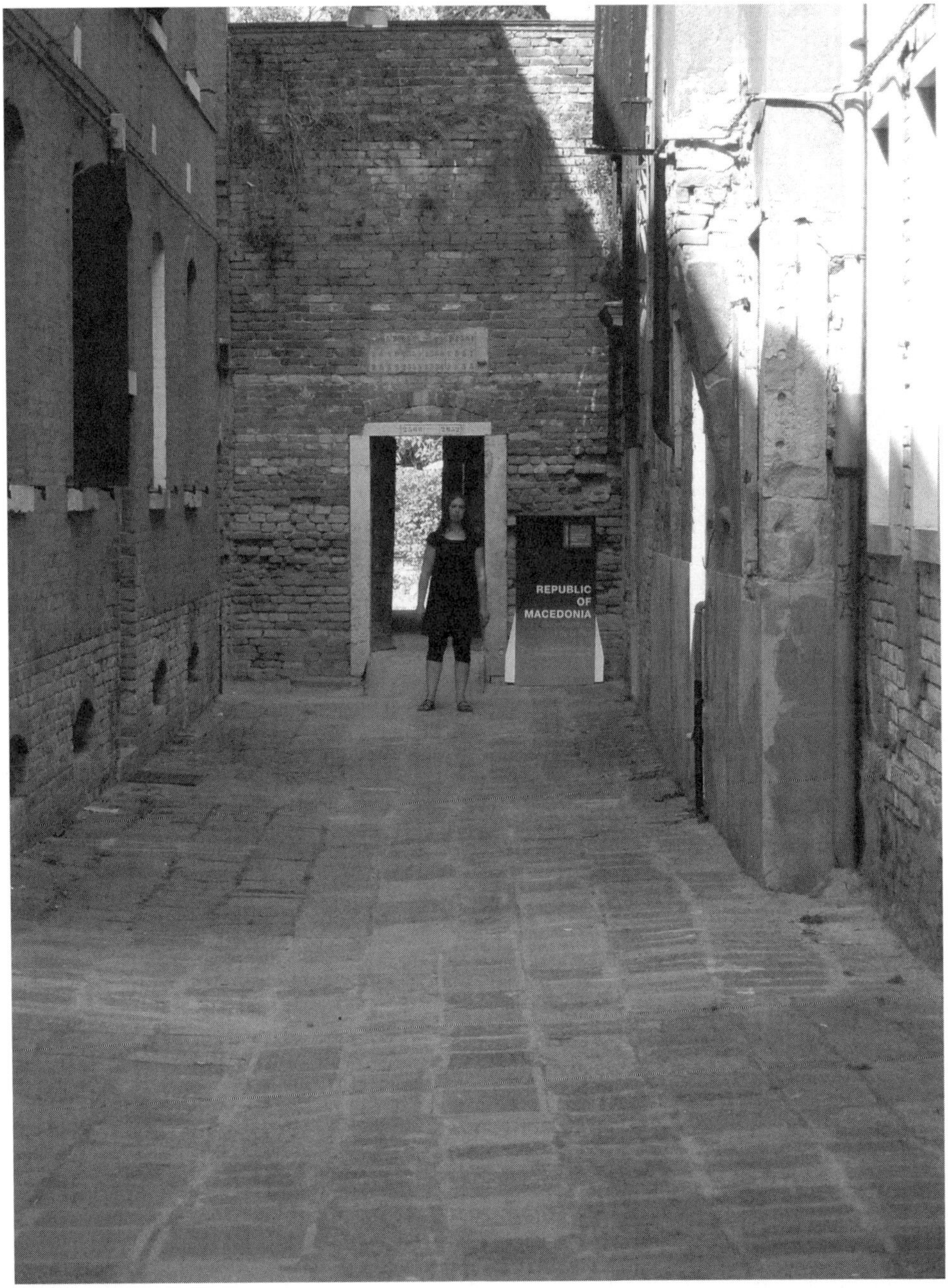

Figure 4.18

Blast Theory. *Ulrike and Eamon Compliant*. Performer waiting for the participant in front of the abandoned Ludovico Church.

Copyright Gabriella Giannachi.

reflected in the screen at the beginning of the piece. The performer, dressed in black and adopting an indeterminate, even relaxed role—more akin to a friend or counselor than an interrogator—invited the participant to sit down and conducted an interview with them. This interview acknowledged that participants may be answering as themselves or as their chosen character, though the majority of players answered as themselves. Participants could then either denounce the violent actions they had chosen to carry out or justify their choices. At the end, as they were taken out of the room, they were asked to pause at the back of the room, right behind the mirror, which so turned out to be a one-way mirror, allowing them to look into the room and see the next player being interviewed.

Like in other Blast Theory works, participants in *Ulrike and Eamon Compliant* were made to inhabit two worlds, the physical world around them and a soundscape that took them back in time by nearly half a century. The two worlds could not be more remote. The Venetian neighborhood was bursting with life, with traders' boats trafficking the busy canals, friends meeting over coffee in open-air bars, children playing football in the squares, and tourists taking photographs of picturesque bridges and churches. On the other hand, the soundscape offered information about imminent danger, betrayal of loved ones, terror, and political failure. The two worlds were both adjacent and superimposed, however, with participants continuously negotiating how to move within and between them.

Ulrike and Eamon Compliant informs our discussion of performance roles in several ways. First, unlike in previous works, participants did not create their own role but rather were required to embrace the uncomfortable persona of a real historical figure, a now-dead terrorist, who had caused the death of innocent others but also suffered a violent death themselves. In fact, the piece aimed at challenging participants to see how far they were prepared to go. Though on the one hand, by their own choice, they could become further and further immersed and implicated into the world of Ulrike Meinhof or Eamon Collins, on the other this meant that they had to finally be held responsible for their actions—a reminder perhaps that participating in a game still means that we should be held accountable for the choices we make within it.

Ulrike and Eamon Compliant highlights a common tension in the performer role: to what extent is the performer asked to play a specific character, either one that they have been given or one that they have created, versus to what extent are they performing as themselves? Role-playing games, ranging from traditional live-action role-play (LARPs) to massively multiplayer online role-playing games (MMORPGs) and more recent experiments with using mixed reality technology to create pervasive LARPs within the IPerG project (e.g., the games Prosopopeia and Kesjartemplet) (Waern 2009), lead the participant down the route of performing a specific character, whereas many of the other case studies in this book such as *Fairground: Thrill Laboratory* invite them to be themselves. Of course, these two possibilities can become blurred, with elements of "real life" filtering through to fictional characters, and maybe even vice versa. Perhaps due to its fine-grained interweaving of fictional game play with everyday life, some players of *Day of the Figurines* reported a blurring of their real selves with their fictional personas. *Ulrike and Eamon Compliant*, however, adopts a different tactic, deliberately engineering a situation in which the performers are required to accept or reject the somewhat uncomfortable character that they were made to encounter.

This work also speaks to our notion of spectatorship. Right at the end of the performance, the participants were briefly asked to become a spectator to the next player's performance, as they looked back through the one-way mirror, but in this case the next player was not aware that he or she was being observed. This constituted a form of anonymous, voyeuristic spectating. To conclude, the most striking aspect of the construction of roles in *Ulrike and Eamon Compliant* is the relationship between the participant, or performer, and the hidden actor, or orchestrator, who appears to follow them through the streets, who speaks to them over the phone and quite literally steers their performance of the piece, which leads us to our next topic: the function of trajectories in the performer, spectator, and orchestrator triangle.

Interview 8: Performing Trajectories

Box 4.2

We ask Blast Theory members Matt Adams (MA) and Nick Tandavanitj (NT), "What role does technology play in giving participants 'license' to play?"

NT: I think there are two kinds of licenses that technology affords. The first is in relation to people using technology that they're familiar with. For example people who've played *Can You See Me Now?*, or who've played third-person action games or other computer games, have licenses because they have a familiarity with technology, and they're able to draw on their own cultural and personal experience of it. The other kind of license that it might afford is when, for example in *Uncle Roy All Around You*, where we handed out PDAs to street players who were often unfamiliar with such a technology, the object becomes a pretext for doing things that participants wouldn't otherwise do, precisely because they were involved in a novel experience.

MA: Affordances of technologies have to do with the way in which the technology enables you to behave, think or do things, filtering your experience and giving you channels through which you must conduct yourself. SMS is a perfect example of a precise set of affordances, most notably that no message can exceed the 160-character limit. But other forms of technology also have limitations, and these lead to affordances that enable you to do certain types of things. A lot of the playful behaviors that we would see in our work, and that you would see in other games, are to do with the subversion or playing around,

Box 4.2 (continued)

or pushing of those limits and lots of early computer games are either exploiting or are vulnerable to simple forms of tricking, cheating, or gaming the system. So people could set up a very simple script to repeat a task over and over again, and earn themselves unlimited amounts of gold or power within a game space. Although we're not working with these types of games in such a rigid way, there are still ways of gaming our systems, and some of those are defined technologically. One of the most obvious examples in *Uncle Roy All Around You* is the anonymity of the system and the fact that you can drop in with new names very easily, and change your identity frequently, which enables you to set up multiple personalities, and play in multiple ways, for instance in an extremely destructive or mischievous way one minute and in a totally untainted way the next.

NT: *Uncle Roy All Around You* gave players a license to go into buildings and ask strangers on the street questions that they wouldn't otherwise have asked, because they have this thing in their hand that acts like an objectification of the game goal, as if to say, "I'm playing a game, here is my device."

MA: Technology has two types of power. It is magic, in that it does things that we don't quite understand. For instance in *Uncle Roy All Around You,* and latterly in *Rider Spoke*, a lot of people assumed that there was a very sophisticated form of location-based technology inside the box, and in fact there was nothing of that kind at all in *Uncle Roy All Around You*, and there was only a very limited and crude tool in *Rider Spoke.* Nevertheless, people invested the technology with a power that inscribed their experience. It's also important to remember that these technologies are often derived from the military—GPS is the most famous example—or from commercial uses. Mobile phones, for example, were tools for executives when they were first brought in. This gave them a power and an agency. Likewise, walking along London streets in 2003 with a PDA gave people a certain kind of kudos, an agency, and it made them look different. This in itself provided a platform for playfulness. People felt they had some degree of authority that the technology gave them. Quite worryingly, they felt that it was the technology that was telling them what to do. They felt that they had permission to act, to do things that they would not normally do. I know of an instance in *Uncle Roy All Around You*, where someone went into an office block, walked up to the reception and said, "I'm here to meet Uncle Roy," and the receptionist was completely baffled, and by way of explanation the player showed them the device and said, "Look, I have it on my screen here, I'm trying to find Uncle Roy's office." That shows how this player felt excused by the fact that they just made a major social *faux pas* because they had just gone to someone who was not part of the game and acted as if they were within the game.

What are the challenges of orchestration? How do you "design" orchestration, particularly in works such as Ulrike and Eamon Compliant in which the technology tends to be managed behind the scenes?

NT: *Ulrike and Eamon Compliant* is an interesting case. Rather than provide interfaces, automate things, or systematize things, we had a lot of people behind the scenes, operat-

Box 4.2 (continued)

ing the show to make it work. In general, the real challenge of orchestration is knowing where you need to pay attention to things as they unravel when a show is live. In *Ulrike and Eamon Complaint*, we lost a connection with a front of house webcam, which was taking photos of people doing the experience, and so we ended up having no photos of participants. Then we started losing walkie-talkie coverage for people who were watching participants walk around Venice. So we had no idea who people were, and the orchestrators who were watching people had no means of contacting each other. Although we had tested each of the parts of the system, without those two pieces we suddenly had no means of managing the flow of participants. We usually test as much as possible but also learn practically, often in real time. So in the design phase of *Ulrike and Eamon Compliant*, we worked out everything in advance and essentially mapped out all the roles and the responses, and how we would deal with things if something went wrong. But only when you get a real member of the public to actually experience the piece do you realize all the things they can do that you had not originally thought of. In this sense, orchestration is a playful exchange between the unpredictability of the public, the natural entropy of the city, and our intentions as artists.

MA: Ju and I play quite a big role in that orchestration process, because we often take on the role of the member of the public. We try to run through all the possible permutations of how people might behave and then think of contingencies for all the possible ways in which they could behave, deal with them, rank them in likelihood of occurrence, and set systems in place that will deal with multiple occurrences of these different variations at the same time. People don't just neatly make one misinterpretation or one alternative or tangential leap at a time—they often do it in multiple ways at a time, and you have to have a very complex set of responses.

A classic example in our location based work is: what do you do when someone gets lost, how do we know they're lost, how do we put them back on the right track, and how do we know that they're back on the right track? Nearly always in our works there will be a number of different gates through which people pass as they get increasingly lost, and we'll go from very small automated nudges to put them back on track through to more drastic forms of correcting them, through to announcing to them that they are certainly lost and they need to get back on track, through to remote human interaction, where we might ring them up and tell them they're lost and guide them back, right the way up to a direct face to face interaction, where one of us physically finds them, stops them, turns them around, and puts them back on the right track. We're also making semiotics in the ways in which we choose to do orchestration, and we try to make the semiotics sit within the work, as a kind of metamessage. It is very difficult to get the balance right, because if you fold it in too neatly, people don't register that in fact they need to change their behavior.

I find that Steve Benford's term "orchestration" is such a fantastic word to describe this process. As an artist, with a background in theater, I can say that everything we do is orchestration, practically as well as creatively and conceptually. We use two types of

Box 4.2 (continued)

orchestration: self-orchestration and directed orchestration. In *Ulrike and Eamon Compliant,* for example, we took tremendous responsibility ourselves, as the orchestrators, to take care of participants, and we would spot if they came off course and do something about it. You, as the participant, had no idea where you were going, you were not able to really judge whether you were off track or not, or at least it was hard to do that, especially in Venice which is, of course, legendary for getting people lost. We had a whole bunch of people on the street who were watching what was happening, eyeballing each participant one at a time, and observing whether they were on track, manually implementing orchestration approaches to route them back on. There was one participant in Venice who was more or less led around the entire experience by one of us, because their sense of direction got sufficiently confused, they just didn't know which way to go. Every time we tried to correct them through our orchestration systems, it didn't work, and ultimately one of us had to act as a one-on-one steward. That shows that we have to design experiences that are able to adapt to people and include dealing with people with very low levels of self-orchestration, where we have to do everything for them.

NT: This reminds me of when we were doing *Uncle Roy All Around You.* One of the first problems we came across was to do with the PDAs disconnecting from the internet. Once a PDA was disconnected, we had no way of tracking down someone, finding them, or even troubleshooting what was happening on their PDA. The first time this happened, people who were out on the streets, members of our team, would approach participants and say "I think you might be having problems, can I have a look at your PDA," at which point they would then stand next to them and go through troubleshooting of a network connection, which means going through various windows, mobile interfaces, possibly restarting the PDA in front of that person. We realized within a short time, that this constituted a break or fault in the experience. We then changed the way we approached participants so that when there was a problem we would find the person, ask them to wait where they were, walk away five steps, stand facing away from them, talk on a walkie-talkie, thus creating a sense of drama, which made the whole thing seem as if it was part of the experience.

What role does ambiguity play in this context?

MA: We always try to create a sense of mystery and ambiguity around what is happening so that in *Uncle Roy All Around You*, for instance, you didn't know whether this person approaching you was part of the game. We are also drawn to using objects by both their real and representational functions. For instance, we might choose costumes that are deliberately ambiguous as to whether they are in fact costumes. In *Rider Spoke*, we are often asked whether it's a coincidence that we're all wearing check shirts, which of course it's not. But the fact that people are uncertain when they look at us, that it might just be a coincidence that three or four people are all wearing check shirts at the same event reflects not just an uncertainty about whether they're costumes or not, but maybe even an uncer-

Box 4.2 (continued)

tainty about who's a member of the team and who is not. And that's always something that we're interested in, to put people in an uncertain relationship as to what the frame of the work is.

What is the role of participant trajectories in your work?

MA: The role of trajectories is a very important part of how we think about our work. One of the things that Ju and I do is relentlessly put ourselves in the role of the participant and drive through the work in a chronological way, taking multiple and different trajectories through it, exploring those shifts in perspective and viewpoint. Traditional drama too is about multiple viewpoints being represented on stage and the kind of tension of those viewpoints being played out. A big influence on my thinking in terms of theatre directing was David Mamet. He talks about the fact that acting is not something you can put on. But you can *do* something, and in order to do something your character needs to seek to achieve something within the scene. And so what you tend to have in the very best scenes are mutually incompatible trajectories. Mamet wouldn't use that term, but I do. Two people look at getting something different from the scene, and the scene reaches a resolution where either one or the other gets what they're trying to get, what they want, or both participants realize that they are not going to get it. This is a very powerful system of decoding good, dramatic scenes, and I worked with this technique as a director and an actor and found it very interesting. What this means in terms of our work is that the game we design are goal-orientated and so often when we set up a game it's about what the participant wants, what they should try to achieve. So in that sense, they are taking on a Mamet-style trajectory in that they are trying to get something within this context.

In most online and computer games, my achievement of my goal is entirely unrelated to whether you can achieve your goal. We can both fail, or both succeed, or one of us can fail and the other succeed, and these multiple outcomes are really all separate. There's no mutual dependency of these things. We're all interacting with a system and the system enables all of these different outcomes. The exceptions are online multiplayer first-person shooter games, where clearly one person wins at the cost of someone else. By setting up these goals, we're giving you a trajectory, which may, for instance, be: I'm trying to find Uncle Roy, I now need to assemble the things that I will need in order to find Uncle Roy. The first thing I need to know is where I am, the next thing I need to know is where Uncle Roy is, the next thing I need to know is in which direction should I head, the next thing I need to know is, is Uncle Roy moving around or is he static? And so on. So you're assembling information. The game play trajectory is about acquiring tools to enable you to complete your goal. In Monopoly, you need to get hold of property and then be able to build on it to then be able to collect rent and so on, as a sort of example in a more traditional kind of game structure. But theatrical trajectories in the David Mamet sense are all about the impossibility in life of getting exactly what we want. The most interesting drama is about the fact that you do not get what you want. The outcomes that you get

Box 4.2 (continued)

come with unexpected corollaries. They're about the nuanced complexities of how we try and attain what we seek in life.

A lot of our work is about these different trajectories all rubbing up against one another and trying to look for the kind of pollutants between these slightly more hermetic forms of trajectory and goal achievement, and the kinds of muddy, complex social and political forms of interaction that constantly thwart our ability to achieve our goals. So in *Desert Rain* you're playing a game where you need to find your target. Everyone can find their target independently. All six players can be successful within that. The next goal of that game is to get your whole team out within twenty minutes. At that point you're completely codependent. You have to work as a team. You have to help other people and your team will always be as slow as the weakest member of the team. And that is inherently quite frustrating, to walk at the pace of the slowest member of a group, to explain something to a group where the key thing about the explanation is that it will be readily comprehensible by the person who is having the most trouble understanding what is being explained.

These are difficult things and yet they are very important political things. I was informed by a political ideology in the 1980s which said: fuck the lower 20 percent of the population, let them go, they're unnecessary; the other 80 percent of the population are the people who matter and are doing things and own things and can be economically useful; and if we can just forget about those remaining 20 percent then we will have economic regeneration. And so the kind of polluting, corrosive effects of that ideology informs all three of us in terms of our thinking about the work we make and what you do about the weakest link, what you do about the slowest mover, and how you can make work that incorporates thinking about that particular question while engaging in game structures which are inherently competitive, Darwinian even, and assert a level of interpenetration between those modes of caring, of thinking, of ethics.

A License to Perform

We now revisit a second of our three core roles: that of the performer. A fundamental characteristic of computer games and other forms of interactive narrative is that by immersing the player in a fictional virtual world of some kind, they place them center stage, transforming them from being a viewer to being an active participant and ultimately to a performer. The emergence of multiplayer games, both those that involve remote online collaboration and also those that take place in local social settings, emphasize this notion of interaction as performance. Role-playing games encourage players to take on particular characters; interactive arcade games such as Dance Dance Revolution enhance the element of public spectacle. However, many of the mixed reality performances covered in this book take the element of public performance much further, deliberately framing their public participants as performers to be watched by others who are framed as spectators, at least until their turn comes to perform, and promoting conditions under which a performance might occur. This framing is perhaps at its most explicit in *Fairground: Thrill Laboratory*, which first uses an actor to demonstrate how to perform, before explicitly selecting an audience member to be cast into the same role and then attaching a highly visible explicit performance technology to them. There can be little surprise then that riders do enter a performance mode, commentating on their own experiences. The framing is different in *Rider Spoke*, in which a rider, or cyclist, is encouraged into a confessional performance in which they tell personal stories to an unseen future audience. As discussed earlier, the nature of cycling, time of day, sense of isolation and vulnerability, and not least the manner and voice of instruction, all encourage the public participant to become a performer. Clearly, the framing of the performance is as relevant to the performer role as it is to the spectator role. So what both of these experiences have in common is that, in their different ways, they grant members of the public a license to perform while also providing a supporting scaffold that makes it possible for them to be able to do this without the need for lengthy training.

Control, or lack of, over oneself is a key issue here, as was clearly seen in *Fairground: Thrill Laboratory*, where the physical nature of the ride could cause participants to lose control of their performance at certain especially intense moments. *Rider Spoke* appears to have had the same effect, as some messages were clearly very deep and genuine performances with people being moved to tears (even though they could delete or record their stories if they wished). Indeed, in contrast to the great control of the professional actor who has trained and rehearsed to play a role rather than themselves, and in parallel with the recent vogue for Reality Television, the inherent attraction of these less controlled performances may lie in their alleged "truthfulness." As we discussed previously, a notable feature of many of these experiences is that the public performers tend to play themselves rather than external characters, and even when they do play external characters, these may become blurred with their own identities over time (e.g., in *Day of the Figurines*) or be posed as a challenge to their own identity (e.g., in *Ulrike and Eamon Compliant*).

A number of strategies can be used to prompt participants to perform. We have already discussed in chapter 4 the role played by interfaces in generating affordances that lead to participation as well as performance. Other dramaturgical factors play an equally important role. For instance, we know that in happenings (Kaprow 1993, 163, as well as in games, second-person narration ("you are") tends to evoke first-person participation ("I am") (see Douglass in Harrigan and Wardrip-Fruin 2007, 135). In fact, to cite Jeremy Douglass on games, game systems describe "an inhabitable experience through assertion (second person) for the purpose of the player's participation, identification, or immersion (first person)" (135). As we know from Fluxus and happenings, the use of instructions, or indeed questions, is also particularly important. We have already seen how instruction of participants, paired with the use of second-person narration, operates in *Day of the Figurines*, *Rider Spoke*, and in *Ulrike and Eamon Compliant*, where this strategy is used not only to manage engagement and disengagement with the work, but also to steer participants between different types of roles and the trajectories they facilitate.

There are other dramaturgical factors that can be employed to prompt performance, such as role and character. We know that in role-playing games (RPGs), players emotionally identify with their own player characters—so much so that they see themselves as sole protagonists of the work. For instance, John Kim notes that "the actions of the other characters may be interesting and relevant, but they are not where the power of the story lies" so much so that "the player does not derive emotional impact primarily from the performances of others, but rather from her own performance" (Kim in Montola and Stenros 2004, 36). This tends to happen in mixed reality performances, too, except that roles are often left deliberately fluid, so that players may change them over time and quickly engage and disengage with the work. Blast Theory often merged established game strategies with others, stemming from theater and experimental performance. Hence, in *Day of the Figurines*, for instance, as well as in *Rider Spoke*, participants were encouraged to switch between roles, thus encountering and indeed even experiencing the work from the varying perspectives. In fact, as we have seen in the case of *Day of the Figurines*, participants themselves could often choose, according to the circumstances of their everyday life, which particular trajectory to use in order to perform the game.

We know that usually license to perform is given by the artistic frame in which the participant is involved. As put by Allan Kaprow, the "ritualisation" of a "mix of lifelike elements and fantasy" (1993, 185), alongside the rejection of naturalistic stage conventions, eliminates the audience and generates an atmosphere not only of participation, but of performance. So, Kaprow noted, "a performance could be simply a cluster of events of varying length in any number of places" so that "changing one's shirt in a park recreation area; walking through a city, crossing streets only with persons wearing red coats; listening for hours to a dripping faucet" could all be considered as examples of performances though the latter, because of their pervasive quality, tended, as in the case of Blast Theory's *Day of the Figurines*, to produce some sense of isolation and even indifference among participants (186). In other words, in mixed reality performance participants enter the work by means of a process of *ritualization* in which the object of ritualization is the participant's relationship with a given technology. This ritualization then allows them to be inside as well as outside of the frame of the work, empowering them to carry out a series of actions in both. Not only does this give them license to perform simultaneously in art and life, so that, for instance, in *Rider Spoke*, participants had to perform the act of cycling while also acting out the work, but also it gives them the impression that they are doing so legitimately, within the frame of the game.

Blast Theory—who, of course, often exploit this fluidity between art and life—utilizes orchestrators right from the beginning of each of its works to set up this process of ritualization, which not only creates a safe frame within which participants may perform, but also informs participants of the technology's potential affordances and presents them with a role model, something in between a character and a performer, that in turn gives them license to act both in role and as themselves. Just as in Schechner's work the act of taking one's shoes off (1973b, 46) constituted the beginning of a process of negotiation (through transactions) that led to the creation of an "agreed space" (82), a space that is "neither inside nor outside" (70), here the relinquishment of personal details represents the beginning of the process of ritualization by which the participant enters into the hybrid spatiotemporal universe that constitutes the work of art but is neither fully inside nor outside of this work. Crucially, this induction, and the subsequent monitoring or orchestration of the work, is what continuously ensures that the participant continues to feel licensed to perform while also occasionally being able to step out of one's role to look at themselves, the work, and its context, from a refreshed perspective.

To conclude, we shall again cite Schechner, who noted over forty years ago that "*audience participation takes place precisely at the point where the performance breaks down and becomes a social event*" (1973b, 40; emphasis in original) and that therefore "to encourage participation is *to demand changes in the social order*" (82; emphasis added). When entering the mixed reality performance space, the participant agrees to become part of a new social order that, precisely because of the hybrid nature of the work, can have an impact on both their performance of the artwork and their performance of everyday life.

Interview 9: Designing Orchestration in HCI

Box 4.3

We ask Martin Flintham from the Mixed Reality Laboratory, "What are orchestration tools and how do they work with respect to different interfaces?"

I define orchestration as the art of guiding or shaping an experience as it unfolds, to ensure its smooth operation and enjoyable, engaging and constant participation for players, rather than leaving them to fend for themselves and assuming that systems are operating correctly. Orchestration tools and processes, then, provide mechanisms for inspecting the different aspects of an experience (both at a system and human level), assessing whether

Box 4.3 (continued)

something is in line with the desired trajectory of the experience, and intervening if necessary.

In general orchestration tools aim to support the following high-level functions with appropriate interfaces and processes:

- *Monitoring* Reviewing what players are doing, what they have been doing in the past, and what they are likely to be doing next, alerting behind-the-scenes crew that something is happening that needs attention.
- *Intervention* Manipulating a player's experience on a number of levels to respond to problems as they occur, or to push the player along the desired trajectory.
- *Improvisation* Supplementing a player's experience with personalized content performed live, or to rapidly prototype new game mechanics or scenarios.
- *Induction* Managing the everyday work of players entering the experience, getting them up to speed with potentially unfamiliar technologies or gameplay.
- *Distributed orchestration* Observing players directly rather than solely from a control room, and sharing additional information based on observations with other members of the team—for example, appearance, manner of movement, indications of problems or confusion.

The first four functions are generally supported by control-room interfaces that hook directly into the main system for the experience—as much of an experience revolves around how players interact with the system, then inspecting the system's model of what is happening is usually primary mechanism for gaining information. As this is a large amount of information, control-room orchestration tools reveal this in a variety of ways:

- showing whether the system/experience is grossly working for all players (i.e., have there been any catastrophic failures?)
- showing the state of players currently participating—where in the experience they are, are they where they should be?
- inspecting a particular player of interest in more detail—examining his or her history of interaction with the system

Distributed orchestration evolved from an informal practice to a defined strategy involving all members of the production crew, primarily using walkie-talkies to communicate and to share information. This enables the crew to compare and contrast the actions of the players in the physical environment with their corresponding interactions with the system—for example, the system shows this player in this location receiving this content; is this actually correct? Finally, the use of walkie-talkies to broadcast information allows all members of the team to maintain a shared awareness of potential problems, even if they do not directly affect them at this immediate time.

What are the technologies and techniques that enable orchestration?

We use walkie-talkies for communication between all members of the team, and, importantly, we adopt a practiced walkie-talkie usage protocol of stating who you are and who

Box 4.3 (continued)

you are talking to. We build the system from the outset with hooks for orchestration interfaces, allowing inspection, insertion of additional content, and modification of existing state and content. We also use bespoke interfaces that reveal these data in a useful form, and additionally gather information to reveal a bigger picture—for example, displaying the location of players on a map in a location-based experience, or the history of their network connectivity to reveal if a player is regularly having network difficulties. Finally, we create a variety of interfaces for the different needs of the production crew, such as interfaces that the development team uses to inspect or maintain the system are unnecessarily detailed for a performer to use, and as a result dedicated performer interfaces are often constructed.

Early orchestration interfaces such as those used for *Uncle Roy All Around You* were implemented as desktop applications, which then moved to web-based interfaces as later systems were implemented as web applications (from *Day of the Figurines* onwards) to allow remote operation by several members of the crew, and as the main system was potentially hosted elsewhere from the venue. Desktop applications and tools were written in Java, and the web-based interfaces were dynamic web pages generated by custom controllers, often making use of AJAX. In some cases, notably *Ulrike and Eamon Compliant*, these controllers were used to generate encoded data in XML, and the web page was replaced by a Flash interface that could viewed using a PDA. Using standard web technologies meant that the interfaces could be used on a variety of different platforms and operating systems seamlessly.

What are the differences between these tools in different works and how do they operate, specifically, in Ulrike and Eamon Compliant *versus, for instance, in* Rider Spoke *and* Uncle Roy All Around You*?*

The key differences between the orchestration tools in these works were primarily driven by where and when the focus of the orchestration work took place.

In *Uncle Roy All Around You*, the use of orchestration tools focused primarily around the control room, in which a large number of centralized monitoring and intervention interfaces were situated, with street performers fanning out to provide an awareness of what was unfolding on the streets. On the whole, orchestration was used as a mechanism to keep track of what was happening to players during the experience, and to respond to unexpected events when players deviated from their expected trajectory, so in this way orchestration can be thought of as largely *reactive* rather than proactive. The orchestration tools and processes were used directly to induct players into the experience, and to regulate their progress through key points where there was a contention for a limited resource—for example, time alone in the office and the ride in the limousine.

In *Rider Spoke*, orchestration during the experience itself consisted only of the induction of players—introducing them to the experience, equipping the bicycles registering them with the system, and logging them out when they returned. The bulk of the orchestration work occurred after each day, when the recordings and data from the day's experience

Box 4.3 (continued)

from each device was uploaded and merged with that from previous days. For this, a web-based orchestration tool was used, which allowed operators to listen to and rank each new recording, and also manually resolve content conflicts (two or more recordings made at the same location on a particular day). This newly merged dataset was then downloaded to each of the devices ready for the next day. The web application was particularly important in that it allowed multiple operators to simultaneously rank the content, perhaps from a different location. In this sense, the orchestration of *Rider Spoke* was a gradual evolution of the content from day to day, with the artists retaining overall control but having the ability to "outsource" the task of ranking—again to potentially remote operators, or those with the correct language background. Over time, the orchestration interface was slightly changed to reflect this, adding instructions informing the operator of the schema with which to rank content—for example, "2. I wouldn't want to listen to this: boring, not specific, not precise, not personal, similar to many other answers."

Finally, the orchestration tools developed for *Ulrike and Eamon Compliant* were designed to support orchestration taking a primary *proactive* role in the operation of the experience, rather than the reactive monitoring role seen in *Uncle Roy All Around You.* This task again involves registering and inducting players (by way of a live phone call), but notably involves actively monitoring players on the streets, their location and their actions as well as their state within the system in order to trigger phone calls to move the experience on. Without this orchestration, the experience would not be able to operate (as opposed to *Uncle Roy All Around You* and *Rider Spoke*, in which potentially a player could largely take part without intervention by the crew). To support this, the orchestration system was designed from the outset to support an interface that could be taken out onto the streets using a networked mobile device. It is also deliberately generic, in that all of the crew use the same orchestration interface to perform all of the available roles (front of house, bridge, bench, control, and so on), allowing them to immediately change and perform actions for a different role if necessary. Furthermore, the interface was designed to distribute some of the information that performers had shared manually between themselves in previous experiences—for example, a description or photograph of each player. As this interface is primarily for use by performers, a significant amount of effort was put into making it robust and intuitive for those members of the crew who did not have detailed technical knowledge of the architecture of the system. It was implemented using Flash to give greater scope for user-interface design than a static web page.

What support do you have to provide and what are the challenges of this kind of work?

The support that I provide is somewhere between technical systems administration and monitoring, and supporting the orchestration task both directly and indirectly. Usually this takes place from some central "control room" position.

The systems I develop to make the experiences work are usually prototypes that are used in a production environment—that is they are often first "tested in anger" during

Box 4.3 (continued)

the premiere of any given experience, and so haven't undergone the testing and refinement that you'd expect from an off-the-shelf commercial software system. This leads to a lot of "edge cases"—errors that aren't found in early testing, and occur only when you throw a constant stream of public players and users at the system. To this end, a lot of my work consists of identifying and responding to these cases, or thinking of strategies for the other members of the crew to use to perform around them.

Second, my role is often one of "meta-orchestration"—listening to the shared walkie-talkie channel (if it's a live experience such as *Ulrike and Eamon Compliant*), and giving instructions of how a problem can be solved with respect to the capabilities of the system, contrasting with the performer, who has a good view of what a player is doing and therefore their immediate capabilities or immediate scenario. One of the main challenges is translating between these two areas—explaining to performers in a language that they can understand what any system problems are and how they should best react to them, and, conversely, trying to interpret anecdotal evidence of problems and trying to logically map that onto my picture of how the system has been built. Often this leads to catchall solutions: "my pda keeps disconnecting"—"turn it off and on again" as performers tend to build (perhaps superstitious) mental models of how things work—"this pda is a good one," and that doesn't fit with my scientific nature). Finally, I tend to have access to a "god view" of the system, and to some extent the players, while the performers typically have access to a subset of this information (again both in terms of actual information—I may have interfaces that show much more than the performers interface, or technical knowledge of what is happening under the hood), and the majority of my time in "control" is spent relaying this information where appropriate, or performing actions on behalf of the performer. For example, in *Uncle Roy All Around You*, this would involve relaying descriptions of players based on their photographs, and sending additional messages to players that a performer thought would be useful to steer the player to their goal.

The key challenges change as an experience tours and evolves. The first outing of an experience typically focuses on technical challenges—compare *Rider Spoke* at the Barbican: the system was very slow and was barely finished, but later gigs focused much more on the task of ranking content to create a good experience. Similarly, with *Day of the Figurines*, the first gig in Berlin was almost about exposing the cracks and limitations in the system, and once these had been resolved, looking back at the bigger picture—how is this scalable and to how many players, how can we refine the content?

With this sort of experience in particular, there are a large number of factors that are outside the control of the system designer (me)—when creating a conventional software system, the possible actions of the user are very well defined, and it is more difficult to act outside of them. Orchestration needs to take into account not only software errors (i.e., Word crashed, did we save the document in time?), but also spurious GPS data, mobile network delays and errors, batteries running out, and all manner of actions that a member

Box 4.3 (continued)

of the public unfamiliar with the technology may do—misunderstanding an instruction, moving too quickly or too slowly, getting lost. Orchestration tools need to both preempt as many of these as possible, but also allow us to react to occurrences that we haven't seen before.

What is the relationship between authoring and orchestration? And what is the relationship between preauthored materials and materials that need to be authored on the fly?

Fundamentally I define authoring and prescripting as occurring before an experience begins, and orchestration or authoring on the fly as occurring dynamically as the experience unfolds. However, it's usually not as clean-cut as this.

Authoring usually refers to content that is configured or loaded into the system before the experience begins—for example, the clue trail in *Uncle Roy All Around You*, the content that players experience in *Day of the Figurines*, the questions in *Rider Spoke*, and the phone calls and call structure in *Ulrike and Eamon Compliant*. In practice, the content is often authored on a "just in time" basis, with content being authored while the experience is running but the day before that particular content goes live—for example authoring day 5 of *Day of the Figurines* on day 4, usually because the authors did not have enough time to author it all in advance. Second, the authors tend to use an "agile" development model, albeit not deliberately, in which content is changed on a day-to-day basis based on the previous days' experience—"people struggled with this part, so we'll change it," or "we're not happy with this part, so we'll change it." The rapid iterative cycle of authoring and testing that occurs before an experience often extends well into the experience itself. However, after the first deployment of the experience, the content often remains static.

Arguably, orchestration is about responding to those edge cases that fall outside the authored scenario, and authors use orchestration in order to gain knowledge of how to adapt their content to cover these circumstances. In an ideal world, there would be no need for orchestration, as the authored content would cover every possible circumstance. As it's not an ideal world, however, orchestration perhaps falls into two categories—handling situations that will always occur—players getting lost, hardware/software failures and performing around them, and which no amount of preauthoring will ever solve, and those that orchestration provides real-world information about how to change authored content so as to minimize those events in the future.

Ulrike and Eamon Compliant requires constant orchestration in order to operate—performers observing players on the streets and triggering the appropriate phone calls. However, arguably this work is "authored," in that the performers know the script—when the player gets to a certain location, trigger the next phone call. The *actual* orchestration of the experience is responding to "outside context" events—when the player cannot be found, or the performer's PDA has disconnected/crashed and another performer, or the control room, has to perform an action on their behalf—going against the authored script.

Box 4.3 (continued)

Day of the Figurines, on the other hand, is heavily authored but not so much orchestrated—as the players are highly limited in their interactions with the system through their use of SMS and keywords, and it is a nontrivial task to inspect each player's interactions with the system (there are lots of them with about two hundred players), and furthermore the authored content unfolds at the same rate for all players (game time)—orchestration mainly consists of identifying systemic problems with the underlying system, rather than manipulating content on a one-to-one basis for each player, as is the case with location-based experiences such as *Uncle Roy All Around You* or *Ulrike and Eamon Compliant*, and taking on board lessons for the next deployment, rather than the next player.

Orchestrating Mixed Reality Performance

Throughout this book, we have seen how mixed reality performances combine rule-based computer games with scripted and improvised theatrical performance. We now consider how our third core performance role, that of orchestrators, is central to shaping participants' experiences in such performances, providing a human component to balance the automated implementation of narrative and game rules by computers. Elements of orchestration can of course be found in traditional theater, where technicians manage props, sets, lighting, and sound from behind the scenes, guided by directors and stage managers. In contemporary performance works, such as those by the Wooster Group, the Builders Association, or Forced Entertainment, performers also often operate the technology and appear center stage while additional technicians operate off-stage technology and remain off-stage. Orchestration also features in some computer games—especially early multiuser dungeons (MUDS) and the more recent descendents, online (and now pervasive) role-playing games—human "game masters" and "wizards," who are often senior members of the playing community, are responsible for dynamically defining and shaping the game as it unfolds (see also McGonigal 2007a). Orchestration in mixed reality performance is a particularly complex task that combines elements on both of these, often involving large distributed teams of technicians and actors working together to carry out multiple tasks throughout the entire duration of the performance. Ethnographic studies of *Desert Rain, Can You See Me Now, Uncle Roy All Around You, Day of the Figurines*, and *Fairground: Thrill Laboratory* (Crabtree et al. 2004; Schnädelbach et al. 2008) have repeatedly emphasized the significance of orchestration, revealing it to be a collaborative process of monitoring and intervening in an experience, supported by its own ecology of technologies. We now draw on these various studies to provide an overview of the general nature of this key role.

In their ethnographic study of *Desert Rain*, Dirk vom Lehn and colleagues at Kings College London highlighted three fundamental aspects of orchestration work that were seen to be vital to maintaining the overall timing and flow of the experience: covertly *monitoring* players' progress; *communicating* in order to decide whether and how to respond to a variety of circumstances (from players getting lost, players progressing too rapidly, to technical failures); and *intervening* to resolve these issues. They showed how orchestration work involved a team of five actors and technicians who worked closely together in order to deal with both the performative and technical aspects of the experience:

Orchestrator 1 (antechamber): meet and brief the players.
Orchestrators 2 and 3 (behind the rain curtains): lead players to cubicles and zip them in. Observe players from behind the rain curtains, cross curtains at the correct moment and hand over swipe card. Lead players to the corridor of sand.
Orchestrator 4 (control center): monitor players' progress through the virtual world and their conversations. Talk to players over audio.
Orchestrator 5 (control center): run, control, and monitor software. Help steer players' avatars using the keyboards. (Koleva et al. 2001, 41)

This team coordinated its actions verbally as well as through a signaling system that used flashlights for communication between a control center and an area behind the six projectors. Boriana Koleva and her colleagues noted that "in order to establish the illusion of traversal," Blast Theory conducted "carefully designed actions that led participants in and out of the different phases of the performance." This included moments in which the company deliberately encouraged the audience "to suspend disbelief." Their study identified three broad types of intervention:

1. Off-face interventions, "conducted by the orchestrator at the control center to advise players about actions in the virtual world." These were usually conducted "in character"; and included attempts to influence players' movements on the footpad, often to encourage players to help each other.
2. Virtual interventions, carried out from the control room through an arrow key on the computer. Players were not aware of the manipulations that would move a player toward or sometimes away from a particular target.
3. Face to face interventions, which were (rarely) carried out by orchestrators who approached the player's cubicle directly to give advice using the footpad. (Koleva et al. 2001, 44)

This study also described how orchestration work relied on various interfaces from six monitors located in the control area that enabled the team to monitor and steer each avatar's movement through the virtual world, to the rain curtains that, due to their asymmetric transparency, enabled orchestrators to covertly observe players on their footpads without being seen in return (see figure 4.19).

Crabtree and his colleagues' study of *Can You See Me Now?* focused on the extensive orchestration work that was required to cope with the effects of the limited coverage

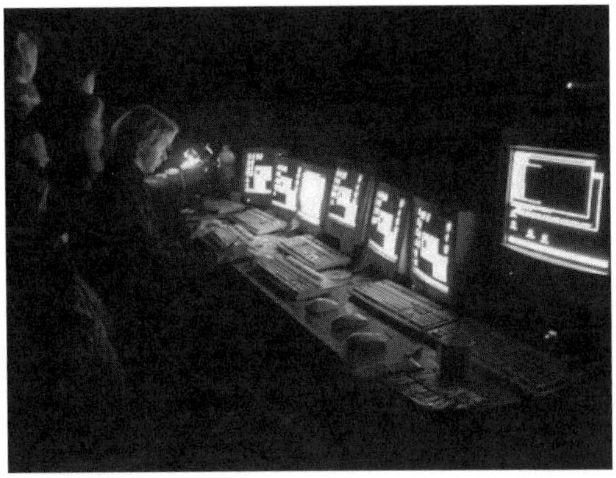

Figure 4.19
Desert Rain. An orchestrator in the control room monitors the six players' avatars via a bank of monitors.
Copyright Blast Theory.

of Wi-Fi and GPS—the "seams" in the technical infrastructure that we discussed earlier. In this case, a team in a central control room (see figure 4.20) used many different interfaces to monitor the positions and connection status of runners on the street, the activities of online players, and also the performance of the game server and supporting infrastructure. Walkie-talkie communication with the distant runners enabled them to discuss their problems as they battled with the technologies on the streets—for example, for advising them on where to go in the city in order to get reconnected. Finally, technicians would sometimes be sent to the streets in order to locate runners and help them deal with especially complex problems face to face.

A subsequent study of *Uncle Roy All Around You* highlighted the additional challenges of managing public participants as they ventured forth into the city streets. As noted earlier, though the ambiguous framing of this experience gave players a license to explore the city and interact with its contents, including bystanders, this also raised new challenges in ensuring that they remained safely on track and did not veer too far from the planned—canonical—trajectory through the experience. This challenge was met by an extensive orchestration team of actors and technicians, distributed across the game zone, who coordinated their activities with those of the players through specialized game management interfaces. In this case, there were two front-of-house orchestrators admitting the audience, briefing them and collecting their data; two orchestrators ensuring the running to schedule of the office, car, and phone booth; and three roving orchestrators deployed on the streets to ensure that players experiencing difficulties were brought back to the game. A game operator was also housed in a central control room to monitor players' interactions with the game and the

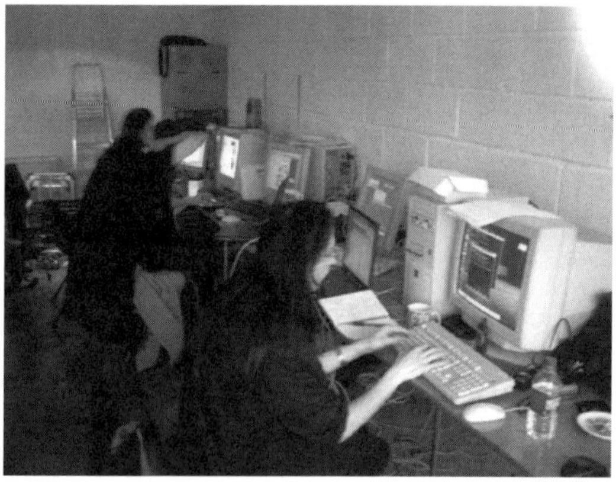

Figure 4.20
The Control Room for the first ever performance of *Can You See Me Now?* showing at least nine different interface displays being used to monitor runners, online players, game servers, GPS, and Wi-Fi.

software, being able to intervene virtually, for instance, by changing the player's game state and sending them improvised text messages. The control room orchestrator used the dedicated interface (see figure 4.21) to track players through the experience. This displays a map of the game environment overlaid with the last reported locations of the current street players. The pop-up window on the right shows a list of current players alongside their histories of periods of network connection (green shading) and disconnection (red shading); a further control enables this operator to change the players' game status or even to improvise text messages to a player that are sent as if in the voice of the game. The study paid particular attention to the challenges of orchestrating the experience of street players as they tried to navigate the city, often getting lost and "*trawling the streets*" to establish a sense of their physical topography and their relation to one another" (Benford, Crabtree, Reeves, et al. 2006, 430; emphasis in original), and also as they experienced frequent disconnections from the game server and hence online players. The first difficulty of orchestrators working the streets in *Uncle Roy All Around You* was to recognize players. This was often achieved through the collaboration between street orchestrators, control, and front of house. If orchestrators lost a player, for instance, they would have had to trace their expected "pathway" through the game zone. This entailed walking and scanning the streets the player is expected to be on. This notion of "an expected pathway" (Benford, Crabtree, Reeves, et al. 2006, 430; Crabtree and Rodden 2007, 487) partly arose from orchestrators' repeated experience of the game, during which they would build up knowledge of

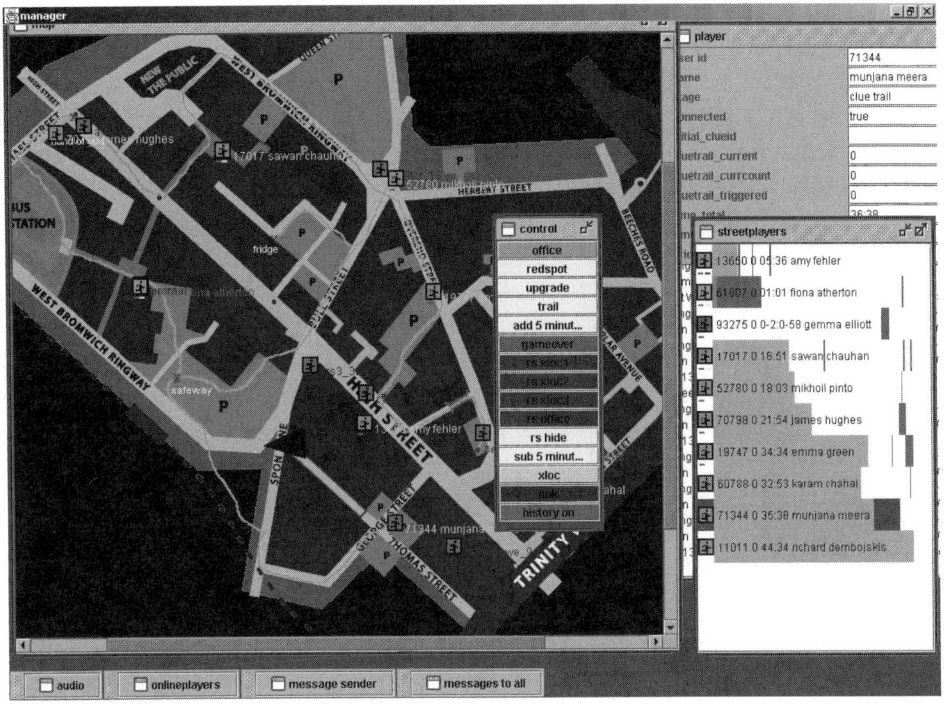

Figure 4.21

Blast Theory. *Uncle Roy All Around You*. Interface for game orchestration used in the control room. Copyright Blast Theory.

players' typical trajectories through a game. However, it was also explicitly built into the structure of the game through the "clue trial." During the three initial implementations of the game in different cities, the designers evolved an approach to creating the clue trial that began with them identifying a few ideal routes from the host organization to the office and designing clue trial to "funnel players along these routes" (Benford, Crabtree, Reeves, et al. 2006, 430). Potential pathways were considered if a player was not where he or she should be; crucial aspects of orchestration in this context consisted of recognizing confused players and shadowing players. When players were not recognized on the streets, they were sometimes recognized through digital traces.

Ulrike and Eamon Compliant raised similar concerns to *Uncle Roy All Around You* as it sent the public out into the streets of a city. In this case, there were four street orchestrators and front-of-house staff responsible for inducting participants. The street orchestrators had a PDA that allowed them to follow players at all times from four strategic points along the game trajectory, the first one near the first bridge, the second one near the second bridge, the third one near the square, and the last one on a bridge near the Ludovico Church. Mapped on the participants' trajectory through the work were areas that triggered sequences of codes and calls. Major orchestration was needed to ensure that the work run smoothly. The orchestrators had to ensure that the participants did not get lost and that the running order of their experience was broadly correct. Orchestrators tried to remain invisible to participants, though they walked past them on at least one occasion. Generally positioned in strategic places (see figures 4.22 and 4.23), they disappeared against the busy background of everyday Venetian life, looking like tourists or even locals, simply passing by, waiting for friends, hanging out at a bar, or using their mobile phones.

There were two distinct aspects of orchestration work in *Day of the Figurines*. First, a small team (typically two people) were present at the venue for ten hours each day during playing time in order to register players and work the table. This orchestration

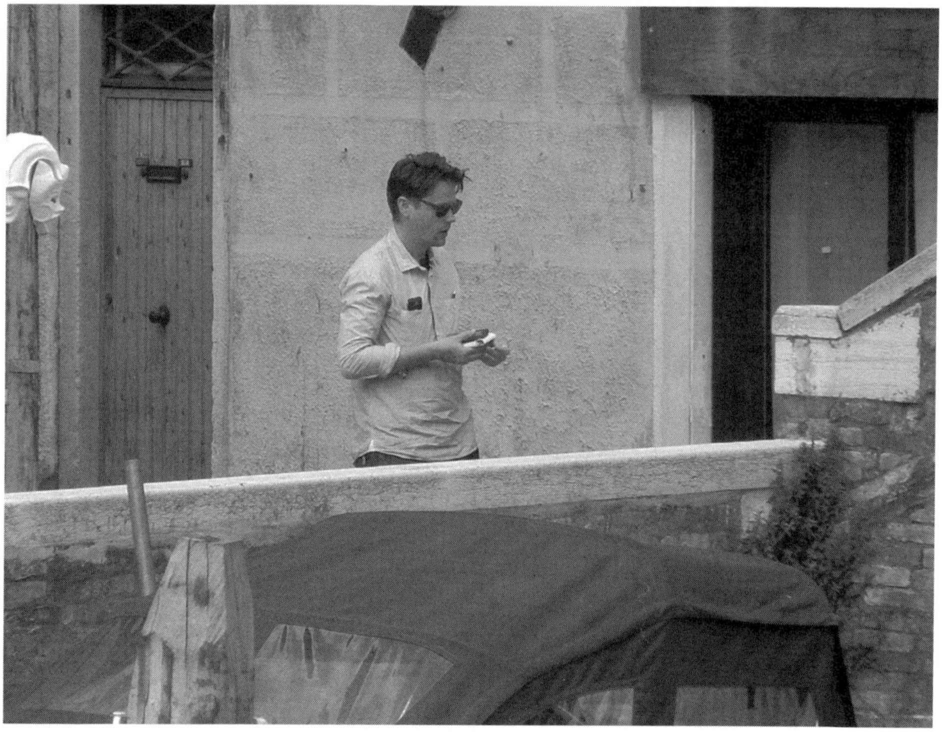

Figure 4.22
Blast Theory. *Ulrike and Eamon Compliant.* Orchestrator by a boat near second bridge. Copyright Gabriella Giannachi.

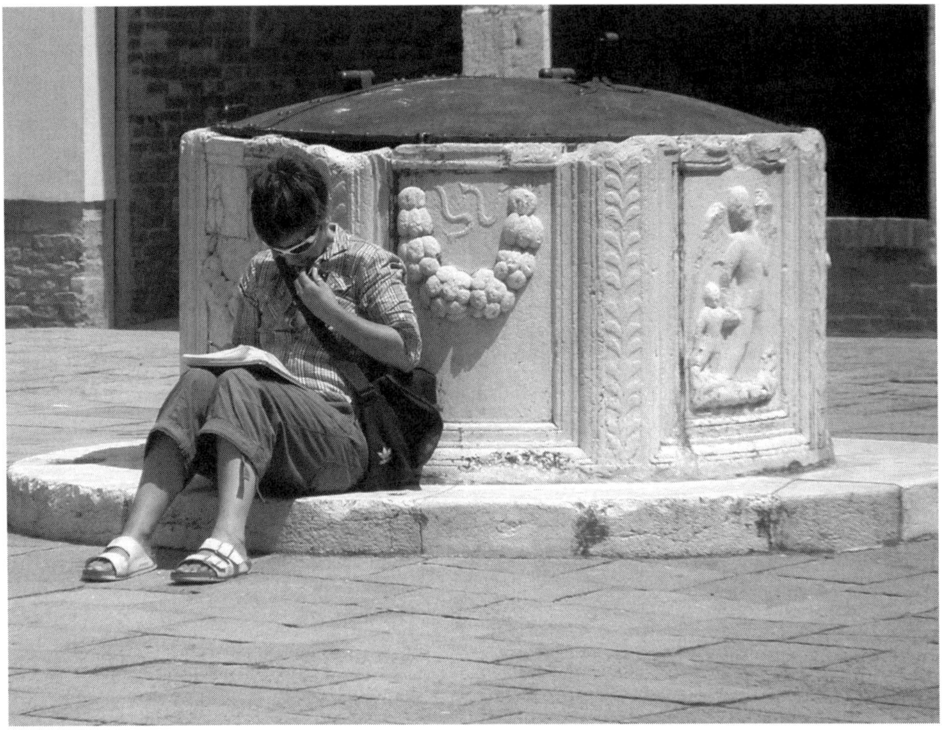

Figure 4.23
Blast Theory. *Ulrike and Eamon Compliant.* Orchestrator by a well in the square.
Copyright Gabriella Giannachi.

work involved engaging potential players who were initially attracted by the spectator interface; helping them register their figurine's details using a local web terminal; placing their figurine on the table (see figure 4.24), briefing them, and ensuring that their phone was receiving game messages; and finally performing the hourly update of the figurines' positions on the table. The second key aspect of orchestration work involved managing the action in the virtual world as the game unfolded. This made use of a series of web-based interfaces that enabled a game master, who might be located anywhere with a web connection, to monitor key online actions, including: joining and leaving the game, being immobilized, being on missions, receiving error messages, and sending help requests. This interface displayed various tables and graphs that summarized the overall state of the game and enabled the orchestrator to quickly identify problem players, while also allowing them to drill down into an individual player's history of messages (see figure 4.25). This orchestrator could also intervene by

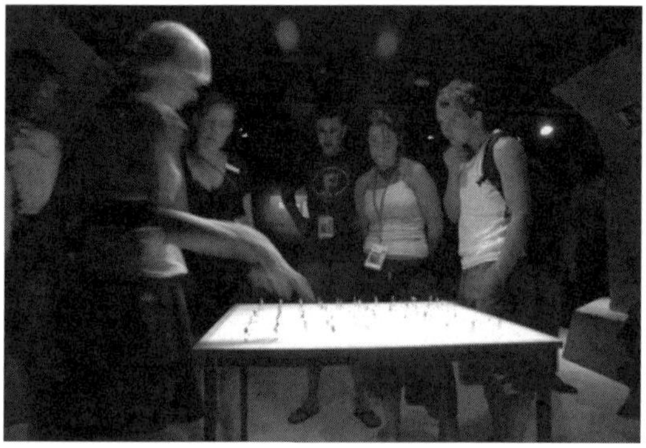

Figure 4.24
Blast Theory. *Day of the Figurines*. Blast Theory orchestration staff inducting the audience at the beginning of the game.

sending the player hand-crafted messages, manually triggering game actions, or even playing as the player for a while.

The study of *Fairground: Thrill Laboratory* highlighted the extensive nature of orchestration work that spanned hosting the experience, operating the ride, and managing the thrill technology, with the team of orchestrators widely distributed throughout the entire site and communicating using walkie-talkies. Key here was the way in which the use of the telemetry system provided an additional channel for orchestration work (in addition to its primary purpose as part of the spectator interface), enabling the team to monitor riders' responses, mainly through the audio and video streams, but also occasionally involving discussions of their heart rate. However, as we saw with the example of the rider asking for the ride to be stopped, this dual use of the audio channel for public performance and orchestration could potentially be problematic, revealing sensitive issues that might normally be dealt with behind the scenes.

Between them these various studies have repeatedly highlighted the importance and complexity of orchestration in mixed reality performance (see also Flintham 2007). In terms of our discussion of performance roles, they lead us to the following conclusions:

• As we saw with both the performer and spectator roles, the orchestrator role is actually an umbrella term for many specialist subroles. These appear to fall into two general classes: technicians or operators who manage the technologies (servers, networks, interfaces, GPS, rides, and so forth) and actors who engage the public at key points, such as giving initial briefings or improvising interventions to help resolve difficulties.

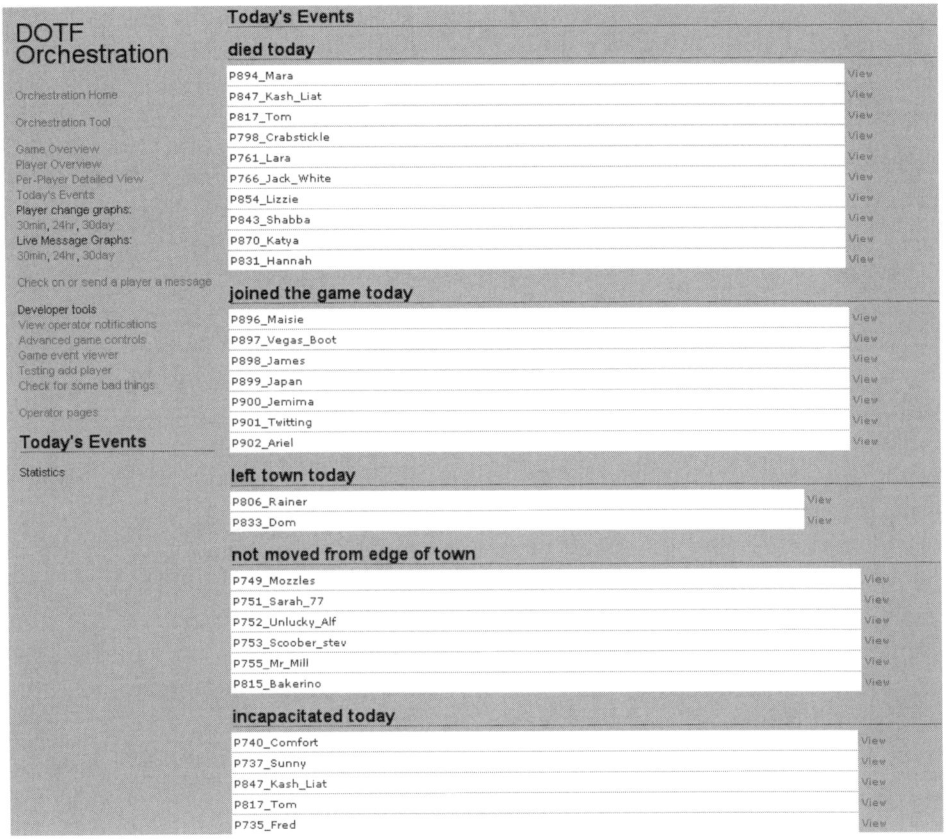

Figure 4.25

Screenshot of part of the *Day the Figurines* web-based orchestration interface showing different lists of players who might warrant further investigation.

Copyright MRL.

Although they are "performing," these actors are really playing the visible public face of the orchestration role, stepping out from behind the scenes to briefly reveal themselves "front stage" before disappearing again. Their role remains one facilitating members of the public to themselves become the primary performers.

• Orchestration work involves a complex variety of tasks, many of which are dependent on the details of a particular performance. That said, vom Lehn's broad division into monitoring, communicating, and intervening (in Koleva, et al. 2001) does appear to provide a high-level breakdown of these tasks that holds across the performances that we have discussed. These tasks need to be supported by specialized interfaces, the design of which is essential to the performance.

• These are nearly always collaborative tasks, requiring coordination among various team members who are often physically distributed. Supporting this distributed collaboration is one of the most difficult challenges for orchestration work and again, requires support through carefully designed technologies.

This discussion of orchestration leads us to two more general points. A core dynamic of mixed reality performance is the way in which interactive (often game-like) structures are combined with scripted and improvised live performance. Rather than being a "bolt-on" activity that tidies up the odd problem, orchestration is in fact an essential human activity required to balance the computer's coding of the "rules of interaction." These kinds of mixed reality performances would simply be unable to function without human orchestrators, just as they could not function without their computer software. To take this a stage further, interactivity and orchestration can be seen as two opposing, but complementary, components in mixed reality performance. Interactivity enables participants to diverge from the scripted track to define their own route through an experience. Orchestration is the counterforce that monitors this divergence and pushes them back toward the scripted route if it threatens to become too great. Artists then need to balance the interactivity and orchestration to create a performance that successfully blends scripted narrative with improvised decision making. This is a core issue, and one that we will return to later in this book when discussing the divergence and convergence of canonical and participant trajectories. Second, the balance between human orchestration and coded rules of interaction may shift during the lifetime of a work. For example, the first public test of *Day of the Figurines* involved a "Wizard of Oz" approach in which there were relatively few hard-coded game rules and in which the orchestration team was heavily involved in improvising responses to players. Subsequent performances coded many of their responses into software, freeing up their time to engage with higher-level orchestration tasks. Orchestration may therefore usefully support the early design and iterative tests of a performance when the rules of interaction are still open and emerging.

Trajectories through an Ecology of Roles

Earlier in this chapter, we introduced the idea that mixed reality performance involves three broad classes of role: performers, spectators, and orchestrators. Although this basic distinction provided a useful departure point for our discussion, it should be clear by now that the structure of roles in mixed reality performance needs to be thought of in more complex terms than this, so we propose to break our three core roles into at least a further level of detail.

We have argued that the nature of the spectator role is largely determined by whether they are inside or outside of the performance frame, leading to a general division into audience (inside the frame) and bystanders (outside of the frame), both of whom need to be addressed by the design of a mixed reality performance. The orchestrator role can usefully be divided into operators, the technicians who are responsible for controlling technologies from behind the scenes, versus actors, who are responsible for directly engaging the public at various key moments. Though conventional theater might not consider front-of-house staff responsible for ticketing and issuing equipment to be actors in the traditional sense, it is interesting to note that these roles are often taken on by professional actors in Blast Theory's works and are carefully scripted and rehearsed. We can conclude that even apparently mundane interactions with participants are vital to their proper engagement with the experience and have to be meticulously acted out. The performer role is perhaps harder to break down in a general way. One division to be seen in many works is a general distinction between "online" and "street" (or perhaps more generally "physical world") performers (typically called "players" in these works), who assume different perspective as part of a collaborative enterprise. Another important distinction we have seen involves whether these performers are playing themselves or are given (or create) a fictional character.

However, such general roles remain abstractions that capture only broad features of mixed reality performance rather than the subtle nuances of individual works. At the finest level of detail, each individual performance establishes its own specific roles that are associated with particular actions and capabilities such as the "online players" and "street players" of *Uncle Roy All Around You* or the "riders" of *Fairground: Thrill Laboratory*, or specific technical orchestration roles within all of these works. In other words, as with the structure of space, time and interfaces before, each mixed reality performance defines its own ecology of roles that fit together as part of a larger hybrid structure. It is also beneficial to think of there being trajectories through these ecologies as different participants move from one role to another during a performance. One common trajectory is from bystander to spectator or audience to performer and then back to audience or spectator (and possibly to bystander). People may initially be unaware of the nature of the performance (bystander), but then enter the performance frame to become a witting audience member, watching as others take their turn before them. Next they may become performers to others as their turns arrive, and finally, they move back to being audience members when their turns finish. Such a trajectory is plainly evident in *Fairground: Thrill Laboratory* and can be seen to some extent in most other performances we have described, and also more generally in people's trajectories through interactive installations in museums and galleries. A second common trajectory is from operator to actor and back again as part of orchestration work, as seen in *Desert Rain* when orchestrators pass through the curtain and back again or in *Uncle Roy All Around You* as they reveal themselves to engage with a street player on the city streets before disengaging and fading into the background again to resume a technical role. There is perhaps another far longer-term sense in which we can see trajectories between roles. The whole evolution of mixed reality performance can be seen as involving a fundamental shifting of roles, at least when compared to those that are evident in conventional theater. Thus the public moves from being audience to being performers (as well as audience to each others' performance), while—to make room for this—traditional actors step away from center stage to adopt an orchestration role that increasingly blurs acting with technical operation. As a final note, events such as *Fairground: Thrill Laboratory*'s Bucking Bronco also hint at the possibilities for technical operators to fall under the spotlight, suggesting that their trajectory could even be toward a more visible performance role.

Conclusion

Informed by a series of case studies, the last four chapters have undertaken an extensive exploration of the structure of mixed reality performance. We have applied the four lenses of space, time, interfaces, and roles, one at a time, to view this structure at a fine level of detail. Though we have used each case study to focus on a specific issue or topic within one of these chapters, it is generally true to say that each of our examples involves spatial, temporal, interface, and role structures that work together as an integrated whole. Thus, as *Day of the Figurines* illustrates the complexities of temporal structure, it also involves spatial, interface, and role structures. So what can we conclude from putting mixed reality performance under the microscope in this way? One obvious conclusion is that these new kinds of performances are complex, "mashing up" many different approaches and technologies to create a structure that might best be described in terms of multiple hybrid ecologies. In large part, they defy previous attempts to express the structure of interactive experience. For example, notions of virtual reality, augmented reality, ubiquity, or even mixed reality from computer science and HCI fail to express the hybrid nature of their spatial structures, let alone deal with the further issues of time, interface, and role. Moreover, though our own apparently neat division into space, time, interfaces, and roles gives a tractable approach to presenting and analyzing our case studies, these aspects are hardly so clearly separated; instead many spaces, times, interfaces, and roles connect together to form a larger, more complex hybrid performance ecology, rather than existing as four separate ecologies. In short, mixed reality performances appear to be structurally complex and hybrid. What is required now therefore is the elaboration of a theoretical approach that can express the essence of how our experiences are constructed so as to inform the design and study of future work in this area. We have already seen the glimmerings of this new structure many times throughout these chapters whenever we mentioned the idea of trajectories running through these hybrid ecologies. The core premise of this book is that mixed reality performances can be described in terms of different kinds of trajectories that interweave and overlap as part of the overall fabric of the user experience. Having reviewed the detail of examples and laid the groundwork for this idea, the concluding chapter will next draw out and develop a theory of trajectories that is intended to help explain the nature of the mixed reality performance.

5 Trajectories through Mixed Reality Performance

In this book we have discussed a diverse collection of interactive experiences that collectively define an emerging genre that we call *mixed reality performance*. We have analyzed the structure of these experiences through the four lenses of space, time, interfaces, and roles. Here we discuss the broader framework we can draw from our analyses of these mixed reality performances. Perhaps, as we have seen, the most immediately remarkable aspect of these mixed reality performances is their hybridity, that is, the ways in which they combine multiple real and virtual spaces, layer different timeframes, employ diverse interfaces, and break down conventional performance roles. Each example that we have studied establishes its own particular ecology of spaces, times, roles, and interfaces through which participants navigate as the experience unfolds. These ecologies defy straightforward classification and deliberately challenge well-established conventions. Spatially, they are not virtual reality, augmented, reality, mixed reality, or ubiquitous computing, but rather a mix of all of these in new ways. Temporally, they slice up story and plot time and recombine them with schedule and interaction time to create unusual structures in which the fictional and real elements are ever more finely interwoven. Moreover, mixed reality performances appear to combine different interface paradigms at will, integrating mobile phones, wearable computers, tangible interfaces, immersive interfaces, and traditional web interfaces. Finally, they challenge traditional performance roles in that audiences become participants, actors become orchestrators, and a fluid and sometimes ambiguous framing implicates unwitting bystanders in the action. So we might conclude that mixed reality performances are complex hybrids of existing paradigms, forms, structures, and technologies, and that established concepts from HCI and performance studies, though clearly relevant, are still insufficient to fully describe how they are designed or experienced. Mixed reality performances do seem to have a core essence—they share a common lineage as well as many specific features. It therefore seems that we may need to adopt a new, possibly quite different perspective if we are to understand them. To this purpose, we now define a framework of concepts that can guide scholars from different disciplines who may wish to study mixed reality performances as well as practitioners and technologies who may wish to create them. Our motivations for doing this (as we revisit in greater detail toward the end of the chapter) are to provide sensitizing concepts to guide future empirical studies; to compile artistic craft knowledge into a form that is useful to a wider range of designers; to identify requirements for new technologies; and ultimately, to establish the foundations for a dramaturgy of interactive user experiences. This then is the goal of this final chapter: to reflect on our previous examples and discussions and to develop a conceptual framework for mixed reality performance.

Why Trajectories?

The idea of trajectories has already been discussed in the introduction and flagged several times during the preceding chapters. The relevance of spatial trajectories through many of these experiences is perhaps obvious, but we have also talked about trajectories through times, interfaces, and roles. This chapter takes the idea of trajectories through mixed reality performance as the fundamental basis for our conceptual framework.

We propose that the essential unifying characteristic of our four user experiences is that they take their participants on journeys. Although these journeys may pass through different places, times, roles, and interfaces, they maintain an overall sense of coherence; of being part of a connected whole. They are steered by the participants, but are also shaped by narratives that are embedded into spatial, temporal, and performative structures by authors. They are further influenced by the dynamic process of orchestration. Finally, they may be undertaken by groups and/or involve encounters among participants. We consider such journeys to define continuous trajectories through the structures of mixed reality performance. Each participant follows his or her own trajectory, which may be shaped and steered, and may cross those of others. In what follows, we identify different kinds of trajectories—canonical, participant, and historic—that define different aspects of participants' journeys through a performance. We consider the key challenges that need to be met when trying to design a coherent trajectory. We also explore how interweaving trajectories can express the social aspects of participation in mixed reality performances.

An important characteristic of trajectories is that they establish a sense of continuity. From a participant's point of view, trajectories may often appear to be continuous, extending backward in time to reveal a coherent history of experience, and forward in time to suggest anticipated routes and possible future actions. Why is continuity such a desirable property? The answer lies in part in the extended nature of mixed reality performances, especially their embedding of digital media into extended physical spaces. In contrast to the use of conventional personal computers, in which users tend to remain seated at one location, the experiences we have studied require participants to travel through physical spaces such as constructed sets in *Desert Rain*; the city streets in *Uncle Roy All Around You*; the space of the ride, museum, and amusement park in *Fairground: Thrill Laboratory*; and an arrangement of tables in *Day of the Figurines*. Any journey through physical space takes noticeable time and is experienced continuously. More generally, carefully establishing a sense of continuity may be particularly important, but also challenging when complex hybrid structures are involved. There is a danger that participants will be overwhelmed and confused by simultaneously traversing multiple spaces, dipping in and out of the experience, wielding diverse interfaces, and passing through different roles, so it becomes critically important to design an overall trajectory through the experience that establishes and sustains a sense of coherence and that enables participants to make meaning from their experience.

This approach of thinking of experiences in terms of continuous trajectories is in direct contrast to one of the most familiar computer experiences today, the World Wide Web, which adopts the paradigm of hypermedia, in which discrete elements are interconnected into complex structures using hyperlinks. Traversal of hyperlinks is nearly instantaneous, in marked contrast to our experiences here, in which the unfolding journey through space and time is a primary aspect of the experience. In looking beyond the "discrete and connected" toward the "continuous and interwoven" we have taken inspiration from the anthropologist Tim Ingold who, in his recent history of lines (2007), has drawn on fields as diverse as geography, genealogy, music, drawing, calligraphy, and weaving to argue for the benefits of thinking in terms of interwoven continuous lines rather than discrete networks. With reference to the tradition of wayfaring, Ingold argues that it is the experience of the journey that matters more than the final destination. He concludes his book with the observation "as in life, what matters is not the final destination, but all the interesting things that occur along the way" (170), an observation that resonates strongly with our view of mixed reality performance. The purpose of these user experiences is not to reach a destination, solve a problem, or complete a task, but rather to experience an engaging journey.

Transitions

We begin our discussion of trajectories in mixed reality performance by focusing on this essential property of continuity. Although trajectories through an experience are ideally continuous, maintaining continuity can raise significant challenges in practice. There may be many critical moments in an experience at which users must cross between spaces, rub up against schedules, take on new roles, or engage with interfaces, which need to be carefully designed if continuity and therefore coherence is to be maintained. We capture this in the idea that there are key *transitions* along each trajectory, moments at which, for whatever reason, continuity is at risk (see figure 5.1). Our

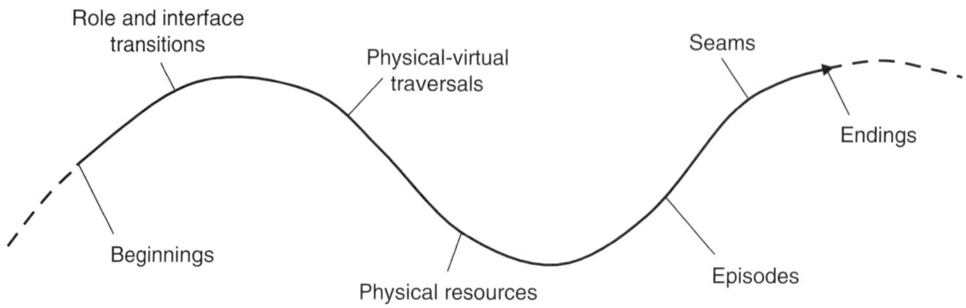

Figure 5.1
Different kinds of transitions that may be encountered along a trajectory.
Copyright MRL.

studies revealed various kinds of transitions as well as the strategies that artists use to carefully manage them.

Beginnings

The first important transition is of course the very start of the trajectory. Beginnings must be designed to introduce the narrative, distinguish between plot and story, define the spatiotemporal framework of the piece, but also to build suspense, brief participants, create affordances, establish the rules of the ritualization and the frame and transactions of the piece, while also dealing with practical concerns such as ticketing, queuing, and admission. Our examples show how an experience actually begins with the first point of contact, when a bystander starts his or her journey toward becoming a spectator and/or participant. Ticketing, queuing, and admissions should therefore be designed to be a wholly integrated part of the experience. We have seen that the beginnings of our experiences often involve carefully structured sequences of actions in which participants are registered and briefed, hand over their personal possessions, and are given equipment that is in return demonstrated to them, as we see for example in *Desert Rain*, *Uncle Roy All Around You*, and *Rider Spoke*. Although the professionals involved may appear to be administrative or technical staff, they are in fact actors and these sequences are scripted, rehearsed, and refined to ensure an appropriate introduction to and framing of the experience.

Endings

The transition out of an experience is also a key moment. This may involve the (re)exchange of equipment and personal possessions. It may also encourage participants to reengage with experience, but through a different trajectory. For example, *Uncle Roy All Around You* provides public terminals at the hosting venue that encourage street players to stay around and subsequently become online players. There is also a need to enable reflection and discussion through the use of souvenirs and replay interfaces: the box of sand in *Desert Rain*, the postcard in *Uncle Roy All Around You*, the souvenir video from *Fairground: Thrill Laboratory*, and viewing a personal history on the web in *Day of the Figurines*. Perhaps it is the highly subjective and personal nature of each participant's trajectory that raises this requirement for some kind of souvenir, often in a tangible form, to provoke reflection and discussion with others later on.

Role and Interface Transitions

Transitions into new roles may involve further briefings to instruct participants, establish mood, and hand over yet more equipment, testing whether it works and instructing participants how to use it. Interfaces are often designed with fluid handover in mind. In *Uncle Roy All Around You*, an actor starts the handheld computer interface, tests it, hands it over, and demonstrates it as part of a briefing. However, this is not always the case, and the handoff of equipment can instead be a long complex process that heightens anticipation along with the sense of the participant taking on their new role. This is especially true where wearable technologies are involved. In *Fairground: Thrill Laboratory*, for example, the time-consuming process of donning the wearable telemetry system is carefully rehearsed so that it serves to raise tension and suspense, and establish the sense that the participant has undergone a transition—that they have become a performer. On the other hand, in *Day of the Figurines* the cartoon-like quality of the figurines suggested the possibility of creating flexible and fluid roles that facilitated engagement over a long period of time.

Traversals between Physical and Virtual Worlds

Becoming immersed in virtual reality can be an especially challenging form of transition, especially when it involves picking up or putting on 3D tracking technologies. For example, viewpoints may swing around wildly and avatars assume distorted postures while participants are donning sensors. Beyond this, participants need to establish an appropriate sense of presence, which may include, among other things, cutting themselves off from the distractions of the everyday physical world. Our previous discussion of traversable interfaces reveals techniques for handling this potentially difficult spatial transition into and out of virtual worlds, as perhaps best illustrated in *Desert Rain*. First, the design of the virtual world is extended outwards to encompass the physical space within which it is embedded, that is, the virtual reality technology is placed in a purpose-built physical set (as we also often see with simulator rides at amusement parks). Second, participants are isolated from physical distractions, in this case through the use of fabric cubicles. The switching on of the rain curtain gives an effect of the virtual world gently materializing in front of the participant, gradually coming into focus. Finally, participants and actors can physically pass through the curtain, establishing the illusion of stepping into and out of the virtual world.

Episodes and Temporal Transitions

A long-term or ongoing experience such as *Day of the Figurines* will involve episodic engagement in which participants repeatedly disengage from and subsequently reengage. These too are important moments of transition and can entail structural micro beginnings and micro endings. The study of *Day of the Figurines* revealed that reengagement can be an especially challenging moment of transition with participants needing to catch up with any missed action while potentially being annoyed by floods of delayed messages. Techniques are required to summarize missed action so as to quickly and effectively reengage participants with the experience and perhaps also to better support them in scheduling and managing episodes.

Transitions into Physical Resources

Another important kind of transition involves gaining access to key physical resources such as the office and limousine in *Uncle Roy All Around You.* There is a natural constraint on how many copies of such resources there can be (there is only one office and one car) and they need to be carefully shared out to avoid contention if they need to be experienced in isolation or can accommodate only limited numbers. For example, it is deeply problematic if two people simultaneously arrive at the limousine, as their sense of having a highly personal and individual experience may be shattered and they will quite possibly begin to relax and chat during what is meant to be in one of the moments of highest dramatic tension in the work. In this respect, physical resources are fundamentally different from virtual ones that can be readily replicated. The orchestrators in *Uncle Roy All Around You* invested considerable effort into slowing down and speeding up players on the clue trail so that they would not arrive at the office and car together.

Transitions across Seams in the Infrastructure

Finally, there is an additional class of transition arising from constraints in the underlying GPS and Wi-Fi infrastructure that supports an experience. Limitations in network coverage resulted in participants in *Can You See me Now?* (and other experiences, too) suffering frequent disconnections with a major impact on their experience. Far from being occasional bugs, these seams in the underlying technical infrastructure are an inherent part of the texture of the material with which the artists are working and require conscious attention during the design and delivery of the experience. Previously, we discussed five different strategies for dealing with this kind of transition, including removal, hiding, managing, revealing, and even exploiting them.

In summary, although trajectories ideally establish a sense of continuity of an experience as it moves through complex hybrid structures, there are various transitional moments that threaten this continuity and that have to be dealt with on the way, either through design or orchestration. Thinking in terms of the key transitions that we identified previously (and others, no doubt) may help researchers in their analyses of mixed reality performances or artists and technologists in designing them.

Canonical and Participant Trajectories

The essence of interactive experiences is that they enable each participant to control his or her own trajectory, making choices and following personal routes. Thus, participants on the streets of the city or in a virtual world can choose which way to turn and where to go next, and those using a mobile phone can choose whether to attend to the experience at a given moment in time or deal with other more pressing matters. Yet this is not an entirely free choice. Artists carefully define one or more ideal routes through the hybrid structures of each experience as part of the overall narrative that they wish to create. *Desert Rain* always begins in the briefing room and ends in the motel room, and even the apparently free exploration of the virtual world is shaped by orchestration. Similarly, street players' explorations of the city in *Uncle Roy All Around You* are expected to follow one of a few envisaged or ideal routes, and significant divergence from these quickly becomes a concern. There is therefore a fundamental creative tension between an author's ideal trajectory through an experience that is embedded into its design and scripting, and each participant's actual trajectory, which emerges as they take part. Our framework accommodates this tension by distinguishing two fundamentally different kinds of trajectory.

A *canonical trajectory* expresses the author's intent: an idealized route that they have designed through the experience. Canonical trajectories express the narrative structure of the experience, but in a way that is mapped down onto the particular spaces, interfaces, and roles that are involved at any given moment in time. They are a blueprint for how the experience is intended to unfold. Many canonical trajectories may be present in each experience. Each class of participant may be associated with its own canonical trajectories (street players and online players in *Can You See Me Now?* and *Uncle Roy All Around You* follow quite different canonical trajectories). Beyond this, there may be several different canonical trajectories that a given class of participant could follow (thus there are multiple prescripted narrative arcs in *Day of the Figurines*, or several anticipated routes through the city in *Uncle Roy All Around You*). Canonical trajectories are expressed in multiple ways in the design of an experience, though maps, scripts, functional and technical system specifications, and so forth and are ultimately embedded in both the system code and performative processes that are rehearsed and then rolled out. Each participant follows his or her own individual *participant trajectory* through an experience. Participant trajectories emerge as a result of the specific choices that are made along the way. Different participants establish distinct participant trajectories, and an individual participant may follow a different participant trajectory each new time he or she takes part.

Canonical and participant trajectories tend to repeatedly diverge and reconverge throughout an experience as participants make individual decisions that lead them away from the ideal (canonical) route, and then the artists work to bring them back at key moments (see figure 5.2). Thus, the rhythm of many of the experiences that we have reported in this book is one of phases of exploration, which often quite deliberately involve getting lost and confused, followed by more tightly managed phases that almost "run on rails" as participants experience carefully scripted and rehearsed sequences (compare the city exploration with the office, phone booth, and limousine in *Uncle Roy All Around You*). This tension between the continual divergence and reconvergence of canonical and participant trajectories is a productive one, providing that they are kept in balance. Too much divergence and the experience may fall into incoherence and the underlying narrative will disappear. Too much convergence and interactivity is lost. Divergence and convergence are driven by two opposing forces. Interactivity is the force that drives convergence, pushing canonical and participant trajectories apart, and orchestration is the opposing force that drives reconvergence, steering them back together. This explains the importance of orchestration to the experiences that we have studied—it is the essential opposing force that balances interactivity in a live performance—and artists and technologists need to recognize this from the very start and design processes and tools to support it.

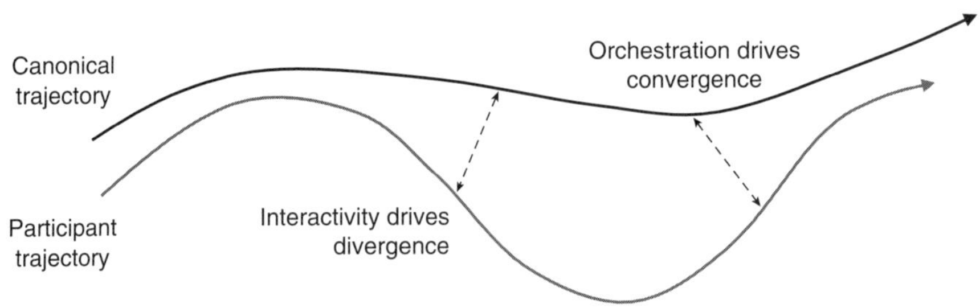

Figure 5.2
Interactive and orchestration shape divergence and convergence between canonical and participant trajectories.
Copyright MRL.

Interweaving Trajectories

All of the mixed reality performances analyzed in this book are inherently collaborative experiences, involving encounters between their various kinds of participants. Sometimes these are face to face, sometimes distributed via online virtual worlds, and sometimes they span the two. Either way, social interaction lies at the heart of their liveness and improvised nature. We can express the social and collaborative characteristics of mixed reality performances by considering how different participant trajectories interweave with one another. As continuous threads, participant trajectories might approach, cross, and leave one another many times throughout an experience. As they approach, so participants should become increasingly aware of one another, be able to communicate, and affect each other's experience. When their trajectories are far apart, participants will be unaware of one another and will not be able to communicate. These ideas are of course familiar in the everyday world, where we encounter one another whenever our trajectories cross in space-time, that is, when we are in the same place at the same time. However, encounters might potentially occur whenever trajectories cross in any of the key structural elements of a mixed reality performance: space, time, roles, or interfaces. Thus, participants might meet one another because they share the same place, are playing at the same time, are using specific interfaces, or are playing particular combinations of roles. For example, we shall discuss in greater detail later in this chapter the various ways in which participants might encounter each other across time in extended episodic experiences such as *Day of the Figurines*.

Although it may often be desirable to bring trajectories together, it is sometimes equally important to steer them apart, so as to create moments of isolation and reflection, minimize distractions and interruptions, or avoid competition for limited resources (e.g., the limousine in *Uncle Roy All Around You*). In *Desert Rain*, players begin their journey together in the briefing room, but are then separated in their individual fabric cubicles and in the virtual world, often lost and confused, before being brought back together again as they cross the hill of sand and enter the final motel room. The study of *Desert Rain* reported how the performers had to carefully control the regrouping of players beyond the virtual world in order to reduce chatting and sustain tension. In *Uncle Roy All Around You*, street players are initially isolated as their explore the city, but then begin a series of encounters with remote online players, and ultimately meet the actor in the limousine. *Rider Spoke* deliberately discourages face-to-face interactions between riders, instead building the experience around a sense of cycling alone through the city at night. However, riders do experience asynchronous encounters with others who previously left messages at the locations they visit. In short, moving between periods of relative isolation and various forms of encounters with others appears to be an important and common dramatic technique within these mixed reality performances. Different combinations of participant trajectories need to be steered together at some points, but equally steered apart at others to create the appropriate "social fabric" for the experience, ensuring that it moves between moments of collaboration and isolation, or that some combinations of players are in contact while others remain separated.

Maintaining social encounters over time can be particularly challenging, especially as individuals pass through various transitions that may disrupt their collaboration (e.g., suffering technical disconnections or choosing to dip in and out of a long-term episodic experience at different times). Maintaining parallel participant trajectories so that participants can sustain a relationship may also be an important, although challenging, aspect of designing and delivering a mixed reality performance. Finally, each individual may be involved in many different ongoing experiences that might affect one another. For example, they might be trying to integrate an ongoing mixed reality performance with other ongoing work and social activities or might even be taking part in several simultaneous mixed reality performances. *Day of the Figurines* is the best example in this book of a long-term experience that needs to be interwoven with other activities. Players' trajectories through *Day of the Figurines* therefore need to be interwoven with their own and others' trajectories through work, family, and social experiences (see figure 5.3). There are interesting possibilities here, such as when two players of the game meet each other face to face in some other work or social activity. Trajectories from different experiences might also be steered together or apart, such as bringing the trajectory of a cultural experience to the foreground in moments of downtime from work and vice versa.

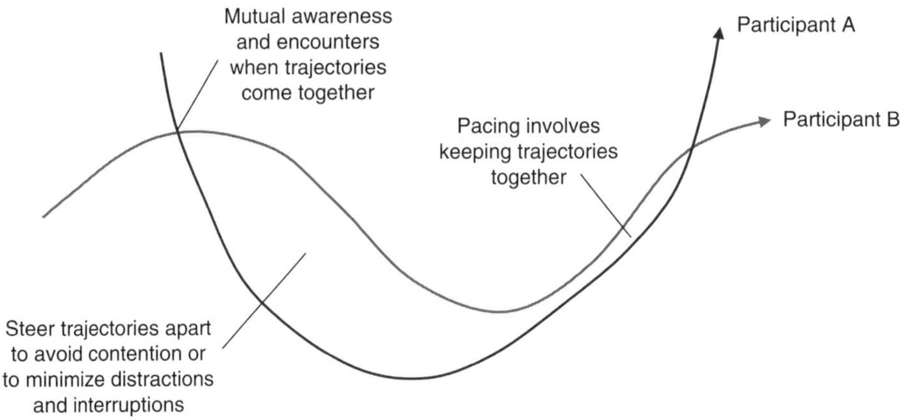

Figure 5.3
Interweaving participant trajectories show encounters and moments of isolation. Copyright MRL.

Trajectories in *Uncle Roy All Around You*

Having introduced the key concepts in our conceptual framework (with the exception of one more concept, the historic trajectory, that we come to later on), we now offer two detailed examples of how they can be used to help understand mixed reality performances. In both cases, we return to performances that have been discussed in previous chapters, but here we use the concepts of trajectories to further explain them.

We begin with *Uncle Roy All Around You*. There are two fundamental kinds of canonical trajectory in this performance: one for the street player and a second for the online player. The essence of the street player's intended journey through the experience is defined by a spatial trajectory through the city, during which they encounter various roles and interfaces. As shown in figure 5.4 this begins at the hosting venue and then heads out to a first location in the city (the "red spot" moment at which the player first presses the "I am here" button to trigger their first clue). From here, the canonical trajectory splits into several likely routes through the city, which the artists have identified in advance and planned the clue trail around. These converge on Uncle Roy's office, after which they pass to the phone booth and finally the limousine. The main interactivity in *Uncle Roy All Around You* lies in deciding where to go next (supported by further interactions with remote online players). Thus, the force of interactivity may take the street player away from the planned (canonical route) and out into

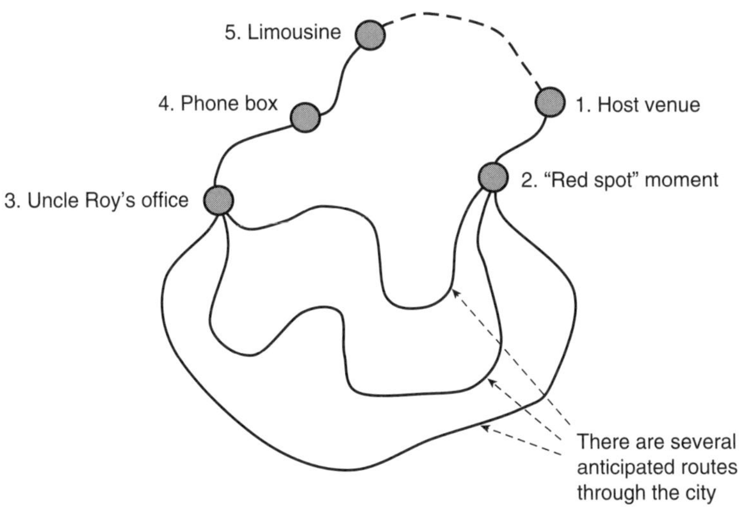

Figure 5.4
Street player spatial trajectory showing planned routes on the clue trail. Copyright MRL.

the wider city. Although an element of exploring side tracks and even of being lost is to be expected, and possibly even somewhat desired, players ultimately have to be steered back toward one of the planned canonical trajectories if they are to reach the office and enjoy a complete and safe experience. This involves various levels of orchestration that are applied in sequence as in figure 5.5, which shows various potential degrees of divergence and convergence between the canonical and participant trajectories of street players. As they begin to diverge from a canonical route, the street player is initially presented with subtle clues that try to steer them back. If they continue to diverge, the clues become more explicit and insistent, telling them that they need to stop, turn around, and head back into the game zone. If this fails to turn them around, then one of the team of actors on the street is sent to find them and bring them back.

Staying with the street player for a moment, there are various transitions that the artists had to consider when designing the canonical trajectory (see figure 5.6). The initial briefing is carefully planned and rehearsed and the PDA interface designed to support rapid handover and learning (role and interface transition). Again, the "red spot" moment is intended to be a first very simple task that teaches players the basic mechanic of the experience before they head out into the city. Wireless disconnections and reconnections (seams) were anticipated and were dealt with by having a stand-alone version of the clue trail running on the PDA even when disconnected so as to maintain a basic level of experience, while also providing a central control room interface that highlighted periods of disconnection along with last known location

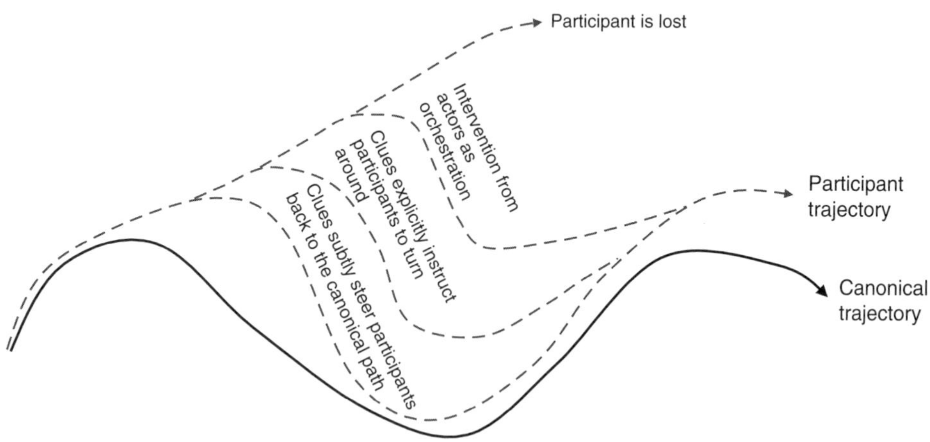

Figure 5.5
Orchestration techniques used during the clue trial.
Copyright MRL.

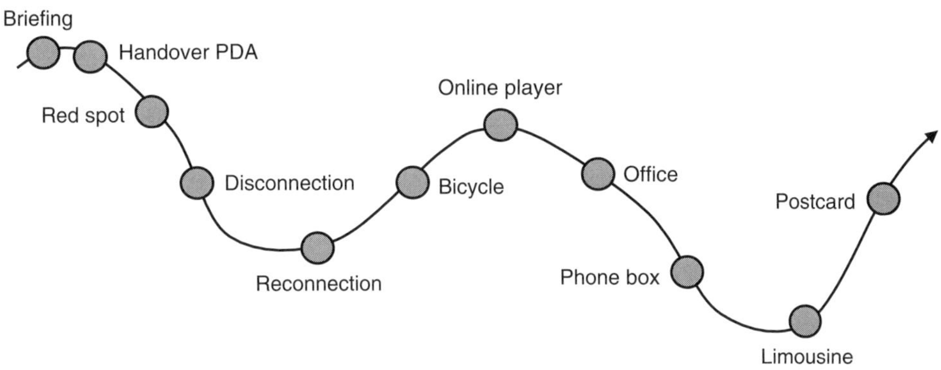

Figure 5.6
Street player canonical trajectory with examples of transitions.
Copyright MRL.

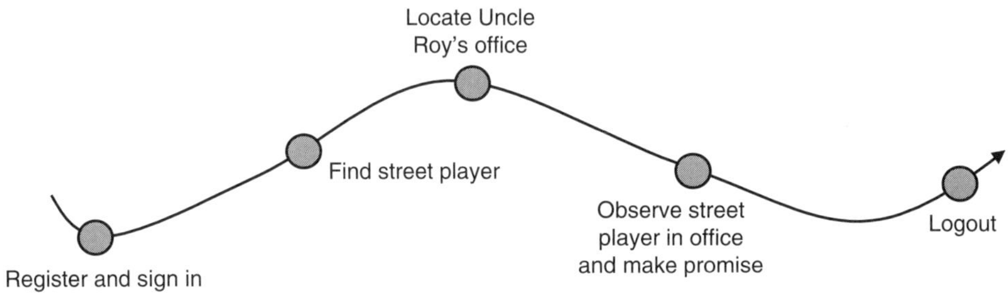

Figure 5.7
Online player canonical trajectory with examples of transitions.
Copyright MRL.

for each player in the game. The bicycle, office, phone booth, and limousine were all examples of transitions into the use of particular physical resources, which required careful management, including sometimes slowing players down so as to avoid contention and face-to-face encounters at these critical points. A further key transitional moment that we deal with shortly involves meeting online players. Finally, the true ending of the experience is the receipt of another player's postcard sometime after the main performance.

Online players have their own canonical trajectory, which also includes a significant spatial element as they explore the virtual model of the city. There are key transitions on this route, as shown in figure 5.7, including registering and signing in, making contact with a street player, locating Uncle Roy's office, observing a street player in the office over the video link, and signing out.

A particularly rich and interesting aspect of *Uncle Roy All Around You* is the way in which it engineers different collaborative relationships between the various kinds of players. These can be expressed in terms of interweaving participant trajectories as depicted by figure 5.8, which shows four example participant trajectories, two for street players and two for online players, and the various ways in which they might cross. Street players may encounter online players, often fleetingly, but also sometimes these would lead to sustained relationships in which the latter guides the former through the city or observe them in the office. For much of the time, street players are meant to be isolated from one another, but they clearly can meet, although this is to be actively avoided around the office, phone booth, and limousine. Online players can also meet in the virtual world, which, on the whole, is seen to be less of a problem.

Although still a relatively high-level discussion, the preceding diagrams and accompanying explanations also manage to capture many of the essential characteristics of *Uncle Roy All Around You* as well as some of the specific challenges that were faced by the artists and the techniques that they employed to overcome them. To our mind,

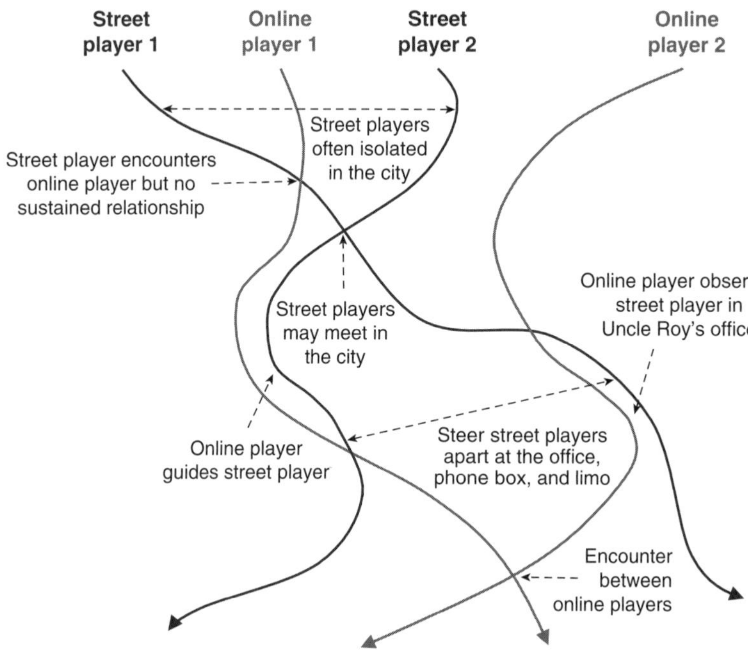

Figure 5.8
Interweaving street and online player participant trajectories.
Copyright MRL.

this provides some evidence that trajectories might be useful for both guiding analyses of mixed reality performances and explaining their results in a structured way. A further question is whether they might also be useful during the design of such performances. Our next example goes some way toward answering this by using trajectories to analyze a performance, but also to consider alternative ways in which it might have been constructed.

Trajectories through Time in *Day of the Figurines*

Our second illustrative example of applying trajectories returns to *Day of the Figurines*. In this case, we use trajectories to help explain, at quite a detailed level, findings from previous studies, and also to explore various alternative designs. Our aim is to both to explore the temporal structure of mixed reality performance, but also to demonstrate how trajectories can be used to relate narrative structures, user interactions, and the underlying construction of networked applications.

Although there are many potential examples of trajectories to be found in *Day of the Figurines*, such as trajectories through its table spectator interface and trajectories through the fictional world and narrative, we focus here on the complexities of its temporal structure, using trajectories to explore some of the issues that were encountered around episodic engagement and pacing. Our core idea here is that trajectories can express various mappings between the hybrid layers of time that are present in *Day of the Figurines* as discussed in chapter 2. Figure 5.9 shows the overall canonical trajectory that lies at the heart of the temporal structure of *Day of the Figurines* through which the authors establish a linear mapping of twenty-four hours of fictional story time onto twenty-four days of actual clock time in the real world. In the terms of chapter 2, this canonical trajectory defines the core plot time of *Day of the Figurines*, that is, the order and timing by which events from the story world are narrated in the real world.

Although this canonical trajectory is linear in *Day of the Figurines*, it might be more complex in other experiences. Story time (ST) might advance at variable rates relative to clock time (CT), speeding up or slowing down as we see in a number of computer games. It might also jump up and down the vertical axis, representing (fictional) time travel in the story universe, such as through flashbacks or players revisiting previous levels in a game. Story time could even progress downward vertically so that it unfolds in reverse as clock time advances. Canonical trajectories might also include branching narrative structures (Murray 1997) that reflect interactive decisions, for example expressing the idea of moving to the next level or repeating the current level according to some success criterion in a game. However, it is not possible for a canonical trajectory to jump or move backward in clock time. In other words, real time travel is not possible, as clock time always moves forward.

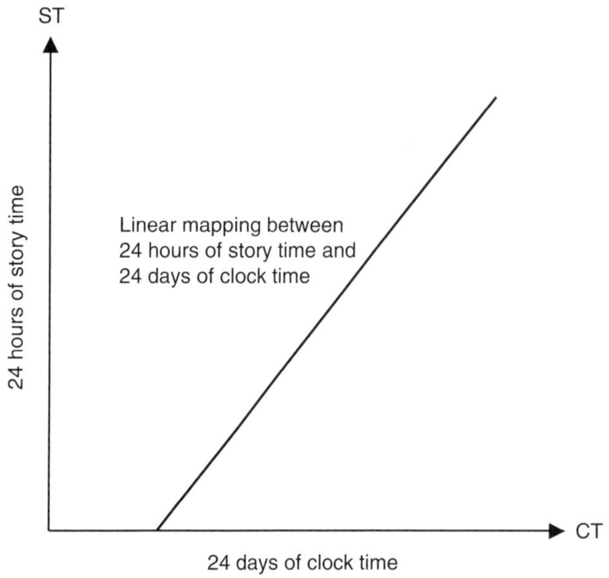

Figure 5.9
The core canonical trajectory underlying *Day of the Figurines* (*DoF*).
Copyright MRL.

Although figure 5.9 captures the author's overall intent for plot time in *Day of the Figurines*, its actual canonical trajectory through time is more complex than this, due to the need to schedule multiple performances of the experience to take place at particular times on particular days (i.e., to deal with the layer of schedule time identified in chapter 2). Figure 5.10 shows a more refined version of the canonical trajectory of time in *Day of the Figurines* that expresses the detailed scheduling of two distinct performances. Each performance consists of twenty-four segments (only five of these are shown in the figure), each of which specifies how one hour of story time is intended to unfold over ten hours of a particular day of clock time. Each distinct performance of *Day of the Figurines* is represented by its own canonical trajectory, potentially defining its own local schedule of opening hours and days. These canonical trajectories could overlap in clock time if multiple performances were ever staged simultaneously.

Again, briefly looking beyond *Day of the Figurines*, multiple canonical trajectories can be used to represent the more complex nested temporal structures of some MMORPGs such as Ultima Online. At the core of Ultima is a shared virtual world that provides a space for social interaction with time unfolding linearly in relation to clock time. However, Ultima also includes additional narrative-driven elements in the form

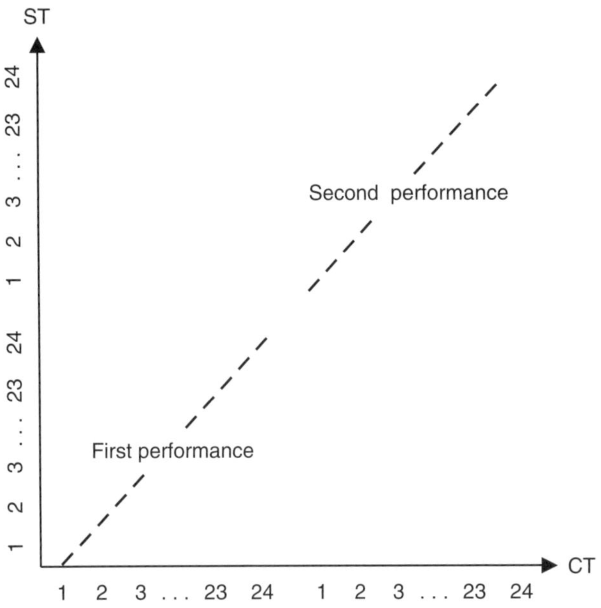

Figure 5.10
Canonical trajectories express scheduling.
Copyright MRL.

of quests that must be completed to particular timescales and that are initiated and shared by groups of players. Quests are then associated with their own localized canonical trajectories that serve to group together a subset of players for a limited duration of clock time. Interestingly, these are also created—or scheduled—on the fly in response to players' actions within the game. In terms of narrative theory, this is an example of multiple canonical trajectories representing plots and subplots.

Up to now, we have considered the intention of the author (or director or scheduler) in defining the temporal structure of an interactive narrative experience. We now consider how participants actually interact with such an experience. Each player in *Day of the Figurines* inscribes his or her own participant trajectory that captures the temporal nature of their individual experience, relating where they actually are in story time as clock time unfolds. Whereas a canonical trajectory describes where an author wants the participant to go (in time), a participant trajectory describes where they actually do go. Though we might expect participant trajectories to generally follow canonical trajectories, they can diverge from them, either as a matter of choice or due to technical constraints such as network disconnections or delays in delivering messages. Participant trajectories therefore express the characteristics of interaction time in the layered temporal framework of chapter 2. Interaction time is primarily determined by the player, and previous HCI research has produced various accounts of factors that shape interaction time in narrative experiences for example studies of how players coordinate their engagement in MMORPGs (Ducheneaut et al. 2007) and how their engagement with long-term mobile games adapts to the patterns of their daily lives, for example, commuting (Bell et al. 2006). In the case of *Day of the Figurines*, interaction time is characterized by episodic patterns of play as we discussed earlier, with players frequently disengaging and reengaging. We now consider what happens when a participant disengages from and subsequently reengages with the game, for example by losing and then regaining their network connection to a remote server that is maintaining the canonical trajectory for their experience. In *Day of the Figurines*, story time appears to freeze for the participant, as they no longer receive information from the server. However, the server actually continues to operate their character in their absence (albeit in a passive mode) so that others can still see it, speak to it, and use objects on it, although it will not respond. This explains why participants often feel ignored by others (who may be disengaged) and why a few experience the more severe problem of "waking up dead" because others have killed them in their absence.

Figure 5.11 shows how we can use canonical and participant trajectories to analyze in depth the *Day of the Figurines* approach to disengagement. Initially, the participant trajectory follows the canonical trajectory until the point of disengagement, where we show it splitting into two threads. One of these represents the server actively maintaining the character along the canonical trajectory (shown by the solid black line).

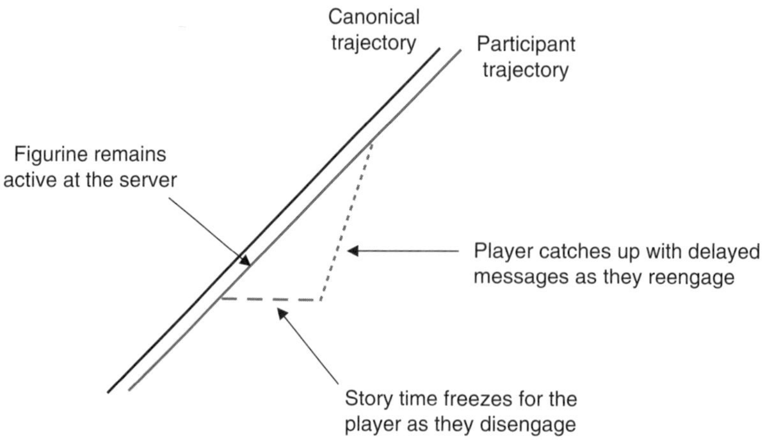

Figure 5.11
Disengagement and reengagement in *Day of the Figurines*.
Copyright MRL.

The other represents the state of the participant's phone, which initially receives no updates, so its local story time is frozen (the gray line). It subsequently receives a series of delayed messages from the server in quick succession as it reconnects, resulting in its local story time rapidly catching up with the canonical story time (the dotted gray line).

Some participants experienced floods of messages upon reengagement. The slope of the dotted line is important in this regard. If it is steep (i.e., delayed messages are delivered quickly on reengagement), then they experience a flood of messages. On the other hand, if it is shallow (they receive the delayed messages gradually), there is a risk that they will try to respond to earlier messages before they see any later ones, trying to interact with the experience as if they were at an earlier point in canonical time than they actually are, which could cause confusion. Further inspection of figure 5.11 reveals other approaches to managing temporary disengagement. In general, a disengagement and subsequent reengagement creates a triangular area of uncertainty in our trajectory diagram as the participant trajectory first becomes separated from the canonical trajectory and then subsequently rejoins it. During this period, there is inconsistency between the participant's notion of story time and that of the central server (and hence other participants), potentially leading to confusion and the need to resynchronize. Figure 5.12 shows how *Day of the Figurine*'s approach is just one of four general "routes" by which this triangle of uncertainty can be negotiated. In route (a), the participant is totally removed from the game for the duration of his or her disengagement. The participants no longer interact with it on their phone and their characters disappear from the server. This avoids floods of update messages upon reengagement as well as the potentially "nasty surprises" that can be experienced in *Day of the Figurines*, although at the cost of the participant missing a chunk of the narrative. This requires a technical mechanism to detect disengagement that is not

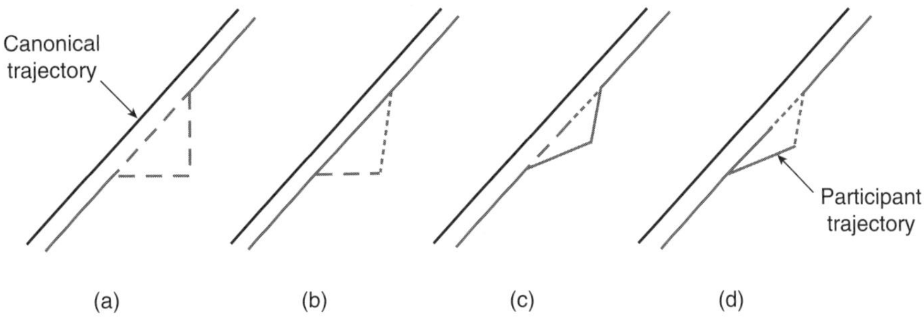

Figure 5.12
Four "routes" around the "uncertainty triangle."
Copyright MRL.

reliably possible with SMS, although can be achieved with many other communication technologies. This approach is typical of MMORPGs such as World of Warcraft.

Route (b) is the current version of *Day of the Figurines* that we have already discussed. Route (c) represents the case in which the participants continue to interact with a local version of their character that runs on their phone but that is no longer visible to other participants via the server. The participants control an independent participant trajectory with its own local story time, which gets resynchronized with the canonical trajectory only as they reengage, at which point they become visible to other players again. This requires that a version of the game can be run independently on the participant's local device, which was not the case in *Day of the Figurines*. Finally, route (d) represents the case in which both the canonical and participant trajectories progress independently. The participant continues to interact with a local version of their character, while the server also continues to maintain a separate version that is visible to others. Both branches of the trajectory have to be resynchronized with each other on reengagement. This approach has the advantage of allowing everyone to progress, but at considerable risk of inconsistency.

What is also interesting here is that our concepts of canonical and participant trajectories speak to discussions in distributed computing about how to synchronize state between different software components (e.g., clients and servers) in a networked application. These four routes can be mapped on to existing approaches to concurrency control in distributed simulation (Fujimoto 2000). Pessimistic concurrency control requires that one component of the system exclusively acquires and locks a resource (the character) before interacting with it. This is the case in route (b) where the server takes control of the character and route (c) where the client does. Route (d), on the other hand, represents optimistic concurrency control, where both client and server update the character independently and resolve any inconsistencies later on.

So far we have seen how temporal trajectories can help analyze the temporal structure of an existing experience, uncovering and helping explain why participants experience various interactional problems when playing episodically. Next we show how these concepts also have the power to help envision new insights and designs. Our first step is to envisage a rolling experience—one that is still driven by a strong narrative, but in which participants can join at many different times. For example, rather than having just a few widely separated performances of *Day of the Figurines*, we could launch a new performance on each day of clock time, enabling participants to join on any day and experience the game over the subsequent twenty-four days. The result would be a rolling structure of twenty-four concurrent games each with its own separate group of participants. This can be represented by twenty-four parallel canonical trajectories, with a new one starting and an old one finishing on each day. This becomes more interesting when we also allow for different paces of play. In his writing about time and HCI, Alan Dix has emphasized the importance of pacing within interactive and collaborative systems arguing that communication breakdowns often occur when the pace of participants' interactions or communication is considerably slower than that of the task that they are trying to achieve (1992). Pacing was clearly an issue in *Day of the Figurines*, as we saw participants adopting different styles and paces of play over twenty-four days. A few played intensively, sending messages nearly every day. However, as we have seen, the majority played episodically, increasing and decreasing the intensity of their interactions according to shifting personal circumstances. To support episodic play, we might extend our rolling game with the following simple pacing rule: any day in clock time during which a participant sends a message to the game is deemed to be an "engaged day," causing story time to advance by one hour, whereas any day when they do not send a message is deemed to be a "disengaged day," during which story time does not advance. A participant who sent a message every day would complete the game in twenty-four days as before. Slower-paced participants, however, would take longer due to missed days of play during which their story time would be paused. They would still require twenty-four days of play to finish, but these would no longer have to be contiguous. They would also encounter different groups of players and possibly different states of the game as they passed through different instances. Figure 5.13 represents this approach using twenty-four parallel canonical trajectories. Two participants join the experience on the same day. Each time one of them disengages for a day, he or she falls back into the next less temporally advanced instance of the game (the next canonical trajectory coming along) where a new set of players is encountered.

Each time such a participant joins a new canonical trajectory, he or she might encounter a new group of participants who are currently following it and who therefore share the same current point in story time. However, although it might be interesting to meet new participants, it could also be frustratingly difficult to maintain

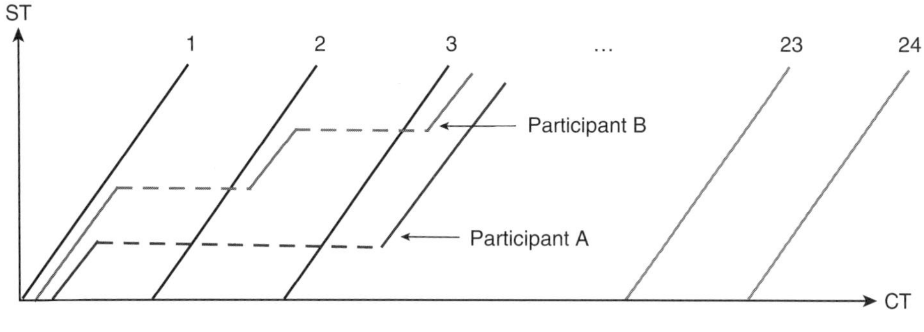

Figure 5.13
A rolling experience with variable pacing.
Copyright MRL.

friendships over the course of a game. Imagine two friends who join on the same day and play regularly, but then one of them skips a day and so falls into the next canonical trajectory. If they both continue to play regularly after that, they will be locked into parallel trajectories, separated by one hour in story time, and will never meet each other again.

Figure 5.14 suggests how we might use multiple canonical trajectories to manage pacing more subtly. Here there are two canonical trajectories with different slopes, one for fast-paced participants and another for slow ones. One participant is initially assigned to the faster-paced trajectory. They disengage briefly at one point and are resynchronized when they reengage. They then disengage for a much longer period. When they reengage for the second time, they are synchronized with the slower canonical trajectory and are henceforth grouped with participants who adopt a slower pace. Essentially, this approach dynamically divides participants into differently paced groups.

Another alternative involves the system managing pacing without an author or scheduler intervening. Figure 5.15 shows a possible design in which the system automatically synchronizes two different participants' trajectories. Participant A and Participant B initially describe similar but slightly divergent participant trajectories. At

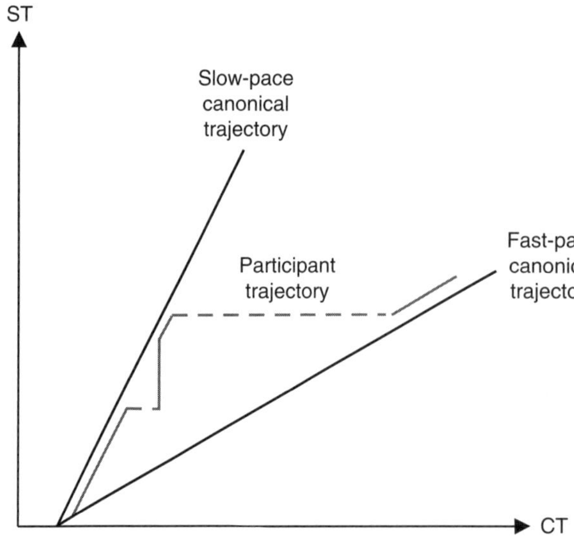

Figure 5.14
Using multiple canonical trajectories to group participants according to their pace of interaction.
Copyright MRL.

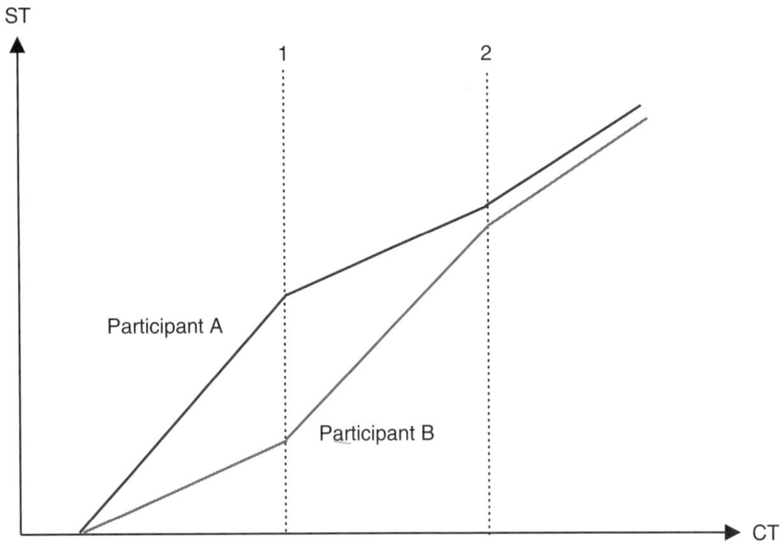

Figure 5.15
Synchronizing two participant trajectories.
Copyright MRL.

Clock Time 1, the system begins to gently steer them back together by subtly speeding up the rate at which Participant A consumes Story Time while slowing down Participant B, until they meet at Clock Time 2, from which point on, their trajectories are held together, enabling them to share the narrative. As an aside, this approach of dynamically synchronizing unfolding participant trajectories relates to previous discussions of the WYSIWIS (What You See Is What I See) and relaxed-WYSIWIS techniques that afford different degrees of relaxation of synchronization in groupware tools such as shared editors (Munson and Dewan 1996; Stefik et al. 1987).

Another more radical possibility is to enable participants to encounter each other even when they are at different times. Figure 5.16 shows two participant trajectories that describe quite different temporal journeys through an experience. An inspection of this figure suggests some interesting potential encounters between these participants, labeled (1) to (4).

At point (1), our two participants share a common temporal trajectory for a while, being coincident in both clock time and story time. In a shared interactive narrative such as *Day of the Figurines*, it would make sense for these participants to encounter one another (subject to other factors such as spatial proximity), as they share a common temporal context; that is, they are seeing the same fictional events unfold around them. At point (2), their paths briefly cross again in both story time and clock

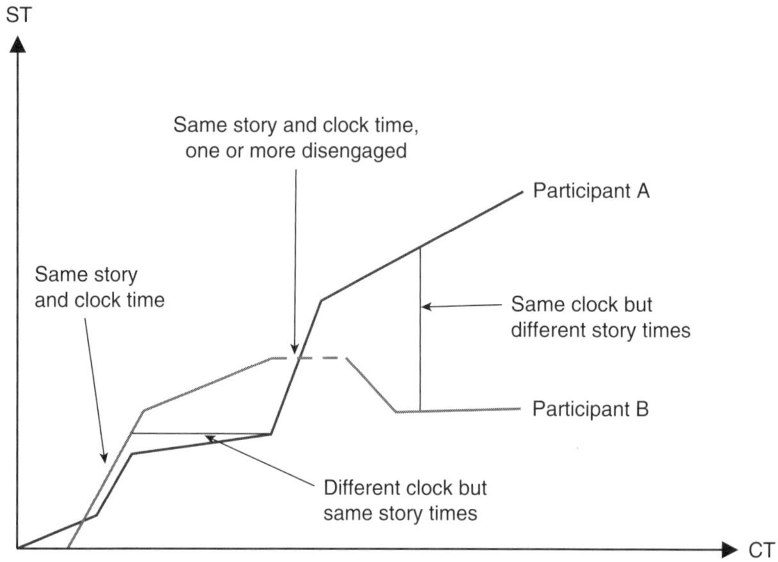

Figure 5.16
Different kinds of encounters in time.
Copyright MRL.

time; however, this time one participant is disengaged while the other participant remains engaged. If we allow them to encounter one another at this point, we need to be aware that one may appear to ignore the other or may affect the other in their absence, as we saw in *Day of the Figurines*, which allows encounters involving disengaged participants. A more unusual possibility is at point (3), where two participants encounter one another even through they are at different story times. This would enable participants from a relative fictional future and past to meet and exchange information. For example, in the proposed rolling version of *Day of the Figurines* that we introduced earlier, two participants might simultaneously (in clock time) be in Kath's Café, but for one it would be 11:00 a.m. in story time, whereas for the other it would be 3:00 p.m. This unconventional scenario opens up new narrative possibilities. For example, players might use a "time portal" object to allow them to discover information about what is going to happen in the future or to leave a warning or hint for those in the past. Finally, point (4) shows an encounter between two participants who are at different clock times. This represents asynchronous communication between participants who actually share a common fictional time. For example, the one participant might see a recording of what one participant did at this moment in story time earlier on in this performance (or even in a previous performance). In other words, we propose that encounters between participants in shared interactive narratives can be mediated according to their proximity in a combination of story time and clock time, and also according to their ongoing levels of engagement. Combining these factors in various ways can establish new narrative possibilities, including the extent to which communication is synchronous or asynchronous (proximity in clock time), whether it reflects a notion of fictional time travel (proximity in story time), and whether participants can be affected in their absence (engagement). If we allow such encounters, then it may be helpful to convey the nature of any time differences to the participants involved, perhaps by extending previous proposals for awareness widgets that reveal the presence and nature of network delays between participants in groupware (Stach et al. 2007).

To draw this section to a close, we have undertaken a detailed discussion of the temporal structure of *Day of the Figurines*—both actual and possible—in terms of various comparisons between canonical and participant trajectories that run through a combination of story time and clock time. We hope that this discussion has served to illustrate the potential usefulness of these concepts to explain the design and experience of mixed reality performance, while also broadening understanding of temporal issues surrounding episodic engagement, pacing, collaboration, and even new possibilities for enabling fictional time travel. Yet it turns out that canonical and participant trajectories are not sufficient to fully express all of the complexities of time in mixed reality performance, especially the challenges involved in recording and replaying live experiences. For this, we need to discuss a third fundamental kind of trajectory.

Historic Trajectories

Chapter 2 finished with a discussion of recording and replaying mixed reality performances in which system recordings (log files) of participants' actions (messages, movements, and interactions) are captured alongside more traditional forms of documentation such as video, and are then synchronized and played back during or after the event. We considered several kinds of audience for this kind of record and replay facility, including participants who wish to discuss and compare their experience with others or who might appreciate souvenirs that stimulate recollection and reflection; artists and curators who wish to establish public archives of the experience, either as physical installations or online, perhaps as part of its legacy or as part of a retrospective exhibition; and scholars from various disciplines, especially the humanities and social sciences, who may wish to study the experiences over the years to come. We presented various examples of how these requirements might be met ranging from physical mementos (the box of sand in *Desert Rain* or postcard in *Uncle Roy All Around You*), to giving people access to their histories of interaction (the *Day of the Figurines* web interface) or creating interactive replays for use during the event (e.g., *Savannah*) or afterwards (e.g., the *Can You See Me Now?* replay interface). This requirement to be able to record and replay mixed reality performance is not reflected in either canonical or participant trajectories, but rather requires the introduction of a third fundamental kind of trajectory, the *historic trajectory*.

If we assume that all interactions with and via the underlying technical system that supports a performance are recorded as they are in *Can You See Me Now?*, *Savannah*, *Day of the Figurines*, and other examples that we have presented, then it becomes possible to synthesize various historic views of what took place. A historic trajectory encapsulates such a synthesis. Each historic trajectory defines one particular view of recorded history, such as from a particular staging of a performance and/or from particular individual's point of view. There might therefore be many different histories or retellings of the performance, each of which is defined by its own historic trajectory. We assume that each participant trajectory that corresponds to a particular journey through the experience is recorded by the system as a system log file (which possibly links into other materials such as video documentation). A historic trajectory then consists of a selection and recomposition of segments from possibly many participant trajectories that provides a particular account of what happened. This might be based upon various criteria such as the participants who were involved, the importance of particular events, or even how recently they occurred. These selected events are then made available to participants, perhaps being scheduled for replay at a particular time and maybe being presented (narrated) in a particular order (which could be different to the one in which they originally occurred). This selection and recomposition might be done by hand, for example, by the participant themselves or some other agent such as a producer might select the most appropriate segments by hand and then stitch them together in the same way that conventional movies are edited together from multiple takes of many different shots. However, what is perhaps more interesting is to consider how this might be done automatically by associating a historic trajectory with a set of "synthesis rules." Thus, in general, a historic trajectory can be defined by a set of rules that encompass

• an initial selection of a set of participant trajectories;
• the further selection of particular segments of these by time, space, or some other criteria;
• a specification of how (e.g., the order in which) these segments are to be recombined;
• a further rule that governs who can access this historic trajectory and when it becomes available to them (e.g., during or after the performance).

As examples of relatively simple historic trajectories, *Day of the Figurines* involved two kinds of automatically generated historic trajectory. The first was when participants reviewed text messages on their phones. The selection here was that each participant could see only their own messages, and these were often further selected (due to limited storage) to be only important or recent messages. These were made available as soon as they had been received, so that the historic trajectory was interwoven with their ongoing participant trajectory, and they were presented through the same medium—their mobile phone. The second was the history of events published on the web. Again, the selection was by participant, but this time all messages were shown. These many different historic trajectories (one for each participant) were scheduled to appear after the event and were translated into a new medium (the web versus a phone). The synthesis rules for these two cases are summarized by table 5.1.

The *Can You See Me Now?* replay interface enabled viewers to dynamically choose to replay two historic trajectories from among the many that were selected from individual players. *Savannah*, on the other hand, allowed its players to move forward and backward through a single historic trajectory that expressed the recorded interactions of all players from the most recently played game level.

These examples of historic trajectories are relatively straightforward, mostly focusing on selecting which players' recorded histories to replay after a performance has taken place and been recorded. There are, however, far richer and more complex ways in which historic trajectories might be used. In particular, previously recorded events might be injected back into the live experience to become part of the live content. In other words, a live performance might potentially include recordings of participants earlier actions to create a kind of temporally looping narrative structure. To understand these more complex *multilayered historic trajectories*, we need to return to the concepts of clock time and story time from our earlier discussion. In general, story time, like the fictional space in which a story is set, is a construct of the author's imagination,

Table 5.1
Comparing historic trajectories for *Day of the Figurines*

Historic trajectory	The participant reviews messages on their phone	The participant reviews messages on the website
Initial selection	Historic trajectory created by selecting all messages sent/received by a particular participant in this instance of the performance.	Historic trajectory crated by selecting all messages sent/received by a particular participant in this instance of the performance.
Further selection of segments	Participants can further select messages by keeping some on their phone and deleting others.	All messages are included.
Order in which segments are recombined	Probably seen in the order they were sent/received, but may vary according to phone.	Seen in the order in which they were processed by the game server.
Who accesses and when	Only available to this participant. Can be viewed during the live performance.	Available to only this participant and only after the performance has finished.

so there is no reason why participants cannot move backward and forward within it, provided that the author can satisfactorily explain this within the story. Traveling in clock time, however, is a different matter. Outside of relativistic effects, participants cannot change or diverge their positions in clock time (though they might try to spoof the system by resetting their local system clocks). What they can do, however, is replay events from previous clock times that have been recorded by the system. Following the same diagrammatic conventions that we used to analyze canonical and participant trajectories through time in *Day of the Figurines*, figure 5.17 shows various possibilities for one participant (Participant A) to view recorded events, some of which have been generated by a second participant (Participant B). At points 1, 2, and 3 they view events that were recorded by Participant A at past, present, and future story times, respectively. Next we note that the act of viewing a previously recorded event can itself be recorded, so that at point 4 Participant B sees a recording of themselves viewing the recorded event from 1.

New narrative possibilities arise when we combine recorded and live events in these kinds of ways. At any moment, a participant may experience a combination of live events that has been scripted to appear at this point in clock time and story time and recorded events that have already happened at some previous clock time. Depending on how these are mixed, the participant will have quite different experiences of fic-

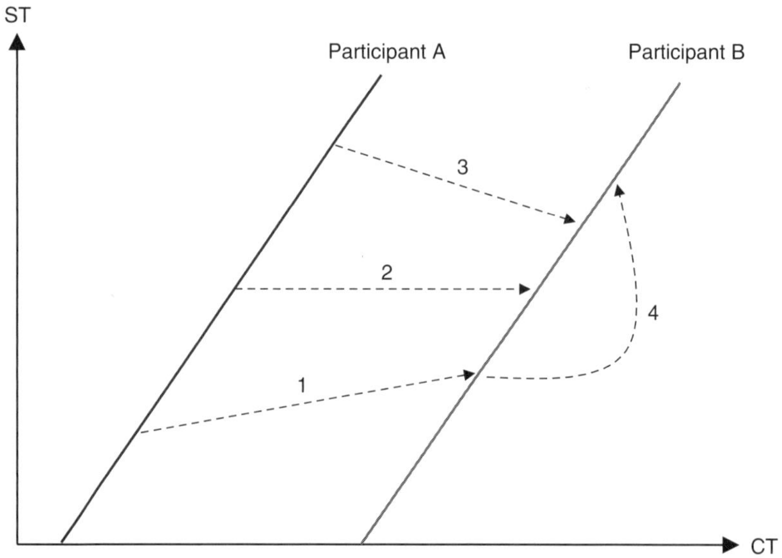

Figure 5.17
Accessing recorded events from the past.
Copyright MRL.

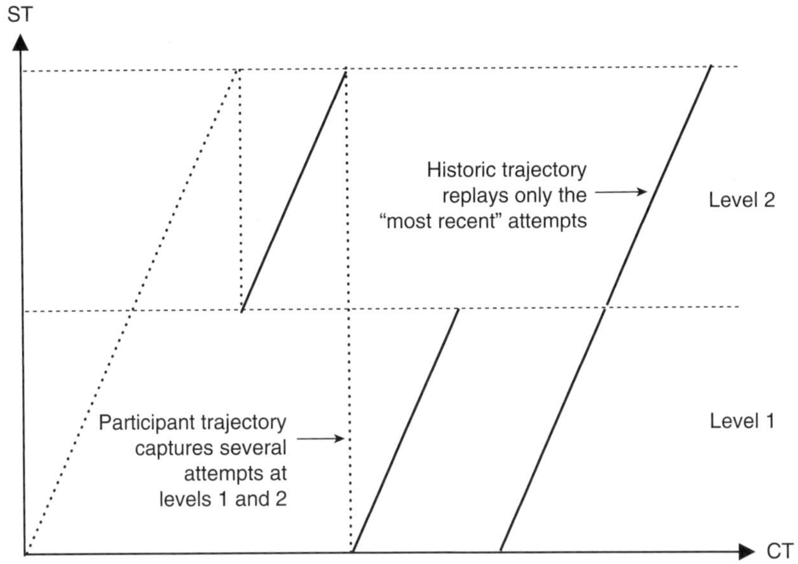

Figure 5.18
Synthesizing a historic trajectory.
Copyright MRL.

tional time travel. If he or she sees only live events, then the experience is like replaying a level in a conventional computer game—he or she travels back to a suitable moment in story time (but not, of course, in clock time) to retry scripted interactions. If the participant sees only recorded events, then he or she can view only the history of his or her own or others' activities from previous clock times. If the participant sees a mixture of the two, then he or she will be able to interact with some elements while only viewing others, as in racing against recorded "ghost" versions of themselves, as we see in computer games such as Gran Turismo, in which players can race virtual cars against recorded versions of themselves from previous games in order to try to improve their times.

It is important to note that recorded events are immutable, which means they cannot be changed, as this would require time travel in clock time. We can, however, appear to change them by overwriting them with new versions (a familiar idea from recording video and audio), which can support interesting narratives that exploit classic time travel paradoxes arising from altering the past through historic trajectories, which synthesize fragments from different recorded participant trajectories. For example, figure 5.18 shows a participant trajectory where a player repeatedly attempts two levels of a computer game that are associated with different story times. In this example, the system synthesizes a historic trajectory from the rule that only the most recently (in clock time) recorded versions of each level should be included (shown by the highlighted segments). The dashed line shows that the player then reviews this historic trajectory at a later time (and also speeded up).

Under this selection rule, the experience works like a multitrack recorder, with participants being able to overwrite the apparent history of events by replaying previous levels. As with multitrack audio recording, care must be taken to avoid jarring anomalies that might become apparent at the transitions between segments, such as the cast of participants (e.g., other players) suddenly changing. This might be achieved by ensuring that any such transitions occur at natural breaks or pauses in the structure of story time (e.g., between chapters, acts, or levels).

There are other potentially interesting selection rules for synthesizing a historic trajectory from recorded participant trajectories. For example, the "best" version of events (e.g., with the highest score) rather than the most recent version might be selected, participants might see their own subjective versions of history composed from only their recorded trajectories, or in the most extreme case they might be able to explore all recorded histories, following different participants' stories and seeing alternative versions and outcomes.

Looking further afield, this idea of multilayered temporal trajectories has parallels in the broader computing literature, as in proposals for managing divergent and reconvergent histories in asynchronous shared document editors. For example, the Timewarp system enabled participants to create and navigate divergent edit histories, including moving backward and forward in a document's history (story time in our terms) before creating a final definitive version (an example of synthesizing a historic trajectory) (Edwards and Mynatt 1997). A later extension to this work involved multiple local edit histories that could be edited independently and/or related to a common overall document history (Edwards et al. 2000), a more complex example of synchronizing multiple trajectories. The MASSIVE-3 collaborative virtual environment platform included a nested recording facility where scenes in one virtual world could be enacted, recorded, and then played back within another live world. This enabled "3D flashbacks" within an interactive narrative (Craven et al. 2001), providing an example of creating a historic trajectory (recording) that subsequently becomes part of a canonical trajectory later on in an experience.

Summary of the Trajectories Conceptual Framework

In this chapter, we have developed a conceptual framework for understanding mixed reality performance in terms of the interleaving of various kinds of trajectories that express different aspects of extended journeys through hybrid ecologies of space, times, interfaces, and roles. Before moving on to consider the wider uses of this framework, we first pause to briefly draw together and summarize the key concepts in the framework (see table 5.2).

Putting Trajectories to Work

In the introduction to this chapter, we identified four possible motivations for developing our conceptual framework. We now revisit and expand on each of these so as to clarify how trajectories might help researchers and practitioners engage with mixed reality performance as an emerging interactive and theatrical form.

Providing Sensitizing Concepts for Future Empirical Studies

Our initial aim has been to provide empirical researchers with sensitizing concepts to guide studies of user experiences. In the words of Herbert Blumer, a sensitizing concept provides a "general sense of reference and guidance in approaching empirical instances" (1954, 7). Or, as Glenn Bowen has recently put it, they can act as "interpretative devices and a starting point for a qualitative study" (2006). Sensitizing concepts can help inspire new studies, suggesting domains to study or themes on which to focus, and can provide an analytic lens through which to look at data from these studies, or indeed from past studies. In this book, we have taken an initial sensitizing concept—that of interactional trajectories—that had emerged from previous research and, by applying it retrospectively to previously published studies of user experiences, have extended and refined it, drawing out many of its subtle nuances. We propose that the resulting conceptual framework can help researchers identify key themes for future studies of cultural experiences. We offer the following as some immediate possibilities:

- studying how continuity is established and sustained in complex user experiences, including revealing the causes, effects and management of breakdowns in continuity due to different kinds of transitions, building on previous studies of seams and their effects
- studying how ecologies of interfaces are assembled, and the nature of trajectories through multiple interfaces that are situated within a surrounding environment, rather than through single interfaces
- exploring the temporal interleaving of multiple ongoing experiences and the nature of episodic engagement, including how participants prioritize competing activities and how they manage, interruptions, accountability, and reengagement
- deepening our understanding of how experiences are framed, from the practicalities of scheduling, admission, and flow in high-throughput experiences, to the role of rituals and briefings and the nature of giving instructions

Future studies might look beyond "cutting-edge" artistic projects for evidence of trajectories in more mainstream applications, such as amusement parks, tour guides,

Table 5.2
Summary of the trajectories conceptual framework

A *trajectory* describes a journey through a user experience, emphasizing its overall continuity and coherence. Trajectories pass through different *hybrid structures* that are combined to create the underlying structure of the performance:

• Multiple physical and virtual spaces may be adjacent, connected, and overlaid to create a *hybrid space* that provides the stage for the experience.
• *Hybrid time* combines story time, plot time, schedule time, interaction time, and perceived time to shape the overall timing of events.
• *Hybrid interfaces* assemble different interfaces in an environment to enable interaction and collaboration.
• *Hybrid roles* define how different individuals engage, including the public roles of participant and spectator (audience and bystander) and the professional roles of actor, operator, and orchestrator.

Our framework defines three distinct kinds of trajectory:

• *Canonical trajectories* express an artist's intended journey through the performance or overall narrative. They may create many canonical trajectories expressing different routes through the performance, perhaps for different kinds of participants, or so that participants can choose among alternative paths.
• *Participant trajectories* express an individual participant's actual route through the experience and may diverge from canonical trajectories due to interactivity (the ability of the participant to choose what to do next). The balancing force of orchestration enables artists to steer a participant's trajectory back toward a canonical trajectory.
• *Historic trajectories* support reflection, replay, and documentation by defining particular views of what happened in a mixed reality performance in the past. They achieve this through synthesis rules that select segments from among recorded participant trajectories, recombine them, and express when and how they become available to others.

Establishing a sense of continuity and coherence involves dealing with various *transitions*, key moments at which trajectories cross the seams in hybrid structure. The following transitions must be carefully designed and managed:

• *Beginnings* frame an experience, through attracting attention, admission, briefing, and handing over equipment as part of the framing of the experience.
• *Endings* use souvenirs and replay interfaces to support reflection, discussion, and the sharing of memories.
• *Role transitions* and *interface transitions* involve handing over equipment and further briefings.
• *Traversals between physical and virtual worlds* are enhanced by matching physical and virtual design and through traversable interfaces.
• *Temporal transitions between episodes* involve periods of disengagement and subsequent reengagement and require succinct summaries of missed action.
• *Transitions into physical resources* that cannot easily be replicated must deal with the challenge of contention when several participants simultaneously try to engage with the resource.
• *Transitions across seams in the infrastructure* must deal with limitations in the underlying technical infrastructure such as partial coverage of sensing systems and wireless communications.
• *Interleaved trajectories* capture the social and collaborative aspects of experiences, identifying possibilities for encounters in space and time, around interfaces, or through roles. They also identify important opportunities for isolation. Interleaved trajectories can also express issues of pacing as well as balancing and prioritizing multiple ongoing activities.

museums, and galleries. Our framework might even help sensitize studies outside of the immediate domain of cultural applications, perhaps in learning, the home, or the workplace. To what extent can these experiences also be understood in terms of trajectories?

A Vehicle for Compiling Craft Knowledge

There is clearly already extensive experience among a variety of artists of designing complex mixed reality performances, but much of it remains "craft knowledge," painstakingly acquired by artists, designers, and performers over years of practice in which they have iteratively refined their ideas and techniques through multiple projects. Such craft knowledge is currently passed onto the next generation of artists and designers through what might be broadly thought of as an apprenticeship model—for example, through the common approach of interns working on projects. Our conceptual framework marks the beginning of an attempt to collect and collate such craft knowledge and to distill its key lessons. This might be of benefit to those wishing to enter the specific and growing field of mixed reality performance, but might also speak to designers and practitioners working in other more tangentially related fields of endeavor. One use of our conceptual framework is therefore to support the compilation of key techniques and examples, both from practice and the literature, in order to ultimately establish design guidelines or "interaction design patterns" (Tidwell 2005) for specific aspects of the user experience. From a more research-oriented perspective, our framework also integrates previously disparate concepts from the literature including virtual reality (Sutherland 1970), ubiquitous computing (Weiser 1991), mixed reality (Milgram and Kishino 1994), tangible and public interfaces (Hornecker and Buur 2006), seamful design (Chalmers and Galani 2004), and interface ecologies (Huang et al. 2006).

One intriguing question for us is whether the diagrammatic expressions of trajectories that we have adopted throughout this chapter actively support design work. Our suspicion is that they do. Drawing trajectories that move through different structures or overlap in different ways helps to focus attention on a wide variety of design cases, as one can inspect all corners of a diagram and ask the question, "What might happen here?" For example, the construction and then inspection of both figures 5.8 and 5.16 brought to the foreground various questions about isolation or unusual encounters that might occur away from the most obvious points at which the trajectories actually cross. We have certainly found this kind of diagrammatic reasoning, which to us inherently emphasizes notions of symmetry and completeness, to be extremely useful for identifying and considering a wide variety of different design possibilities. As has been recently pointed out by Tim Ingold's study of lines (2007), which we discuss in the introduction, as well as Franco Moretti's research on the use of graphs, maps, and trees in literature, in which he presents a new way to redefine aesthetic concepts through mathematical models (2005), we suggest that such diagrams are able to paint the possible design space that is associated with a particular issue and thereby encourage not only designers, but also researchers in the arts and humanities, HCI, and the social sciences to explore it widely.

Identifying Requirements for New Technologies

In addition to helping collate existing techniques, reflection on our framework can also reveal gaps where there are requirements for new interaction techniques, tools, and platforms. The following are three immediate possibilities:

1. We currently lack techniques to support the fluid disengagement from and reengagement with ongoing long-term experiences. We require new techniques to help participants schedule episodes of engagement, to predict likely engagement from their patterns of activity, and to summarize missed action upon reengaging.
2. In spite of the use of souvenirs and simple histories, there is a gap for new tools and techniques that can record complex user experiences and then make these available to participants for reflection and discussion. Indeed, it is not even clear what it means to record such an experience—how can we capture all relevant interactions and events in hybrid experiences?
3. Orchestration is clearly an important process and, as noted previously, a necessary counterbalance to interactivity. However, each new experience currently relies on its own bespoke interfaces for monitoring and intervening in experiences. We require tools that can more easily (perhaps even semiautomatically) generate orchestration interfaces from the specification of an experience. Orchestration tools also need to deal with the dynamic scheduling of limited physical resources.

Enabling a Dramaturgy of Interactive User Experiences

As the field of HCI increasingly engages with practicing artists in order to explore new forms of cultural user experience, so it becomes important to consider whether it also needs to engage with those academic disciplines outside of HCI that have traditionally studied such experiences. The fields of drama and performance studies offer interesting paradigms to HCI. These fields involve dramaturgy; the art or technique of dramatic composition or theatrical representation, that is, the craft that shapes and studies the principal structural elements of a drama or performance; and the study of performance as both an aesthetic and social gathering. Conventionally, dramaturgies have focused on the drama or action represented on a stage, concentrating, for instance, on practitioners' use of space, time, plot, story, and character within that action, and its effect on an audience (Pfister 1998). Ideas from dramaturgy, adapted with concepts from performance studies, have shaped our framework and potentially have much to offer HCI. In turn, the emerging forms of interactive user experience that we discussed in this book have created the necessity for new methodologies and dramaturgies in performance and theater studies that are able to interpret interactive experiences, multiuser platforms, and hybrid forms (Hagebölling 2004). Ultimately, our framework is intended to bridge between HCI and performance studies, acting as a *"boundary object"* (Star 1989) that establishes a common language to support new interdisciplinary perspectives on complex interactive user experiences.

Trajectories beyond Mixed Reality Performance

The theory of trajectories that we have developed in this chapter has emerged from a series of studies of *mixed reality performance*, a new form of interactive experience that integrates digital media with physical settings and also combines interactivity with live action. Though the primary goals of our book have been to define and document mixed reality performance as an emerging genre and to provide concepts to explain how it works, it is also important consider how our concepts of trajectories relate to other kinds of experience. There are two motivations for this. First, we have argued that mixed reality performance is an inherently hybrid form that draws on various elements of other forms of experience such as installations, theater, and games. Surely concepts that explain mixed reality performance also speak to these related kinds of experience? Second, artistic experiences of the kind documented here may be at the leading edge of innovation into cultural and leisure applications of computing—where artists lead, the mainstream may eventually follow—so the ideas and techniques that we have described here may eventually see much more widespread adoption.

The first place to look for wider applications of our ideas is in the "creative industries," a broad catch-all term that encompasses different cultural, leisure, and entertainment sectors. Perhaps the most obvious applications of our concepts are to be found in those sectors of the creative industries that inherently address extended spatial settings and can therefore most immediately benefit from an integration of digital media into the everyday physical world. Museums, galleries, exploratoria, sites of historical or scientific special interest, and similar visiting experiences are increasingly concerned with the design of interactive installations and the association of digital media with locations and artifacts in the real world (e.g., location-based tours and guides). Previous studies of interactives in museums and galleries had already highlighted the idea that there are interactional trajectories through such experiences (Hornecker and Buur 2006), and our work in this book offers a widening and substantial generalization of this. Our discussions of spectator interfaces, ecologies of interfaces, extended spatial structures, and recording and replaying experiences should be of direct relevance to the design and study of new forms of visiting experience. The theme park, as a particular kind of extended visiting experience, is of particular relevance here. *Fairground: Thrill Laboratory* already shows a direct connection between our ideas of trajectories and this particular setting, but we envisage much wider possibilities. At one level, the design of individuals rides clearly embodies a strong notion of trajectory, with a carefully designed flow of experience through initial queuing and the main ride, and from there into a shop where there is the possibility to purchase souvenirs and mementos. More generally, the wider design of the theme park as an extended but integrated spatial and temporal experience might be considered in terms of many different of interleaved trajectories that reflect the social experiences of different groups of visitors.

Games have emerged as a major sector of the creative industries, spanning diverse genres from conventional console and PC-based video games to MMPORGs and casual games. Of particular relevance here are emerging genres such as augmented reality games (see Bernandes et al. 2008; Flintham et al. 2003), alternate reality games (see Montola 2005), and pervasive games (see Montola, Stenros, and Waern 2009) that aim to unchain the player from the spatial and temporal constraints of the fixed console and instead move the gaming experience out into the real world. Many of the examples that we have described in the book are at the forefront of this trend, and several have received recognition in the games industry for breaking new ground. Our concepts of trajectories should therefore be directly relevant to the study and design of games, helping explain the complexities of their narrative and social structures (typified by our discussion of temporal structure in chapter 2 and this chapter) and also identifying the key challenges that have to be met as they increasingly become interwoven with the everyday physical world around us.

Thinking in terms of trajectories may also be relevant to other sectors of the creative industries, such as film, television, and music. The spread of mobile computing means that these traditionally linear media are becomingly increasingly finely sliced and accessed in a variety of different settings and while on the move, so they essentially take on a more interactive form (in which the interactivity arises from when, where, and how to access them), raising questions of how they can best be interwoven with other ongoing threads of activity. Here, our concepts of trajectories may provide new insights into the scheduling of such media, the design of increasingly episodic structures, their juxtaposition with physical settings, and issues of spectatorship that arise when they are consumed or shared in pubic settings.

Looking beyond the creative industries, trajectories, which are already adopted in stations and airports to direct flow, are increasingly used in a whole variety of subject areas, including medicine and business. In medicine, for instance, they have been employed to define an "ongoing course of action" that could be useful for the understanding of the way staff work because it allows for the identification of key transitions, cycles, plans, and management (Graham, Cheverst, and Rouncefield 2005, 16). Different types of trajectories have been identified, such as psychological trajectories indicating "the disease process itself," temporal trajectories, marking "day-to-day activities," social trajectories, indicating "the social consequences of dependency," and sentimental trajectories, marking "emotions concerning confrontation of the disease" (Strauss in Graham, Cheverst, and Rouncefield 2005, 16). For instance, Anselm Strauss defines a trajectory as "(1) the course of any experience phenomenon as it evolves over time (an engineering project, a chronic illness, dying, a social revolution, or national problems attending mass or 'uncontrollable' immigration) and (2) the actions and interactions contributing to this evolution" (1993, 53). Trajectories in this sense can define a process spanning from design to management. So Graham identifies three subcategories to describe how trajectories are conceptualized, designed, and managed (Graham, Cheverst, and Rouncefield 2005, 17). Equally broad is Geraldine Fitzpatrick's *Locales Framework* (1998), which uses Strauss's model of activity (1993) and defines trajectories as indicating the emergence of a possible course of action through time and the involvement of multiple actors. This model is based on five "aspects": foundations, civic structure, individual views, mutuality, and interaction trajectory. The latter, Paul Dourish notes, introduces the idea of trajectory as "a way of understanding how social worlds develop, how people enter and leave, and how the activities in which they engage contribute to the various courses of action in which the social world is engaged." For this reason, he notes, the temporal aspect of trajectories allows for the consideration of schedules and other dynamic aspects of action that "are more than simply sequence" (2001, 93–94).

There are other sectors of activity that might benefit from thinking in terms of trajectories through experience. The design of new interactive learning experiences might benefit from discussions of spatial integration, record and replay, pacing, and new approaches of collaboration. Architecture and planning are increasingly concerned with how digital media can enhance our experience and understanding of the spatial structures that we inhabit, including analyzing and designing trajectories through structures at multiple levels of scale from individual buildings to cities. In a similar vein, the transportation sector is fundamentally concerned with the design of spatial trajectories, including an emerging focus on designing the "end-to-end" experience of entire journeys that connect across multiple forms of transportation. Finally, and even more broadly, a variety of service industries are increasingly concerned how to connect multiple components to create new services, especially with regard to the emerging world of digital services in which processes can potentially be very rapidly combined and restructured. Recent work in this area has argued for new service design methods that can bridge what are referred to as the "front stage" and "backstage" of service provision, and thus better manage the delivery of service encounters to customers, especially with regard to how humans might improvise interactions with customers against a backdrop of increasingly automated backend processes, proposals that have potentially strong resonances with our discussions of trajectories, interaction, and orchestration (Glushko and Tabas 2009). Related to all of these is a growing movement within HCI to consider how all forms of interaction with computers might be considered in terms of a holistic user experience that extends far beyond the bounds of conventional usability and interaction design (Law et al. 2008). Ultimately, this may turn out to be the wider target for our theory of trajectories that can provide an approach to designing holistic and extended user experiences that gracefully interweave our use of computers with our experience of diverse settings and our social encounters with other people. Clearly, this book has taken only a first step along this particular route, by drawing out an initial conceptual framework from the study of a new and distinctive kind of experience. Much remains to be done to see whether and how the concepts of trajectories that we have outlined here can be applied beyond mixed reality performance to other areas of the creative industries, to other sectors altogether, and in the long term, as a framework to guide the design of the interactive user experience, whatever its application.

Conclusion

For over ten years now, groups of artists working at the cutting edge of theater, live art, and game design have been experimenting with interactive technologies to create new theatrical experiences that mix real worlds with virtual worlds and also interactivity with live action. The inherently "mixed" nature of what we choose to call mixed reality performances—continually mixing diverse spaces, time scales, roles, and interfaces in new ways to create complex hybrid structures—may appear to challenge classification, and can make these experiences difficult to comprehend, especially when seen through the conventional theoretical lenses provided by the fields of human computer interaction and performance studies. This is not to say, however, that such experiences do not belong to a common genre or that they are beyond study. Rather, as we have argued throughout this book, they demand a new theoretical approach, one that is able to accommodate their inherent hybridity yet is also able to articulate what they have in common.

The book proposes that mixed reality performance—and perhaps other forms of interactive experience that share the same characteristics of hybrid space, time, interfaces, and roles—can be most usefully understood in terms of trajectories. As lines or threads through experience, trajectories emphasize the journey more than the destination and naturally reflect the importance of continuity and the interweaving of social experience. Although the basis for thinking of many different kinds of experiences in terms of trajectories can already be seen in diverse disciplines, we have attempted to develop a detailed and structured conceptual framework around trajectories that might provide sensitizing concepts with which to ground studies; that act as a vehicle for distilling and compiling craft knowledge; that help identify requirements for new or missing technologies; and that potentially provide guidelines to help with the creation of similar experiences. There are several key aspects to our theory. First, mixed reality performances can be understood in terms of three fundamental types of trajectory: canonical trajectories express artists intended narratives or journeys through a work; participant trajectories express the actual journeys that different individuals undertake; and historic trajectories synthesize different views of what took place as the experience is subsequently replayed. The relationship between canonical and participant trajectories as they diverge and reconverge throughout an experience reflects the inherent tension between the force of interactivity on the one hand and orchestration on the other. Second, trajectories must be carefully overcome key transitions, moments at which, for various reasons, the continuity of experience is at risk and has to be carefully sustained. Key transitions include beginnings, endings, role and interface handovers, real-virtual traversals, managing access to physical resources, and dealing with the so-called "seams" in the underlying technical infrastructure. Third, the interweaving of participant trajectories can reflect the different possibilities for encounters but also isolation in social experiences, across space and time, and around common roles and interfaces.

Beyond the theory, our other driving concern has been to document the work of the artists who are creating and defining mixed reality performance. The artist company Blast Theory in particular has been at the forefront of this field for over ten years and in collaboration with Nottingham's Mixed Reality Laboratory has produced a series of landmark works including *Desert Rain, Can You See Me Now?, Uncle Roy All Around You, Day of the Figurines, Rider Spoke*, and *Ulrike and Eamon Compliant*, all of which were documented herein. The evolving nature of the collaboration between these parties is also of general interest, as is the emergence of the methodology of "research in the wild" in which artist-led practice provides opportunities for ethnographic studies that in turn underpin theatrical work. It is also interesting how these activities feed into each other in various other ways over both short and longer time scales. Of course, other artists are also involved in this growing area, and we have documented the work of some of these, such as Brendan Walker, and various other collaborative research projects, and have referred to many other interesting and powerful examples of work in the field.

Of the longer-term or wider impact of this body of work, of course, only time will tell. However, we end by noting that where artists lead the mainstream may eventually follow. Mixed reality performance may perhaps appear to be a niche theatrical genre at the current time, practiced by a small group of artists, some of whom might not even recognize this term as applying to their work. However, what these artists are trying to do with emerging technologies is both fascinating and deeply imaginative. They are creating new forms of interactive experience and in so doing are challenging many existing conventions and paradigms. Thus, the complex spatial, temporal, performative, and interactional characteristics of the works documented in this book may point toward new kinds of applications in which online and physical are interwoven in different ways over multiple time scales. Perhaps there are ideas, technologies, designs, or templates here for future applications in more mainstream forms of leisure or entertainment, or perhaps even beyond, in health care, transportation, customer services, or many other sectors of the future digital economy. The artists themselves may or may not be concerned with such applications, but it is certainly of interest to wider research communities to consider them and to understand what mixed reality performances can tell us about the design of the "user experience" in general. We hope that by documenting this unique and challenging body of work and by providing theoretical foundations for understanding and designing them, we will be able to inspire a variety of communities, from human computer interaction to performance studies and beyond, to gain new insights into the relationships between people, interactive technologies, and new forms of experience.

References

Adams, K. 2006. "The threshold of the real: A site for participator resistance in Blast Theory's *Uncle Roy All Around You* (2003)." *Body, Space and Technology*. Available at <http://people.brunel.ac.uk/bst/vol0601/kateadams/kateadamspdf.pdf> (accessed September 2008).

Adams, M. 2005. Interview with G. Giannachi. London, April 11, 2005, Giannachi's private archive.

Adams, M. 2007. Email to G. Giannachi and S. Benford, September 11, 2007, private archive.

Adams, M., S. Benford, and G. Giannachi. 2008. Pervasive presence: Blast Theory's *Day of the Figurines*. *Contemporary Theatre Review* 18 (2): 219–257.

Adams, M., and J. Row Farr. 2001. Blast Theory: *Desert Rain* und andere Performance-Environments. In *Maschinen, medien, performances*, edited by M. Leeker, 732–749. Berlin: Alexander Verlag.

Adams, M., M. Flintham, L. Oppermann, and S. Benford. 2007. "Workpackage WP17 CCG R*ider Spoke*." Available at <http://www.pervasive-gaming.org/press1.php> (accessed June 2009).

Allen, R. C. 1992. *Channels of discourse, reassembled: Television and contemporary criticism*. London: Routledge.

Anastasi, R., N. Tandavanitj, M. Flintham, A. Crabtree, M. Adams, J. Row Farr, J. Iddon, et al. 2002. "*Can You See Me Now?* A citywide mixed-reality gaming experience." Available at <http://www.cs.nott.ac.uk/~sxi/papers/tech02.pdf> (accessed September 2008).

Armstrong, S. 1999. Want to replay the Gulf War as a video game? *Sunday Times*, October 31.

Armstrong, S. 2003. Strange brain. *Sunday Times*, June 9.

Attali, J. 1982. *Histories du temps*. Paris: Fayard.

Bannon, L., S. Benford, J. Bowers, and C. Heath. 2005. Hybrid design creates innovative museum experiences. *Communications of the ACM* 48 (3) (March): 62–65.

Barfield, W., T. Sheridan, D. Zeltzer, and M. Slater. 1995. Presence and performance within virtual environments. In *Virtual environments and advanced interface design*, edited by W. Barfield and T. Furness III, 473–513. Oxford: Oxford University Press.

Barfield, W., and S. Weghorst. 1993. The sense of presence within virtual environments: A conceptual framework. In *Human computer interaction: Software and hardware interfaces*, edited by G. Salvendy and M. Smith, 699–704. Amsterdam: Elsevier.

Barkhuus, L., M. Chalmers, P. Tennent, M. Hall, M. Bell, S. Sherwood, and B. Brown. 2005. Picking pockets on the lawn: The development of tactics and strategies in a mobile game. In *UbiComp 2005: Ubiquitous Computing*, edited by M. Beigl, S. Intille, and H. Tokuda, 358–374. LNCS 3660. Berlin, Heidelberg, and New York: Springer.

Bateson, G. 1955. A theory of play and fantasy. *A.P.A. Psychiatric Research Reports* 2: 39–51.

Baudrillard, J. 1991. *The Gulf War did not take place*. Translated by Power Institute and P. Patton. Sydney: Power Publications.

Bell, M., M. Chalmers, L. Barkhuus, M. Hall, S. Sherwood, P. Tennent, B. Brown, D. Rowland, and S. Benford. 2006. Interweaving mobile games with everyday life. In *Proceedings of the ACM CHI 2006 Conference on Human Factors in Computing Systems, Games, and Performances*, vol. 1, 417–426. Montreal: ACM Press.

Bellotti, V., M. Back, W. K. Edwards, R. E. Grinter, A. Henderson, and C. Lopes. 2002. Making sense of sensing systems: Five questions for designers and researchers. In *Proceedings of the SIGCHI Conference on Human Factors in Computing Systems: Changing Our World, Changing Ourselves*, 415–422. Minneapolis, Minn.: ACM Press.

Benford, S., ed. 2006. "WP12: City as Theatre deliverable D12.4 evaluation of the first City as Theatre public performance," Version 2. Release date: February 10, 2006. Available at <http://www.pervasive-gaming.org/index_swf.html> (accessed June 2006).

Benford, S. 2007. "D12.6 Evaluation of *Day of the Figurines* II. Final report of the City as Theatre showcase." Available at <http://www.pervasive-gaming.org/index.php> (accessed September 2010).

Benford, S., R. Anastasi, M. Flintham, H. Schnädelbach, B. Koleva, S. Izadi, M. Fraser, et al. 2004. "Towards a citywide mixed reality performance." Available at <http://www.blasttheory.co.uk/bt/documents/Twds%20a%20city%20Mixed%20Reality%20Game.pdf> (accessed September 2010).

Benford, S., J. Bowers, P. Chandler, L. Ciolfi, M. Flintham, M. Fraser, C. Greenhalgh, et al. 2001. Unearthing virtual history: Using diverse interfaces to reveal hidden virtual worlds. In *Ubicomp 2001: Ubiquitous Computing*, edited by G. D. Abowd, B. Brumitt, and S. Shafer, 225–230. LNCS 2201. Berlin, Heidelberg, and New York: Springer.

Benford, S., A. Crabtree, M. Flintham, A. Drozd, R. Anastasi, M. Paxton, N. Tandavanitj, M. Adams, and J. Row Farr. 2006. *Can You See Me Now? ACM Trans. Computer-Human Interaction* 13 (1): 100–133.

Benford, S., A. Crabtree, M. Flintham, D. Rowland, B. Gaver, M. Adams, J. Row Farr, N. Tandavanitj, A. Oldroyd, and J. Sutton. 2004. *Provoking reflection through artistic games.* In *Proceedings of the 2004 CHI Conference on Human Factors in Computing Systems* (Workshop 19. Social

Learning through Gaming). Vienna: ACM Press. Available at <http://www.blasttheory.co.uk/bt/documents/Reflection%20thru%20Artistic%20Games.pdf> (accessed September 2010).

Benford, S., A. Crabtree, S. Reeves, M. Flintham, A. Drozd, J. Sheridan, and A. Dix. 2006. The frame of the game: Blurring the boundary between fiction and reality in mobile experiences. In *Proceedings of the ACM CHI 2006 Conference on Human Factors in Computing Systems, Games, and Performances*, vol. 1, 427–436. Montreal: ACM Press.

Benford, S., and L. Fahlén. 1993. A spatial model of interaction in large virtual environments. In *Proceedings of the Third European Conference on Computer-Supported Cooperative Work (ECSCW '93)*, 109–124. Milan: Kluwer.

Benford, S., M. Flintham, and A. Drozd. 2006. "The design and experience of the location-based performance *Uncle Roy All Around You*." *Leonardo* 14:3. Available at <http://leoalmanac.org/journal/vol_14/lea_v14_n03-04/roy.html> (accessed September 2010).

Benford, S., M. Flintham, A. Drozd, R. Anastasi, D. Rowland, N. Tandavanitj, M. Adams, J. Row Farr, A. Oldroyd, and J. Sutton. 2004. "*Uncle Roy All Around You*: Implicating the city in a location-based performance." In *Proceedings of the ACM CHI 2004 Conference on Human Factors in Computing Systems, Games, and Performances*. Available at <http://www.amutualfriend.co.uk/papers/3.Uncle_Roy_at_ACE.pdf> (accessed September 2008).

Benford, S., and G. Giannachi. 2008. Temporal trajectories in shared interactive narratives. In *Proceedings of CHI 2008*, 73–82. Florence: ACM Press.

Benford, S., G. Giannachi, B. Koleva, and T. Rodden. 2009. From interaction to trajectories: Designing coherent journeys through user experiences. In *Proceedings of the 27th International Conference on Human Factors in Computing Systems (CHI 2009*), 709–718. Boston: ACM Press.

Benford, S., and C. Greenhalgh, M. Craven, G. Walker, T. Regan, and J. Morphett, J. 2000. Inhabited TV: Broadcasting interaction from within collaborative virtual environments. *ACM Transactions on Computer-Human Interaction (TOCHI)* 7 (4): 510–547.

Benford, S., C. Greenhalgh, G. Reyard, C. Brwon, and B. Koleva. (September 1998). Understanding and constructing shared spaces with mixed-reality boundaries. *ACM Transactions on Computer-Human Interaction* 5 (3): 185–223.

Benford, S., G. Reynard, C. Greenhalgh, D. Snowdon, and A. Bullock. 2000. A poetry performance in a collaborative virtual environment. *IEEE Computer Graphics and Applications* 20 (3): 66–75.

Benford, S., D. Rowland, M. Flintham, A. Drozd, R. Hull, J. Reid, J. Morrison, and K. Facer. 2005. Life on the edge: Supporting collaboration in location-based experiences. In *Proceedings of the ACM CHI 2005 Conference*, 721–730. Portland, Ore.: ACM Press.

Benford, S., D. Rowland, M. Flintham, R. Hull, J. Reid, J. Morrison, K. Facer, and B. Clayton. 2004. "*Savannah:* Designing a location-based game simulating lion behaviour." International Conference on Advances in Computer Entertainment Technology. Available at <http://www.mobilebristol.com/PDF/MobileBristol-2004-03.pdf> (accessed October 2008).

Benford, S., W. Seager, M. Flintham, R. Anastasi, D. Rowland, J. Humble, D. Stanton, et al. 2004. The error of our ways: The experience of self-reported position in a location-based game. In *UbiComp 2004: Ubiquitous Computing*, edited by N. Davies, E. D. Mynatt, and I. Siio, 721–730. LNCS 3205. Berlin, Heidelberg, and New York: Springer.

Benjamin, W. [1955] 1992. Theses on the philosophy of history. In *Illuminations*, translated by H. Zohn, 245–255. London: Fontana Press.

Bernandes, J., R. Tori, R. Nakamura, D. Calife, and A. Tomoyose. 2008. Augmented reality games. In *Extending experiences: Structure, analysis and design of computer game player experience*, edited by O. Leino, H. Wirman, and A. Fernandez, 228–246. Lapland: LUP.

Björk, S. 2007. Changing urban perspectives: Illuminating cracks and drawing illusionary lines. In *Space time play: Computer games, architecture and urbanism: The next level*, edited by F. von Borries, S. Walz, and M. Böttger, 276–289. Basel: Birkhaüser.

Blast Theory. 2000. "*Desert Rain.*" Available at <http://www.blasttheory.co.uk/bt/work_desertrain.html> (accessed September 2010).

Blast Theory. 2002. *Desert Rain*, catalogue.

Blast Theory. 2003. "*Can You See Me Now?*" Available at <http://www.blasttheory.co.uk/bt/work_cysmn.html> (accessed September 2008).

Blast Theory. 2005. "*Uncle Roy All Around You.*" Available at <http://www.blasttheory.co.uk/bt/work_uncleroy.html> (accessed September 2010).

Blast Theory. 2008. "*Flypad.*" Available at <http://www.blasttheory.co.uk/bt/work_flypad.html> (accessed February 2009).

Blast Theory. 2009. "*Ulrike and Eamon Compliant.*" Available at <http://www.blasttheory.co.uk/bt/work_ulrikeandeamoncompliant.html> (accessed September 2010).

Blumer, H. 1954. What is wrong with social theory. *American Sociological Review* 18:3–10.

Bolter, J. D., and R. Grusin. 2000. *Remediation*. Cambridge, Mass.: MIT Press.

Borries, F. von, S. Walz, and M. Böttger, eds. 2007. *Space time play: Computer games, architecture and urbanism: The next level*. Basel: Birkhäuser.

Bowen, G. 2006. "Grounded theory and sensitizing concepts." *International Journal of Qualitative Methods* 5 (3) (September). Available at <http://www.ualberta.ca/~iiqm/backissues/5_3/PDF/bowen.pdf> (accessed January 2010).

Bowers, J. 1999. "Production tools for electronic arenas: Event management and content production." eRENA D4.3/D4.4 CID, KTH. August.

Bowers, J., and S. O. Hellström. 2000. Simple interfaces to complex sound in improvised music. In *Proceedings of CHI 2000, Extended Abstracts*, 125–126. The Hague: ACM Press.

Bowers, J., J. Pycock, and J. O'Brien. 1996. Talk and embodiment in collaborative virtual environments. In *Proceedings of the SIGCHI Conference on Human Factors in Computing Systems (CHI '96)*, 58–65. Vancouver: ACM Press.

Capra, M., and S. Benford. 2007. "*Day of the Figurines*: Informing the Development of Tangible Spectator Interfaces." WP12: City as Theatre, deliverable D12.7. Available at <http://www.pervasive-gaming.org/index.php> (accessed February 2009).

Castells, M. 1996. *The rise of the network society*. Oxford: Blackwell.

Castells, M., J. Fernández-Ardèvol, J. Linchuam Qiu, and A. Sey. 2007. *Mobile communication and society*. Cambridge, Mass.: MIT Press.

Chalmers, M., and A. Galani. 2004. Seamful interweaving: Heterogeneity in the theory and design of interactive systems. In *Proceedings of the 2004 ACM Symposium on Designing Interactive Systems*, 243–252. Cambridge, Mass.: ACM Press.

Chamberlain, A., and S. Benford. 2008. "Deliverable D17.3 cultural console game, final report." Available at <http://www.pervasive-gaming.org/press1.php> (accessed June 2009).

Chamberlain, A., D. Rowland, J. Foster, and G. Giannachi. 2010. Riders have spoken: Replaying and archiving pervasive performances. *Leonardo* 43 (1): 88.

Chen, J. 2007. Flow in games (and everything else). *Communications of the ACM* 50 (4) (April): 31–34.

Clarke, R. 2001. Reigning territorial plains: Blast Theory's "*Desert Rain*." *Performance Research* 6 (2): 43–50.

COMIC. Available at <http://www.comp.lancs.ac.uk/computing/research/soft_eng/comic/> (accessed December 2009).

Communications Research Group. Available at <http://www.crg.cs.nott.ac.uk> (accessed January 2010).

Costello, B., L. Muller, S. Amitani, and E. Edmonds. 2005. Understanding the experience of interactive art: Iamascope in Beta_space. In *Proceedings of the 2nd Australasian Conference on Interactive Entertainment*, vol. 123, 49–56. Sydney: Creativity and Cognition Studios Press.

Crabtree, A. 2003. *Designing collaborative systems: A practical guide to ethnography*. Berlin: Springer.

Crabtree, A., in M. Capra and S. Benford. 2007. "*Day of the Figurines*: Informing the development of tangible spectator interfaces." WP12: City as Theatre, deliverable D12.7 version. Available at <http://www.pervasive-gaming.org/index.php> (accessed February 2009).

Crabtree, A., S. Benford, C. Greenhalgh, P. Tennant, M. Chalmers, and B. Brown. 2006. Supporting ethnographic studies of ubiquitous computing in the wild. In *Proceedings of ACM Designing Interactive Systems (DIS 2006)*, 60–69. Penn State, Penn.: ACM Press.

Crabtree, A., S. Benford, T. Rodden, C. Greenhalgh, M. Flintham, R. Anastasi, A. Drozd, M. Adams, J. Row Farr, N. Tandavanitj, and A. Steed. 2004. Orchestrating a mixed reality game "on the ground." In *Proceedings of the 2004 CHI Conference on Human Factors in Computing Systems*, 391–398. Vienna: ACM Press.

Crabtree, A., and T. Rodden. 2007. Hybrid ecologies: Understanding cooperative interaction in emerging physical-digital environments. *Personal and Ubiquitous Computing* 12 (7): 481–493.

Crang, M., P. Crang, and J. May. 1999. *Virtual geographies: Bodies, space and relations*. London: Routledge.

Craven, C., I. Taylor, A. Drozd, J. Purbrick, C. Greenhalgh, S. Benford, M. Fraser, J. Bowers, K. Jaa-Aro, B. Lintermann, and M. Hoch. 2001. Exploiting interactivity, influence, space, time to explore non-linear drama in virtual worlds. *CHI 2001*: 30–37.

Cruz-Neira, C., D. J. Sandin, T. A. DeFant, R. V. Kenyon, and J. C. Hart. 1992. The Cave: Audio visual experience virtual environment. *CACM* 35 (6): 65–72.

Davies, C., and J. Harrison. 1996. *Osmose*: Towards broadening the aesthetics of virtual reality. *ACM Computer Graphics: Virtual Reality* 30 (4): 25–28.

de Certeau, M. 1984. *The practice of everyday life*. Translated by S. Rendall. Berkeley: University of California Press.

Deleuze, G. 1993. *The fold*. Translated by B. Conley. London: Continuum.

Deleuze, G., and F. Guattari. 1988. *A thousand plateaus*. Translated by B. Massumi. London: Athlone Press.

Deligny, F. 1975. *Voix et Voir, Recherches*, no. 8 (April).

de Souza e Silva, A. 2003. "From MUDS as space to space as a MUD." Conference proceedings, University of California Irvine. Available at <http://www.humanities.uci.edu/visualstudies/everyday/papers.html> (accessed October 2008).

de Souza e Silva, A. 2004. Location based mobile games: Blurring the borders between physical and virtual spaces. In *Proceedings of the 12th International Symposium of Electronic Arts* (*ISEA 2004*), 14–22. Helsinki: ISEA.

de Souza e Silva, A. 2006. From cyber to hybrid: Mobile technologies as interfaces of hybrid spaces. *Space and Culture* 9 (3): 261–278.

de Souza e Silva, A. 2009. Hybrid reality and location-based gaming: Redefining mobility and game spaces in urban environments. *Simulation & Gaming* 40 (3): 404–424.

Dinkla, S. 1997. *Pioniere interaktiver Kunst von 1970 bis heute*. Karlsruhe: Edition ZKM, Cantz Verlag.

Dinkla, S. 2001. Auf dem Weg zu einer performativen Interaktion. In *Maschinen, Medien, Performances: Theater and der Schnittstelle zu digitalen Welten*, edited by M. Leeker, 126–141. Berlin: Alexander Verlag.

Dix, A. 1987. The myth of the infinitely fast machine. In *People and computers III*, edited by D. Diaper and R. Winder, 215–228. Cambridge: Cambridge University Press.

Dix, A. 1992. Pace and interaction. In *Proceedings HCI '92 People and Computers VII*, 193–207. Cambridge: Cambridge University Press.

Dixon, S. 2007. *Digital performance*. Cambridge, Mass.: The MIT Press.

Dodson, S. 2004. *"Uncle Roy All Around You." Icon Magazine*. Available at <http://www.iconeye.com/index.php?option=com_content&view=article&id=2705&Itemid=64> (accessed September 2008).

Dourish, P. 2001. *Where the action is*. Cambridge, Mass.: MIT Press.

Dourish, P. 2006. Re-Space-ing Place: "Place" and "space" ten years on. In *Proceedings of the ACM Conference on Computer Supported Cooperative Work (CSCW '96)*, 299–308. Banff, Canada: ACM Press.

Ducheneaut, N., N. Yee, E. Nickell, and R. Moore. 2007. The life and death of online gaming communities: A look at guilds in *World of Warcraft*. In *CHI 2007*, 839–848. San Jose: ACM Press.

Edwards, W. K., T. Igarashi, A. LaMarca, and E. Mynatt. 2000. A temporal model for multi-level undo and redo. In *Proceedings of the 13th annual ACM Symposium on User Interface Software and Technology (UIST)*, 31–40. San Diego, Calif.: ACM Press.

Edwards, W. K., and E. Mynatt. D. 1997. Timewarp: Techniques for autonomous collaboration. In *CHI 97*, 218–225. Atlanta: ACM Press.

Eisenstein, S. [1943] 1968. *The film sense*. London: Faber and Faber.

Equator. Available at <http://www.equator.ac.uk> (accessed December 2009).

eRENA. Available at <http://www.nada.kth.se/erena> (accessed December 2009).

Escape. Available at <http://escape.lancs.ac.uk> (accessed December 2009).

Evans, R. [1978] 1997. Figures, doors, and passages. In *Translations from drawing to building and other essays*, by R. Evans, 55–93. Cambridge, Mass.: MIT Press.

Facer, K., R. Joiner, J. Reid, R. Hull, and D. Kirk. 2004. *Savannah*: Mobile gaming and learning. *Journal of Computer Assisted Learning* 20:399–409.

Fischer, J. E., and S. Benford. 2009. Inferring player engagement in a pervasive experience. In *Proceedings of the 27th International Conference on Human Factors in Computing Systems (CHI 2009)*, 1903–1906. Boston: ACM Press.

Fitzpatrick, G. 1998. "The locales framework: Understanding and designing for cooperative work." PhD thesis, University of Queensland, CRC for Enterprise Distributed Systems Technology. Available at <http://www.cogs.susx.ac.uk/users/geraldin/Publications/localesFramework.pdf> (accessed July 2009).

Flintham, M. 2007. "Supporting mobile mixed reality experiences." PhD thesis, University of Nottingham. Available at <http://etheses.nottingham.ac.uk/632/> (accessed November 2009.

Flintham, M., S. Benford, R. Anastasi, T. Hemmings, A. Crabtree, C. Greenhalgh, N. Tandavaniti, M. Adams, and J. Row Farr. 2003. Where on-line meets on-the-streets: experiences with mobile mixed reality games. In *Proceedings of the SIGCHI Conference on Human Factors in Computing Systems*, 569–576. Fort Lauderdale, Fla.: ACM Press.

Flusser, V. 1992. Entwurf von Relationen. In Soft urbanism, by E. Sikiaridi and F. Vogelaar, in *Open 11/hybrid space*, edited by H. Rheingold, 82–94. Rotterdam: NAI Publishers.

Flynn, B. 2000. "Toward an aesthetics of navigation: Spatial organisation in the cosmology of the adventure game." *M/C: A Journal of Media and Culture* 3.5. Available at <http://journal.media-culture.org.au/0010/navigation.php> (accessed December 2008).

Foreman, R. 1992. *Unbalancing acts: Foundations for a theater*. New York: Pantheon.

Foucault, M. [1976] 1978. *The history of sexuality*, Vol. 1. Translated by R. Hurley. New York: Random House.

Fraser, M., D. Stanton, K. Ng, S. Benford, C. O'Malley, J. Bowers, G. Taxén, K. Ferris, and J. Hindmarsh. 2003. Assembling history: Achieving coherent experiences with diverse technologies. In *Proceedings of the European Conference on Computer-Supported Cooperative Work (ECSCW '03)*. Helsinki: Kluwer.

Fujimoto, R. M. 2000. *Parallel and distributed simulation systems*. New York: John Wiley and Sons.

Fuller, M. 2005. *Media ecologies: Materialist energies in art and technoculture*. Cambridge, Mass.: MIT Press.

Gaver, W. W. 1991. Technology affordances. In *ACM CHI 1991*, 79–84. New York: ACM.

Gaver, W. W. 1992. The affordances of media space. In *Proceedings of the ACM Conference on Computer-Supported Cooperative Work (CSCW '92)*, 17–24. Toronto: ACM Press.

Gaver, W. W., J. Beaver, and S. Benford. 2003. Ambiguity as a resource for design. In *Proceedings of the SIGCHI Conference on Human Factors in Computing Systems*, 233–240. Ft. Lauderdale, Fla.: ACM Press.

Ghali, A., S. Benford, S. Bayoumi, J. Green, and T. Pridmore. 2003. Visually-tracked flashlights as interaction devices. In *Human-Computer Interaction: INTERACT '03*, edited by M. Rauterberg, M. Menozzi, and J. Wesson, 487–494. Amsterdam: IOS Press.

Giannachi, G. 2004. *Virtual theatres: An introduction*. London: Routledge.

Giannachi, G. 2007. *The politics of new media theatre: Life®™*. London: Routledge.

Giannachi, G. 2010. Lynn Hershman in conversation with Gabriella Giannachi, San Francisco, Nov. 26, 2009. *Leonardo* 43 (3): 232–233.

Giannachi, G., and S. Benford. 2008. Temporal expansion in Blast Theory's *Day of the Figurines. P. A. Journal* 30 (3): 60–69.

Gibson, J. J. 1979. *The ecological approach to visual perception.* New York: Houghton Mifflin.

Glushko, R. J., and L. Tabas. 2009. Designing service systems by bridging the "front stage" and "back stage." *Information Systems and e-Business Management* 7 (4): 407–427.

Goffman, E. 1959. *Presentation of self in everyday life.* New York: Doubleday.

Goffman, E. 1974. *Frame analysis.* Cambridge, Mass.: Harvard University Press.

Gold, R. 1993."This is not a pipe." Special issue on computer augmented environments: Back to the real world. *Communications of the ACM* 36 (7): 72.

Goldberg, K., ed. 2000. *The robot in the garden: Telerobotics and telepistemology in the age of the Internet.* Cambridge, Mass.: MIT Press.

Graham, C., K. Cheverst, and M. Rouncefield. 2005. Technology for the humdrum: Trajectories, interactional needs and care setting. In *Proceedings of OZCHI 2005,* 16–25. Narrabundah: Computer-Human Interaction Special Interest Group (CHISIG) of Australia.

Grau, O. 2003. *Virtual art: From illusion to immersion.* Cambridge, Mass.: MIT Press.

Green, J., H. Schnädelbach, B. Koleva, S. Benford, T. Pridmore, K. Medina, E. Harris, and H. Smith. 2003. Camping in the digital wilderness: Tents and flashlights as interfaces to virtual worlds. In *Proceedings of Human Factors in Computing Systems (CHI '03), Extended Abstracts.* New York: ACM.

Greenhalgh, C., J. Bowers, G. Walker, J. Wyver, S. Benford, and I. Taylor. 1999. Creating a live broadcast from a virtual environment. In *Proceedings of the 26th Annual Conference on Computer Graphics and Interactive Techniques (SIGGRAPH '99),* 275–384. Los Angeles: ACM.

Greenhalgh, C., J. Purbrick, S. Benford, M. Craven, A. Drozd, and I. Taylor. 2000. Temporal links: Recording and replaying virtual environments. In *Proceedings of the 8th ACM International Conference on Multimedia,* 67–74. Marina del Rey, Calif.: ACM.

Guattari, F. 2000. *The three ecologies.* Translated by I. Pinder and P. Sutton. London: The Athlone Press.

Hageblling, H. 2004. *Interactive dramaturgies.* Berlin: Springer.

Hansen, M. 2006. *Bodies in code.* London: Routledge.

Harrigan, P., and N. Wardrip-Fruin, eds. 2007. *Second person: Role-playing and story in games and playable media.* Cambridge, Mass.: MIT Press.

Harrison, S., and P. Dourish. 1996. Re-Place-ing Space: The roles of place and space in collaborative systems. In *Proceedings of the ACM Conference on Computer-Supported Cooperative Work (CSCW '96),* 69–76. Cambridge. Mass.: ACM Press.

Hassan, R., and R. Purser. 2007. *24:7 time and temporality in the network society*. Stanford: Stanford University Press.

Heath, C., P. K. Luff, D. vom Lehn, J. Hindmarsh, and J. Cleverly. 2002. Crafting participation: Designing ecologies, configuring experience. *Visual Communication* 1 (1): 9–34.

Hershman, L. 1975. *Re:Forming familiar environments*, May 16, 1975. Lynn Hershman (with E. Coppola). Box 22. Lynn Hershman papers, M452. Dept. of Special Collections, Stanford University Libraries, Stanford, Calif.

Hershman, L. 2005. The raw data diet: All-consuming bodies and the shape of things to come. *Leonardo* 38 (3): 208–212.

Hillier, B., and J. Hanson. 1984. *The social logic of space*. Cambridge: Cambridge University Press.

Hindmarsh, J., M. Fraser, C. Heath, S. Benford, and C. Greenhalgh. 2000. Object-focused interaction in collaborative virtual environments. *ACM Transactions on Computer-Human Interaction (TOCHI)* 7 (4): 477–509.

Hindmarsh, J., C. Heath, D. vom Lehn, and J. Cleverly. 2002. Creating assemblies: Aboard the ghost ship. In *Proceedings of the 2002 ACM Conference on Computer-Supported Cooperative Work (CSCW '02)*, 156–165. New Orleans: ACM.

Horizon. Available at <http://www.horizon.ac.uk> (accessed December 2009).

Hornecker, E., and J. Buur. 2006. Getting a grip on tangible interaction: A framework on physical space and social interaction. In *Proceedings of ACM CHI 2006 Conference on Human Factors in Computing Systems, Games, and Performances*, vol. 1, 437–446. Montreal: ACM.

Huang, E., E. Mynatt, and J. Trimble. 2006. Displays in the wild: Understanding the dynamics and evolution of a display ecology. In *Proceedings of the Fourth International Conference on Pervasive Computing*, 321–336. LNCS 3968. Berlin, Heidelberg, and New York: Springer.

Hughes, J., V. King, T. Rodden, and H. Andersen. 1994. Moving out from the control room: Ethnography in system design. In *Proceedings of the 1994 ACM Conference on Computer Supported Cooperative Work (CSCW '94)*, 429–439. Chapel Hill: ACM.

Huizinga, J. 1955. *Homo Ludens: A study of the play element in culture*. Boston: Beacon Press.

Ingold, T. 2000. *The perception of the environment: Essays in livelihood, dwelling and skill*. London: Routledge.

Ingold, T. 2007. *Lines: A brief history*. London: Routledge.

IperG. Available at <http://www.pervasive-gaming.org/index.php> (accessed January 2010).

Iseard, N. 2009. My life in travel: Brendan Walker, thrill engineer. *The Observer*, March 29.

Ishii, H., and B. Ullmer. 1997. Tangible bits: Towards seamless interfaces between people, bits, and atoms. In *ACM CHI 1997*, 234–241. Atlanta: ACM.

Jackson, M. 1989. *Paths toward a clearing: Radical empiricism and ethnographic enquiry*. Bloomington: Indiana University Press.

Juul, J. 2004. Introduction to game time. In *First person: New media as story, performance and game*, edited by N. Wardrip-Fruin and P. Harrigan, 131–142. Cambridge, Mass.: MIT Press.

Kandinsky, W. [1947] 1979. *Point to plane*. Translated by H. Dearstyne and H. Rebay. New York: Dover Publications.

Kaprow, A. 1993. *The blurring of art and life*. Edited by J. Kelley. Berkeley: University of California Press.

Kelly, H., Howell, K., Glinert, E., Holding, L., Swain, C., Burrowbridge, A., Roper, M. 2007. How to build serious games. *Communications of the ACM* 50 (7): 44–49.

Kluitenberg, E. 1996. The network of weaves. In *Open 11/Hybrid Space*, edited by H. Rheingold, 7–16. Rotterdam: NAI Publishers.

Koleva, B., H. Schnädelbach, S. Benford, and C. Greenhalgh. 2000. Traversable interfaces between real and virtual worlds. In *Proceedings of Human Factors in Computing Systems (CHI 2000)*, 233–240. The Hague: ACM.

Koleva, B., I. Taylor, S. Benford, M. Fraser, C. Greenhalgh, H. Schnädelbach, D. vom Lehn, C. Heath, J. Row Farr, and M. Adams. 2001. "Orchestrating a mixed reality performance: *Desert Rain*." In *Proceedings of the SIGCHI Conference on Human Factors in Computing Systems*, 38–45. Seattle: ACM Press. Available at <http://www.ahds.ac.uk/creating/guides/new-media-tools/koleva.htm> (accessed May 2009).

Kozel, S. 2008. *Closer: Performance, technologies, phenomenology*. Cambridge, Mass.: MIT Press.

Kraan, A. 2006. To act in public through geo-annotation. In *Open 11/Hybrid Space*, edited by H. Rheingold, 38–49. Rotterdam: NAI Publishers.

Kuzuoka, H., G. Ishimoda, and T. Nishimura. 1995. Can the GestureCam be a surrogate? In *Proceedings of the 1995 European Conference on Computer-Supported Cooperative Work (ECSCW '95)*. Stockholm: Kluwer.

Lamont, P., and R. Wiseman. 1999. *Magic in theory: An introduction to the theoretical and psychological elements of conjuring*. Hatfield, UK: University of Hertfordshire Press.

Laurel, B. 1993. *Computers as Theatre*. Reading, Mass.: Addison-Wesley.

Law, E., and J. Kort, V. Roto, M. Hassenzahl, and A. Vermeeren. 2008. Towards a shared definition of user experience. In *CHI 2008: ACM Proceedings*, 2395–2398. Florence: ACM.

Lefebvre, H. [1974] 1992. *The production of space*. Translated by D. Nicholson-Smith. Oxford: Blackwell.

Lewis, G. 2007. The virtual discourses of Pamela Z. *Journal of the Society of American Music* 1 (1): 55–77.

Libeskind, D. 1992. *Extension to the Berlin Museum with Jewish Museum Departments*. Berlin: Ernst & Sohn.

Libeskind, D. 1999. *Jewish Museum Berlin*. Münich: Prestel.

Manovich, L. 2001. *The language of new media*. Cambridge, Mass.: MIT Press.

Manovich, L. 2006. The poetics of augmented space: Learning from Prada. *Visual Communication* 5 (2): 219–240.

Mauss, M. [1954] 2000. *The gift: Forms and functions of exchange in archaic societies*. Translated by W. D. Halls. New York: Norton.

McCloud, S. 1993. *Understanding comics: The invisible art*. New York: Harper Collins.

McGonigal, J. 2006. "This might be a game: Ubiquitous play and performance at the turn of the twenty-first century." PhD diss., University of California, Berkeley. Available at <http://avantgame.com/dissertation.htm> (accessed December 2009).

McGonigal, J. 2007a. The puppet master problem: Design for real-world, mission-based gaming. In *Second person: Role-playing and story in games and playable media*, edited by P. Harrigan and N. Wardrip-Fruin, 251–263. Cambridge, Mass.: MIT Press.

McGonigal, J. 2007b. Ubiquitous gaming: A vision for the future of enchanted spaces. In *Space time play: Computer games, architecture and urbanism: The next level*, edited by F. Borries, S. Walz, and M. Böttger, 233–237. Basel: Birkhäuser.

Milgram, P. and F. Kishino. 1994. A taxonomy of mixed reality visual displays. *IEICE Transactions on Information Systems*, E77–D12, 449–455.

Montola, M. 2005. "Exploring the edge of the magic circus: defining pervasive games." In *Proceedings of DAC 2005*. Available at <http://users.tkk.fi/mmontola/publication.html> (accessed January 2010).

Montola, M., and J. Stenros. 2004. *Beyond role and play: Tools, toys and theory for harnessing the imagination*. Vantaa, Ropecon. Available at <http://www.ropecon.fi/brap/> (accessed November 2009).

Montola, M., J. Stenros, and A. Waern. 2009. *Pervasive games theory and design: Experiences on the boundary between life and play*. Burlington, Mass.: Morgan Kaufmann.

Moretti, F. 2005. *Graphs, maps, trees*. London: Verso.

Munson, J., and P. Dewan. 1996. A concurrency control framework for collaborative systems. In *Proceedings of the 1996 ACM Conference on Computer-Supported Cooperative Work (CSCW '96)*, 278–287. Boston: ACM.

Murray, J. 1997. *Hamlet on the holodeck: The future of narrative in cyberspace*. Cambridge. Mass.: MIT Press.

Norman, D. 2002. *The design of everyday things*. New York: Basic Books.

Novak, M. [1991] 1993. Liquid architectures in cyberspace. In *Cyberspace: First steps*, edited by M. Benedikt, 225–254. Cambridge, Mass.: MIT Press.

Paulos, E., and J. Canny. 1998. PRoP: Personal roving presence. In *Proceedings of the SIGCHI Conference on Human Factors in Computing* Systems (*CHI '98*), edited by C.-M. Karat, A. Lund, Joëlle Coutaz, and John Karat, 296–303. New York: ACM Press/Addison-Wesley.

Perrella, S., ed. 1998. *Hypersurface architecture*. London: Architectural Design.

Pfister, M. 1998. *The theory and analysis of drama*. Translated by J. Halliday. Cambridge: Cambridge University Press.

Pinhanez, C. 2001. Using a steerable projector and a camera to transform surfaces into interactive displays. In *CHI '01 Extended Abstracts on Human Factors in Computing Systems*, 369–370. Los Angeles, Calif.: ACM.

Price, C. 2003. *The square book*. Chichester, UK: Wiley & Sons.

Reeves, S. 2005. "*Flypad*." Available at <http://www.mrl.nott.ac.uk/~str/doc/report_0605.pdf> (accessed February 2009).

Reeves, S., S. Benford, C. O'Malley, and M. Fraser. 2005. Designing the spectator experience. In *Proceedings of Conference on Human Factors in Computing Systems (CHI 2005)*, 741–750. Portland, Ore.: ACM.

Rieser, M., and A. Zapp. 2002. *New screen media/cinema/art/narrative*. London: BFI/ZKM.

Rinman, M. L. 2002. "Forms of interaction in mixed reality nedia performance: A study of the artistic event *Desert Rain*." TRITA-NA-0214, CID-168. Stockholm: KTH.

Rosen, C. 2002. *Notes: The hidden world of the pianist*. Harmondsworth, UK: Penguin Press.

Russell, I. 2007. "Now I can see you: The politics of presence." Available at <http://humanitieslab.stanford.edu/NewMedia/278> (accessed September 2008).

Salen, S., and E. Zimmerman. 2004. *Rules of play*. Cambridge, Mass.: MIT Press.

Schechner, R. 1968. Six axioms for environmental theatre. In *The Drama Review: Thirty years of commentary on the avant-garde*, edited by B. McNamara and J. Dolan, 151–171. Ann Arbor: UMI.

Schechner, R. 1973a. Performance and the social sciences. *Drama Review* 17:5–36.

Schechner, R. 1973b. *Environmental theater*. New York: Hawthorn.

Schechner, R. 1993. *The future of ritual*. London: Routledge.

Schnädelbach, H., S. R. Egglestone, S. Reeves, S. Benford, B. Walker, and M. Wright. 2008. Performing thrill: Designing telemetry systems and spectator interfaces for amusement rides. In *CHI 2008: ACM Proceedings*, 1167–1176. Florence: ACM.

Schnädelbach, H., B. Koleva, M. Flintham, M. Fraser, P. Chandler, M. Foster, S. Benford, C. Greenhalgh, S. Izadi, and T. Rodden. 2002. The Augurscope: A mixed reality interface for outdoors. In *Proceedings of Human Factors in Computing Systems (CHI 2002)*, 9–16. New York: ACM.

Schnädelbach, H., B. Koleva, M. Paxton, M. Twidale, S. Benford, and R. Anastasi. 2006. The Augurscope: Refining its design. *Presence* 13 (3): 278–293.

Schnädelbach, H., A. Penn, P. Steadman, S. Benford, B. Koleva, and T. Rodden. 2006. "Moving office: Inhabiting a dynamic building." Paper presented at the CSCW conference, Banff, Canada, 313–322.

Schnädelbach, H., A. Penn, and P. Steadman. 2007. "Mixed reality architecture: A dynamic architectural topology." Paper presented at the Space Syntax Symposium, Istanbul, Turkey.

Schwartz, I. 1997. A Testing Ground for Interactivity: The Water Pavilions by Lars Spuybroek and Kas Oosterhuis. *Archis* (September): 9–13.

Shaw, J., H. Staff, J. Row Farr, M. Adams, D. vom Lehm, C. Heath, M. L. Rinman, I. Taylor, and S. Benford. 2000. "Staged mixed reality performance '*Desert Rain*' by Blast Theory." eRENA Deliverable D7b.3. Available at <http://www.erena.kth.se> (accessed January 2010).

Sheridan, J. G. 2006. "Digital live art: Mediating wittingness in playful arenas." PhD thesis, University of Lancaster. Available at <http://www.jennifersheridan.com/dla.html> (accessed January 2010).

Sheridan, T. B. 1992a. Musings on telepresence and virtual presence. *Presence* 1 (1): 120–125.

Sheridan, T. B. 1992b. Defining our terms. *Presence* 1 (2): 272–274.

Slater, M. 2003. "A note on presence terminology." *Presence Connect,* vol. 3. Available at <http://presence.cs.ucl.ac.uk/presenceconnect/articles/Jan2003/melslaterJan27200391557/melslaterJan27200391557.html> (accessed December 2008).

Slater, M., and M. Usoh. 1994. Representations systems, perceptual position, and presence in immersive virtual environments. *Presence* 2 (3): 221–233.

Sorkin, M. 1992. *Variations on a theme park: The new American city and the end of public space.* Cambridge, Mass.: Blackwell.

Stach, T., C. Gutwin, D. Pinelle, and P. Irani. 2007. Improving recognition and characterization in groupware with rich embodiments. In *CHI 2007,* 11–20. New York: ACM Press.

Stanislavski, C. [1936] 1980. *An actor prepares.* Translated by E. A. Hapgood. London: Methuen.

Star, S. L. 1989. Institutional ecology, "translations," and boundary objects: Amateurs and professionals in Berkeley's Museum of Vertebrate Zoology. *Social Studies of Science* 19 (3): 387–420.

Steed, A., S. Benford, N. Dalton, C. Greenhalgh, I. MacColl, C. Randell, and H. Schnädelbach. 2002. "Mixed-reality interfaces to immersive projection systems." In *Proceedings of the Immersive Projection Technology Workshop,* March 2002, Orlando. Available at <http://www.cs.ucl.ac.uk/research/equator/papers/mixed_interface_final.pdf> (accessed August 2009).

Stefik, M., D. Bobrow, G. Foster, S. Lanning, and D. Tatar. 1987. WYSIWIS revised: Early experiences with multiuser interfaces. *ACM TOIS* 5 (2): 147–167.

Steuer, J. 1992. Defining virtual reality: Dimensions determining telepresence. *Journal of Communication* 42:73–93.

Stewart, J., B. Bederson, and A. Druin. 1999. Single display groupware: A model for co-present collaboration. In *Proceedings of Human Factors in Computing Systems (CHI 1999)*, 286–293. New York: ACM.

Strauss, A. 1993. *Continual permutations of action*. New York: Aldine de Gruyter.

Sudnow, D. 1978. *Ways of the hand: The organization of improvised conduct*. London: Routledge & Kegan Paul.

Sutherland, I. E. 1970. Computer displays. *Scientific American* 222 (6): 57–81.

Thomson, P. 1970. Games and plays: An approach to Ionesco. *Educational Theatre Journal* 22 (1): 60–70.

Tidwell, J. 2005. *Designing interfaces*. Sebastopol, Calif.: O'Reilly Media.

Tromble, M., ed. 2005. *The art and films of Lynn Hershman Leeson*. Berkeley: University of California Press.

Tschumi, B. 1996. *Architecture and disjunction*. Cambridge, Mass.: MIT Press.

Tyler, P. E. 1991. Powell says U.S. will stay in Iraq. *New York Times,* March 23.

Ultima. Available at <http://www.uoherald.com> (accessed September 2007).

Varela, F. J. 1999. "The specious present: A neurophenomenology of time consciousness." In *Naturalizing Phenomenology*, edited by J. Petiot, F. J. Varela, B. Pachoud, and J.-M. Roy, 266–314. Stanford: Stanford University Press. Available at <http://www.franzreichle.ch/images/Francisco_Varela/Human_Consciousness_Article02.htm> (accessed January 2010).

vom Lehn, D., C. Heath, and H. Knoblauch. 2001. Configuring exhibits. In *Verbal art across cultures*, edited by H. Knoblauch and H. Kotthoff, 281–297. Tübingen: Gunter Narr Verlag.

Waern, A., M. Montola, and J. Stenros. 2009. The three-sixty illusion: Designing for immersion in pervasive games. In *Proceedings of the 27th International Conference on Human Factors in Computing Systems (CHI 2009)*, 1549–1558. Boston: ACM Press.

Wagner, R. 1986. *Symbols that stand out for themselves*. Chicago: University of Chicago Press.

Walker, B. 2005. *The taxonomy of thrill*. London: Aerial Publishing.

Walker, B., H. Schnädelbach, S. R. Egglestone, A. Clark, T. Orbach, M. Wright, K. H. Ng, A. French, T. Rodden, and S. Benford. 2007. Augmenting amusement rides with telemetry. In *ACE 2007*, 115–122. Salzburg: Shaker Verlag.

Wardrip-Fruin, N., and P. Harrigan, P., eds. 2004. *First person: New media as story, performance and game*. Cambridge, Mass.: MIT Press.

Weiser, M. 1991. The computer for the twenty-first century. *Scientific American* (September): 94–104.

Williams, D. 2009. "Blast Theory: Small secrets in public spaces." *Realtime* 90:32. Available at <http://www.realtimearts.net/article/issue90/9413> (accessed June 2009).

Williams, A., E. Kabisch, and P. Dourish. 2005. From interaction to participation: Configuring space through embodied interaction. In *UbiComp 2005: Ubiquitous Computing*, edited by M. Beigl, S. Intille, and H. Tokuda, 287–304. LNCS 3660. Berlin, Heidelberg, and New York: Springer.

Wilson, S. 2002. *Information arts: Intersections of art, science, and technology*. Cambridge, Mass.: MIT Press.

Zellner, P. 1999. *Hybrid space: New forms in digital architecture*. London: Thames and Hudson.

Žižek, S. 2002. *Welcome to the desert of the real: Five essays on September 11 and related dates*. London: Verso.

Zuckerman, M. 1979. *Sensation seeking: Beyond the optimal level of arousal*. Hillsdale, N.J.: Lawrence Erlbaum.

Index